HENRY DAVID THOREAU

A Year in Thoreau's Journal 1851

With an Introduction & Notes by

H. DANIEL PECK

PENGUIN BOOKS

PENGUIN BOOKS
Published by the Penguin Group
Penguin Books USA Inc., 375 Hudson Street,
New York, New York 10014, U.S.A.
Penguin Books Ltd, 27 Wrights Lane, London W8 5TZ, England
Penguin Books Australia Ltd, Ringwood, Victoria, Australia
Penguin Books Canada Ltd, 10 Alcorn Avenue,
Toronto, Ontario, Canada M4V 3B2
Penguin Books (N.Z.) Ltd, 182–190 Wairau Road,
Auckland 10, New Zealand

Penguin Books Ltd, Registered Offices:
Harmondsworth, Middlesex, England

First published in Penguin Books 1993

1 3 5 7 9 10 8 6 4 2

This edition published by arrangement with Princeton University Press, publishers of Henry
D. Thoreau, *Journal, Volume 3: 1848–1851,* Copyright © 1990 by Princeton University Press,
and Henry D. Thoreau, *Journal, Volume 4: 1851–1852,* Copyright © 1992 by Princeton
University Press.

The map on page 338 is reproduced with permission from *Faith in a Seed* by Henry D. Thoreau,
edited by Bradley F. Dean. Published by Island Press, Washington, D.C. and Covelo, California.

COMMITTEE ON
SCHOLARLY EDITIONS
AN APPROVED EDITION
MODERN LANGUAGE
ASSOCIATION OF AMERICA

®

LIBRARY OF CONGRESS CATALOGING IN PUBLICATION DATA
Thoreau, Henry David, 1817–1862.
[Journal. Selections]
A year in Thoreau's journal, 1851/ Henry David Thoreau;
with an introduction & notes by H. Daniel Peck.
p. cm.
Includes bibliographical references.
ISBN 0 14 03.9085 5
1. Thoreau, Henry David, 1817–1862—Diaries.
2. Authors, American—19th century—Diaries. I. Peck, H. Daniel.
II. Title.
PS3053.A2 1993
818'.303—dc20
[B] 93–30735

Printed in the United States of America
Set in Bembo

Contents

Introduction

How can a two-million-word journal, written during a period of twenty-four years, be called a work of literature? The question arises from an emerging, twofold consensus among scholars: that Thoreau's Journal is perhaps his most important work, more important even than *Walden*, and that the writer himself unmistakably regarded it as an integral form of expression. Supporting these observations is the remarkable beauty of the Journal's prose. As Alfred Kazin once remarked, "It is not natural for a man to write this well every day."

While Thoreau's complete Journal was first published in 1906, by Houghton Mifflin in fourteen volumes, only in our time has its large significance in American literature been recognized. Part of that recognition owes to the publication, begun during the 1980s and continuing in this decade, of an authoritative modern edition. The modern edition, published by Princeton University Press, is far more inclusive and faithful to the format of Thoreau's original manuscript Journal than was the 1906 edition. This Penguin Classics volume excerpts from the Princeton Edition of Thoreau's Journal the full calendar year 1851. By presenting an uninterrupted text of the Journal, rather than brief selections from different periods, this volume invites readers to encounter not only the Journal's characteristic themes but also its distinctive mode of daily writing.

Though systematic study of the Journal's literary qualities did not begin until the 1980s, the impetus for such study was given by the American intellectual historian Perry Miller during the 1950s. Miller was the first scholar to observe Thoreau's self-conscious and overt aesthetic purposes for his Journal. In viewing this document as "a deliberately constructed work of art," Miller pointed to a Journal entry of January 27, 1852, in which Thoreau speculates that "thoughts written down thus in a journal might be printed in the same form with greater advantage—than if the related ones were brought together into separate essays. They are now allied to life—& are seen by the reader not to be far fetched— It is more simple—less artful."

Recently scholars have confirmed Miller's recognition of Thoreau's artistic intentions for his Journal by showing that in 1850 the writer generally ceased tearing out pages from his Journal for use in drafting essays, books, and lectures. Instead, he began to copy out such material, thereby preserving his Journal intact. The passage from January 1852 cited by Miller thus seems to characterize Thoreauvian practices and intentions that had been in place for at least a year when that passage was written.

Closely related to this development is the fact that in 1850 Thoreau initiated a daily discipline to which he was faithful for the rest of his life: he would generally walk in the fields, hills, and forests around Concord during the afternoons—often taking notes as he walked—and give the mornings to reading and to writing out, in his Journal, observations from his walks. The Journal was, to use a famous phrase from *Walden*, Thoreau's "morning work," and it proceeded rhythmically with his afternoon walks. These activities fed one another, and, in their reciprocity, enacted an essential openness toward experience and the world.

Sometimes, Thoreau would write out several days' walks in a single morning session, and in many of his entries he would employ the present tense, creating the fiction of observing the natural world just now. All these developments suggest strongly that by 1850, and certainly by 1851, Thoreau had begun to see his Journal as an integral work—a "lifework" that henceforth would be his central literary concern.

We may, thus, divide the Journal's development into two major phases. The first phase falls between 1837, when Thoreau graduated from Harvard, and 1850, shortly after the publication of his first book, *A Week on the Concord and Merrimack Rivers* (1849). The second phase extends from 1850 until the Journal closes in 1861, the year before Thoreau's death from tuberculosis at the age of forty-four. By the end, he had produced forty-seven manuscript volumes. The year 1851, presented here, takes up the greater part of four of these volumes.

In its earlier phase, from 1837 through about 1849, the Journal Thoreau left behind is fragmentary, with many torn out, missing pages; the earliest volumes are copies he made from their originals, now lost to us. But the early Journal is fragmentary in other ways as well. Though an invaluable record of Thoreau's youthful reading and thinking, the Journal of this period lacks the clear sense of literary and philosophical purpose that evidences itself in the second phase.

Even so, Thoreau's Journal from its earliest moments is a fascinating document. The very first entry, written October 22, 1837, begins, " 'What are you doing now?' he asked, 'Do you keep a journal?'–So

I make my first entry to-day." The unnamed "he" is almost certainly Ralph Waldo Emerson, Thoreau's mentor until their falling out in the late 1840s, and the passage suggests the spiritual purposes that drove Emerson and others in his circle to keep a journal.

For the Concord Transcendentalists, a journal was the most responsive of literary forms, the form most likely to catch one's inspiration in the moment of its inception, and journal keeping became for a time almost a required practice for Emersonians such as Margaret Fuller and Bronson Alcott. None of these figures, however, adhered to the discipline of journal keeping longer or with greater dedication than Thoreau. The seriousness of his endeavor is expressed by the idealistic headings that structure Thoreau's Journal entries in the early years, headings such as "Solitude," "Beauty," "Truth," and "Harmony." Eventually, such thematic headings drop away and the entries become more flowing, while retaining their quality of earnest intellectual and spiritual inquiry. The developing organic form of the Journal in the 1840s does not, however, prepare us for the depth, eloquence, and complexity that emerge so strikingly in the early 1850s. These are the qualities that give the Journal claim to being Thoreau's greatest work, and, arguably, the greatest of all writers' journals.

The reasons behind the Journal's full maturation in the early 1850s are difficult to ascertain. For Perry Miller, with his characteristic animus toward Thoreau, the writer's decision to invest himself so deeply in a private form of writing was simply a matter of "sour grapes," a feeble rationalization for the failure of his published works, especially that of his first book, *A Week on the Concord and Merrimack Rivers*. *A Week*, which recounted a voyage taken by Thoreau and his brother John in 1839, was too digressive for most contemporary readers, and few copies were sold.

Undoubtedly Thoreau was disappointed by the commercial failure of *A Week*, yet disappointment alone cannot explain the remarkable flowering of the Journal in the early 1850s. The energy and eloquence that readers will encounter in this volume seem to proceed, rather, from the momentum of journal keeping itself. That is, the activity of writing a journal produced for Thoreau intellectual discoveries that, in turn, taught him the artistic and moral possibilities of the form. And, in a different sense than Perry Miller intended, these discoveries are not unrelated to Thoreau's first book. *A Week on the Concord and Merrimack Rivers*, for all its sunny and triumphant aspects (readers of this volume will note Thoreau's characterization of it as an "unroofed book" [88]), is deeply elegiac.

By voyaging on the river of time, *A Week* commemorates Thoreau's brother John, who died tragically in 1842, and New England's lost Native-American and colonial past. It is a book of memory, structured, in the manner of Hesiod, by the days of the week. The writing of *A Week* may have confirmed for Thoreau the efficacy of the "day" as a formal structure for the remembrance and commemoration of experience. Such confirmation is suggested by the following Journal passage from early 1851: "I would fain keep a journal which should contain those thoughts & impressions which I am most liable to forget that I have had   Which would have, in one sense the greatest remoteness—in another the greatest nearness, to me" (7).

In August of the same year, Thoreau asks a question in his Journal whose urgency dramatizes the hazards of forgetting: "What if a man were earnestly & wisely to set about recollecting & preserving the thoughts which he has had! How many perchance are now irrecoverable!–Calling in his neighbors to aid him" (166). What was at stake for Thoreau was the continuity of experience, the sense of relation between past and present that constitutes a life. While Thoreau's Journal is not an autobiography in any strict, formal sense, his use of it to "recollect" and "preserve" experience reveals his deeply felt autobiographical impulses.

Walden (1854), published three years after these Journal passages were written, is also a book of recollection, but in a different sense. It celebrates the two years (1845–47) almost a decade earlier that Thoreau had spent at the Pond, and filters the meanings of that experience as he reflected upon it during the following decade. Between 1845 and 1854, Thoreau produced at least seven drafts of *Walden* (not including the printer's copy), three of them written by 1850 and the final four written largely between early 1852 and 1854.

Thus, the period between 1850 and 1852, when the Journal comes into its full maturity, is also a period when Thoreau is quietly reconceiving *Walden*, working on it only intermittently. This coincidence between the hiatus in *Walden*'s composition and the emergence of the mature Journal suggests an important relation between the two works, a relation that is far more intimate and fluid than scholars generally have recognized. Increasingly, we are coming to see this relation as a form of dialogue, and we no longer view the Journal merely as a "source" for the "texts" of works like *Walden* and *A Week*. Rather, all these works should be understood as texts, speaking to one another and to readers in their own distinctive modes, about the public and

private issues that preoccupied Thoreau in these highly generative
years.

A Week and *Walden* speak to these issues as "books" (they are the
only full-length books completed and brought to publication by Thoreau), and both redeem the experiences they recount through recog-
nizable nineteenth-century narrative techniques of development and
closure. The Journal is no less redemptive than are *A Week* and *Walden*,
but, unlike them, its mode is open and provisional. It always stands at
the forward edge of experience, enacting daily the goal expressed in
Walden: "to toe that line" between "past and future."

Thoreau's books (including works like *Cape Cod* that he clearly
intended for book-length publication), as well as his lectures and published essays, served his public, moral, and oracular purposes. They
were written, as he puts it in *Walden*, "to wake my neighbors up,"
and to address the condition of "quiet desperation" that he saw all
around him in commercial and agricultural New England. The Journal
served these same purposes, in the sense that Thoreau often used it to
compose passages that eventually found their way into his published
works; readers of this volume will encounter a number of such familiar
passages. But, more important, the Journal was a forum for meditation,
a private sphere in which his imagination could range freely.

In any case, the new emphases of Thoreau's Journal in the early
1850s are strikingly in accord with the new directions in which he was
taking *Walden* at this time. Just as Thoreau appears now to recognize
a distinctive commemorative dimension of his Journal, he also completes in this period some of the most hauntingly elegiac portions of
Walden, such as the "Former Inhabitants" subchapter. The way in
which memory might serve to retrieve "the landscape of my infant
dreams," as Thoreau puts it in *Walden*, is reflected in many Journal
entries of 1851. On June 11th, for example, he writes, "I can sometimes recall to mind the quality the immortality of my youthful life—
but in memory is the only relation to it" (66).

That Thoreau was reading Wordsworth in these years merely con-
firms the deepening of his commitment to the redemptive power of
memory, a pervasive theme of Romanticism, and to the form of
writing—his Journal—that best served his own purposes of recollection.
By the early 1850s, Thoreau's Journal had become a way of keeping
time in two senses: it could vividly mark the rhythms of life and nature
because its observations were always made in the present, and it could
preserve such moments for later consideration. That this process of

keeping time was for Thoreau a form of art, the art of memory, is evident in the following passage written in 1853:

> It is surprising how any reminiscence of a different season of the year affects us— When I meet with any such in my journal it affects me as poetry and I appreciate that other season and that particular phenomenon more than at the time.— The world so seen is all one spring & full of beauty.— You only need to make a faithful record of an average summer day's experience & summer mood—& read it in the winter—& it will carry you back to more than that summer day alone could show—only the rarest flavor—the purest melody—of the season thus comes down to us.

As this passage suggests, another important correspondence between the Journal of the early 1850s and the later versions of *Walden* is the emphasis both place upon natural process. In this period, Thoreau gives *Walden* a more overt seasonal structure than it had in earlier versions, a development that parallels his increasing use of his Journal to study seasonal change. He begins now to index his Journal volumes for recurring natural phenomena, thereby anticipating the Journal's later use in developing a grand calendar of nature that remained incomplete at his death.

Such a calendar is one of several long-term natural history projects whose development Thoreau was entertaining in 1851. On June 11th, he had an idea for "A Book of the seasons—each page of which should be written in its own season & out of doors or in its own locality wherever it may be" (67). The scientific and philosophical impetus for such projects is suggested by the entry for August 21st, in which Thoreau writes that the "related yet distinct" properties of plants "suggest a history to Nature—a Natural *history* in a new sense" (173).

The great passage describing the flow of earth from the railroad cut, in the "Spring" chapter of *Walden*, was first drafted in the Journal during a mid-winter thaw in December of 1851 (see page 325 of this volume). Indeed, the entire year 1851, as reflected in the Journal, was a time during which Thoreau intensified his study of nature, both in his reading and in his direct observations. During this year, he read Darwin's *Voyage of the Beagle*, William Bartram's *Travels*, and the work of other naturalists such as Kalm, Cuvier, Agassiz, and Gould. A biography of Linnaeus also absorbed him during this period.

Going hand in hand with Thoreau's reading of naturalists during 1851 was his direct experience in nature. The activity that most fully opened the natural world to him was walking, and Thoreau was a ceaseless and inspired walker (his work as a surveyor, described at various points throughout the Journal of 1851, was the ideal vocation for such a person). His great essay "Walking" explains the symbolic significance of this activity for him, how it became a form of spiritual "sauntering." Though not published until 1862, a month after Thoreau's death, "Walking" was largely drafted in his Journal during 1851, and readers will find in this volume many passages familiar to them from that work. Yet here in the Journal, in their original form, these passages reveal the actual environments from which the essay's generalizations proceed. They remind us that Thoreau's walks were vividly experienced, highly tactile encounters with the hills, swamps, fields, and forests surrounding Concord.

It was the moonlit aura of these settings, as Thoreau experienced it in a number of nighttime walks, that most deeply engaged him between the spring and fall of 1851. By defamiliarizing the landscape through the prism of moonlight, he felt he had discovered nature's timeless, mythic dimension. As he writes on September 7th, "the chaster light of the moon . . . tells of . . . an antiquity superior to time—unappreciable by time" (209). Thoreau's moonlit walks, which often extended from dusk until dawn, are recounted in an extraordinary series of Journal entries contained in this volume. They provide some of the most lyrical prose in all of his writings, and, by themselves, make 1851 an exceptional year in the Journal's development. The following passage was written on June 11th:

> I now descend round the corner of the grain field—through the pitch-pine wood in to a lower field, more inclosed by woods—& find my self in a colder damp & misty atmosphere, with much dew on the grass—I seem to be nearer to the origin of things   There is something creative & primal in the cool mist—this dewy mist does not fail to suggest music to me—unaccountably—fertility the origin of things— An atmosphere which has forgotten the sun—where the ancient principle of moisture prevails. (65)

So consistently mysterious and evocative are Thoreau's accounts of his moonlit walks that we must wonder what process of deep self-examination, what probing for his own "origins," motivated these excursions. Yet they also bear a clear relation to his evolving study natural process. The night, far from obscuring nature, opened a cle view of it. On September 5th, Thoreau writes, "This [moon]li this hour takes the civilization all out of the landscape" (201). the day might open a more focused, particularized view of the world, the night revealed nature's most fundamental structures. On June 15th, Thoreau observes: "After walking by night several times—I now walk by day—but I am not aware of any crowning advantage in it. I see small objects better, but it does not enlighten me any. The day is more trivial" (82–83).

Thoreau's perceptions during the summer of 1851 of nature's largest, mythic dimensions, as opposed to its "trivial" aspects, correspond to his growing impatience in this period with the methods and perspective of science. The limitation of science is a theme that sounds throughout 1851, beginning with an entry written on January 7th: "Science does not embody all that men know—only what is for men of science" (3). The problem, as Thoreau states it again on September 5th, is that "[t]he man of science discovers no world for the mind of man with all its faculties to inhabit" (201). On November 1st, he advises himself, "See not with the eye of science—which is barren" (276). And on December 25th, employing a famous distinction derived from Kant and Coleridge, he observes that science "enriches the understanding but robs the imagination" (319). The issue, as Thoreau focuses it in an entry of August 5th, was "how" one sees: "The astronomer is as blind to the significant phenomena—or the significance of phenomena as the wood-sawyer who wears glasses to defend his eyes from sawdust—   The question is not what you look at—but how you look & whether you see" (146).

Paradoxically, Thoreau's growing distrust of science—a departure from his earlier confidence in its methods—occurs at the same time that his own empirical study of nature intensifies. Readers of this volume will note his rapt attention during 1851 to a host of natural phenomena: trees (especially during the spring months), reflections in water, ice formations, sunsets, and, most of all, seasonal variation as manifested in plants, atmospheric conditions, and other features of the landscape. Sometimes Thoreau's observations surprise him, as indicated by a passage written on September 12th: "I can hardly believe that there is so great a diffirence between one year & another as my journal shows. The 11th of this month last year the river was as high as it commonly is in the spring—over the causeway on the Corner Road. It is now quite low. Last year Oct 9th the huckleberries were fresh & abundant on Conantum—   They are now already dried up" (222).

As careful as such observations are, Thoreau distinguished his own close study of nature from the "barren" gaze of science, because his approach served a larger, spiritual vision. Unlike the aggressive, probing scientist, Thoreau was prepared to await nature's revelations patiently.

As he puts it in an entry of September 7th, "If by watching all day & all night—I may detect some trace of the Ineffable—then will it not be worth the while to watch?" (206). Thus, while the Journal is often given to focused observations of nature, these observations always implicitly belong to a quest for truth, for knowledge of the "higher laws" to which Thoreau aspires in *Walden*.

Thoreau believed that his Journal could ultimately provide, in the language of a passage from November 10th, "a true and absolute account of things—-of the evening & the morning & all the phenomena between them" (287). By recording natural phenomena every day, and at every season, he would create a record of the natural past that, seen in relation to the present, would gradually chart nature's longest, most enduring patterns.

In other words, seasonal variation as such was not the final object of Thoreau's study. Rather, he would learn from such variation the "constant phenomenon" (285), as he calls it in an entry of November 9th. The grand design of the seasons and the spiritual harmony that it reflected, so eloquently evoked in *Walden*, would actually be experienced and vividly understood in the Journal over the long course of its development. The resulting vision, capacious and profound, is suggested by the following passage written on June 13th, in which Thoreau is observing reflections of moonlight on the surface of a pond:

> The pyramid or sheaf of light which we see springing from near where we stand only—in fact is the outline of that portion of the shimmering surface which an eye takes in—to myriad eyes suitably placed, the whole surface of the pond would be seen to shimmer, or rather it would be seen as the waves turned up their mirrors to be covered with those bright flame like reflections of the moon's disk like a myriad candles every where issuing from the waves—i.e. if there were as many eyes as angles presented by the waves. (75)

The "myriad eyes" whose vision might take in the whole shimmering surface of the pond perceive the world as would the mind of God. This is the cosmic view that Thoreau hopes to achieve in his Journal, through slowly, incrementally, building up a vast inventory of perspectives. In this way, his empirical observations are always implicitly working toward an understanding of cosmos. Yet, grounding this search for truth was Thoreau's fidelity to lived experience. He would search out nature's higher laws not as a metaphysician but as a naturalist, and in translating "facts" into "truths," as he describes this process in *Walden*, he was suspicious of moving too quickly. His caution is apparent in an entry of December 25th, where he writes, "Let me not be in haste to detect the *universal law*, let me see more clearly a particular instance" (320).

The Journal's characteristic rhythm of observation and reflection suggests Thoreau's approach to uncovering nature's truths. During May of 1851, for example, close descriptions of trees and the processes of their growth are interwoven with generalizations about the human relation to nature. In the entry for May 21st, following descriptions of ash, pine, and wild holly trees, we come suddenly to an extended passage in which Thoreau claims, "I think that the existence of man in nature is the divinest and most startling of all facts" (48).

Large generalizations like this are often stated in the Journal with great certainty. Yet the Journal's open, provisional form always allowed for the possibility that such "truths" could be unsettled, revised, or even overturned. (Needless to say, Thoreau did not always see human beings as the lords of creation.) Like Walt Whitman's loosely structured catalogues of experience, Thoreau's Journal allowed him to contradict himself, to follow his inspiration wherever it might lead—even into the dead ends of the imaginative life.

The period immediately following Thoreau's 34th birthday, during the summer of 1851, was such a time. His Journal entry for July 19th begins, "Here I am 34 years old, and yet my life is almost wholly unexpanded" (113). But such dead ends were never really dead, since another day's entry always awaited writing; there was always more "morning work" to do. And, in fact, Thoreau's midsummer birthday doldrums in 1851 gave way by autumn to a joyous sense of recovery and fullness of spirit. On November 1st, he could say, "I love my life. I warm toward all nature" (276), and a week later exclaim, "Here ever springing—never dying with perrennial root I stand" (283).

The Journal's insistent provisionality may seem at odds with Thoreau's search for divinity in nature. From a literary perspective, this discrepancy between the Journal's open form and its quest for ultimate knowledge is one of the most interesting things about it. In its very nature, the Journal is always directed to the occasion that life presents just now. Its literary "moment" is the present instant of time, and its open form suggests a view of reality in which meanings are unfixed, plural, and provisional. Indeed, the Journal's dailiness, its ceaseless experimentation, the play of its language—these qualities suggest modern thought, particularly the thought of early twentieth-century process philosophy, such as that espoused by William James, Alfred North Whitehead, and John Dewey.

Thoreau himself could not have understood the full procedural and philosophical implications of his journal keeping, because he remained wedded to his great nineteenth-century Romantic dream of knowing "an entire heaven and an entire earth," as he puts it in a Journal entry of 1856. Yet the provisional method of the Journal is itself an expression of his restlessness with the philosophical idealism of his age. In the Journal, he strives to understand the actual *processes* of nature, and to *embody* truth in the world of things. Nowhere in Thoreau's writings is his struggle toward a new worldview more apparent than in the Journal. And in his yearning for contact with the actual, living earth, he also creates a legacy for future generations of nature writers from John Muir to Annie Dillard and Barry Lopez.

All this suggests that we should read the Journal as much for the manner of its saying as for what it says. And, in any case, Thoreau's Journal is not a "memoir," a record of public life and times. The life whose meditations it records was uneventful, at least in the terms of the "restless, nervous, bustling, trivial Nineteenth Century," as Thoreau calls his era in *Walden*. The drama of his life was, to an extraordinary degree, internal, and the Journal was the stage on which this drama unfolded. "Say's I to my-self should be the motto of my Journal" (289), Thoreau writes in an entry of November 11th.

If the self reflected in Thoreau's Journal is primarily engaged in an interior monologue, that same self also, necessarily, makes a relation to other people and to public events. Inevitably, these people and events have a presence in the Journal, and 1851 is not an uninteresting year for those concerned with the public dimension of Thoreau's life. Readers of this volume will follow the exciting narrative of his sending a fugitive slave to Canada (247); they will hear his description of the telegraph's installation in Concord (188); and they will witness his responses to a number of the public issues of his time, such as feminism, about which he heard a lecture in late December (327). And there is gossip in these pages, about the Transcendentalists and other New England personages, including Margaret Fuller, Bronson Alcott, and Thoreau's friend and walking companion William Ellery Channing. Thoreau's reflections on Channing's human frailties provide some of the Journal's more charming and amusing moments.

Transcending gossip are Thoreau's agonized remarks in his Journal, during 1851, about his deteriorating friendship with Emerson. These remarks, in which Emerson is unnamed, often lead to a more general consideration of how deeply problematical friendship was for Thoreau. Certainly, one reason it was so problematical for him is the impossibly high standards he set for human relationships. "Friendship is the unspeakable joy & blessing that results to two or more individuals who from constitution sympathise" (313), he writes on December 21st.

So idealized and demanding were Thoreau's expectations of friends that it is no wonder they disappointed him. Clearly, he left them no margin for error, and he allowed no medium of expression through which broken friendships might be repaired. As he puts the matter on December 17th, "To explain to a friend is to suppose that you are not intelligent of one another. If you are not, to what purpose will you explain?" (311).

From his relationships with women Thoreau desired an even greater purity than he demanded from his male friends, and the resulting difficulties with women and with the idea of marriage are evident in the Journal during 1851. "Does not the history of chivalry and Knight-errantry," Thoreau asks on April 30th, "suggest or point to another relation to woman than leads to marriage—yet an elevating and all absorbing one—perchance transcending marriage? . . . Man is capable of a love of woman quite transcending marriage" (34). Here too, is it any wonder that many of the women he describes in the Journal are disappointing to him?

The Journal of 1851 also offers us glimpses of Thoreau's struggle for vocation during a period when his career as a writer seemed stalled. On September 7th, he writes, "I feel myself uncommonly prepared for *some* literary work, but I can select no work" (204). Earlier, on July 19th, in a passage that later found its way into *Walden*, he had written, "When formerly I was looking about to see what I could do for a living—some sad experience in conforming to the wishes of friends being fresh in my mind to tax my ingenuity—I thought often & seriously of picking huckleberries—that surely I could do, and its small profits might suffice" (115). During this same month, he was finding "some advantage in being the humblest cheapest least dignified man in the village" (94).

But even during such periods of ironic self-appraisal, Thoreau does not lose sight of his central vocation as a writer. In these years, the Journal itself was his principal vehicle of written expression, and during 1851 we often find him self-consciously honing his skills. On November 12th, Thoreau urges himself, "Write often . . . upon a thousand themes—rather than long at a time. . . . Those sentences are good and well discharged which are like so many little resiliencies from the spring floor of our life" (289). And on December 20th, he remarks, "Say the thing with which you labor—it is a waste of time for the writer to use his talents merely. Be faithful to your genius—write in the strain that interests you most— Consult not the popular taste" (312).

Thoreau's struggle for vocation, it might be said, was ultimately resolved *in* the Journal. In this resonant verbal space, he brought his gift for writing to his quest for the spiritual truths that nature might reveal. "My profession," he writes in an entry of September 7th, "is to be always on the alert to find God in nature—to know his lurking places" (207). In 1851 Thoreau was approaching the final decade of his life, and this decade was given to the most intense search for nature's meanings ever undertaken by an American writer. The Journal is a record of that search.

—H. Daniel Peck

Suggestions for Further Reading

While a large body of interpretation surrounds works such as *Walden*, few studies have focused on Thoreau's Journal. The following studies, many of them recent, are either devoted to the Journal, or include significant discussion of it as a work in its own right.

Baym, Nina. "Thoreau's View of Science." *Journal of the History of Ideas* 26 (1965): 221–34.

Burbick, Joan. *Thoreau's Alternative History: Changing Perspectives on Nature, Culture, and Language.* Philadelphia: University of Pennsylvania Press, 1987.

Cameron, Sharon. *Writing Nature: Henry Thoreau's "Journal."* New York: Oxford University Press, 1985.

Delbanco, Andrew. "The Skeptical Pilgrim." In the *New Republic*, July 6, 1992, 37–41.

Golemba, Henry. *Thoreau's Wild Rhetoric.* New York: New York University Press, 1990.

Howarth, William. *The Book of Concord: Thoreau's Life as a Writer.* New York: Penguin Books, 1982.

Kazin, Alfred. "Thoreau's Journals." *Thoreau: A Century of Criticism*, ed. Walter Harding. Dallas: Southern Methodist University Press, 1954.

Lebeaux, Richard. *Thoreau's Seasons.* Amherst: University of Massachusetts Press, 1984.

Miller, Perry. *Consciousness in Concord: The Text of Thoreau's Hitherto "Lost Journal" (1840–1841) Together with Notes and a Commentary.* Boston: Houghton Mifflin, 1958.

Neufeldt, Leonard. "*Praetextus* as Text: Editor-Critic Responses to Thoreau's Journal," *Arizona Quarterly* 46 (Winter 1990): 27–72.

Peck, H. Daniel. " 'Better Mythology': Perception and Emergence in Thoreau's Journal," *North Dakota Quarterly* (Special Issue: "Nature Writers/Writing"), Vol. 59 (Spring 1991): 33–44.

Peck, H. Daniel. *Thoreau's Morning Work: Memory and Perception in "A Week on the Concord and Merrimack Rivers," the Journal, and "Walden."* New Haven: Yale University Press, 1990.

Richardson, Jr., Robert D. *Henry Thoreau: A Life of the Mind.* Berkeley: University of California Press, 1986.

Rossi, William. "The Journal, Self-Culture, and the Genesis of 'Walking,' " *Thoreau Quarterly* 16 (Summer/Fall 1984): 138–55.

Sattelmeyer, Robert. *Thoreau's Reading: A Study in Intellectual History, With Bibliographical Catalogue.* Princeton: Princeton University Press, 1988.

Schneider, Richard J. *Henry David Thoreau.* Boston: Twayne Publishers, 1987.

A Note on the Text

The text of this volume is taken from volumes three and four of Princeton University Press's developing edition of Thoreau's Journal: *Journal 3: 1848–1851*, ed. Robert Sattelmeyer, Mark R. Patterson, and William Rossi (1990); *Journal 4: 1851–1852*, ed. Leonard N. Neufeldt and Nancy Craig Simmons. These volumes, as well as the Princeton Edition's other Journal volumes, include historical and textual introductions, extensive annotation, indexes to topics treated in the Journal, tables indicating Thoreau's alterations, and cross-references to published versions of material that was written first in the Journal. The extract on page xii of the Introduction, based on a transcript of the manuscript, is reproduced with permission of the Thoreau Textual Center. The General Editor of the Journal is Robert Sattelmeyer, and the Editor-in-Chief of The Writings of Henry D. Thoreau is Elizabeth Hall Witherell.

While the four manuscript journals that encompass the year 1851 are largely intact, a few pages and portions of pages did not survive. The position and length of the missing passages are indicated in the text with italicized notes.

A YEAR IN
THOREAU'S JOURNAL:
1851

Thoreau made his first Journal entry of 1851 on January 2nd, while on a brief trip away from Concord. He had gone to Cape Cod, where he lectured at the Bigelow Mechanic Institute in Clinton, Massachusetts, on January 1st. On the 1st he also toured the textile mills at Clinton, and the mills' operations are the primary subject of his January 2nd entry. Thoreau's observation of the Concord landscape— "The catkins of the alders are now frozen stiff!!"—that opens the January 5th entry indicates that by this date his attention had fully returned to his native village.

Jan 2nd 1851

Saw at Clinton last night a room at the Gingham mills which covers 1⅞ acres & contains 578 looms not to speak of spindles both throttle & mule— The rooms all together cover 3 acres. They were using between 3 & 400 horse-power—and kept an engine of 200 horse power with a wheel 23 feet in diameter & a hand ready to supply deficiencies which have not often occurred.

Some portion of the machinery—I think it was where the cotton was broken up lightened up & mixed before being matted together—revolved 1800 times in a minute.

I first saw the pattern room where patterns are made by a hand loom. There were two styles of warps ready for the woof or filling. The operator must count the threads of the woof—which in the mill is done by the machinery.

It was the ancient art of weaving the Shuttle flying back & forth, putting in the filling. As long as the warp is the same it is but one "style" so called.

The cotton should possess a long staple & be clean & free from seed.— The sea-island cotton has a long staple and is valuable for thread. Many bales are thoroughly mixed to make the goods of one quality— The cotton is then torn to pieces & thoroughly lightened up by cylinders armed with hooks & by fans. Then spread a certain weight on a square yard—& matted together & torn up & matted together again two or 3 times over.

Then the matted cotton fed to a cylindrical card—a very thin web of it which is gathered into a copper trough making six (the six card machines) flat ropelike bands which are united in to one at the railway head & drawn And this operation of uniting & drawing or stretching goes on from one machine to another until the thread is spun. which is then dyed—(calico is printed after being woven) having been wound off on to reels & so made into skeins—dyed & dried by steam Then by machinery wound on to spools for the warp & the woof—from a great many spools the warp is drawn off over cylinders and different colored threads properly mixed & arranged. Then the ends of the warp are drawn through the harness of the loom by hand. The operator knows the succession of red blue green &c threads having the numbers given her and draws them through the harness accordingly keeping count. Then the woof is put in or it is *woven*!!

Then the inequalities or nubs are picked off by girls— If *they* discover any imperfection they tag it and if necessary the wages of the weaver are reduced. Now, I think, it is passed over a red hot iron cylinder & the fuz singed off— Then washed with wheels with cold water. Then the water forced out by centrifugal force within horizontal wheels. Then it is starched— The ends stitched together by machinery. Then stretched smooth, dried, & ironed by machinery. Then measured folded & packed.

This the agent Forbes says is the best Gingham mill in this country—the goods are better than the imported— The English have even stolen their name Lancaster mills calling theirs "Lancasterian"

The machinery is some of it peculiar——part of the throttle spindls? for instance.

The Coach lace mill—only place in this country where it is made by machinery—made of thread of different materials—as cotton—worsted—linnen—as well as colors—the raised figure produced by needles inserted woof fashion. Well worth examining further. Also pantaloon stuffs made in same mill—& dyed after being woven—the woolen not taking the same dye with the cotton—hence a slight particolored appearance. These goods are sheared i.e. a part of the nap taken off—making them smoother— Pressed between paste boards.

The Brussels carpets made at the Carpet Factory said to be the best in the world. Made like coach lace only wider.

Erastus (?) Bigelow inventor of what is new in the above machinery. & with his brother & another owner of the carpet factory.

I am struck by the fact that no work has been shirked when a piece of cloth is produced, every thread has been counted in the finest web—it has not been matted together—the operator has suceeded only by patience perseverance and fidelity.

The direction in which a rail-road runs, though intersecting another at right angles, may cause that one will be blocked up with snow & the other be comparatively open—even for great distances, depending on the direction of prevailing winds & valleys— There are the Fitchburg & Nashua & Worcester.

Jan. 4th

The longest silence is the most pertinent question most pertinently put. Emphatically silent. The most important questions—whose answers—concern us more than any—are never put in any other way.

It is difficult for two strangers mutually well disposed so truly to bear themselves toward each other that a feeling of falseness & hollowness shall not soon spring up between them. The least anxiety to behave truly vitiates the relation.

I think of those to whom I am at the moment truly related—with a joy never expressed & never to be expressed, before I fall asleep (at night.)

Jan 5th—51

The catkins of the alders are now frozen stiff!!

Almost all that my neighbors call good, I believe in my soul to be bad. If I repent of anything it is of my good behavior. What demon possessed me that I behaved so well.

You may say the wisest thing you can—old man—you who have lived seventy years not without honor of a kind— I hear an irresistible voice, the voice of my destiny which invites me away from all that

Jan 7th

The snow is sixteen inches deep at least but is a mild & genial afternoon—as if it were the beginning of a January thaw. Take away the snow and it would not be winter but like many days in the fall. The birds acknowledge the difference in the air—the jays are more noisy & the chicadees are oftener heard.

Many herbs are not crushed by the snow.

I do not remember to have seen fleas except when the weather was mild & the snow damp.

I must live above all in the present—

{Seven-eighths page missing}

on a rail may be, in the midst of the affairs of nature & of God— He had not fallen astern—he had got up early Where he was it was always seasonable to

{Seven-eighths page missing}

woodchoppers than to read books of natural history. What they know is very slow to get into books. Science does not embody all that men know—only what is for men of science. The Woodman tells me how he caught trout in a box trap—how he made his troughs for maple sap of pine logs—& the spouts of sumack or white ash which have a large pith.

The knowledge of an unlearned man is living & luxuriant like a forest—but covered with mosses & lichens and for the most part inaccessible & going to waste—the knowledge of the man of science is like timber collected in yards for public works which stub supports a green sprout here & there—but even this is liable to dry rot.

I felt my spirits rise when I had got off the road into the open fields & the sky had a new appearance. I stepped along more buoyantly. There was a warm sunset over the wooded valleys—a yellowish tinge on the pines Reddish dun colored clouds like dusky flames stood over it And then streaks of blue sky were seen here & there— The life the joy that is in blue sky after a storm— There is no account of the blue sky in history. Before I walked in the ruts of travel—now I adventured. This evening a fog comes up from the south.

If I have any conversation with a scamp in my walk my afternoon is wont to be spoiled.

The squirrels & apparently the rabbits have got all the frozen apples in the hollow behind Miles'. The rabbits appear to have devoured what the squirrels dropped & left I see the tracks of both leading from the woods on all sides to the apple trees.

Jan 8th

The smilax green briar berries still hang on like small grapes— The thorn of this vine is very perfect like a straight dagger

The light of the setting sun falling on the snow banks today made them glow almost yellow

The hills seen from Fair Haven Pond make a wholly new landscape Covered with snow & yellowish green or brown pines & shrub oaks they look higher & more massive. Their white mantle relates them to the clouds in the horizon & to the sky. Perchance what is light colored looks loftier than what is dark.

You might say of a very old & withered man or woman that they hang on like a shrub-oak leaf almost to a second spring. There was still a little life in the heel of the leaf-stalk

Jan 10th

The snow shows how much of the *mts* in the horizon are covered with forest— I can also see plainer as I stand on a hill what proportion of the township is in forest.

Got some excellent frozen thawed apples off of Anursnack— Soft

& luscious as a custard—and free from worms & rot Saw a partridge
budding—but they did not appear to have pecked the apples

There was a remarkable sunset a mother of pearl sky seen over
the Price farm Some small clouds as well as the edges of large ones
most brilliantly painted with mother of pearl tints through &
through. I never saw the like before. Who can foretel the sunset—
what it will be?

The near and bare hills covered with snow look like
mountains—but the mts in the horizon do not look higher than
hills.

I frequently see a hole in the snow where a partridge has squatted
the mark or form of her tail very distinct.

The chivalric & heroic spirit which once belonged to the
chevalier or rider only seems now to reside in the walker— To
represent the chivalric spirit we have no longer a knight—but a
walker errant— I speak not of Pedestrianism, or of walking a
thousand miles in a thousand successive hours—

The Adam who daily takes a turn in his garden

methinks I would not accept of the gift of life If I were required
to spend as large a portion of it sitting bent up or with my legs
crossed as the shoemakers and tailors do. As well be tied head &
heels together & cast into the sea— Making acquaintance with my
extremities

I have met with but one or two persons in the course of my life
who understood the art taking walks daily—not exercize—the legs or
body merely—nor barely to recruit the spirits but positively to
exercise both body & spirit—& to succeed to the highest & worthiest
ends by the abandonment of all specifics ends.— who had a genius,
so to speak, for sauntering—— And this word saunter by the way is
happily derived "from idle people who roved about the country [in
the middle ages] and asked charity under pretence of going à la
sainte terre," to the holy land—till perchance the children exclaimed
There goes a sainte terrer a holy lander— They who never go to
the holy land in their walks as they pretend, are indeed mere idlers
& vagabonds—

{*Two leaves missing*}

than usually jealous of my freedom I feel that my connexions with
& obligations to society are at present very slight & transient. Those
slight labors which afford me a livelihood & by which I am
serviceable to my contemporaries are as yet a pleasure to me and I

am not often reminded that they are a necessity. So far I am successful—and only he is successful in his business who makes that pursuit which affords him the highest pleasure sustain him. But I foresee that if my wants should be much increased the labor required to supply them would become a drudgery— If I should sell both my forenoons & afternoons to society neglecting my peculiar calling there would be nothin left worth living for. I trust that I shall never thus sell my birth-right for a mess of pottage

F. Andrew Michaux says that "the species of large trees are much more numerous in North America than in Europe: in the U S there are more than 140 species that exceed 30 feet in height——; in France there are but 30 that attain this size, of which 18 enter into the composition of the forests, & seven only are employed in building."

The perfect resemblance of the Chestnut Beech & hornbeams in Europe & the U S rendered a separate figure unnecessary.
He says the white oak "is the only oak on which a few of the dried leaves persist till the circulation is renewed in the spring."
Had often heard his father say that "the fruit of the common European walnut, in its natural state, is harder than that of the American species just mentioned [the Pacanenut Hickory] and inferior to it in size & quality."

The arts teach us a thousand lessons. Not a yard of cloth can be woven without the most thorough fidelity in the weaver. The ship must be made *absolutely* tight before it is launched.

It is an important difference between two characters that the one is satisfied with a happy but level success but, the other as constantly elevates his aim. Though my life is low, if my spirit looks upward habitually at an elevated angle—it is, as it were redeemed— When the desire to be better than we are is really sincere we are instantly elevated, and so far better already
I lose my friends of course as much by my own ill treatment & ill valuing of them (prophaning of them cheapening of them) as by their cheapening of themselves—till at last when I am prepared to them justice I am permitted to deal only with the memories of themselves—their ideals still surviving in me—no longer with their actual selves—

We exclude ourselves— As the child said of the stream in which he bathed head or foot V Confucius

It is something to know when you are addressed by divinity and not by a common traveller.

I went down cellar just now to get an armful of wood—and passing the brick piers with my wood & candle—I heard methought a common place suggestion—but when as it were by accident—I reverently attended to the hint—I found that it was the voice of a God who had followed me down cellar to speak to me.

How many communications may we not lose through inattention?

I would fain keep a journal which should contain those thoughts & impressions which I am most liable to forget that I have had Which would have, in one sense the greatest remoteness—in another the greatest nearness, to me.

'Tis healthy to be sick sometimes,

I do not know but the reason why I love some Latin verses more than whol English poems—is simply in the elegant terseness & conciseness of the language—an advantage which the individual appears to have shared with his nation.

When we can no longer ramble in the fields of Nature, we ramble in the fields of thought & literature. The old become readers — Our heads retain their strength when our legs have become weak.

English literature from the days of the minstrels to the Lake Poets Chaucer & Spencer & Shakspeare & Milton included breathes no quite fresh & in this sense wild strain It is an essentially tame & civilized literature reflecting Greece and Rome. Her wilderness is a greenwood her wild man a Robinhood. There is plenty of genial love of nature in her poets but

Her chronicles inform us when her wild animals, but not when the wild man in her became extinct
There was need of America

I cannot think of any poetry which adequately expresses this yearning for the wild. the *wilde*.

Ovid says

Nilus in extremum fugit perterritus orbem,
Occuluitque caput, quod adhuc latet.–
Nilus terrified fled to the extremity of the globe,
And hid his head, which is still concealed–

And we moderns must repeat–quod adhuc latet.

Phaeton's Epitaph

Hic situs est Phaëton, currûs auriga paterni;
Quem si non tenuit, magnis tamen excidit ausis.

His sister Lampetie–

subitâ radice retenta est.

All the sisters were changed to trees while They were in vain
beseeching Their mother not to break their branches

cortex in verba novissima venit.

His brother Cycnus lamenting the death of Phaeton–killed by
Joves lightning–& the metamorphosis of his sisters–was changed into
a Swan–

Nec se caeloque, Iovique
Credit, ut injustè missi memor ignis ab illo.

Reason why the swan does not fly–

Nor trusts himself to the heavens
Nor to Jove, as if remembering the fire unjustly sent by him

i.e. against Phaeton.

precibusque minas regaliter addit.
II-397

Jove–

royally adds threats to prayers.

Callisto–

Miles erat Phoebes

i.e. a huntress

––(neque enim coelestia tingi
Ora decet lachrymis) II-621

> For it it is not becoming that the faces
> of the celestials be tinged with tears

How much more fertile a Nature has Grecian Mythology its root
in than English Literature! The nature which inspired mythology still
flourishes— Mythology is the crop which the old world bore before
its soil was exhausted— The west is preparing to add its fables to
those of the east. A more fertile nature than the Mississippi valley.
None of your four hour nights for me me— The wise man will take
a fool's allowance— The corn would not come to much if the
nights were but four hours long
The soil in which those fables grew is deep and inexhaustible.
Lead cast by the Balearian sling.

> Volat illud, et incandescit eundo;
> Et quos non habuit, sub nubibus invenit, ignes.
> II-728
> That flies & grows hot with going,
> And fires which it had not finds under the clouds.

The old world with its vast deserts—& its arid & elevated steppes
& table lands contrasted with the new world with its humid & fertile
valleys & savannahs & prairies—& its boundless primitive forests— Is
like the exhausted Ind corn lands contrasted with the peat meadows,
America requires some of the sand of the old world to be carted
onto her rich but as yet unassimilated meadows

I went some months ago to see a panorama of the Rhine It was
like a dream of the Middle ages— I floated down its historic stream
in something more than imagination under bridges built by the
Romans and repaired by later heroes past cities & castles whose very
names were music to me made my ears tingle—& each of which was
the subject of a legend. There seemed to come up from its waters &
its vine-clad hills & vallys a hushed music as of crusaders departing
for the Holy Land— There were Ehrenbreitstein & Rolandseck &
Coblentz which I knew only in history. I floated along through the
moonlight of history under the spell of enchanment It was as if I
remembered a glorious dream as if I had been transported to a
heroic age & breathed an atmospher of chivalry Those times
appeared far more poetic & heroic than these
Soon after I went to see the panorama of the Mississippi and as I
fitly worked my way upward in the light of today—& saw the
steamboats wooding up—& loooked up the Ohio & the Missouri &

saw its unpeopled cliffs–& counted the rising cities–& saw the
Indians removing west across the stream & heard the legends of
Dubuque & of Wenona's Cliff–still thinking more of the future than
of the past or present–I saw that this was a Rhine stream of a dif
kind that the foundations

{*One leaf missing*}

all this West–which our thoughts traverse so often & so freely. We
have never doubted that their prosperity was our prosperity– It is
the home of the younger-sons As among the Scandinavians the
younger sons took to the seas for their inheritance and became the
Vikings or Kings of the Bays & colonized Ice land & Greenland &
probably discovered the continent of America

    Guyot says–"the Baltic Sea has a depth of only 120 feet between
the coasts of Germany and those of Sweeden;" p 82
    "The Adriatic, between Venice & Trieste, has a depth of only
130 feet."
    "Between France & England, the greatest depth does not exceed
300 feet;"
    He says
    The most extensive forest "the most gigantic wilderness" on the
earth is in the basin of the Amazon & extends almost unbroken
more than 1500 miles
    South America the kingdom of palms no where a greater no' of
species "This is a sign of the preponderating development of leaves
over every other part of the vegetable growth; of that expansion of
foliage, of that leafiness, peculiar to warm & moist climates. America
has no plants with slender shrunken leaves, like those of Africa and
New Holland. The Ericas, or heather, so common, so varied, so
characteristic of the flora of the Cape of Good Hope, is a form
unknown to the New World. There is nothing resembling those
Metrosideri of Africa, those dry Myrtles (Eucalyptus) and willow-
leaved acacias, whose flowers shine with the liveliest colors, but their
narrow foliage, turned edgewise to the vertical sun, casts no
shadow."

my own
    The white man derives his nourishment from the earth from the
roots & grains The potatoe & wheat & corn & rice & sugar–which
often grow in fertile & pestilential river bottoms fatal to the life of

the cultivator The Indian has but a slender hold on the earth— He
derives his nourishment in great part but indirectly from her through
the animals he hunts

  —"compared with the Old World, the New World is the humid
side of our planet, the *oceanic, Vegetative* world, the passive element
awaiting the excitement of a livelier impulse from without."

{*One leaf missing*}

  "For the American, this task is to work the virgin soil,"—
  "Agriculture here already assumes proportions unknown
everywhere else."

Feb 9th 1851

The last half of January was warm & thawy. The swift streams
were open & the muskrats were seen swimming & diving &
bringing up clams leaving their shells on the ice. We had now
forgotten summer & autumn, but had already begun to anticipate
spring. Fishermen improved the warmer weather to fish for pickerel
through the ice— Before it was only the Autumn landscape with a
thin layer of snow upon it we saw the withered flowers through it—
but now we do not think of autumn when we look on this snow
That earth is effectually buried— It is mid winter. Within a few days
the cold has set in stronger than ever though the days are much
longer now. Now I travel across the fields on the crust which has
frozen since the Jan. thaw—& I can cross the river in most places. It
is easier to get about the country than at any other season— Easier
than in summer because the rivers & meadows are frozen—& there is
no high grass or other crops to be avoided—easier than in Dec
before the crust was frozen

  Sir John Mandeville says—"In fro what partie of the earth that
men dwell, outher aboven or benethen, it seemeth always to hem
that dwellen there, that they gon more right than any other folk."
  Again—"And yee shulle undirstonde, that of all theise contrees,
and of all theise yles, and of all the dyverse folk, that I have spoken
of before, and of dyverse laws and of dyverse beleeves that thei have,
yit is there non of hem alle, but that thei have sum resoun within
hem and understondinge, but gif it be the fewere."

  I have heard that there is a Society for the Diffusion of Useful
Knowledge— It is said that Knowledge is power and the like—

Methinks there is equal need of a society for the diffusion of useful Ignorance—for what is most of our boasted so called knowledge but a conceit that we know something which robs us of the advantages of our actual ignorance—

In What consists the superiority of that

{*One leaf missing*}

auctoritatis. Habemus enim hujusmodi senatûs-consultum, veruntamen inclusum in tabulis, tanquam gladium in vaginâ reconditum; quo ex senatûs-consulto, confestim interfectum te esse, O Business, convenit. Vivis; et vivis, non ad deponendam, sed ad confirmandam, audaciam. Cupio, Patres Conscripti, me esse clementem: cupio in tantis rei-*privatae* periculis, me non dissolutum videri: sed jam me ipse inertiae nequitiaeque condemno.

Castra sunt in Italiâ, contra rem-*privatam*, in Etruriae faucibus collocata: crescit in dies singulos hostium numerus: eorum autem imperatorem castrorum, ducemque hostium, intra moenia, atque adeò in senatu, videmus, intestinam aliquam quotidie perniciem rei-privatae molientem."

For a man's ignorance sometimes is not only useful but beautiful while his knowledge is oftentimes worse than useless beside being ugly.

In reference to important things whose knowledge amounts to more than a consciousness of his ignorance Yet what more refreshing & inspiring knowledge than this?

How often are we wise as serpents without being harmless as doves.

Donne says "Who are a little wise the best fools be Cudworth says "we have all of us by nature μαντευμά τι (as both Plato & Aristotle call it) a certain divination, presage and parturient vati-cination in our minds, of some higher good & perfection than either power or knowledge." — — Aristotle himself declares, that there is λόγου τι κρεῖττον, which is λόγου ἀρχὴ, something better than reason & knowledge, which is the principle and original of all."

Lavater says "Who finds the clearest not clear, thinks the darkest not obscure"

My desire for knowledge is intermittent but my desire to commune with the spirit of the universe—to be intoxicated even with the fumes, call it, of that divine nectar—to bear my head

through atmospheres and over heights unknown to my feet—is
perennial & constant.

It is remarkable how few events or crises there are in our minds'
histories—   How little *exercised* we have been in our mind—how few
experiences we have had   I would fain be assured that I am growing
apace & rankly—though

{Two leaves missing}

society—to that culture—that interaction of man on man which is a
sort of breeding in & in and produces a merely English nobility a
puny & effoete nobility, a civilization which has a speedy limit.

The story of Romulus & Remus being suckled by a wolf is not a
mere fable; the founders of every state which has risen to eminence
have drawn their nourishment and vigor from a similar source. It is
because the children of the empire were not suckled by wolves that
they were conquered & displaced by the children of the northern
forests who were.

America is the she wolf to day and the children of exhausted
Europe exposed on her uninhabited & savage shores are the
Romulus & Remus who having derived new life & vigor from her
breast have founded a new Rome in the west.

It is remarkable how few passages comparatively speaking there
are in the best literature of the day which betray any intimacy with
nature.

It is apparent enough to me that only one or two of my
townsmen or acquaintances (not more than one in many thousand
men in deed—) feel or at least obey any strong attraction drawing
them toward the forest or to nature, but all almost without
exception gravitate exclusively toward men or society. The young
men of Concord and in other towns do not walk in the woods but
congregate in shops & offices—   They suck one another—   Their
strongest attraction is toward the mill dam.

A thousand assemble about the fountain in the public square—the
town pump—be it full or dry clear or turbid, every morning but not
—one in a thousand is in the meanwhile drinking at that fountain's
head.

It is hard for the young aye & the old man in the outeskirts to
keep away from the Mill dam a whole day—but he will find some
excuse as an ounce of cloves that might be wanted or a new
England Farmer still in the office—to tackle up the horse—or even go

afoot but he will go at some rate— This is not bad comparatively this is because he cannot do better. In spite of his hoeing & chopping he is unexpressed & undeveloped.

I do not know where to find in any literature whether ancient or modern—any adequate account of that Nature with which I am acquainted. Mythology comes nearest to it of any.

The actual life of men is not without a dramatic interest at least to the thinker. It is not altogether prosaic. 70,000 pilgrims proceed annually to Mecca from the various nations of Islám. But this is not so significant as the far simpler & more unpretending pilgrimage to the shrines of some obscure individual which yet makes no bustle in the world

I believe that adam in paradise was not so favorably situated on the whole as is the backwoodsman in America— You all know how miserably the former turned out—or was turned out—but there is some consolation at least in the fact that it yet remains to be seen how the western Adam Adam in the wilderness will turn out—

> In Adams fall
> We sinned all.
> In the new Adam's rise
> We shall all reach the skies.

Infusion of hemlock in our tea, if we must drink tea—not the poison hemlock—but the hemlock spruce I mean—or perchance the Arbor Vitae—the tree of life is what we want.

Wednesday Feb 12th

A beautiful day with but little snow or ice on the ground. Though the air is sharp, as the earth is half bare the hens have strayed to some distance from the barns. The hens standing around their lord & pluming themselves and still fretting a little strive to fetch the year about.

A thaw has nearly washed away the snow & raised the river & the brooks & flooded the meadows covering the old ice which which is still fast to the bottom

I find that it is an excellent walk for variety & novelty & wildness to keep round the edge of the meadow—the ice not being strong enough to bear and transparent as water—on the bare ground or snow just between the highest water mark and the present water line A narrow meandering walk rich in unexpected views & objects.

The line of rubbish which marks the higher tides withered flags &

reeds & twigs & cranberries is to my eyes a very agreeable &
significant line which nature traces along the edge of the meadows.

It is a strongly marked enduring natural line which in summer
reminds me that the water has once stood over where I walk
Sometimes the grooved trees tell the same tale. The wrecks of the
meadow which fill a thousand coves and tell a thousand tales to
those who can read them Our prairial mediterranean shore. The
gentle rise of water around the trees in the meadow—where oaks &
maples stand far out in the sea— And young elms sometimes are
seen standing close around some rocks which lifts its head above the
water—as if protecting it preventing it from being washed away
though in truth they owe their origin & preservation to it. It first
invited & detained their seed & now preserves the soil in which they
grow. A pleasant reminiscence of the rise of waters To go up one
side of the river & down the other following this way which
meanders so much more than the river itself— If you cannot go on
the ice—you are then gently compelled to take this course which is
on the whole more beautiful—to follow the sinuosities of the
meadow. Between the highest water mark & the present water line
is a space generally from a few feet to a few rods in width. When
the water comes over the road, then my spirits rise—when the fences
are carried away. A prairial walk— Saw a caterpillar crawling about
on the snow

The earth is so bare that it makes an impression on one as if it
were catching cold.

I saw today something new to me as I walked along the edge of
the meadow—every half mile or so along the channel of the river I
saw at a distance where apparently the ice had been broken up while
freezing by the pressure of other ice—thin cakes of ice forced up on
their edges & reflecting the sun like so many mirrors whole fleets of
shining sails. giving a very lively appearance to the river—Where for
a dozen rods thin flakes of ice stood on their edges—like a fleet
beating upstream against the sun—a fleet of ice-boats

It is remarkable that the cracks in the ice on the meadows
sometimes may be traced a dozen rods from the water through the
snow in the neighboring fields.

It is only necessary that man should start a fence that nature
should carry it on & complete it. The farmer can not plough quite
up to the rails or wall which he himself has placed—& hence it often
becomes a hedge-row & sometimes a coppice.

I found to-day apples still green under the snow— And others

frozen and thawed sweeter far than when sound. a sugary
sweetness.

There is something more than association at the bottom of the
excitement which the roar of a cataract produces. It is allied to the
circulation in our veins We have a waterfall which corresponds
even to Niagara somewhere within us. It is astonishing what a rush
& tumult a slight inclination will produce in a swolen brook. How
it proclaims its glee—its boisterousness—rushing headlong in its
prodigal course as if it would exhaust itself in half an hour—how it
spends itself— I would say to the orator and poet Flow freely &
lavishly as a brook that is full—without stint—perchance I have
stumbled upon the origin of the word lavish. It does not hesitate to
tumble down the steepest precipice & roar or tinkle as it goes,—for
fear it will exhaust its fountain.— The impetuosity of descending
waters even by the slightest inclination! It seems to flow with ever
increasing rapidity.

It is difficult to believe what Philosophers assert that it is merely a
difference in the form of the elementary particles, as whether they
are square or globular—which makes the difference between the
steadfast everlasting & reposing hill-side & the impetuous torrent
which tumbles down it.

It is worth the while to walk over sproutlands—where oak &
chestnut sprouts are mounting swiftly up again into the sky— And
already perchance their sere leaves begin to rustle in the breeze &
reflect the light on the hills sides—

> "Heroic underwoods that take the air
> With freedom, nor respect their parent's death"

I trust that the walkers of the present day are conscious of the
blessings which they enjoy in the comparative freedom with which
they can ramble over the country & enjoy the landscape—anticipating
with compassion that future day when possibly it will be partitioned
off into so called pleasure grounds where only a few may enjoy the
narrow & exclusive pleasure which is compatible with ownership.
When walking over the surface of Gods earth—shall be construed to
mean trespassing on some gentleman's grounds. When fences shall be
multiplied & man traps & other engines invented to confine men to
the public road. I am thankfull that we have yet so much room in
America.

Feb 13th

Skated to Sudbury. A beautiful summerlike day. The meadows
were frozen just enough to bear—— Examined now the fleets of ice
flakes close at hand. They are a very singular & interesting
phenomenon which I do not remember to have seen I should say
that when the water was frozen about as thick as pasteboard—a
violent gust had here & there broken it up & while the wind &
waves held it up on its edge—the increasing cold froze it in firmly.
So it seemed for the flakes were for the most part turned one way—
i.e. standing on one side you saw only their edges on another—the
N E or S W—their sides— They were for the most part of a
triangular form—like a shoulder of mutton? sail slightly scolloped—
like shells They looked like a fleet of a thousand mackeral fishers
under a press of sail careering before a smacking breeze. Sometimes
the sun & wind had reduced them to the thinness of writing paper
and they fluttered & rustled & tinkled merrily. I skated through
them & strewed their wrecks around.

They appear to have been elevated expressly to reflect the sun
like mirrors—to adorn the river & attract the eye of the walker
skater. Who will say that Their principal end is not answered when
they excite the admiration of the skater? Every half mile or mile as
you skate up the river you see these crystal fleets. Nature is a great
imitator & loves to repeat herself. She wastes her wonders on the
town. It impresses me as one superiority in her art, if art it may be
called, that she does not require that man appreciate her—takes no
steps to attract his attention.

The trouble is in getting on & off the ice— When you are once
on you can go well enough It melts round the edges

Again I saw today half a mile off in Sudbury a sandy spot on the
top of a hill—where I prophesied that I should find traces of the
Indians. When within a dozen rods I distinguished the foundation of
a lodge—and merely passing over it I saw many fragments of the
arrowhead stone— I have frequently distinguished these localities
half a mile—gone forward & picked up arrowheads. Examined by the
botany All its parts—the first flower I have seen, the ictodes
foetidum

Saw in a warm muddy brook in Sudbury—quite open & exposed
the skunk cabbage spathes above water— The tops of the spathes
were frostbitten but the fruit sound— There was one partly
expanded— The first flower of the season—for it is a flower— I
doubt if there is month without its flower.

Also mosses—mingled red & green—the red will pass for the blossom.

As for antiquities— One of our old deserted country roads marked only by the parallel fences & a cellar hole with its bricks where the last inhabitant died the victim of intemperance 50 years ago with its bare & exhausted fields stretching around—suggests to me an antiquity greater & more remote from America than the tombs of Etruria.— I insert the rise & fall of Rome in that parenthesis.

It is important to observe not only the subject of our pure & unalloyed joys—but also the secret of any dissatisfaction one may feel.

In society—in the best institutions of men—I remark a certain precocity— When we should be growing children—we are already little men. Infants as we are we make haste to be weaned from our great mother's breast & cultivate our parts by intercourse with one another.

I have not much faith in the method of restoring impoverished soils which relies on manuring mainly—& does not add some virgin soil or muck

Many a poor sore eyed student that I have heard of would grow faster both intellectually & physically if instead of sitting up so very late to study, he honestly slumberd a fool's allowance.

I would not have every man cultivated—any more than I would have every acre of earth cultivated. Some must be preparing a mould by the annual decay of the forests which they sustain.

Saw half a dozen cows let out & standing about in a retired meadow as in a cow yard.

Feb 14th

Consider the farmer, who is commonly regarded as the healthiest man— He may be the toughest but he is not the healthiest. He has lost his elacticity—he can neither run nor jump— Health is the free use & command of all our faculties—& equal development— His is the health of the ox—an over worked buffalo— His joints are stiff. The resemblance is true even in particulars. He is cast away in a pair of cowhide boots—and travels at an ox's pace—indeed in some places he puts his foot into the skin of an ox's shin. It would do him good to be thoroughly shampooed to make him supple. His health is an insensibility to all influence— But only the healthiest man in the world is sensible to the finest influence— He who is affected by more or less of electricity in the air—

We shall see but little way if we require to understand what we see— How few things can a man measure with the tape of his understanding—how many greater things might he he be seeing in the meanwhile.

One afternoon in the fall Nov 21st I saw Fair Haven Pond with its island & meadow between the island & the shore, a strip of perfectly smooth water in the lee of the island & two hawks sailing over it—(and something more I saw which cannot easily be described which made me say to myself that it the landscape could not be improved.) I did not see how it could be improved. Yet I do not know what these things can be; (for) I begin to see such objects only when I leave off understanding them—and afterwards remember that I did not appreciate them before. But I get no further than this. How adapted these forms & colors to our eyes, a meadow & its islands. What are these things? Yet the hawks & the ducks keep so aloof, & nature is so reserved! We are made to love the river & the meadow as the wind (is made) to ripple the water

There is a difference between eating for strength & from mere gluttony. The Hottentots eagerlly devour the marrow of the Koodoo & other antelopes raw, as a matter of course—& herein perchance have stolen a march on the cooks of Paris. The eater of meats must come to this. This is better than stall fed cattle & slaughter-house pork. Possibly they derive a certain wild-animal vigor therefrom which the most artfully cooked meats do not furnish.

We learn by the January thaw that the winter is intermittent and are reminded of other seasons— The back of the winter is broken

Feb. 15th

Fatal is the discovery that our friend is fallible—that he has prejudices. He is then only prejudiced in our favor. What is the value of his esteem who does not justly esteem another?

Alas! Alas! When my friend begins to deal in confessions—breaks silence—makes a theme of friendship—(which then is always something past) and descends to merely human relations As long as there is a spark of love remaining cherish that alone—only *that* can be kindled into a flame.

I thought that friendship—that love was still possible between—I thought that we had not withdrawn very far asunder— But now that my friend rashly thoughtlessly—prophanely speaks *recognizing* the distance between us—that distance seems infinitely increased.

Of our friends we do not incline to speak to complain to others—we would not disturb the foundations of confidence that may still be.

Why should we not still continue to live with the intensity &

rapidity of infants. Is not the world—are not the heavens as
unfathomed as ever? Have we exhausted any joy—any sentiment?

The author of Festus well exclaims

> "Could we but think with the intensity
> We love with, we might do great things, I think.

Feb 16th

Do we call this the land of the free? What is it to be free from
King Geo the IV. and continue the slaves of prejudice? What is it be
born free & equal & not to live. What is the value of any political
freedom, but as a means to moral freedom. Is it a freedom to be
slaves or a freedom to be free, of which we boast. We are a nation
of politicians—concerned about the outsides of freedom—the means &
outmost defences of freedom— It is our children's children who
may perchance be—essentially free.

We tax ourselves unjustly— There is a part of us which is not
represented— It is taxation without representation— We quarter
troops upon ourselves. In respect to virtue or true manhood we are
essentially provincial not metropolitan—mere Jonathans

We are provincial because we do not find at home our standards—
because we do not worship truth but the reflection of truth.
because we are absorbed in & narrowed by trade & commerce &
agriculture which are but means & not the end.

We are essentially provincial, I say, & so is the English parliament
—mere country bumpkins they betray themselves—when any more
important question arises for them to settle— Their natures are
subdued to what they work in. The finest manners in the world are
awkwardness & fatuity when contrasted with a finer intelligence.—
They appear but as the fashions of past days—mere courtliness—small
clothes out of date—& knee buckles—an attitude merely.

The vice of manners is that they are continually deserted by the
character—they are castoff clothes or shells—claiming the respect of
the living creature.

You are presented with the shells instead of the meat—and it is no
excuse generally that in the case of some fish the shells are of more
worth than the meat. The man who thrusts his manners upon me
does as if he were to insist on introducing me to his cabinet of
curiosities, when I wish to see himself. Manners are conscious.
Character is unconscious.

My neighbor does not recover from his formal bow so soon as I
do from the pleasure of meeting him.

Feb 18th Tuesday

Ground nearly bare of snow pleasant day with a strong south wind. Skated though the ice was soft in spots—saw the skunk cabbage in flower—gathered nuts & apples on the bare ground still sound & preserving their colors red & green—many of them.

Yesterday the river was over the road by Hubbard's bridge.

Surveyed White Pond yesterday Feb— 17th

There is little or nothing to be remembered written on the subject of getting an honest living. Neither the New testament nor Poor Richard speaks to our condition. I cannot think of a single page which entertains—much less answers the questions which I put to myself on this subject. How to make the getting our living poetic—! for if it is not poetic—it is not life but death that we get

Is it that men are too disgusted with their experience to speak of it? Or that commonly they do not question the common modes.

The most practically important of all questions, it seems to me, is how shall I get my living—& yet I find little or nothing said to the purpose in any book. Those who are living on the interest of money inherited—or dishonestly i.e. by false methods acquired are of course incompetent to answer it.

I consider that society with all its arts, has done nothing for us in this respect.— One would think from looking at literature—that this question had never disturbed a solitary individual's musings.

Cold and hunger seem more friendly to my nature than those methods which men have adopted & advise to ward them off—

If it were not that I desire to do something here (accomplish some work) I should certainly prefer to suffer and die rather than be at the pains to get a living by the modes men propose.

There may be an excess even of informing light

Niepce a Frenchman announced that "No substance can be exposed to the sun's rays without undergoing a chemical change." Granite rocks & stone structures & statues of metal &c—"are" says Rob. Hunt "all alike destructively acted upon during the hours of sunshine, and, but for provisions of nature no less wonderful, would soon perish under the delicate touch of the most subtile of the agencies of the universe." But Niepce showed says Hunt "that those bodies which underwent this change during daylight, possessed the power of restoring themselves to their original conditions during the hours of night, when this excitement was no longer influencing them" So in the case of the Daguerreotype "The picture which we receive to-night, unless we adopt some method of securing its permanency, fades away before the morning, & we try to restore it

in vain.--(infers) "the hours of darkness are as necessary to the
inorganic creation as we know night & sleep are to the organic
kingdom."

Such is the influence of "actinism" that power in the sun's rays
which produces a chemical effect.

Feb 25th–51

A very windy day–a slight snow which fell last night was melted
at noon–a strong gusty wind The waves on the meadows make a
fine show– I saw at Hubbards bridge that all the ice had been
blown up stream from the meadows and was collected over the
channel against the bridge in large cakes These were covered and
intermingled with a remarkable quantity of the meadow's crust.
There was no ice to be seen up stream and no *more* down stream.
The meadows have been flooded for a fortnight–and *this* water has
been frozen barely thick enough to bear once (one day) only– The
old ice on the meadows was covered several feet deep–– I
observed from the bridge a few rods off northward what looked like
an island directly over the channel– It was the crust of the meadow
afloat. I reached with a little risk and found it to be 4 rods long by
one broad–the surface of the meadow with cranberry vines &'c all
connected & in their natural position and no ice visible but around
its edges– It appeared to be the frozen crust (which was separated
from the unfrozen soil as ice is from the water beneath) buoyed up?
perchance by the ice around its edges frozen to the stubble– Was
there any pure ice under it? Had there been any above it? Will
frozen meadow float? Had ice which originally supported it from
above melted except about the edges? When the ice melts or the soil
thaws of course it falls to bottom wherever it may be. Here is
another agent employed in the distribution of plants– I have seen
where a smooth shore which I frequented for bathing was in one
season strewn with these hummocks bearing the button bush with
them which have now changed the character of the shore. There
were many rushes & lily pad stems on the ice. Had the ice formed
about them as they grew–broke them off when it floated away & so
they were strown about on it?

Wednesday Feb 26th

Examined the floating meadow again today. It is more than a foot
thick the under part much mixed with ice–ice & muck– It
appeared to me that the meadow surface had been heaved by the
frost & then the water had run down & under it & finally when the
ice rose lifted it up–wherever there was ice enough mixed with it to
float it. I saw large cakes of ice with other large cakes the latter as

big as a table on top of them. Probably the former rose while the
latter were already floating about. The plants scattered about were
bullrushes & lily-pad stems.– Saw 5 red-wings & a songsparrow?
this afternoon.

Feb 27

Saw today on Pine Hill behind Mr. Joseph Merriam's House a
Norway pine. The first I have seen in Concord– Mr Gleason
pointed it out to me as a singular pine which he did not know the
name of. It was a very handsome tree about 25 feet high. F. Wood
thinks that he has lost the surface of 2 acres of his meadow by the
ice.– Got 15 cartloads out of a hummock left on another meadow
Blue joint was introduced into the first meadow where it did not
grow before.

Of two men, one of whom knows nothing about a subject, and
what is extremely rare, knows that he knows nothing–and the other
really knows something about it, but thinks that he knows all–
What great advantage has the latter over the former? Which is the
best to deal with?

I do not know that knowledge amounts to anything more
definite than a novel & grand surprise on a sudden revelation of the
insufficiency of all that we had called knowledge before. An
indefinite sence of the grandeur & glory of the Universe. It is the
lighting up of the mist by the sun

But man cannot be said to know in any higher sense, than he can
look serenely & with impunity in the face of the sun.

A culture which imports much muck from the meadows &
deepens the soil not that which trusts to heating manures &
improved agricultural implements only.

How when a man purchases a thing he is determined to get &
get hold of it using how many expletives & how long a string of
synonomous or similar terms signifying possession in the legal
process– What's mine's my own. An old Deed of a small piece of
swamp land which I have lately surveyed at the risk of being mired
past recovery says "that the said Spaulding his Heirs & Assigns, shall
and may from time, & at all times forever hereafter, by force &
virtue of these presents, lawfully, peaceably and quietly have, hold,
use, occupy, possess and enjoy the said swamp &c"

Magnetic iron being anciently found in *Magnesia* hence–magnes
or magnet employed by Pliny & others– Chinese appear to have

discovered the magnet very early   A D 121 & before? used by
them to steer ships in 419—mentioned by an Icelander 1068—in a
French poem 1181 In Torfaeus Hist of Norway 1266—used by
DeGama in 1427   leading stone hence load stone

The peroxide of hydrogen or ozone at first thought to be a
chemical curiosity merely is found to be very generally diffussed
through nature.

The following bears on the floating ice which has risen from the
bottom of the meadows— Robert Hunt says "Water conducts heat
downward but very slowly; a mass of ice will remain undissolved but
a few inches under water, on the surface of which, ether, or any
other inflammable body, is burning. If ice swam beneath the surface,
the summer sun would scarcely have power to thaw it; and thus our
lakes & seas would be gradually converted into solid masses"

The figures of serpents of griffins flying dragons and other
embellishments of heraldry—the eastern idea of the world on an
elephant that on a tortoise & that on a serpent again &c usually
regarded as mythological in the com. sense of that word—are thought
by Hunt? to "indicate a faint & shadowy knowledge of a previous
state of organic existence"—such as geology partly reveals.

The fossil tortoise has been found in Asia large enough to support
an elephant.

Ammonites, snake-stones, or petrified snakes have been found
from of old—often decapitated.

In the N part of Grt Britain the fossil remains of encrinites are
called "St. Cuthbert's beads."—"fiction dependant on truth."

Westward is Heaven or rather heavenward is the west. The way
to heaven is from east to west around the earth   The sun leads &
shows it   The stars too light it.

Nature & man   Some prefer the one others the other; but that is
all dè gustibus— It makes no odds at what well you drink, provided
it be a well-head.

Walking in the woods it may be some afternoon the shadow of
the wings of a thought flits across the landscape of my mind   And I
am reminded how little eventful is our lives   What have been all
these wars & survivors of wars and modern discoveries &
improvements so called a mere irritation in the skin. But this shadow
which is so soon past & whose substance is not detected suggests
that there are events of importance whose interval is to us a true
historic period.

The lecturer is wont to describe the 19th century—the American the last generation in an offhand & triumphant strain—wafting him to Paradise spreading his fame by steam & telegraph—recounting the number of wooden stopples he has whittled But who does not perceive that this is not a sincere or pertinent account of any man's or nation's life. It is the hip hip hurrah & mutual admiration society style. Cars go by & we know their substance as well as their shadow. They stop & we get into them. But those sublime thoughts passing on high do not stop & we never get into them. Their conductor is not like one of us.

I feel that the man who in his conversation with me about the life of man in New England lays much stress on rail-roads telegraphs & such enterprises does not go below the surface of things   He treats the shallow & transitory as if it were profound & enduring in one of the minds avatars in the intervals between sleeping & waking —aye even in one of the interstices of a Hindoo dynasty perchance such things as the 19th century with all its improvements may come & go again. Nothing makes a deep & lasting impression but what is weighty

Obey the law which reveals and not the law revealed.

I wish my neighbors were wilder.

A wildness whose glance no civilization could endure.

He who lives according to the highest law—is in one sense lawless That is an unfortunate discovery certainlly that of a law which binds us where we did not know that we were bound. Live free—child of the mist. He who for whom the law is made who does not obey the law but whom the law obeys—reclines on pillows of down and is wafted at will whither he pleases—for man is superior to all laws both of heaven & earth. (when he takes his liberty.)

Wild as if we lived on the marrow of antelopes devourd raw

There would seem to be men in whose lives there have been no events of importance more than in the beetles which crawls in our path.

March 19th

The ice in the pond is now soft and will not bear a heavy stone thrown from the bank— It is melted for a rod from the shore. The ground has been bare of snow for some weeks, but yesterday we had a violent N E snow storm which has drifted worse than any the past winter. The spring birds ducks & geese &c had come—but now the spring seems far off.

No good ever came of obeying a law which you had discovered.

March 23rd For a week past the elm buds have been swolen
The willow catkins have put out. The ice still remains in Walden
though it will not bear. Mather Howard saw a large meadow near
his house which had risen up. but was prevented from floating
away by the bushes.

March 27 Walden is ⅔ broken up It will probably be quite
open by to-morrow night.

March 30th Spring is already upon us. I see the tortoises or
rather I hear them drop from the bank into the brooks at my
approach— The catkins of the alders have blossomed The pads are
springing at the bottom of the water—the Pewee is heard & the lark.

"It is only the squalid savages and degraded boschmen of creation
that have their feeble teeth & tiny stings steeped in venom, and so
made formidable." ants—centipedes, and mosquitos—spiders, wasps,
and scorpions— Hugh Miller.
To obtain to a true relation to one human creature is enough to
make a year memorable.

The man for whom law exists—the man of forms, the
conservative, is a tame man.

A recent English writer (De Quincey) endeavoring to account for
the atrocities of Caligula and Nero—their monstrous & anomalous
cruelties—and the general servility & corruption which they imply—
Observes that it is difficult to believe that "the descendants of a
people so severe in their habits" as the Romans, "could thus
rapidly" have degenerated—that "in reality the citizens of Rome
were at this time a new race brought together from every quarter of
the world, but especially from Asia"
A vast "proportion of the ancient citizens had been cut off by the
sword and such multitudes of emancipated slaves from Asia had been
invested with the rights of citizens, "that, in a single generation,
Rome became almost transmuted into a baser metal." As Juvenal
complained—"the Orontes had mingled its impure waters with those
of the Tiber." & "Probably, in the time of Nero, not one man in
six was of pure Roman descent." Instead of such says another "came
Syrians, Cappadocians, Phyrgians, and other enfranchised slaves"—

"these in half a century had sunk so low, that Tiberius pronounced her (Rome's) very senators to be *homines ad servitutem natos*, men born to be slaves."

So one would say, in the absence of particular genealogical evidence, that the vast majority of the inhabitants of the City of Boston—even—those of senatorial dignity—the Curtises—Lunts—Woodbury's and others—men not descendants of the men of the revolution the Hancocks Adamses Otises but some "syrians Cappadocians & Phyrgians," merely, *homines ad servitutem natos* men born to be slaves

There is such an office if not such a man as the Governor of Massachusetts— What has he been about the last fortnight? He has probably had as much as he could do to keep on the fence during this moral earthquake. It seems to me that no such keen satire, no such cutting insult could be offered to that man, as the absence of all inquiry after him in this crisis. It appears to have been forgotten that there was such a man or such an office. Yet no doubt he has been filling the gubernatorial chair all the while— One Mr Boutwell—so named perchance because he goes about well to suit the prevailing wind

In '75 2 or 300s of the inhabitants of Concord assembled at one of the bridges with arms in their hands to assert the right of 3 millions to tax themselves, & have a voice in governing themselves— About a week ago the authorities of Boston, having the sympathy of many of the inhabitants of Concord assembled in the grey of the dawn, assisted by a still larger armed force—to send back a perfectly innocent man—and one whom they knew to be innocent into a slavery as complete as the world ever knew Of course it makes not the least difference I wish you to consider this who the man was—whether he was Jesus christ or another—for in as much as ye did it unto the least of these his brethen ye did it unto him Do you think *he* would have stayed here in *liberty* and let the black man go into slavery in his stead? They sent him back I say to live in slavery with other 3 millions mark that—whom the same slave power or slavish power north & south—holds in that condition. 3 millions who do not, like the first mentioned, assert the right to govern themselvs but simply to run away & stay away from their prison-house.

Just a week afterward those inhabitants of this town who especially sympathize with the authorities of Boston in this their deed caused the bells to be rung & the cannons to be fired to celebrate the courage & the love of liberty of those men who assembled at the bridge. As if *those* 3 millions had fought for the right to be free themselves—but to hold in slavery 3 million others

Why gentlemen even consistency though it is much abused is sometimes a virtue.

Every humane & intelligent inhabitant of Concord when he or she heard those bells & those cannon thought not so much of the events of the 19th of April 1775 as of the events of the 12 of april 1851

I wish my townsmen to consider that whatever the human law may be neither an individual nor a nation can ever deliberately commit the least act of injustice without having to pay the penalty for it A government which deliberately enacts injustice—& persists in it!—it will become the laughing stock of the world.

Much as has been said about American slavery, I think that commonly we do not yet realize what slavery is— If I were seriously to propose to congress to make mankind into sausages, I have no doubt that most would smile at my proposition and if any believed me to be in earnest they would think that I proposed something much worse than Congress had ever done. But gentlemen if any of you will tell me that to make a man into a sausage would be much worse (would be any worse), than to make him into a slave—than it was then to enact the fugitive-slave law—I shall here accuse him of foolishness—of intellectual incapacity—of making a distinction without a difference.

The one is just as sensible a proposition as the other.

When I read the account of the carrying back of the fugitive into slavery, which was read last sunday evening—and read also what was not read here that the man who made the prayer on the wharf was Daniel Foster of *Concord* I could not help feeling a slight degree of pride because of all the towns in the Commonwealth Concord was the only one distinctly named as being represented in that tea-party—and as she had a place in the first so would have a place in this the last & perhaps next most important chapter of the Hist of Mass. But my second feeling,—when I reflected how short a time that gentleman has resided in this town,—was one of doubt & shame—because the *men* of Concord in recent times have done nothing to entitle them to the honor of having their town named in such a connexion.

I hear a good deal said about trampling this law under foot— Why one need not go out of his way to do that— This law lies not at the level of the head or the reason— Its natural habitat is in the

dirt. It was bred & has its life only in the dust & mire—on a level
with the feet & he who walks with freedom unless with a sort of
quibbling & Hindoo mercy he avoids treading on every venomous
reptile—will inevitably tread on it & so trample it under foot.

It has come to this that the friends of liberty the friends of the
slave have shuddered when they have understood, that his fate has
been left to the legal tribunals so called of the country to be decided.
The people have no faith that justice will be awarded in such a case
—the judge may decide this way or that, it is a kind of accident at
best— It is evident that he is not a competent authority in so
important a case. I would not trust the life of my friend to the
judges of all the supreme Courts in the world put together—to be
sacrificed or saved by precedent— I would much rather trust to the
sentiment of the people, which would itself be a precedent to
posterity— In their vote you would get something worth having at
any rate, but in the other case only the trammelled judgment of an
individual—of no significance be it which way it will.

I think that recent events will be valuable as a criticism on the
administration of justice in our midst—or rather as revealing what are
the true sources of justice in any community. It is to some extent
fatal to the Courts when the people are compelled to go behind the
courts They learn that The courts are made for fair-weather & for
very civil cases—

{One leaf missing}

let us entertain opinions of our own—let us be a town & not a
suburb—as far from Boston in this sense as we were by the old Road
which lead through Lexington—a place where tyranny may ever be
met with firmness & driven back with defeat to its ships.

Concord has several more bridges left of the same sort which she
is taxed to maintain— Can she not raise men to defend them?

As for measures to be adopted among others I would advise
abolitionists to make as earnest and vigorous and persevering an
assault on the Press, as they have already made and with effect too—
on the Church— The Church has decidedly improved within a year
or two.— aye even within a fortnight—but the press is almost
without exception corrupt. I believe that in this country the press
exerts a greater and a more pernicious influence than the Church
We are not a religious people but we are a nation of politicians we
do not much care for—we do not read the Bible—but we do care for

& we do read the newspaper— It is a bible which we read every
morning & every afternoon standing & sitting—riding & walking— It
is a bible which lies on every table & counter which every man
carries in his pocket which the mail & thousands of missionaries are
continually dispersing— It is the only book which America has
printed and is Capable of exerting an almost inconceivable influence
for good or for bad. The editor is preacher whom you voluntarily
support your tax is commonly one cent—& it costs nothing for
pew-hire. But how many of these preachers preach the truth— I
repeat the testimony of many an intelligent traveller as well as my
own convictions when I say that probably no country was ever ruled
by so mean a class of tyrants as are the editors of the periodical press
in *this* country.

Almost without exception the tone of the press is mercenary &
servile— The Commonwealth & the Liberator are the only papers as
far as I know which make themselves heard in condemnation of the
cowardice & meanness of the authorities of Boston as lately
exhibited. The other journals almost without exception—as the
Advertiser the Transcript—the Journal—the Times—Bee—Herald—&c
by their manner of referring to & speaking of the Fugitive-slave law
or the carrying back of the slave—insult the common sense of the
country And they do this for the most part because they think so to
secure the approbation of their patrons & also one would think
because they are not aware that a sounder sentiment prevails to any
extent.

But thank fortune this preacher can be more easily reached by the
weapons of the Reformer than could the recreant Priest—the *free*
men of New England have only to—refrain from purchasing &
reading these sheets have only to withhold their cents to kill a score
of them at once.

Mahomet made his celestial journey in so short a time that "on
his return he was able to prevent the complete overturn of a vase of
water, which the angel Gabriel had struck with his wing on his
departure."

When he took refuge in a cave near Mecca being on his flight
(Hegira) to Medina. "By the time that the Koreishites [who were
close behind] reached the mouth of the cavern, an acacia tree had
sprung up before it, in the spreading branches of which a pigeon had
made its nest, and laid its eggs, and over the whole a spider had
woven its web."

He said of himself. "I am no king, but the son of a Koreishite woman, who ate flesh dried in the sun."

He exacted—"a tithe of the productions of the earth, where it was fertilized by brooks & rain; and a twentieth part where its fertility was the result of irrigation."

Ap. 22nd 1851.

Had Mouse-ear in blossom for a week—observed the crowfoot on the cliff in abundance & the saxifrage

The wind last Wednesday—Ap 16th—blew down a hundred pines on Fair Haven Hill.

Having treated my friend ill, I wished to apologize; But not meeting him I made an apology to myself.

It is not the invitation which I hear, but which I feel, that I obey.

Ap. 26 1851

The judge whose words seal the fate of a man for all time and furthest into eternity is not he who merely pronounces the verdict of the law, but he, whoever he may be, who from a love of truth and unprejudiced by any custom or enactment of men, utters a true opinion or *Sentence* concerning him. He it is that *sentences* him. More fatal as affecting his good or ill fame is the utterance of the least inexpugnable truth concerning him, by the humblest individual, than the sentence of the supremest court in the land.

Gathered the May flower & cowslips yesterday—& saw the houstonia violets &c. Saw a Dandelion in blossom

Are they Americans—are they New Englanders—are they inhabitants of Concord—Buttricks—& Davises and Hosmers by name—who read and support the Boston Herald? Advertiser Traveller Journal—Transcript—&c &c Times Is that the Flag of our Union?

Could slavery suggest a more complete servility? Is there any dust which such conduct does not lick and make fouler still with its slime? Has not the Boston Herald acted its part well served its master faithfully— How could it have gone lower on its belly— How can a man stoop lower than he is low—do more than put his extremities in the place of that head he has. Than make his head his *lower* extremity.

And when I say the Boston Herald I mean the Boston Press with such few & slight exceptions as need not be made

When I have taken up this paper or the Boston times—with my cuffs turned up I have heard the gurgling of the sewer through every column—I have felt that I was handling a paper picked out of the public sewers—a leaf from the gospel of the gambling house—the groggery & the brothel—harmonizing with the gospel of the Merchant's exchange

I do not know but there are some who if they were tied to the whipping post—and could but get one hand free would use it to ring the bells & fire the cannon to celebrate their liberty.

—It reminded me of the Roman Saturnalia on which even the slaves were allowed to take some liberty— So some of you took the liberty to ring & fire—that was the extent of your freedom—and when the sound of the bells died away—your liberty expired—and when the powder was all expended your liberty went off in smoke.

Now a days men wear the fools cap and call it a liberty-cap.

The joke could be no broader if the inmates of the prisons were to subscribe for all the powder to be used in such salutes. & hire their jailors to do the firing & ringing for them.

Ap 29th 1851

Every man perhaps is inclined to think his own situation singular in relation to Friendship. Our thoughts would imply that other men *have* friends, though we have not. But I do not not know of two whom I can speak of as standing in this relation to one another— Each one makes a standing offer to mankind— On such & such terms I will give myself to you—but it is only by a miracle that his terms are ever accepted.

We have to defend ourselves even against those who are nearest to friendship with us.

What a difference it is!—to perform the pilgrimage of life in the society of a mate—and not to have an acquaintance among all the tribes of men!

What signifies the census—this periodical numbering of men—to one who has no friend?

I distinguish between my *actual* and my *real* communication with individuals. I *really* communicate with my friends, and congratulate myself & them on our relation—and rejoice in their presence & society—oftenest when they are personally absent. I remember that not long ago as I laid my head on my pillow for the night I was visited by an inexpressible joy that I was permitted to know & be related to such mortals as I was then related to—& yet no special event

{One leaf missing}

that I could think of had occurred to remind me of any with whom I was connected—and by the next noon perchance those essences that had caused me joy would have receded somewhat. I experienced a remarkable gladness in the thought that they existed— Their existence was then blessed to me. Yet such has never been my actual relation to any.

Every one experiences that while his relation to another actually may be one of distrust & disappointment he may still have relations to him ideally & so really—in spite of both He is faintly conscious of a confidence & satisfaction somewhere. & all further intercourse is based on this experience of success,

The very dogs & cats incline to affection in their relation to man. It often happens that a man is more humanely related to a cat or dog than to any human being. What bond is it relates us to any animal we keep in the house but the bond of affection. In a degree we grow to love one another.

Ap. 30th 1851

What is a chamber to which the sun does not rise in the morning? What is a chamber to which the sun does not set at evening? Such are often the chambers of the mind for the most part

Even the cat which lies on a rug all day—commences to prowl about the fields at night—resumes her ancient forest habits. the most tenderly bred grimalkin steals forth at night. Watches some bird on its perch for an hour in the furrow like a gun at rest. She catches no cold—it is her nature. Carressed by children & cherished with a saucer of milk.

Even she can erect her back & expand her tail & spit at her enemies like the wild cat of the woods. sweet sylvia

What is the singing of birds, or any natural sound, compared with the voice of one we love.

To one we love we are related as to nature in the spring. Our dreams are mutually intelligible. We take the census, and find that there is one.

Love is a mutual confidence whose foundation no one knows. The one I love surpasses all the laws of nature in sureness— Love is capable of any wisdom

> "He that hath love & judgment too
> Sees more than any other doe." ?

By our very mutual attraction—& our attraction to all other spheres kept properly asunder. Two planets which are mutually attracted—being at the same time attracted by the sun—presume equipoise & harmony.

Does not the history of chivalry and Knight-errantry suggest or point to another relation to woman than leads to marriage—yet an elevating and all absorbing one—perchance transcending marriage? As yet men know not one another—nor does man know woman.

I am sure that the design of my maker—when he has brought me nearest to woman—was not the propagation of the species—but perchance the development of the affections—and something akin to the maturation of the species. Man is capable of a love of woman quite transcending marriage.

I observe that the New York Herald advertises situations wanted by "respectable young women" by the column—but never—by respectable young men—rather "intelligent" and "smart" ones—from which I infer that the public opinion of New York does not require young men to be respectable in the same sense in which it requires young women to be so.

May it consist with the health of some bodies to be impure?

May 1st 1851

Observed the Nuphar Advena Yellow Water Lily in blossom Also the Laurus Benzoin or Fever Bush Spice wood near Wm Wheeler's in Lincoln—resembling the Witch Hazel. It is remarkable that this aromatic shrub—though it grows by the road side—& does not hide itself may be as it were effectually concealed—though it blossoms every spring— It may be observed only once in many years.

The blossom buds of the peach have expanded just enough to give a slight peach tint to the orchards.

In regard to purity, I do not know whether I am much worse or better than my acquaintants. If I confine my thought to myself—I appear—whether by constitution or by education, irrevocably impure, as if I should be shunned by my fellow men, if they knew me better —as if I were of two inconsistent natures—but again when I observe how the mass of men speak of woman and of chastity—with how little love and reverence—I feel that so far I am unaccountably better than they. I think that none of my acquaintants has a greater love and admiration for chastity than I have. Perhaps it is necessary that one should actually stand low himself in order to reverence what is high in others

All distant landscapes—seen from hill tops are veritable pictures— which will be found to have no actual existence to him who travels to them— "Tis distance lends enchantment to the view." It is the bare *land*-scape without this depth of atmosphere to glass it. The distant river reach seen in the north from the Lincoln Hill, high in

the horizon—like the ocean stream flowing round Homer's shield—
the rippling waves reflecting the light—is unlike the same seen near at
hand. Heaven intervenes betwen me and the object—by what license
do I call it Concord River. It redeems the character of rivers to see
them thus— They were worthy then of a place on Homer's
shield—

As I looked today from mt Tabor in Lincoln to the Waltham Hill
I saw the same deceptive slope—the near hill melting into the further
—inseparably indistinguishably—it was one gradual slope from the base
of the near hill to the summit of the further one—a succession of
copsewoods—but I knew that there intervened a valley 2 or 3 miles
wide studded with houses & orchards & drained by a considerable
stream. When the shadow of a cloud passed over the nearer hill—I
could distinguish its shaded summit against the side of the
other.

I had in my mind's eye a silent grey tarn which I had seen the
summer before? high up on the side of a *mt* Bald Mt where the half
dead spruce trees stood far in the water draped with wreathy mist as
with esnea moss—made of dews—where the Mt spirit bathed. Whose
bottom was high above the surface of other lakes Spruces whose
dead limbs were more in harmony with the mists which draped
them.

The forenoon that I moved to my house—a poor old lame fellow
who had formerly frozen his feet—hobbled off the road—came &
stood before my door with one hand on each door post looking
into the house & asked for a drink of water. I knew that rum or
something like it was the only drink he loved but I gave him a dish
of warm pond water which was all I had, nevertheless, which to my
astonishment he drank, being used to drinking.

Nations! what are nations?— Tartars! and Huns! and Chinamen—
like insects they swarm— The historian strives in vain to make them
memorable. It is for want of a man that there are so many men— It
is individuals that populate the world.

The Spirit of Lodin

> "I look down from my height on nations,
> And they become ashes before me;——
> Calm is my dwelling in the clouds;
> Pleasant are the great fields of my rest."

Man is as singular as god.

There is a certain class of unbelievers who sometimes ask me such questions as—if I think that I can live on vegetable food alone, and to strike at the root of the matter at once I am accustomed to answer such "Yes, I can live on board nails" If they cannot understand that they cannot understand much that I have to say. That cuts the matter short with them. For my own part I am glad to hear of experiments of this kind being tried—as that a young man tried for a fortnight to see if he could live on hard raw corn on the ear—using his tooth for his only mortar— The squirrel tribe tried the same (experiment) and succeeded. The human race is interested in these experiments—though a few old women may be alarmed—who own their thirds in mills.

Khaled would have his weary soldiers vigilant still; apprehending a mid night sally from the enemy "Let no man sleep," said he, We shall have rest enough after death,"—
Would such an exhortation be understood by Yankee soldiers?

Omar answered the dying Abu Beker "Oh successor to the apostle of God! spare me from this burden. I have no need of the Caliphat." But the Caliphat has need of you!" replied the dying Abu Beker

"Heraclius had heard of the mean attire of the Caliph Omar, and asked them why, having gained so much wealth by his conquests, he did not go richly clad like other princes? They replied, that he cared not for this world, but for the world to come, and sought favor in the eyes of God alone. "In what kind of a palace does he reside?" asked the emperor. "In a house built of mud" "Who are his attendants?" "Beggars and the poor". "What tapestry does he sit upon?" "Justice and equity". "What is his throne?" "Abstinence and true knowledge" What is his treasure?" "Trust in God" "And who are his guard?" "The bravest of the Unitarians".
It was the custom of Ziyad once governor of Bassora, "wherever he held sway, to order the inhabitants to leave their doors open at night, with merely a hurdle at the entrance to exclude cattle, engaging to replace any thing that should be stolen: and so effective was his police, that no robberies were committed."
Abdallah was "so fixed and immovable in prayer, that a pigeon once perched upon his head mistaking him for a statue."

Monday May 6th 1851

The Harivansa describes a "substance called *Poroucha*, a spiritual substance known also under the name of Mahat, spirit united to the five elements, soul of beings, now enclosing itself in a body like ours, now returning to the eternal body; it is mysterious wisdom, the perpetual sacrifice made by the virtue of the *Yoga*, the fire which animates animals, shines in the sun, and is mingled with all bodies. Its nature is to be born and to die, to pass from repose to movement. The spirit led astray by the senses, in the midst of the creation of Brahma, engages itself in works and knows birth, as well as death. — — The organs of the senses are its paths, and its work manifests itself in this creation of Brahma. Thought tormented by desires, is like the sea agitated by the wind. Brahma has said; the heart filled with strange affections is to be here below purified by wisdom — — Here below even, clothed already as it were in a luminous form, let the spirit, though clogged by the bonds of the body, prepare for itself an abode sure and permanent. — — He who would obtain final emancipation must abstain from every exterior action. The operation which conducts the pious and penitent Brahman to the knowledge of the truth, is all interior, intellectual, mental. They are not ordinary practices which can bring light into the soul.

The Mouni who desires his final emancipation, will have care evening and morning to subdue his senses, to fix his mind on the divine essence, and to transport himself by the force of his soul to the eternal abode of Vichnou. — — Although he may have engaged in works, he does not wear the clog of them, because his soul is not attached to them. A being returns to life in consequence of the affection which he has borne for terrestrial things: he finds himself emancipated, when he has felt only indifference for them. — —

The Richis mingle with nature, which remains strange to their senses. Luminous & brilliant they cover themselves with a humid vapor, under which they seem no more to exist, although existing always, like the thread which is lost and confounded in the woof.

Free in this world, as the birds in the air, disengaged from every kind of chain, — —

Thus the Yogin, absorbed in contemplation, contributes for his part to creation: he breathes a divine perfume, he hears wonderful things. Divine forms traverse him without tearing him, and united to the nature which is proper to him, he goes he acts, as animating original matter.

———————

Like some other preachers—I have added my texts—(derived) from
the Chineses & Hindoo scriptures—long after my discourse was
written.

A commentary on the Sankhya Karika says "By external
knowledge worldly distinction is acquired; by internal knowledge,
liberation."

The Sankhya Karika says By attainment of perfect knowledge,
virtue & the rest become causeless; yet soul remains awhile invested
with body, as the potter's wheel continues whirling from the effect
of the impulse previously given to it."

I rejoice that horses & steers have to *broken* before they can be
made the slaves of men—and that men themselves have some wild
oats still left to sow before they become submissive members of
society— Undoubtedly all men are not equally fit subjects for
civilization and because the majority like dogs & sheep are tame by
inherited disposition, is no reason why the others should have their
natures broken that they may be reduced to the same level— Men
are in the main alike, but they were made several in order that
might be various— If a low use is to be served one man man will
do nearly or quite as well as another, if a high one individual
excellence is to be regarded. Any man can stop a hole to keep the
wind away—but no other man can serve that use which the author
of this illustration did.

Confucius says
"The skins of the tiger and the leopard when they are tanned, are
as the skins of the dog & the sheep tanned"
But it is not the part of a true culture to tame tigers anymore
than it is to make sheep ferocious. It is evident then that tanning
skins for shoes and the like is not the best use to which they can
be put.

How important is a constant intercourse with nature and the
contemplation of natural phenomenon to the preservation of Moral
& intellectual health. The discipline of the schools or of business—can
never impart such serenity to the mind. The philosopher
contemplates human affairs as calmly & from as great a remoteness as
he does natural phenomena— The ethical philosopher needs the
discipline of the natural philosopher. He approaches the study of

mankind with great advantages who is accustomed to the study of
nature.—

The Brahman Saradwata, says the Dharma Sacontala, was at first
confounded on entering the city—"but now," says he, "I look on it,
as the freeman on the captive, as a man just bathed in pure water,
on a man smeared with oil and dust."

May 10th

Heard the Snipe over the meadows this evening

May 12th

Heard the Golden robin & the Bobolink

But where she has her seat whether in Westport or in Boxboro,
not even the assessors know— Inquire perchance of that dusky
family on the cross road which is said to have Indian blood in their
veins—or perchance where this old cellar hole now grassed over is
faintly visable Nature once had her dwelling— Ask the crazy old
woman who brings huckleberries to the village, but who lives no
body knows where.

If I have got false teeth, I trust that I have not got a false
conscience. It is safer to employ the dentist than the priest—to repair
the deficiencies of Nature.

By taking the ether the other day I was convinced how far
asunder a man could be separated from his senses You are told that
it will make you unconscious—but no one can imagine what it is to
be unconscious—how far removed from the state of consciousness &
all that we call "this world" until he has experienced it. The value
of the experiment is that it does give you experience of an interval
as between one life and another— A greater space than you ever
travelled. you are a sane mind with out organs—groping for organs—
which if it did not soon recover its old sense would get new ones—
You expand like a seed in the ground. You exist in your roots—like
a tree in the winter. If you have an inclination to travel take the
ether—you go beyond the furthest star.

It is not necessary for them to take ether who in their sane &
waking hours are ever translated by a thought—nor for them to see
with their hindheads—who sometimes see from their foreheads—nor
listen to the spiritual knockings who attend to the intimations of
reason & conscience.

May 16th.

Heard the whipporwill this evening. A splendid full moon
tonight. Walked from 6½ to 10 pm. Lay on a rock near a meadow

which had absorbed and retained much heat, so that I would warm
my back on it, it being a cold night.

I found that the side of a sand hill was cold on the surface—but
warm 2 or 3 inches beneath.

If there is a more splendid moonlight than usual only the belated
traveller observes it— When I am outside on the outskirts of the
town—enjoying the still majesty of the moon I am wont to think
that all men are aware of this miracle—that they too are silently
worshipping this manifestation of divinity elsewhere—but when I go
into the house I am undeceived, they are absorbed in checquers or
chess or novel, though they may have been advertised of the
brightness through the shutters.

Talk of demonstrating the rotation of the earth on its axis—see the
moon rise, or the sun!

In the moonlight night what intervals are created—! The rising
moon is related to the near pine tree which rises above the forest—&
we get a juster notion of distance. The moon is only somewhat
further off & to one side. There may be only three objects—myself—a
pine tree & the moon nearly equidistant.

The moonlight reveals the beauty of trees. By day it is so light &
in this climate so cold commonly that we do not perceive their
shade. We do not know when we are beneath them.

According to Michaux the canoe Birch Betula Papyracea ceases
below the 43° of lat.

Sections of the wood from just below the 1st ramification are
used to inlay mahogany—in these parts

It is brought from Maine for fuel.

Common White Birch B. Populifolia not found S of Virginia—
Its epidermis incapable of being divided like the canoe Birch & the
European White.

The common alder Alnus serrulata blooms in January.

The Locust Robinia Pseudo-acacia was one of the earliest trees
introduced into Europe from America—(by one Robin about 1601)
now extensively propagated in Eng—France & Germany.

used for trunnels—to the exclusion of all others in the mid & S
states— Instead of decaying acquire hardness with time.

Sunday May 18th

Ladies slipper almost fully blossomed. The log of a Canoe birch
on Fair Haven cut down the last winter—more than a foot in
diameter at the stump. One foot in diameter at 10 ft from the

ground. I observed that all parts of the epidermis exposed to the air & light were white—but the inner surfaces freshly exposed were a buff or Salmon color. Sinclair says that in winter it is white throughout. But this was cut before the sap flowed?!! Was there any sap in the log? I counted about 50 rings. The shrub oaks are now blossoming. The scarlet tanagers are come The oak leaves of all colors are just expanding—& are more beautiful than most flowers. The hickory buds are almost leaves. The landscape has a new life & light infused into it. The deciduous trees are springing to countenance the pines which are evergreen. It seems to take but one summer day to fetch the summer in. The turning point between winter & summer is reached. The birds are in full blast. There is a peculiar freshness about the landscape—you scent the fragrance of new leaves—of hickory & sassafras &c. And to the eye the forest presents the tenderest green

The blooming of the apple trees is becoming general.

I think that I have made out two kinds of poplar— The populus tremuloides or American aspen—& the p. grandidentata or Large Am. aspen. whose young leaves are downy.

Michaux says that the locust begins to convert its sap into perfect wood from the 3d year: which is not done by the oak, the chestnut, the beeech and the elm till after the tenth or the fifteenth year.

He[n] quotes the saying "The foot of the owner is the best manure for his land." "*He" is Aug. L Hillhouse who writes the account of the olive at the request of Michaux

The elder Michaux found the Balsam Poplar P. Balsamifera very abundant on lake St John and the Saguenay R where it is 80 feet high & 3 ft in diametr. This, however, is distinct from the P. Candicans Heart-leaved B. P which M finds here abouts though never in the woods, & does not know where it came from.

He praises the Lombardy poplar because, its limbs being compressed about the trunk it does not interfere with the walls of a house nor obstruct the windows

No wood equal to our black ash for oars. so pliant & elastic & strong 2nd only to hickory for handspikes used also for chair bottoms & middles

The French call the Nettle tree *bois inconnu.*

Our white elm Ulmus Americana "the most magnificent vegetable of the temperate zone

The Pinus Mitis—yellow pine or spruce pine—or short-leaved pine — A 2 leaved pine widely diffused—but not found northward

beyond certain districts of Connecticut & Massachusetts.— In New
Jersey 50 or 60 ft high & 15 to 18 inch in diam.—sometimes 3 leaves
on fresh shoots—smallest of pine-cones—seeds cast first year. very
excellent wood—for houses—masts decks yards beams & cabins.—
next in durability to the Long-Leaved Pine.— called at Liverpool
New York Pine.— Its regular branches make it to be called Spruce
pine sometimes.

Pinus Australis or Long-leaved Pine an invaluable tree—called
(Yellow pine—Pitch p. & Broom P. where it grows) in the North—
Southern P and red p. in Eng Georgia Pitch p. First appears at
Norfolk Virginia thence stretches 600 miles SW 60 or 70 ft high by
15 to 18 inch—leaves a foot long 3 in a sheath—negroes use them for
brooms— Being stronger more compact and durable because the
resin is equally distributed—and also fine grained & susceptible of a
bright polish, it is preferred to every othe pine
   In naval architecture most esteemed of all pines—keels—beams—side
planks trunnels—&c for decks preferred to yellow pine.—& flooring
houses. Sold for more at Liverpool than any other P.
   Moreover it supplies nearly all the resinous matter used
& exported.— others which contain much pitch are more
dispersed. At present (1819) this business is confined to North
Carolina
   M. says the branches of resinous trees consist almost wholly of
wood, of which the organization is even more perfect than in the
body of the tree. They use dead wood for the tar &c. in which it
has accumulated.

Says the vic. of Brunswick Me & Burlington V.t. are the most N
limits of the Pitch pine or P. rigida. (I saw what I should have called
a P. pine at Montmorency)

White Pine P. strobus most abundant bet. 43d & 47th degrees
180 ft by 7-$\frac{8}{12}$ the largest. "The loftiest and most valuable" of the
productions of the N.A. forest

The black spruce is called Epinette noire & Epinette à la bière in
Canada. From its strength best substitute for oak and larch. Used *here*
for rafters & preferred to hemlock.— tougher than white Pine but
more liable to crack.

————

The White spruce Abies alba called Epinette Blanche in Canada—
not so large as the last & wood inferior.

Hemlock Spruce Abies Canadensis called Pérusse in Canada— In
Maine Vermont & upper N Hampshire = ¾ of the evergreen woods
—the rest being Black spruce. Belongs to cold regions, begins to
appear about Hudson's Bay. Its fibre makes the circuit of stocks 15
to 20 inch in diam. in ascending 5 or 6 feet— Old trees have their
circles separated and the boards are *shaky*. Decays rapidly when
exposed to the air. It is firmer though coarser than the white pine—
affords tighter hold to nails. Used in Maine for threshing floors—
resisting indentation—most common use sheathing of houses to be
covered with clapboards.— used for laths

White cedar Cupressus Thyoides—"The perfect wood resists the
succession of dryness & moisture longer than that of any other
species" hence for shingles

Larch Larix Americana—in Canada—Epinette rouge. *Tamarack* by
the Dutch Male aments appear before the leaves—wood superior to
any pine or spruce in strength & durability. used in Maine for
knees.

Cedar of Lebanon Larix cedrus largest & most majeestic of
resinous trees of the old world and one of the finest veg.
productions of the globe.

Cedar island in Lake Champ.—North. limit of red cedar Juniperus
virginiana. Eastward not beyond Wiscasset. seeds mature at begin of
fall & *sown at once*—shoot next spring. Gin made from them.

Arbor vitae Thuya Occidentalis the only species of Thuya in the
New World Lake St John in Canada its N limit abounds between
48° 50' & 45°. The posts last 35 or 40 yrs, & the rails 60 or 3 or 4
times as long as those of any other species. In North N E states the
best for fences—last longer in clay than sand.

The superiority of mahogany in the fineness of its grain & its
hardness which make it susceptible of a brilliant polish. Native trees
in north states used in cabinet making are Black—Yellow—& canoe
birches—Red-flowering curled maple—birds eye do—wild cherry &
sumac.

———————

The circle of peck & other measures made at Hingham—of Black
Red or Grey oak—are "always of a dull blue color—produced by the
gallic acid of the wood acting upon the iron vessel in which it is
boiled."

White-ash used for sieve rims—rake heads & handles—scythe
handles pullies &c.—rake teeth of the Mockernut Hickory.

In New York & Philadelphia "the price [of wood for fuel] nearly
equals & sometimes exceeds that of the best wood in Paris, though
this immense capital annually requires more than 300,000 cords, and
is surrounded to the distance of 300 miles by cultivated plains."   said
in book of 1819.

May 19th

Found the arum triphyllum & the nodding trillium or wake
Robin in Conant's swamp. An ash also in bloom there—& the
sassafras quite striking

—Also the Fringed Polygala by Conantum wood.

Sinclair says the hornbeam is called swamp beech in Vermont.

Tuesday May 20th 1851

There is no doubt a perfect analogy between the life of the
human being and that of the vegetable—both of the body & the
mind.

The botanist, Gray, says—

"The organs of plants are of two sorts:—1. those of *Vegetation*,
which are concerned in growth,—by which the plant takes in the
aerial and earthy matters on which it lives, and elaborates them into
the materials of its own organized substance; 2. those of *Fructification*
or *Reproduction*, which are concerned in the propagation of the
species."

So is it with the human being— I am concerned first to come to
my *Growth* intellectually & morally; (and physically, of course, as a
means to this, for the body is the symbol of the soul) and, then to
bear my *Fruit*—do my *Work*—*Propagate* my kind, not only physically
but *morally*—not only in body but in mind.

"The organs of vegetation are the *Root, Stem, & Leaves*. The *Stem*
is the axis and original basis of the plant."

"The first point of the stem preëxists in the embryo (i.e. in the
rudimentary plantlet contained within the seed): it is here called the
radicle." Such is the rudiment of mind—already partially developed—
more than a bud but pale—having never been exposed to the light—

& slumbering coiled up—packed away in the seed—unfolded (consider
the still pale—rudimentary infantine radicle-like thoughts of some
students, which who knows what they might expand to if they
should ever come to the light & air.—if they do not become rancid
& perish in the seed. It is not every seed that will survive a thousand
years.   Other thoughts further developed but yet pale & languid—
like shoots grown in a cellar.)

"The plant——develops from the first in two opposite directions,
viz. upwards [to expand in the light & air] to produce & continue
the stem (or *ascending axis*), and downwards [avoiding the light] to
form the root, (or *descending* axis. The former is ordinarily or in great
part aerial, the latter subterranean."

So the mind develops from the first in two opposite directions—
upwards to expand in the light & air; & downwards avoiding the
light to form the root. One half is aerial the other subterranean. The
mind is not well balanced & firmly planted like the oak which has
not as much root as branch—whose roots like those of the white
pine are slight and near the surface. One half of the minds
development must still be root—in the embryonic state—in the womb
of nature—more unborn than at first. For each successive new idea or
bud—a new rootlet in the earth. The growing man penetrates yet
deeper by his roots into the womb of things. The infant is
comparatively near the surface. just covered from the light— But
the man sends down a tap root to the centre of things.

The mere logician the mere reasoner who weaves his arguments
as a tree its branches in the sky—not being equally developed in the
roots, is overthrown by the first wind.

As with the roots of the Plant so with the roots of the Mind—
The branches & branchlets of the root "are mere repetitions for the
purpose of multiplying the absorbing points, which are chiefly the
growing or newly formed extremities, sometimes termed *spongelets*. It
bears no other organs."

So this organ of the minds development the *Root*, bears no organs
but spongelets or absorbing points

Annuals which perish root & all the first season—especially have
slender & thread-like fibrous roots. But biennials are particularly
characterised by distended fleshy roots containing starch—a stock for
future growth—to be consumed during their second or flowering
season—as carrots radishes—turnips.

Perennials frequently have many thickened roots clustered together—tuberous or palmate roots—fasciculated or clustered as in the Dahlia, Paeony &c

Roots may spring from any part of the stem under favorable circumstances "that is to say in darkness & moisture, as when covered by the soil or resting on its surface."

I.E. the most clear & etherial ideas (Antaeus like) readily ally themselves to the earth—to the primal womb of things— They put forth roots as soon as branches they are eager to be *soiled* No thought soars so high that it sunders these apron strings of its mother. The thought that comes to light—that pierces the Empyrean on the other side is wombed & rooted in darkness—a moist & fertile darkness—its roots in Hades like the tree of life.

No idea is so soaring but it will readily put forth roots—wherever there is an air & light seeking bud about to expand it may become in the earth a darkness seeking root. even swallows & birds of paradise *can* walk on the ground.

To quote the sentence from Gray—entire

"Roots not only spring from the root-end of the primary stem in germination, but also from any subsequent part of the stem under favorable circumstances, that is to say, in darkness & moisture, as when covered by the soil or resting on its surface."

No thought but is connected as strictly as a flower, with the earth — The mind flashes not so far on one side—but its rootlets its spongelets find their way instantly on the other side into a moist darkness. uterine—a low bottom in the heavens even miasma-exhaling to such immigrants as are not acclimated. A cloud is uplifted to sustain its roots. Imbossomed in clouds as in a chariot the mind drives through the boundless fields of space.— Even there is the dwelling of Indra.

I might have quote the following with the last—of roots

"They may even strike in the open air and light, as is seen in the copious aerial rootlets by which the Ivy, the Poison Ivy, and the Trumpet Creeper climb and adhere to the trunks of trees or other bodies; and also in Epiphytes or Air-plants, of most warm regions, which have no connection whatever with the soil, but germinate & grow high in air on the trunks or branches of trees, &.; as well as in some terrestrial plants, such as the Banian and Mangrove, that send off aerial roots from their trunks or branches, which finally reach the ground"

So if our light & air seeking tendences extend too widely for our original root or stem we must send downward new roots to ally us to the earth.

Also there are parasitic plants which have their roots in the branches or roots of other trees as the mistletoe—the Beech drops &c There are minds which so have their roots in other minds as in the womb of nature— If indeed most are not such?!

Wednesday May 21st

Yesterday I made out the black and the white Ashes— A double male White ash in Miles' swamp and 2 black ashes with sessile leaflets— A female White ash near RR—in Stows land. The White Ashes by Mr Pritchards have no blossoms, at least as yet

If I am right the *black* ash is improperly so called from the color of its bark being lighter than the white— Though it answers to the description in other respects even to the elder-like odor of the leaves, I should like still to see a description of the Yellow Ash which grows in Maine.

The day before yesterday I found the male sassafras in abundance but no female.

The leaves of my new pine on Merriams or Pine Hill are of intermediate length between those of the Yellow Pine & the Norway Pine— I can find no cone to distinguish the tree by. But as the leaves are *semi cylindrical* & not *hollowed* I think it must be the red or Norway Pine—though it does not look very red—& is *spruce*! answering perhaps to the description of the Yellow Pine which is sometimes called Spruce Pine.

To day examined the flowers of the Nemopanthus Canadensis—a genus of a single species says Emerson— It bears the beautiful crimson velvety berry of the swamps—& is what I have heard called the cornel. Common name Wild Holly.

I have heard now within a few days that peculiar dreaming sound of the frogs which belongs to the summer—their midsummer nights dream.

Only that thought & that expression are good which are musical.

I think that we are not commonly aware that man is our contemporary. That in this strange outlandish world—so barren so prosaic—fit not to live in but merely to pass through. that even here so divine a creature as man does actually live. Man the crowning fact —the god we know. While the earth supports so rare an inhabitant there is somewhat to cheer us. Who shall say that there is no God, if there is a *just* man.

It is only within a year that it has occurred to me that there is such a being actually existing on the globe. Now that I perceive that it is so—many questions assume a new aspect. We have not only the idea & vision of the divine ourselves but we have brothers, it seems who have this idea also— Methinks my neighbor is better than I; and his thought is better than mine— There is a representative of the divinity on earth—of all things fair & noble are to be expected. We have the material of heaven here. I think that the standing miracle to man is man—behind the paling—yonder come rain or shine —hope or doubt—there dwells a man. an actual being who can sympathize with our sublimest thoughts.

The revelations of nature are infinitely glorious & cheering— hinting to us of a remote future—of possibilities untold—but startlingly near to us some day we find a fellow man.

The frog had eyed the heavens from his marsh, until his mind was filled with visions, & he saw more than belongs to this fenny earth— He mistrusted that he was become a dreamer & visionary— leaping across the swamp to his fellow what was his joy & consolation to find that he too had seen the same sights in the heavens—he too had dreamed the same dreams

From nature we turn astonished to this *near* but supernatural fact

I think that the existence of man in nature is the divinest and most startling of all facts— It is a fact which few have realized.

I can go to my neighbors & meet on ground as elevated as we could expect to meet upon if we were now in heaven.

> "And we live,
> We of this mortal mixture, in the same law
> As the pure colourless intelligence
> Which dwells in Heaven, & the dead Hadëan shades."

I do not think that man can—understand the *importance* of man's existence—its bearing on the other phenomena of life untill it shall become a remembrance to him the survivor that such a being or such a race once existed on the earth. Imagine yourself alone in the world a musing wondering reflecting spirit *lost* in thought— And imagine thereafter the creation of man! Man made in the image of God!

Looking into a book on dentistry the other day I observed a list of authors who had written on this subject. There were Ran & Tan and Yungerman—& I was impressed by the fact that there was nothing in a name— It was as if they had been named by the child's

rigmarole of Iery ichery van tittle tol tan &c— I saw in my mind a
herd of wild creatures swarming over the earth—and to each one its
own herdsman had affixed some barbarous name or sound or
syllables, in his own dialect—so in a thousand languages— Their
names were seen to be as meaningless exactly as bose or Tray the
names of dogs. Men get named no better.

We seem to be distinct ourselves, never repeated—& yet we bear
no names which express a proportionate distinctness—they are quite
accidental.— Take away their names & you leave men a wild herd
distinguished only by their individual qualities.

It is as if you were to give names in the Caffre dialect to the
individuals in a herd of spring-bocks—or Gnus

We have but few patronymics but few Christian names in
proportion to the number of us. Is it that men ceased to be original
when genuine & original names ceased to be given. Have we not
enough character to establish a new patronymic

Methinks it would be some advantage to philosophy if men were
named merely in the gross as they are known. It would only be
necessary to know the genus & perchance the species & variety—to
know the individual.

I will not allow *mere names* to make distinctions for me but still
see men in herds for all *them*. A familiar name cannot make a man
less strange to me. It may be given to a savage who retains in secret
his own wild title earned in the woods. I see that this neighbor who
wears the familiar epithet of William or Edwin takes it off with his
jacket—it does not adhere to him when asleep or when in anger—or
aroused by any passion or inspiration— I seem to hear pronounced
by some of his kin at such a time his original wild name in some
jaw breaking or else melodious tongue As the names of the Poles
and Russians are to us, so are ours to them.

Our names are as cheap as the names given to dogs— We know
what are dogs names— We know what are men's names. Some
times it would be significant and truer—it would lead to
generalization—it would avoid exaggeration—to say *There was a man
who said or did*—instead of designating him by some familiar, but
perchance delusive name.

We hardly believe that every private soldier in a Roman army
had a name of his own

It is interesting to see how the names of famous men are
repeated. even of great poets & philosophers. The poet is not know

today even by his neighbors to be more than a common man— He
is perchance the butt of many The proud farmer looks down—&
boorishly ignores him but perchance in course of time the poet will
have so succeeded—that some of the farmer's posterity—though
equally boorish with their ancestor will bear the poets name. The
boor names his boy Homer & so succumbs unknowingly to the
bard's victorious fame— Anything so fine as poetic genius he cannot
more directly recognize. The unpoetic farmer names his child
Homer.

You have a wild savage in you—and a savage name is perchance
somewhere recorded as yours.

Friday May 23d–51

And wilder still there grows elsewhere I hear a native and
aboriginal crab apple *Malus* as MX or as Emerson has it *Pyrus
Coronaria* in southern states and also *Angustifolia* in the middle states.—
Whose young leaves "have a a bitter & slightly aromatic taste" MX.
—whose beautiful flowers perfume the air to a great distance. "The
apples——are small, green & intensely acid, and very odoriferous.
Some farmers make cider of them, which is said to be excellent:
they make very fine sweet-meats also, by the addition of a large
quantity of sugar." MX Celebrated for "the beauty of its flowers,
and for the sweetness of its perfume." MX

MX says that the wild apple of Europe has yielded to cultivation
nearly 300 species in France alone. Emerson says referring to Loudon
"in 1836, the catalogue & the gardens of the London Horticultural
Society, contained upwards of 1400 distinct sorts, and new ones are
every year added."

But here are species which they have not in their catalogue—not
to mention the varieties which the crab might yield to
cultivation.

This genus so kind to the human race the malus or pyrus—
Rosaceae the family or others say Pomaceae. Its flowers are perhaps
the most beautiful of any tree. I am frequently compelled to turn &
linger by some more than usually beautiful ⅔ expanded blossoms—
If such were not so common—its fame would be loud as well as
wide. Its most copious & delicious blossoms.

But our wild apple is wild perchance like myself who belong not
to the aboriginal race here—but have strayed into the woods from
the cultivated stock—where the birds where winged thoughts or
agents have planted or are planting me. Even these at length furnish
hardy stocks for the orchard.

You might call one M. oculata. another M. Iridis—M. cum parvuli daemonis oculis or imp-eyed. Blue-jay apple—or M. Corvi Cristati.

wood-dell apple—M. Silvestrivallis. Field-dell apple M. Campestri-vallis Meadow apple M. pratensis. Rock meadow apple saxopratensis Partridge or Grouse apple or bud— Apple of the Hesperides malum Hesperidum. Woodside ap. Wood apple M. silvatica The Truant's ap. m. cessatoris. Saunterer's ap. M. erronis vel Vagabundi The way side ap. M trivialis. Beauty of the air Decus Aeris—December eating—

Frozen thawed—gelato soluta or gelataregelata— The Concord Appl M. Concordiensis. The brindled apple Wine of New England. M. vinosa The Chickaree apple. The Green Apple M. viridis.— The dysentery or cholera morbus apple

Distantly related things are strangely near in fact Perchance this window seat in which we sit discoursing Transcendentalism—with only Germany & Greece—stretching behind our minds—was made so deep because this was a few years ago a garrison house—with thick log walls bullet proof—behind which men sat to escape the wild red man's bullet. & the arrow & the Tomahawk. & bullets fired by Indians are now buried in its walls. Pythagoras seems near compared with them.

Sat May 24th

Our most glorious experiences are a kind of regret. Our regret is so sublime that we may mistake it for triumph. It is the painful plaintively sad surprise of our Genius remembering our past lives and contemplating what is possible.

It is remarkable that men commonly never refer to, never hint at, any crowning experiences—where the common laws of their being were unsettled—and the divine & eternal laws prevailed in them. Their lives are not revolutionary—they never recognize any other than the local and temporal authorities

It is a regret so divine & inspiring so genuine—based on so true & distinct a contrast—that it surpasses our proudest boasts and the fairest expectations.

My most sacred and memorable life is commonly on awaking in the morning—I frequently awake with an atmosphere about me as if my unremembered dreams had been divine—as if my spirit had journeyed to its native place, and in the act of reentering its native body had diffused an elysian fragrance around

The Genius says "Oh! That is what you were! That is what you

may yet be!" It is glorious for us to be able to regret even such an
existence.

A sane & growing man revolutionizes every day. What
institutions of man can survive a morning experience A single
nights sleep—if we have indeed slumbered & grown in our sleep—
puts them behind us like the river Lethe. It is no unusual thing for
him to see the kingdoms of this world pass away.

It is an interesting inquiry to seek for the medicines which will
cure our ails in the plants which grow around us. At first we are not
disposed to believe that man & plants are so intimately related. Very
few plants have been medically examined— And yet this is the
extent of most mens botany and it is more extensive than would at
first be supposed. The botanist is startled by some countryman's
familiarity with an obscure plant to him rare & strange. He who has
been an observer for some years knows not what it is, but the
unobserving countryman, who sees nothing but what is thrust upon
him or the old woman who rarely goes out of the house shows an
easy familiarity with it—& can call it by name.

I am struck by the fact that though any important individual
experience is rare—though it is so rare that the individual is conscious
of a relation to his maker transcending time & space & earth—though
any knowledge of or communication from "Providence" is the rarest
thing in the world— Yet men very easily,—regarding themselves in
the gross speak of carrying out the designs of Providence as nations.
How often the Saxon man talks of carrying out the designs of
Providence—as if he had some knowledge of Providence & his
designs.

Men allow themselves to associate Providence & design of
Providence with their dull prosaic every day thoughts of things

That language is usurped by the stalest and deadest prose which
can only report the most choice poetic experience

This "Providence" is the stalest jest in the universe. The office-
boy sweeps out his office "by the leave of Providence."

                                    May 25th

A fine freshening air a little hazy that bathes & washes everything
—saving the day from extreme heat. Walked to the hills south of
Wayland. by the road by Dea. Farrar's. 1st vista just beyond
Menans? looking west—down a valley with a verdant-columned elm
at the extremity of the vale—& the blue hills & horizon beyond
These are the resting places in a walk. We love to see any part of

the earth tinged with blue—cerulean the color of the sky. The celestial color. I wonder that houses are not oftener located mainly that they may command particular rare prospects—every convenince yielding to this. The farmer would never suspect what it was you were buying, & such sites would be the cheapest of any. A site where you might avail yourself of the art of nature for these thousand years Which could never be materially changed—or taken from you a noble inheritance for your children. The true sites for human dwellings are unimproved— They command no price in the market. Men will pay something to look into a travelling showman's box—but not to look upon the fairest prospects on the earth. A vista where you have the near green horizon contrasted with the distant blue one terrestrial with celestial earth. The prospect of a vast horizon must be accessible in our neighborhood. Where men of enlarged views may be educated.— An unchangeable kind of wealth a *real* estate—

There we found the celandine in blossom & the Ranunculus bulbosus which we afterward saw *double* in Wayland—having nine petals.

The pyrus arbutifolia—variety melanocarpa—Gray makes also the variety erythrocarpa Is this the late red choke berry of the swamps— & is the former the earlier black one of the swamps?

By Farrars' the Nepeta Glechoma a kind of mint Linnaeus calls it G. Hederacea looks some what like catnep

The marsh marigold—caltha palustris improperly called cowslip.

The white oak Quercus alba. And the commonest scrub oak the bear or Black oak—Q. Illicifolia—

The Chinquapin or Dwarf Chestnut oak the smallest of our oaks— Q. prinoides

The crataegus coccinea?—or scarlet fruited Thorn?

Another glorious vista with a wide horizon at the yellow Dutch House just over the Wayland line by the Black spruce Heavy & dark as night which we could see 2 or 3 miles as a land mark now at least before the deciduous trees have fully expanded their leaves it is remarkably black— It is more stoutly & irregularly branched than Holbrooks spruces has a much darker foliage—but the cone scales of both are slightly waved or notched are they then both black spruce? The cones are enough alike & the thickness of the leaves—their color enough unlike. Here is a view of the Jenkin's House—the fish pole house & Wachuset beyond

Noticed what I think must be a young poison sumack abundant

by the roadside in woods—with last years berries—with small greenish
yellow flowers but leaves not pinnatified 3 together From 1 to 2 ft
high— What is it?

Alnus serrulata the common alder with a greyish stem leaves
smooth on both sides—

Alnus incana the speckled alder downy on under side of leaves.

The hard-berried plant seems to be Andromeda ligustrina? of
Gray A. Paniculata of Bigelow—Lyonia Paniculata of Emerson

Thyme leaved veronica little bluish white streak pettalled flower
by roadsides—silene Pensylvanica

What is the orange yellow aster-like flower of the meadows now
in blossom with a sweet smelling stem when bruised?

What the delicate pinkish & yellowish flower with hoary green
stems & leaves of rocky hills.

Saw Bunker Hill monument & Charlestown from the wayland
hills and across the vallies to Milton Hill— Westward or W by S on
island in a pond or in the river (!Which see!) A grand horizon.
Probably saw the elm between Wayland & Weston which is seen so
far in the horizon from the N W part of Sudbury. A good a rare
place this must be to view the sudbury or Wayland meadows a little
earlier.

Came back across lots to the Black-spruce

Now at 8½ o clock PM—I hear the dreaming of the frogs— So it
seems to me & so significantly passes my life away. It is like the
dreaming of frogs in a summer evening.

May 27th

I saw an organ grinder this morning before a rich man's house—
thrilling the street with harmony—loosening the very paving stones &
tearing the routine of life to rags & tatters— When the lady of the
house shoved up a window & in a semi-philanthropic tone inquired
if he wanted anything to eat— But he very properly it seemed to
me kept on grinding & paid no attention to her question—feeding
her ears with melody unasked for— So the world shove up its
window and interrogates the poet—& sets him to gauging ale casks,
in return— It seemed to me that the music suggested that the
recompense should be as fine as the gift—— It would be much
nobler to enjoy the music though you paid no money for it—than to
presume always a beggarly relation

It is after all perhaps the best instrumental music that we have.

May 28th

The trees now begin to shade the streets. When the sun gets high in the sky the trees give shade. With oppressive heats come refreshing shadows.

The butter cups spot the churchyard.

May 29th

It is evident that the virtues of plants are almost completely unknown to us— And we esteem the few with which we are better acquainted unreasonably above the many which are comparatively unknown to us. Bigelow says—"It is a subject of some curiosity to consider, if the knowledge of the present Materia Medica were by any means to be lost, how many of the same articles would again rise into notice and use. Doubtless a variety of new substances would develop unexpected powers, while perhaps the poppy would be shunned as a deleterious plant, and the cinchona might grow unmolested upon the mountains of Quito."

Sawyer regards Nux vomica among the most valuable.

B. says 1817 "We have yet to discover our anodynes & our emetics, although we abound in bitters, astringents, aromatics, and demulcents. In the present state of our knowledge we could not well dispense with opium and ipicacuanha, yet a great number of foreign drugs, such as gentian, columbo, chamomile, kino, catechu, cascarilla, canella, &c. for which we pay a large annual tax to other countries, might in all probability be superceded by the indigenous products of our own. It is certainly better that our own country people should have the benefit of collecting such articles, than that we should pay for them to the Moors of Africa, or the Indians of Brazil."

The Thorn apple Datura stramonium (Apple of Peru—Devil's Apple—Jamestown Weed) "emigrates with great facility, and often springs up in the ballast of ships, and in earth carried from one country to another." It secretes itself in the hold of vessels—& migrates—it is a sort of cosmopolitan weed a roving weed what adventures— What historian knows when first it came into a country!

He quotes Beverly's Hist. of Virginia as saying that some soldiers in the days of Bacon's rebellion—having eaten some of this plant— which was boiled for salad by mistake—were made natural fools & buffoons by it for 11 days, without injury to their bodies??

The root of a biennial or perennial will accumulate the virtues of the plant more than any other part.

B says that Pursh states that the sweetscented Golden Rod
Solidago odora "has for some time (i.e. before 1817] been an article
of exportation to China, where it fetches a high price." And yet it is
known to very few New Englanders.

"No botanist, says B. even if in danger of starving in a wilderness,
would indulge his hunger on a root or fruit taken from an unknown
plant of the natural order *Luridae*, of the *Multisiliquae*, or the
umbelliferous aquatics. On the contrary he would not feel a moment's
hesitation in regard to any of the *Gramina*, the fruit of the *Pomaceae*,
and several other natural families of plants, which are known to be
uniformly innocent in their effects"

The aromatic flavor of the Checquer Berry is also perceived in
the *Gaultheria hispidula*; in *Spiraea ulmaria* and the root of *Spiraea
lobata*–and in the birches.

He says Ginseng, Spigelia, Snake-root, &c. form considerable
articles of exportation.

The odor of Skunk cabbage is perceived in some N.A. currants–
as Ribes rigens of MX on high *mts*–

At one time the Indians above Quebec & Montreal were so taken
up with searching for Ginseng that they could not be hired for any
other purpose. It is said that both the Chinese & the Indians named
this plant from its resemblance to the figure of a man

The Indians used the bark of Dirca palustris or Leather Wood for
their cordage. It was after the long continued search of many
generations that these qualities were discovered.

Of Tobacco, *Nicotiana Tabacum*, B. says after speaking of its
poisonous qualities "Yet the first person who had courage &
patience enough to persevere in its use, until habit had overcome his
original disgust, eventually found in it a pleasing sedative, a soother
of care, and a material addition to the pleasures of life. Its use, which
originated among savages, has spread into every civilized country; it
has made its way against the declamations of the learned, and the
prohibitions of civil & religious authority, and it now gives rise to an
extensive branch of agriculture, or of commerce, in every part of the
globe."

Soon after its introduction into Europe–"The rich indulged in it
as a luxury of the highest kind; and the poor gave themselves up to
it, as a solace for the miseries of life."

Several varieties are cultivated.

In return for many foreign weeds we have sent abroad, says B.
"The Erigeron Canadense & the prolific families of Ambrosia &
Amaranthus."

"The Indians were acquainted with the med. properties of more than one species of Euphorbia"

Night shade is called bitter sweet.

Poke also called Garget

V   root of Arum Triphyllum—Dragon Root or Ind. turnip
V   Gold Thread   Coptis trifolia
V   sanguinaria Canadensis or Blood Root
V   Conium Maculatum   Hemlock
V   Cicuta maculata   Am. Hemlock
V   Asarum Canadense   Wild Ginger snake root—colt's foot—
V   Hyoscyamus Niger   Henbane
V   sweetscented Golden rod
V   Panax quinquefolium   Ginseng.
V   Polygala Senega   Seneca snake root
V   veratrum viride   Am. Hellebore
V   Dirca palustris   Leather Wood.

I noticed the button bush May 25th around an elevated pond or mudhole—its leaves just beginning to expand— This slight amount of green contrasted with its—dark craggly naked looking stem & branches—as if subsiding waters had left them bare—looked Dantesque —& infernal. It is not a handsome bush at this season it is so slow to put out its leaves & hide its naked & unsightly stems.

The Andromeda ligustrina is late to leave out.

malus excelsa—amara—florida—palustris—gratissima—ramosa—spinosa ferruginea—aromatica—aurea—rubigenosa—odorata—tristis—officinalis!! herbacea—vulgaris—aestivalis—autumnalis riparia—odora—versicolor— communis—farinosa—super septa pendens malus scpium virum Nov. Angliae—succosa saepe formicis preoccupata—vermiculosa aut verminosa—aut a vermisbus corrupta vel erosa—Malus semper virens et viridis viridis—cholera—morbifera or dysenterifera—(M. sylvestrispaludosa—excelsa et ramosa superne difficilis conscendere (aut adoepere), fructus difficillimus stringere—parvus et amara.) Pîcis perforata or perterebata—rupestris—agrestis arvensis—Assabettia— Railroad apple—Musketaquidensis—dew apple rorifera. The apple whose fruit we tasted in our youth which grows passim et nusquam, — Our own particular apple malus numquam legata vel stricta. (Malus cujus fructum ineunte aetate gustavi quae passim et nusquam viget) cortice muscosâ Malus viae-ferreae

Friday May 30th

There was a Concord man once who had a fox hound named
Burgoyne—he called him Bugīne. A good name

May 31st Pedestrium solatium in apricis locis.—nodosa

Tuesday June 3d

Lectured in Worcester last Saturday—& walked to *As* or
Hasnebumskit Hill in Paxton the next day. Said to be the highest land
in Worcester County except Wachusett

Met Mr. Blake—Brown—Chamberlin—Hinsdale—Miss Butman?
Wyman—Conant.

Returned to Boston yesterday—conversed with John Downes—
who is connected with the Coast Survey—is printing tables for
Astronomical Geodesic & other uses. He tells me that he once saw
the common sucker in numbers piling up stones as big as his fist.
(like the piles which I have seen) taking them up or moving them
with their mouths.

Dr. Harris suggests that the Mt Cranberry which I saw at Ktaadn
was the vaccinium Vitis idaea cowberry because it was edible & not
the uva ursi—or bear berry—which we have in Concord.

Saw the uvularia perfoliata perfoliate bellwort in Worcester near
the hill—an abundance of Mt Laurel on the hills now budded to
blossom & the fresh lighter growth contrasting with the dark green
An abundance of very large chequer berries or partridge berries as
Bigelow calls them on Hasnebumskit—sugar maples about there. A
very extensive view but the western view not so much wilder as I
expected. See Barre about 15 miles off & Rutland &c &c Not so
much forest as in our neighborhood—high swelling hills—but less
shade for the walker— The hills are green—the soil springer & it is
written that water is more easily obtained on the hills than in the
valleys.— Saw a Scotch fir the pine so valued for tar & naval uses in
the North of Europe.

Mr Chamberlin told me that there was no corporation in
Worcester except the banks (which I suspect may not be literally
true) & hence their freedom & independence. I think it likely there
is a gass company to light the streets at least.

John Mactaggart finds the ice thickest not in the largest lakes in
Canada nor in the smallest where the surrounding forests melt it.

He says that the surveyor of the Boundary line between England
& US on the Columbia River saw pine trees which would require
16 feet in the blade to a cross cut saw to do anything with
them.

I examined today a large swamp white oak in Hubbards Meadow which was blown down by the same storm which destroyed the Light House.

At 5 feet from the ground it was 9¾ feet in circumference The first branch at 11½ feet from ground—and it held the first diameter up to 23 feet from the ground. Its whle height measured on the ground was 80 feet. & its breadth about 66 ft. The roots on one side were turned up with the soil on them—making an object very conspicuous a great distance off, the highest part being 18 feet from the ground—and 14 ft above centre of trunk. The roots which were small and thickly interlaced were from 3 to 9 inches beneath the surface (in other trees I saw them level with the surface) and thence extended 15 to 18 inches in depth (i.e. to this depth they occupied the ground) They were broken off at about 11 feet from the centre of the trunk—and were there on an average one inch in diameter, the largest being 3 inches in diam. The longest root was broken off at 20 feet from the centre, and was there ¾ of an inch in diameter The tree was rotten within. The lower side of the soil (what was originally the lower) which clothed the roots for 9 feet from the centre of the tree, was white & clayey to appearance—& a sparrow was sitting on 3 eggs within the mass. Directly under where the massive trunk had stood and within a foot of the surface you could apparently strike in a spade & meet with no obstruction—to a free cultivation. There was no tap root to be seen. The roots were encircled with dark nubby rings. The tree which still had a portion of its roots in the ground & held to them by a sliver on the leeward side was alive and had leaved out though on many branches the leaves were shrivelled again.

Quercus Bicolor of Big. Q. Prinus discolor MX.f.

I observed the grass waving to day for the first time—the swift Camilla on it— It might have been noticed before— You might have seen it now for a week past on grain fields.

Clover has blossomed

I noticed the Indigo weed a week or two ago pushing up like asparagus. Methinks it must be the small Andromeda? that the dull red mass of leavs in the swamp mixed perchance with the Rhodora— with its dry fruit like appendages as well as the Andromeda Paniculata else called ligustrina & the clethra— It was the Golden Senecio Senecio Aureus which I plucked a week a go in a meadow in Wayland The earliest methinks of the aster and autumnal looking yellow flowers. Its bruised stems enchanted me with their indescribable sweet odor—like I cannot think what

The phaseolus vulgaris includes several kinds of bush beans of which those I raised were one.

Friday June 6th

Gathered last night the strong—rank penetrating scented Angelica

Under the head of the Cicuta Maculata or American Hemlock— "It is a rule sanctioned by the observations of medical botanists, that umbelliferous plants, which grow in or about the water, are of a poisonous nature." He does not say that the Angelica is poisonous but I suppose that it is. It has such a rank offensive & killing odor as make me think of the ingredients of the witchs cauldron It did not leave my hands, which had carried it, long after I had washed them— A strong—penetrating—lasting & sickening odor.

Gathered tonight the Cicuta Maculata American Hemlock—the veins of the leafets ending in the notches & the root fasciculated.

Big. says "The leaves of the Solidago odora have a delightfully fragrant odor, partaking of that of anise and sassafras, but different from either."

June 7th

My practicalness is not to be trusted to the last. To be sure, I go upon my legs for the most part, but being hard pushed & dogged by a superficial common sense which is bound to near objects by beaten paths—I am off the handle as the phrase is—I begin to be transendental and show where my heart is. I am like those Guinea fowl which Charles Darwin saw at the Cape de Verd Islands— He says "They avoided us like partridges on a rainy day in September, running with their heads cocked up; and if pursued, they readily took to the wing." Keep your distance, do not infringe on the interval between us, and I will pick pick up lime & lay real terrestrial eggs for you, & let you know by cackling when I have done it.

When I have been asked to speak at a temperance meeting my answer has been—I am too transendental to serve you in your way— They would fain confine me to the rum sellers & rum drinkers of whom I am not one, and whom I know little about.

It is a certain faery land where we live—you may walk out in any direction over the earth's surface—lifting your horizon—and every where your path—climbing the convexity of the globe leads you between heaven & earth——not away from the light of the sun & stars—& the habitations of men. I wonder that I even get 5 miles on my way—the walk is so crowded with events—& phenomena. How many questions there are which I have not put to the inhabitants!

But how far can you carry *your* practicalness—how far does your knowledge really extend— When I have read in deeds only a hundred years old the words "to enjoy & possess—he and his assigns, *forever*" I have seen how shortsighted is the sense which conducts from day to day. When I read the epitaphs of those who died a century ago they seem deader even than they expected.

A days seems proportionally a long part of your "forever & a day."

There are few so temperate & chaste that they can afford to remind us even at table that they have a palate & a stomach.

We believe that the possibility of the future far exceeds the accomplishment of the past. We review the past with the commonsense—but we anticipate the future with transcendental senses. In our sanest moments we find ourselves naturally expecting far greater changes than any which we have experienced within the period of distinct memory—only to be paralleled by experiences which are forgotten— Perchance there are revolutions which create an interval impassable to the memory.

With reference to the near past we all occupy the region of common sense, but in the prospect of the future we are, by instinct, transcendentalists.

We affirm that all things are possible but only these things have been to our knowledge. I do not even infer the future *from what I know of the past*. I am hardly better acquainted with the past than with the future. What is new to the individual may be familiar to the experience of his race. It must be rare indeed that the experience of the individual transcends that of his race. It will be perceived that there are two kinds of change—that of the race & that of the individual within the limits of the former—

One of those gentle straight down rainy days—when the rain begins by spotting the cultivated fields as if shaken from a pepper box—a fishing day—when I see one neighbor after another—having donned his oil cloth suit walking or riding past with a fish-pole—having struck work—a day & an employment to make philosophers of them all.

When introduced to high life I cannot help perceiving how it is as a thing jumped at—and I find that I do not get on in my enjoyment of the fine arts which adorn it—because my attention is

wholly occupied with the jump, remembering that the greatest
genuine leap on record—, due to human muscles alone, is that of
certain wandering Arabs who cleared 25 ft on level ground. The first
question which I am tempted to put to the proprietor of this great
impropriety—is—"Who boosts you?" Are you one of the 99 who fail
or the 100th who succeeds?

Sunday June 8th

In F. A. Michaux i.e. the younger Michaux's Voyage A l'ouest
des Monts Alléghanys—1802 printed at Paris 1808

He says the common inquiry in the newly settld west was

"From what part of the world have you come? As if these vast
and fertile regions would naturally be the point of union and the
common country of all the inhabitants of the globe"

The current of the Ohio is so swift in the spring that it is not
necessary to row—indeed rowing would do more harm than good,
since it would tend to turn to the ark out of the current onto to
some isle or sand bar—where it would be entangled amid floating
trees— This has determined the form of the bateux—which are not
the best calculated for swiftness but to obey the current. They are
from 15 to 50 feet long by 10 to 12 & 15 with square ends & a roof
of boards like a house at one end— The sides are about 4½ feet
above the water "I was alone on the shore of the Monongahela,
when I perceived, for the first time, in the distance, five or six of
these bateaux which were descending this river. I could not
conceive what those great square boxes were which abandoned to
the current, presented alternately their ends, their sides, & even their
angles As they came nearer I heard a confused noise but without
distinguishing anything, on account of the elevation of the sides. It
was only on ascending the bank of the river that I perceived, in
these bateaux, many families carrying with them their horses, cows,
poultry, dismounted carts, plows, harnesses, beds, agricultural
implements, in short all that constitute the moveables of a household
& the carrying on of a farm" But he was obliged to paddle his log
canoe "sans cesse" because of the sluggishness of the current of the
Ohio in April 1802

A Vermonter told him that the expense of clearing land in his
state was always defrayed by the potash obtained from the ashes of
the trees which were burnt—and sometimes people took land to clear
on condition that they should have what potash they could make.

After travelling more than 3000 miles in North America—he says
that no part is to be compared for the "force végétative des forêts"

to the region of the Ohio between Wheeling & Marietta. 36 miles
above the last place he measured a plane tree on the bank of the
Ohio which at four feet from the ground was 47 in circ. It is true it
was "renflé d'une manière prodigieuse" Tulip & plane trees his
father had said attained the greatest diameter of N A Trees.

Ginseng was then the only "territorial" production of Kentucky
which would pay the expense of transportation *by land* to
Philadelphia. They collected it from spring to the first frosts.

Even hunters carried for this purpose, beside their guns, a bag & a
little "pioche" From 25 to 30 "milliers pesant" were then
transported annually & this commerce was on the increase. Some
transported it themselves from Kentucky to China i.e. without
selling it the merchants of the seaboard— Traders in Kentucky gave
20 to 24 "sous" the pound for it.

They habituated their wild hogs to return to the house from time
to time by distributing corn for them once or twice a week— So I
read that in Buenos Ayres they collect the horses into the corral
twice a week to keep them tame in a degree

Gathered the first strawberries to day.

Observed on Fair Haven a tall Pitch Pine, such as some call
Yellow P— very smooth yellowish & destitute of branches to a great
height. The outer & darker colored bark appeared to have scaled off
leaving a fresh & smooth surface—at the ground all round the tree I
saw what appeared to be the edges of the old surface scales
extending to two inches more in thickness. The bark was divided
into large smooth plates 1 to 2 feet long & 4 to 6 inches wide.

I noticed that the cellular portion of the bark of the canoe birch
log, from which I stripped the epidermis a week or two ago—was
turned a complete brick red color very striking to behold—&
reminding me of the red man—and all strong natural things—the color
of our blood somewhat.— under the epidermis it was still a sort of
buff The different colors of the various parts of this bark, at various
times, fresh or stale are extremely agreeable to my eye

I found the White Pine top full of staminate blossom buds not
yet fully grown or expanded.— with a rich red tint like a tree full of
fruit—but I could find no pistillate blossom—

The fugacious petalled cistus—& the pink—& the lupines of various
tints are seen together.

Our outside garments which are often thin & fanciful & merely
for show—are our epidermis—hanging loose & fantastic like that of

the Yellow birch—which may be cast off without harm our thicker
& more essential garments are our cellular integument when this is
removed the tree is said to be girdled & dies— Our shirt is the liber
or true bark. beneath which is found the alburnum or sap wood—
while the heart in old stocks is commonly rotten or has disappeared.
As if we grew like trees, and were of the exogenous kind.

June 9th

James Wood Senior told me today that Asa? Melvins father told
him that he had seen alewives caught (many of them) in the
meadow which we were crossing on the west of Bateman's Pond,
where now there is no stream, and though it is wet you can walk
every where—also are shad— He thinks that a great part of the
meadow once belonged to the pond.

Gathered the Linnaea borealis

Wednesday June 11th

Last night—a beautiful summer night not too warm moon not
quite full—after 2 or 3 rainy days. Walked to Fair Haven by RR
returning by Potter's pasture & Sudbury Road. I feared at first that
there would be too much white light—like the pale remains of day
light—and not a yellow gloomy dreamier light—that it would be like
a candle light by day but when I got away from the town & deeper
into the night, it was better. I hear whippoorwills & see a few fire
flies in the meadow

I saw by the shadows cast by the inequalities of the clayey sandbank in the Deep Cut, that it was necessary to see objects by moon
light—as well as sunlight—to get a complete notion of them— This
bank had looked much more flat by day when the light was
stronger, but now the heavy shadows revealed its prominences. The
prominences are light made more remarkable by the dark shadows
which they cast.

When I rose out of the deep Cut into the old Pigeon place field,
I rose into a warmer stratum of air it being lighter. It told of the
day, of sunny noon tide hours, an air in which work had been done
—which men had breathed. It still remembered the sunny banks—of
the laborer wiping his brow—of the bee humming amid flowers—the
hum of insects Here is a puff of warmer air which has taken its
station on the hills which has come up from the sultry plains of
noon

I hear the nighthawks uttering their sqeaking notes high in the air
now at nine o'clock PM—and occasionally what I do not remember
to have heard so late—their booming note. It sounds more as if
under a cope than by day—the sound is not so fugacious going off to

be lost amid the spheres but is echoed hollowly to earth—making the low roof of heaven vibrate— Such a sound is more confused & dissipated by day.

The whippoorwill suggests how wide asunder the woods & the town— Its note is very rarely heard by those who live on the street, and then it is thought to be of ill omen—only the dwellers on the outskirts of the village—hear it occasionally— It sometimes comes into their yards— But go into the woods in a warm night at this season—& it is the prevailing sound— I hear now 5 or 6 at once— It is no more of ill omen therefore here than the night & the moonlight are. It is a bird not only of the woods but of the night side of the woods. New beings have usurped the air we breathe—rounding nature filling her crevices with sound— To sleep where you may hear the whipporwill in your dreams.

I hear from this upland from which I see Wachusett by day—a wagon crossing one of the bridges— I have no doubt that in some places to-night I could hear every carriage which crossed a bridge over the river within the limits of concord—for in such an hour & atmosphere the sense of hearing is wonderfully assisted & asserts a new dignity—& become the Hearalls of the story— The late traveller cannot drive his horse across the distant bridge but this still & resonant atmosphere tells the tale to my ear. Circumstances are very favorable to the transmission of such a sound— In the first place planks so placed & struck like a bell swung near the earth emit a very resonant & penetrating sound—add that the bell is in this instance hung over water, and that the night air, not only on account of its stillness, but perhaps on account of its density—is more favorable to the transmission of sound. If the whole town were a raised planked floor—what a din there would be!

I hear some whipporwills on hills—others in thick wooded vales—which ring hollow & cavernous—like an apartment or cellar with their note.— as when I hear the working of some artisan from within an apartment.

I now descend round the corner of the grain field—through the pitch-pine wood in to a lower field, more inclosed by woods—& find my self in a colder damp & misty atmosphere, with much dew on the grass— I seem to be nearer to the origin of things— There is something creative & primal in the cool mist—this dewy mist does not fail to suggest music to me—unaccountably—fertility the origin of things— An atmosphere which has forgotten the sun—where the ancient principle of moisture prevails.

The woodland paths are never seen to such advantage as in a

moonlight night so embowered—still opening before you almost
against expectation as you walk—you are so completely in the woods
& yet your feet meet no obstacles. It is as if it were not a path but
an open winding passage through the bushes which your feet find.

Now I go by the spring and when I have risen to the same level
as before find myself in the warm stratum again

—The woods are about as destitute of inhabitants at night as the
streets in both there will be some night walkers— Their are but
few wild creatures to seek their prey. The greater part of its
inhabitants have retired to rest.

Ah that life that I have known! How hard it is to remember what
is most memorable! We remember how we itched, not how our
hearts beat. I can sometimes recall to mind the quality the
immortality of my youthful life—but in memory is the only relation
to it.

The very cows have now left their pastures & are driven home to
their yards—I meet no creature in the fields.

I hear the night singing bird breaking out as in his dreams, made
so from the first for some mysterious reason.

Our spiritual side takes a more distinct form like our shadow
which we see accompanying us

I do not know but I feel less vigor at night—my legs will not
carry me so far—as if the night were less favorable to muscular
exertion—weakened us somewhat as darkness turns plants pale—but
perhaps my experience is to be referred to being already exhausted
by the day and I have never tried the experiment fairly. It was so
hot summer before last that the Irish laborers on the RR worked by
night instead of day for a while—several of them having been killed
by the heat & cold water. I do not know but they did as much
work as ever by day. Yet methinks nature would not smile on such
labors.

Only the Hunter's & Harvest moons are famous—but I think that
each full moon deserves to be & has its own character well marked.
— One might be called the midsummer night moon

The wind & water are still awake at night you are sure to hear
what wind there is stirring. The wind blows—the river flows without
resting— There lies Fair Haven lake undistinguishable from
fallen sky.

The pines seem forever foreign; at least to the civilized man—not
only their aspect but their scent—& their turpentine.

So still & moderate is the night—no scream is heard whether of fear or joy—no great comedy nor tragedy is being enacted. The chirping of crickets is the most universal if not the loudest sound.

There is no French revolution in Nature.— no excess— She is warmer or colder by a degree or two.

By night no flowers—at least no variety of colors— The pinks are no longer pink—they only shine faintly reflecting more light Instead of flowers under foot stars over head.

My shadow has the distinctness of a 2nd person—a certain black companion bordering on the imp—and I ask "Who is this?" Which I see dodging behind me as I am about to sit down on a rock

No one to my knowledge has observed the minute differences in the seasons— Hardly two nights are alike— The rocks do not feel warm tonight for the air is warmest—nor does the sand particularly. A Book of the seasons—each page of which should be written in its own season & out of doors or in its own locality wherever it may be—

When you get into the road though far from the town & feel the sand under your feet—it is as if you had reached your own gravel-walk—you no longer hear the whipporwill nor regard your shadow—for here you expect a fellow traveller— You catch yourself walking merely The road leads your steps & thoughts alike to the town— You see only the path & your thoughts wander from the objects which are presented to your senses— You are no longer in place.

In Charles Darwins Voyage of a Naturalist round the World— commenced in 1831— He gave to Ehrenberg some of an impalpably fine dust which filled the air at sea near the Cape de Verd Islands & he found it to consist in great part of "infusoria with siliceous shields, and of the siliceous tissue of plants"—found in this 67 dif organic forms.— The infusoria with 2 exceptions inhabitants of fresh water. Vessels have even run on shore owing to the obscurity. Is seen a thousand miles from Africa— Darwin found particles of stone above a thousandth of an inch square.

Speaking of St. Paul's Rocks Lat 58' N Long. 29° 15' W   "Not a a single plant, not even a lichen, grows on this islet; yet it is inhabited by several insects & spiders. The following list completes, I believe, the terrestrial fauna: a fly (Olfersia) living on the booby, and a tick which must have come here as a parasite on the birds; a small brown moth, belonging to a genus that feeds on feathers; a beetle (Quedius), and a woodlouse from beneath the dung; and lastly numerous spiders, which I suppose prey on these small attendants and scavengers of the waterfowl. The often-repeated description of

the stately palm and other noble tropical plants, then birds, and lastly
man, taking possession of the coral islets as soon as formed, in the
Pacific, is probably not quite correct; I fear it destroys the poetry of
this story, that feather & dirt-feeding and parasitic insects and spiders
should be the first inhabitants of newly formed oceanic land."

At Bahia or San Salvador Brazil took shelter under a tree "so
thick that it would never have been penetrated by common English
rain" but not so there.

of A partridge near the mouth of the Plata– "A man on horse
back, by riding round & round in a circle, or rather in a spire, so as
to approach closer each time, may knock on the head as many as he
pleases."– refers to Hearne's Journey, p.383 for "In Arctic North
America the Indians catch the Varying Hare by walking spirally
round & round it, when on its form: the middle of the day is
reckoned the best time, when the sun is high, and the shadow of the
hunter not very long"

In the same place

"General Rosas is also a perfect horseman–an accomplishment of
no small consequence in a country where an assembled army elected
its general by the following trial: A troop of unbroken horses being
driven into a corral, were let out through a gateway, above which
was a cross-bar: it was agreed whoever should drop from the bar on
one of these wild animals, as it rushed out, and should be able,
without saddle or bridle, not only to ride it, but also to bring it back
to the door of the corral, should be their general. The person who
succeeded was accordingly elected, and doubtless made a general fit
for such an army. This extraordinary feat has also been performed by
Rosas."

Speaks of the Gaucho sharpening his knife on the back of the
armadillo before he kills him.

Alcide d'Orbigny–from 1825 to 33 in S. Am. now (1846)
publishing the results on a scale which places him 2d to Humboldt
among S. Am. travellers.

Hail in Buenos Ayres as large as small apples–killed 13 deer beside
ostriches–which last also it blinded.–&c &c Dr Malcomson told
him of hail in India in 1831 which "much injured the cattle"
Stones flat one ten inches in circumference. passed through
windows making round holes.

A difference in the country about Monte Video & somewhere
else attributed to the manuring & grazing of the cattle. refers to
Atwater as saying that the same thing is observed in the prairies of

N. America "where coarse grass, between five and six feet high,
when grazed by cattle, changes into common pasture land"
V Atwater's words in Sill. N. A. Journ. V. 1. p 117

I would like to read Azara's Voyage Speaks of the fennel & the
cardoon (Cynara cardunculus) introduced from Europe, now very
common in those parts of S. America. The latter occurs now on
both sides the Cordillera, across the Continent. In Banda Oriental
alone "very many (probably several hundred) square miles are
covered by one mass of these prickly plants, and are impenetrable by
man or beast. Over the undulating plains, where these great beds
occur, nothing else can now live. --I doubt whether any case is on
record of an invasion on so grand a scale of one plant over the
aborigines."

Horses first landed at the La Plata in 1535 Now these, with
cattle & sheep have altered the whole aspect of the country
vegetation &c.- "The wild pig in some parts probably replaces the
peccari; packs of wild dogs may be heard howling on the wooded
banks of the less frequented streams; and the common cat, altered
into a large and fierce animal, inhabits rocky hills."

At sea eye being 6 ft above level horizon is 2⅘ miles dist. "In
like manner, the more level the plain, the more nearly does the
horizon approach within these narrow limits; and this, in my
opinion, entirely destroys that grandeur which one would have
imagined that a vast level plain would have possessed."

Darwin found a tooth of a *native horse* contemporary with the
mastodon—on the Pampas of Buenos Ayres—though he says there is
good evidence against any horse living in America at the time of
Columbus- He speaks of their remains being common in N
America. Owen has found Darwin's tooth similar to one Lyell
brought from the U States—but unlike any other fossil or living &
named this American horse equus curvidens—from a slight but
peculiar curvature in it.

The great table land of Southern Mexico makes the division
between N & S America with ref. to the migration of animals

Quotes Capt. Owen's Surveying voyage for saying that at the
town of Benguela on the west coast of Africa in a time of great
drought a number of elephants entered in a body to possess
themselves of the wells, after a desperate conflict & the loss of one
man the inhabitants—3000—drove them off. During a great drought
in India says Dr Malcomson, "a hare drank out of a vessel held by
the adjutant of the regiment."

The Guanacos wild llama—& other animals of this genus—have the habit of dropping their dung from day to day in the same heap— The Peruvian Indians use it for fuel and are thus aided in collecting it.

Rowing up a stream which takes its rise in a mountain you meet at last with pebbles which have been washed down from it when many miles distant. I love to think of this kind of introduction to it.

The only quadruped native to the Falkland Islands is a large wolf-like fox. As far as he is aware, "there is no other instance in any part of the world of so small a mass of broken land, distant from a continent, possessing so large an aboriginal quadruped peculiar to itself."

In the Falkland Isles where other fuel is scarce they frequently cook their beeef with the bones from which the meat has been scraped

Also They have "a green little bush about the size of common heath, which has the useful property of burning while fresh & green."

Saw a cormorant play with its fishy prey as a cat with a mouse, 8 times let go & dive after it again.

Seminal propagation produces a more original individual than that by buds layers & grafts.

Some inhabitants of Tierra del Fuego having got some putrid whale's blubber in time of famine "an old man cut off thin slices and muttering over them, broiled them for a minute, and distributed them to the famished party, who during this time preserved a profound silence." This was the only evidence of any religious worship among them. It suggests that even the animals may have something divine in them & akin to revelation. Some inspiration, allying them to man as to God.

"Nor is it easy to teach them our superiority except by striking a fatal blow. Like wild beasts they do not appear to compare numbers; for each individual, if attacked, instead of retiring, will endeavor to dash your brains out with a stone, as certainly as a tiger under similar circumstances would tear you."

"We were well clothed, and though sitting close to the fire, were far from too warm; yet these naked savages, though further off, were observed, to our great surprise, to be streaming with perspiration at undergoing such a roasting."

Ehrenberg examined some of the white paint with which the Fuegians daub themselves—and found it to be composed of infusoria, including 14 polygastrica, and 4 phytolitharia, inhabitants of fresh water—all old & known forms!!

Again of the Fuegians "Simple circumstances—such as the beauty of scarlet cloth or blue beads, the absence of women, our care in washing ourselves—excited their admiration far more than any grand or complicated object, such as our ship. Bougainville has well remarked concerning these people, that they treat the "chef-d'oeuvres de l'industrie humaine, comme ils traitent les loix de la nature, et ses phénonomènes."

He was informed of a tribe of foot-Indians now changing into horse-Indians—apparently in Patagonia.

"With the exception of a few berries, chiefly of a dwarf arbutus, the natives (i.e. of T. del-Fuego) eat no Vegetable food besides this fungus." [Cyttaria Darwinii] the "only country where a cryptogamic plant affords a staple article of food."

No reptiles in T. del Fuego nor in Falkland Islands.

Describes a species of kelp there—Macrocystis pyrifera— "I know few things more surprising than to see this plant growing and flourishing amidst those great breakers of the Western Ocean, which no mass of rock, let it be ever so hard, can long resist.——A few [stems] taken together are sufficiently strong to support the weight of the large loose stones to which, in the inland channels, they grow attached, and yet some of these stones were so heavy that when drawn to the surface, they could scarcely be lifted into a boat by one person." Capt. Cook thought that some of it grew to the length of 360 ft "The beds of this sea-weed even when not of great breadth," says D. "make excellent natural floating breakwaters. It is quite curious to see, in an exposed harbor, how soon the waves from the open sea, as they travel through the straggling stems, sink in height, and pass into smooth water."

Number of living creatures of all orders whose existence seems to depend on the kelp—a volume might be written on them. If a forest were destroyed anywhere so many species would not perish as if this weed were—& with the fish would go many birds & larger marine animals, and hence the Fuegian himself perchance.

Tree-ferns in Van Diemen's Land (Lat 45°) 6 feet in circ.

Missionaries encountered icebergs in Patagonia in lat. corresponding to the Lake of Geneva, in a season corresponding to June in Europe. In Europe—the most southern glacier which comes down to the sea is on coast of Norway lat 67° 20° or 1230 nearer the pole.

erratic boulders not observed in the inter tropical parts of the world.– due to ice-bergs or glaciers.

Under Soil perpetually frozen in N. A. in 56° at 3 feet in Siberia in 62° at 12 to 15 ft

In an excursion from Valparaiso to the base of the Andes– "We unsaddled our horses near the spring and prepared to pass the night. The evening was fine, and the atmosphere so clear, that the masts of the vessels at anchor in the bay of Valparaiso, although no less than 26 geographical miles distant, could be distinguished clearly as little black streaks."

Anson had been surprised at the distance at which his vessels were discovered from the coast without knowing the reason–the great height of the land and the transparency of the air.

Floating islands from 4 to 6 ft thick in lake Tagua-tagua in central Chile–blown about.

June 12th

Listen to music religiously as if it were the last strain you might hear.

There would be this advantage in travelling in your own country even in your own neighborhood, that you would be so thoroughly prepared to understand what you saw– You would make fewer traveller's mistakes. Is not he hospitable who entertains thoughts?

June 13th

Walked to Walden last night (moon not quite full) by rail-road & upland wood path, returning by Wayland Road. Last full moon the elms had not leaved out, cast no heavy shadows & their outlines were less striking & rich in the streets at night. (I noticed a night before night before last from Fair Haven how valuable was some water by moonlight like the river & Fair Haven pond though far away–reflecting the light with a faint glimmering sheen, as in the spring of the year The water shines with an inward light like a heaven on earth. The silent depth & serenity & majesty of water– strange that men should distinguish gold & diamonds–when these precious elements are so common. I saw a distant river by moon light making no noise, yet flowing as by day–still to the sea, like melted silver reflecting the moon light–far away it lay encircling the earth How far away it may look in the night and even from a low hill how miles away down in the valley! As far off off as Paradise and the delectable country! There is a certain glory attends on water by night. By it the heavens are related to the earth– Undistinguishable from a sky beneath you–

And I forgot to say that after I reach the road by Potters barns—o further by potters Brook—I saw the moon sudden reflected full from a pool— A puddle from which you may see the moon reflected—& the earth dissolved under your feet.

The magical moon with attendant stars suddenly looking up with mild lustre from a window in the dark earth.

I observed also the same night a halo about my shadow in the moon light, which I referred to the accidentally lighter color of the surrounding surface, I transferred my shadow to the darkest patches of grass & saw the halo there equally. It serves to make the outlines of the shadow more distinct.) But now for last night—A few fireflies in the meadow— Do they shine though invisibly by day?—is there candle lighted by day?

It is not night fall till the whipporwills begin to sing.— As I entered the deep cut I was affected by beholding the first faint reflection of genuine & unmixed moonlight on the eastern sand bank while the horizon yet red with day was tinging the western side— What an interval—between those two lights! The light of the moon in what age of the world does that fall upon the earth? The moon light—was as the earliest & dewy morning light & the daylight tinge reminded me much more of the night.— There were the old & new dynasties opposed contrasted—and an interval between which time could not span.— Then is night when the daylight yields to the night light It suggested an interval a distance not recognized in history. Nations have flourished in that light.

When I had climbed the sand bank on the left—I felt the warmer current or stratum of air on my cheek like a blast from a furnace.

The white stems of the pines which reflected the weak light—standing thick & close together while their lower branches were gone, reminded me that the pines are only larger grasses which rise to a chaffy head—& we the insects that crawl between them. They are particularly grass-like.

How long do the gales retain the heat of the sun! I find them retreated high up the sides of hills, especially on open fields or cleared places. Does perchance any of this pregnant air survive the dews of night?— Can any of it be found remembering the sun of yesterday even in the morning hours. Does perchance some puff some blast survive the night on elevated clearings surrounded by the forest?

The bull-frog belongs to summer The different frogs mark the seasons pretty well— The peeping hyla—the dreaming frog & the

13

—I believe that all may be heard at last occasionally together.
partridges drumming to night as late as 9 o'clock— What
y-space penetrating & filling sound—! why am I never
nearer to its source!

We do not commonly live our life out & full—we do not fill all
our pores with our blood—we do not inspire & expire fully &
entirely enough so that the wave the comber of each inspiration shall
break upon our extremest shores—rolling till it meets the sand which
bounds us—& the sound of the surf come back to us. Might not a
bellows assist us to breathe. That our breathing should create a wind
in a calm day. We do not live but a quarter part of our life—why do
we not let on the flood—raise the gates—& set all our wheels in
motion— He that hath ears to hear let him hear. Employ your
senses.

The newspapers tell us of news not to be named even with that
in its own kind which an observing man can pick up in a solitary
walk.— as if it gained some importance & dignity by its publicness.
Do we need to be advertised each day that such is still the routine
of life?

The tree-toad's too is a summer sound.

I hear just as the night sets in faint notes from time to time from
some sparrow? falling asleep. A vesper hymn— And later in the
woods the chuckling rattling sound of some unseen bird on the near
trees.

The Night hawk booms wide awake.

By moonlight we see not distinctly even the surface of the earth—
but our daylight experience supplies us with confidence.

As I approached the pond down hubbard's path (after coming out
of the woods into a warmer air) I saw the shimmering of the moon
on its surface—and in the near now flooded cove the water-bugs
darting circling about made streaks or curves of light. The moon's
inverted pyramid of shimmering light commenced about 20 rods off
—like so much micaceous sand— But I was startled to see midway in
the dark water a bright flame like more than phosphorescent light
crowning the crests of the wavelets which at first I mistook for fire
flies & and thought even of cucullos— It had the appearance of a
pure smokeless flame ½ dozen inches long issuing from the water &
bending flickeringly along its surface— I thought of St Elmo's lights
& the like—but coming near to the shore of the pond itself—these
flames increased & I saw that it was so many broken reflections of
the moon's disk, though one would have said they were of an

intenser light than the moon herself—from contrast with the
surrounding water they were— Standing up close to the shore &
nearer the rippled surface I saw the reflections of the moon sliding
down the watery concave like so many lustrous burnished coins
poured from a bag—with inexhaustible lavishness—& the lambent
flames on the surface were much multiplied seeming to slide along a
few inches with each wave before they were extinguished—& I saw
how farther & farther off they gradually merged in the general sheen
which in fact was made up of a myriad little mirrors reflecting the
disk of the moon—with equal brightness to an eye rightly placed.
The pyramid or sheaf of light which we see springing from near
where we stand only—in fact is the outline of that portion of the
shimmering surface which an eye takes in—to myriad eyes suitably
placed, the whole surface of the pond would be seen to shimmer, or
rather it would be seen as the waves turned up their mirrors to be
covered with those bright flame like reflections of the moon's disk
like a myriad candles every where issuing from the waves—i.e. if
there were as many eyes as angles presented by the waves—and these
reflections are dispersed in all directions into the atmosphere flooding
it with light— No wonder that water reveals itself so far by night—
even further in many states of the atmosphere than by day. (I
thought it first it some unusual phosphorescence. In some positions
these flames were star like points brighter than the brightest stars.
Suddenly a flame would show itself in a near and dark space
precisely like some inflammable gass on the surface. As if an
inflammable gass made its way up from the bottom.

I heard my old musical—simple-noted owl. The sound of the
dreaming frogs prevails over the others. Occasionally a bull-frog near
me made a obscene noise a sound like an eructation near me. I
think they must be imbodied eructations. They suggest flatulency.

The pond is higher than ever—so as to hinder fishermen—& I
could hardly get to the true shore here on account of the bushes

I pushed out in a boat a little & heard the chopping of the waves
under its bow. And on the bottom I saw the moving reflections of
the shining waves—faint streaks of light revealing the shadows of the
waves or the opaqueness of the water—

As I climbed the hill again toward my old beanfield—I listened to
the ancient familiar immortal dear cricket sound under all others—
hearing at first some distinct chirps—but when these ceased—I was
aware of the general earth song which my hearing had not heard
amid which these were only taller flowers in a bed—and I wondered

if behind or beneath this there was not some other chant yet more
universal. Why do we not hear when this begins in the spring? &
when it ceases in the fall!—or is it too gradual.

After I have got into the road I have no thought to record—all
the way home— The walk is comparatively barren. The leafy elm
sprays seem to droop more by night!?

Saturday June 14th

Full moon last night. Set out on a walk to Conantum at 7 pm. A
serene evening—the sun going down behind clouds, a few white or
slightly shaded piles of clouds floating in the eastern sky—but a broad
clear mellow cope left for the moon to rise into— An evening for
poets to describe. Met a man driving home his cow from pasture
and stopping to chat with his neighbor.— Then a boy who had set
down his pail in the road to stone a bird most perseveringly—whom
I heard afterward behind me telling his pail to be quiet in a tone of
assumed anger because it squeaked under his arm.— As I proceed
along the back Road I hear the lark still singing in the meadow. &
the bobolink—& the Goldrobin on the elms & the swallows
twittering about the barns. A small bird chasing a crow high in the
air who is going home at night All nature is in an expectant
attitude— Before Goodwin's House—at the opening of the Sudbury
Road The swallows are diving at a tortoise shell cat who curvets &
frisks rather awkwardly as if she did not know whether to be scared
or not— And now having proceeded a little way down this Road,
the sun having buried himself in the low cloud in the west and
hung out his crimson curtains How quietly we entertain the
possibility of joy—of—re creation, of light into our souls—we should
be more excited at the pulling of a tooth.

I hear while sitting by the wall the sound of the stake driver at a
distance—like that made by a man pumping in a neighboring farm
yard—watering his cattle—or like chopping wood before his door on
a frosty morning—& I can imagine him driving a stake in a meadow
— The pumper— I immediately went in search of the bird—but
after going ⅓ a mile it did not sound much nearer—and the two
parts of the sound did not appear to proceed from the same place—
What is the peculiarity of these sounds which penetrates so far on
the keynote of nature. At last I got near to the brook in the
meadow behind Hubbard's wood, but I could not tell if were
further or nearer than that— When I got within half a dozen rods of
the brook it ceased—and I heard it no more— I suppose that I scared
it. As before I was further off than I thought—so now I was nearer

than I thought. It is not easy to understand how so small a creature can make so loud a sound by merely sucking in or throwing out water—with pump-like lungs— As yet no moon but downy piles of cloud scattered here and there in the expectant sky.

Saw a blue flag blossom in the meadow while waiting for the stake driver.

It was a sound as of gulping water.

Where my path crosses the brook in the meadow there is a singularly sweet scent in the heavy air bathing the brakes where the brakes grow— The fragrance of the earth—as if the dew were a distillation of the fragrant essences of nature. When I reach the road The farmer going home from town invites me to ride in his high-set wagon—not thinking why I walk—nor can I shortly explain— He remarks on the coolness of the weather. The angelica is budded a handsome luxuriant plant. And now my senses are captivavated again by a sweet fragrance as I enter the embowered willow causeway—and I know not if it be from a particular plant or all to together— Sweet-scented vernal grass—or sweet briar— Now the sun is fairly gone—& I hear the dreaming frog & the whipporwill from some *darker* wood. It is not far from 8. & the cuccoo. The song-sparrows sing quite briskly among the willows—as if it were spring again—& the blackbirds harsher note resounds over the meadow, and the veery's comes up from the wood. Fishes are dimpling the surface of the river—seizing the insects which alight—a solitary fisherman in his boat inhabits the scene. As I rise the hill beyond the bridge, I found myself in a cool fragrant dewey up country mountain morning air—a new region— (When I had issued from the willows onto the bridge it was like coming out of night into twilight the river reflected so much light) The moon was now seen rising over fair haven & at the same time reflected in the river pale & white like a silvery cloud —barred with a cloud not promising how it will shine anon Now I meet an acquaintance coming from a remote field in his hay-rigging with a jag of wood—who reins up to show me how large a wood chuck he has killed, which he found eating his clover. But now he must drive on, for behind comes a boy taking up the whole road with a huge roller drawn by a horse—which goes lumbering & bouncing along—getting out of the way of night, and making such a noise as if it had the contents of a tinker shop in its bowels—& rolls the whole road like a newly sown grain field.

In conants orchard I hear the faint cricket-like song of a sparrow—saying its vespers—as if it were a link between the cricket & the bird

– The robin sings now though the moon shines silverly–and the veery jingles its trille

I hear the fresh & refreshing sound of falling water–as I have heard it in new Hampshire– It is a sound we do not commonly hear.

I see that the white weed is in blossom which as I had not walked by day for some time I had not seen before.

How moderate–deliberate is nature–how gradually the shades of night gather & deepen giving man ample leisure to bid farewell to day–conclude his day's affairs & prepare for slumber.– The twilight seems out of proportion to the length of the day– Perchance it saves our eyes. Now for some hours the farmers have been getting home.

Since the alarm about mad dogs a couple of years ago–there are comparatively few left to bark at the traveller & bay the moon.

All nature is abandoned to me.

You feel yourself your body your legs more at night–for there is less beside to be distinctly known–& hence perhaps you think yourself more tired than you are.– I see indistinctly oxen asleep in the fields–silent in majestic slumber–like the sphinx–statuesque Egyptian reclining. What solid rest–how their heads are supported! A sparrow or a cricket makes more noise. From conants summit I hear as many as 15 whippoorwills–or whip-or-I-will's at once–the succeeding cluck–sounding strangely foreign like a hewer at work elsewhere.

The moon is accumulating yellow light & triumphing over the clouds–but still the west is suffused here & there with a slight red tinge–marking the path of the day. Though inexperienced ones might call it night, it is not yet– Dark heavy clouds lie along the western horizon exhibiting the forms of animals and men–while the moon is behind a cloud. Why do we detect these forms so readily–? Whales or giants reclining busts of heroes–Michael Angelic. There is the gallery of statuary the picture gallery of man–not a board upon an Italian's head but these dark figures along the horizon. The board some Titan carries on his head– What firm & heavy outlines for such soft & light material!

How sweet & encouraging it is to hear the sound of some artificial music from the midst of woods or from the top of a hill at night–borne on the breeze from some distant farm house–the human voice or a flute– That is a civilization one can endure– worth having– I could go about the world listening for the strains

of music. Men use this gift but sparingly methinks. What should we
think of a bird which had the gift of song but sang but used it only
once in a dozen years! like the tree which blossoms only once in a
century. Now the daw bug comes humming by the first I have
heard this year. In 3 month It will be the harvest moon—I cannot
easily believe it. Why not call this the Traveller's Moon? It would
be as true to call the last (the May) the Planter's moon as it is to call
Septembers the Harvest moon— For the farmers use one about as
little as the other. Perhaps this is the Whippoorwill's Moon. The
bull-frog now which I have not heard before this evening—it is
nearly 9— They are much less common & their note more
intermittent than that of the dreamers.

I scared up a bird on a *low* bush—perchance on its nest— It is rare
that you you start them at night from such places.

Peabody says that the Night Hawk retires to rest about the time
the whipporwill begins its song— The whipporwill begins now at
7½ I hear the Night Hawk after 9 o'clock. He says it flies low in
the evening—but it also flies high as it must needs do to make the
booming sound.

I hear the lowing of cows occasionally—& the barking of dogs.
The Pond by moonlight which may make the object in a walk,
suggests little to be said— Where there was only one firefly in a
dozen rods—I hastily ran to one—which had crawled up to the top of
a grass head & exhibited its light—& Instantly another sailed in to it
showing its light also—but my presence made them extinguish their
lights—the latter retreated & the former—crawled slowly down the
stem. It appeared to me That the first was a female who thus
revealed her place to the male who was also making known his
neighborhood as he hovered about—both showing their lights that
they might come together It was like a mistress who had climbed
to the turrets of her castle & exhibited there a blazing taper for a
signal—while her lover had displayed his light on the plain. If
perchance she might have any lovers abroad.

Not much before 10 o'clock does the moonlight night begin.
When man is asleep & day fairly forgotten—then is the beauty of
moon light seen over lonely pastures—where cattle are silently
feeding. Then let me walk in a diversified country—of hill and dale
with heavy woods one side—& copses & scattered trees & bushes
enough—to give me shadows— Returning a mist is on the river.
The river is taken into the womb of nature again.

Now is the clover month—but haying is not yet begun.

Evening

Went to Nawshawtuct by North branch—overtaken by a slight
shower The same increased fragrance from the ground sweet fern
&c as in the night—& for the like reason probably.

The houstonias still blossom freshly as I believe they continue to
do all summer—. The Fever root in blossom—pictured in B's Med.
Bot. Triosteum perfoliatum near the top of Hill under the wall looks
somewhat like a milkweed. The viburnum dentatum very regularly
toothed just ready to blossom somestimes called arrow wood.

Nature seems not have designed that man should be much abroad
by night and in the moon proportioned the light fitly. By the
faintness & rareness of the light compared with that of the sun she
expresses her intention with regard to him

Sunday June 15th

Darwin still

Finds run away sailors on the Chonos Archipelago who he
thought "had kept a very good reckoning of time" having lost only
4 days in 15 months

Near same place on the islands of the Archipelago—he found wild
potatoe the tallest 4 ft high—tubers generally small—but one 2 inch in
Diam. "resembled in every respect and had the same smell as English
potatoes; but when boiled they shrunk much, & were watery &
insipid, without any bitter taste."

Speaking of the surf on the coast of Chiloe—"I was assured that,
after a heavy gale, the roar can be heard at night even at Castro, a
distance of no less than twenty-one sea miles, across a hilly and
wooded country."

Subsidence & elevation of the W Coast of S America & of the
Cordilleras "Daily it is forced home on the mind of the geologist,
that nothing, not even the wind that blows, is so unstable as the
level of the crust of this earth."

Would like to see Sir Francis Head's ? travels in S America—
Pampas perhaps

Also Chamber's Sea Levels

  "   Travels of Spix & Von Martius

It is said that hydrophobia was first known in S. America in 1803

At the Galapagos the tortoises going to any place travel night &
day & so get there sooner than would be expected—about 8 miles in
2 or 3 days— He rode on their backs.

The productions of the Galapagos Archipelago from 5 to 600
miles from America—are still of the American type.— "It was most

striking to be surrounded by new birds, new reptiles, new shells, new insects, new plants, and yet, by innumerable trifling details of structure, and even by the tones of voice & plumage of the birds, to have the temperate plains of Patagonia, or the hot, dry deserts of Northern Chile, vividly brought before my eyes."

What is most singular—not only are the plants &c to a great extent peculiar to these islands, but each for the most part has its own kinds. though they are within sight of each other.

Birds so tame there they can be killed with a stick. I would suggest that from having dealt so long with the inoffensive & slow moulded tortoise they have not yet inquired an instintive fear of man who is a new comer.

Methinks tortoises lizards &c for wild creatures are remarkable for the nearness to which man approaches them & handles them as logs—coldblooded lumpish forms of life—only taking care not to step into their mouths. An aligator has been known to have come out of the mud like a mud volcano where was now the floor of a native's hut.

"The common dock is widely disseminated, [in New Zealand] and will, I fear, forever remain a proof of the rascality of an Englishman, who sold the seeds for those of the tobacco plant."

The New Hollanders a little higher in the scale of civilization than the Fuegians.

Puzzled by a "well rounded fragment of greenstone, rather larger than a man's head" which a captain had found on a small coral circle or atoll near Keeling Island "where every other particle of matter is calcareous." about 600 miles from Summatra D agrees with Kotzebue (V Kotzebue) who states that "the inhabitants of the Radack Archipelago, a group of lagoon-islands in the midst of the Pacific, obtained stones for sharpening their instruments by searching the roots of trees which are cast upon the beach."—and "laws have been established that such stones belong to the chief, and a punishment is inflicted on any one who attempts to steal them." Let geologists look out "Some natives carried by Kotzebue to Kamtschatka collected stones to take back to their country."

Found no bottom at 7200 ft & 2200 yds from shore of Keeling Island—a coral isle

His theory of the formation of Coral isles by the subsidence of the land appears probable.— He concludes that "the great continents are, for the most part, rising areas; and—the central parts of the great oceans are sinking areas."

Not a *private* person on the island of Ascension—the inhabitants
are paid & victualled by the Brit. government—springs cisterns &c are
managed by the same "Indeed, the whole island may be compared
to a huge ship kept in first rate order."
V Circumnavig. of Globe up to Cook.
V. Voyages Round the World since Cook.

The author of the article on Orchids in the Eclectic says that "a
single plant produced three different flowers of genera previously
supposed to be quite distinct."
Saw the first wild rose today on the west side of the Rail Road
causeway. The white weed has suddenly appeared and the clover
gives whole fields a rich & florid appearance The rich red & the
sweet scented white The fields are blushing with the red species as
the western sky at evening.– The blue-eyed grass well named looks
up to heaven–– And the yarrow with its persistent dry stalks &
heads–is now ready to blossom again– The dry stems & heads of
last years tansy stand high above the new green leaves
I sit in the shade of the pines to hear a wood thrush at noon–the
ground smells of dry leaves–the heat is oppressive. The bird begins
on a low strain i.e. it first delivers a strain on a lower key–then a
moment after anothe a little higher–then another still varied from
the others–no two successive strains alike, but either ascending or
descending. He confines himself to his few notes in which he is
unrivalled. As if his kind had learned this and no more anciently.
I perceive as formerly a white froth dripping from the pitch-pines
just at the base of the new shoots– It has no taste.
The pollywogs in the Pond are now full-tailed.
The hickory leaves are blackened by a recent frost–which reminds
me that this is near their northern limit.
It is remarkable the rapidity with which the grass grows The
25th of May I walked to the hills in Wayland and when I returned
across lots do not remember that I had much occasion to think of
the grass, or to go round any fields to avoid treading on it– But
just a week afterward at Worcester it was high & waving in the
fields & I was to some extent confined to the road & the same was
the case here. Apparently in one month you get from fields which
you can cross without hesitation–to haying time– It has grown you
hardly know when. be the weather what it may sunshine or storm–
I start up a solitary wood-cock in the shade in some copse–goes off
with a startled rattling hurried note.
After walking by night several times–I now walk by day–but I

am not aware of any crowning advantage in it. I see small objects better, but it does not enlighten me any. The day is more trivial.

(What a careful gardener nature is! She does not let the sun come out suddenly with all his intensity after rain & cloudy weather—but graduates the change to suit the tenderness of plants)

I see the tall crowfoot now in the meadows—Ranunculus acris—with a smooth stem— I do not notice the bulbosus which was so common a fortnight ago. The rose colored flowers of the Kalmia Angustifolia lambkill just opened & opening— The Convalaria bifolia growing stale in the woods.— the Hieracium venosum veiny-leaved Hawkweed with its yellow blossoms in the woodland path The Hypoxis erecta Yellow Bethlehem star where there is a thick wiry grass in open paths should be called yellow-eyed grass methinks The Pyrola asarifolia with its pagoda-like stem of flowers i.e. broad leaved winter green. The Trientalis Americana like last in the woods—with its starlike white flower & pointed whorled leaves— The Prunella too is in blossom & the rather delicate Thesium umbellatum a white flower—

The solomons seal with a greenish drooping raceme of flowers at the top I do not identify.

I notice today the same remarkable bunchy growth on the fir—(in wheildons garden) that I have noticed on the pines & cedars—) the leaves are not so thickly set & are much stiffer.

I find that I postpone all actual intercourse with my friends to a certain real intercourse which takes place commonly when we are *actually* at a distance from one another

{One-fifth page blank}

Sunday June 22nd 1851

Is the shrub with yellow blossoms which I found last week near the Lincoln Road while surveying for E Hosmer and thought to be Xylosteum ciliatum or fly Honeysuckle the same with the Yellow Diervilla which I find in Laurel glen today?

The birch is the surveyor's tree— It makes the best stakes to look at through the sights of a compass except when there is snow on the ground. Their white bark was not made in vain. In surveying woodlots I have frequent occasion to say this is what they were made for.

I see that Dugan has trimmed off & peeled the limbs of the willows on the Turnpike to sell at the Acton Powder-Mill. I believe they get 8 dollars a cord for this wood.

J. Hapgood of Acton got me last Friday to compare the level of

his cellar bottom with his garden—for as he says when Robbins &
Wetherbee keep the water of Nashoba brook back so as to flood his
garden it comes into his cellar. I found that part of the garden five
inches lower than the cellar bottom. Men are affected in various
ways by the actions of others If a man far away builds a dam I have
water in my cellar He said that the water was some times a foot
deep in the garden.

We are enabled to criticise others only when we are diffirent
from & in a given particular superior to them ourselves. By our
aloofness from men and their affairs we are enabled to overlook &
criticise them. There are but few men who stand on the hills by the
road-side. I am sane only when I have risen above my common
sense— When I do not take the foolish view of things which is
commonly taken. When I do not live for the low ends for which
men commonly live. Wisdom is not common. To what purpose
have I senses if I am thus absorbed in affairs

My pulse must beat with nature After a hard day's work without
a thought turning my very brain in to a mere tool, only in the quiet
of evening do I so far recover my senses as to hear the cricket which
in fact has been chirping all day. In my better hours I am conscious
of the influx of a serene & unquestionable wisdom which partly
unfits and if I yielded to it more rememberingly would wholly unfit
me for what is called the active business of life—for that furnishes
nothing on which the eye of reason can rest. What is that other
kind of life to which I am thus continually allured?—which alone I
love? Is it a life for this world? Can a man feed and clothe himself
gloriously who keeps only the truth steadily before him,? who calls
in no evil to his aid? Are there duties which necessarily interfere
with the serene perception of truth? Are our serene moments mere
foretastes of heaven joys gratuitously vouchsafed to us as a
consolation—or simply a transient realization of what might be the
whole tenor of our lives?

To be calm to be serene—there is the calmness of the lake when
there is not a breath of wind—there is the calmness of a stagnant
ditch. So is it with us. Sometimes we are clarified & calmed
healthily as we never were before in our lives—not by an opiate—but
by some unconscious obedience to the all-just laws—so that we
become like a still lake of purest crystal and without an effort our
depths are revealed to ourselves All the world goes by us & is
reflected in our deeps. Such clarity! obtained by such pure means!
by simple living—by honesty of purpose—we live & rejoice. I awoke
into a music which no one about me heard—whom shall I thank for

it? The luxury of wisdom! the luxury of virtue! are there any intemperate in these things? I feel my maker blessing me. To the sane man the world is a musical instrument— The very touch affords an exquisite pleasure.

As I walk the Rail road causeway I notice that the fields & meadows have acquired various tinges as the season advances the sun gradually using all his paints— There is the rosaceous evening red tinge of red clover like an evening-sky gone down upon the grass— The white-weed tinge— The white clover tinge, which reminds me how sweet it smells. The tall butter-cup stars the meadow on another side telling of the wealth of daisies— The blue-eyed grass so beautiful near at hand imparts a kind of slate or clay blue tinge to the meads.

It is hot noon— The white pines are covered with froth at the base of the new shoots, as I noticed the pitch pines were a week ago —as if they perspired. I am threading an open pitch & white pine wood—easily traversed—where the pine needles redden all the ground which is as smooth as a carpet still the blackberries love to creep over this floor, for it is not many years since this was a blackberry field— And I hear around me but never in sight the many wood-thrushes—whetting their steel-like notes— Such keen singers It takes a fiery heat— Many dry pine leaves added to the furnace of the sun to temper their strains— Always they are either rising or falling to a new strain. After what a moderate pause they deliver themselves again saying ever a new thing—avoiding repetition— Methinks answering one another While most other birds take their siesta—the wood-thrush discharges his song.

The domestic ox has his horns tipped with brass, this & his shoes are the badges of servitude which he wears—as if he would soon get to jacket & trowsers— I am singularly affected when I look over a herd of reclining oxen in their pasture—& find that every one has these brazen balls on his horns— They are partly humanized so It is not pure brute There is art added. Where are these balls sold? Who is their maker. The bull has a ring in his nose. The Lysimachia Quadrifolia—exhibits its small yellow blossoms now in the woodpath

Butter & eggs has blossomed—

The Uvularia Vulgaris or bladderwort—a yellow pealike flower has blossomed in stagnant pools.

June 23d

It is a pleasant sound to me the squeaking & the booming of night-hawks flying over high open fields in the woods. They fly like like butterflies not to avoid birds of prey but apparently to secure their own insect prey— There is a particular part of the railroad just below the shanty where they may be heard & seen in greatest numbers. But often you must look a long while before you can detect the mote in the sky from which the note proceeds.

The common cinquefoil—potentilla simplex—greets me with its simple & unobtrusive yellow flower in the grass. The P. argentea Hoary Cinquefoil also is now in blossom P. sarmentosa—Running Cinquefoil we had common enough in the spring.

—

Thursday June 26th

—

The slight reddish toppd grass (red-top?) now gives a reddish tinge to some fields like sorrel.

Visited a menagerie this afternoon I am always surprised to see the same spots & stripes on wild beasts from Africa & asia. & also from South America—on the Brazilian tiger and the African Leopard, and their general similarity. All these wild animals—Lions tigers—chetas—Leopards &c Have one hue tawny & commonly spotted or striped— What you may call pard color. A color & marking which I had not associated with America These are wild animals (beasts) What constitutes the difference between a wild beast & a tame one? How much more human the one than the other!— Growling scratching roaring—with whatever beauty & gracefulness still untameable this Royal Bengal tiger or this leopard. They have the character & the importance of another order of men. The majestic lion—the King of beasts—he must retain his title.

I was struck by the gem-like changeable greenish reflections from the eyes of the grizzley bear— So glassy that you never saw the surface of the eye— They quite demonic. Its claws though extremely large & long look weak & made for digging or pawing earth & leaves. It is unavoidable the idea of transmigration not merely a fancy of the poets—but an instinct of the race.

June 29th

There is a great deal of white clover this year. In many fields where there has been no clover seed sown for many years at least, it is more abundant than the red and the heads are nearly as large. Also pastures which are close cropped and where I think there was little or no clover last year are spotted white with a humbler growth—

And everywhere by road sides garden borders &c even where the sward is trodden hard—the small white heads on short stems are sprinkled every where— As this is the season for the swarming of bees—and this clover is very attractive to them, it is probably the more difficult to secure them—at any rate it is the more important to secure their services now that they can make honey so fast. It is an interesting inquiry why this year is so favorable to the growth of clover!

I am interested to observe how old-country methods of farming resources are introduced among us. The irish laborer for instance seeing that his employer is contemplating some agricultural enterprise —as ditching—or fencing suggests some old country mode with he has been familiar from a boy—which is often found to be cheaper as well as more ornamental than the common— And Patrick is allowed to accomplish the object his own way—and for once exhibits some skill and has not to be shown—but working with a will as well as with pride—does better than ever in the old country. Even the Irish man exhibits what might be mistaken for a Yankee knack—exercising a merely inbred skill derived from the long teachings and practice of his ancestors.

I saw an Irish man building a bank of sod where his employer had contemplated building a bank wall—piling up very neatly & solidly with his spade & a line the sods taken from the rear & coping the face at a very small angle from the perpendicular— intermingling the sods with bushes as they came to hand which would grow & strengthen the whole. It was much more agreeable to the eye as well as less expensive than stone would have been—& he thought that it would be equally effective as a fence & no less durable. But it is true only experience will show when the same practice may be followed in this climate & in Ireland—whether our atmosphere is not too dry to admit of it. At any rate it was wise in the farmer thus to avail himself of any peculiar experience which his hired laborer possessed, That was what he *should* buy.

Also I noticed the other day where one who raises seeds when his ropes & poles failed had used ropes twisted of straw to support his plants—a resource probably suggested & supplied by his foreign laborers. It is only remarkable that so few improvements or resources are or are to be adopted from the old world.

I look down on rays of prunella by the road sides now— The panicled or privet Andromeda with its fruit-like white flowers— Swamp-pink I see for the first time this season.

—The Tree Primrose (Scabish) Oenothera biennis a rather coarse yellow flower with a long tubular calyx naturalized extensively in Europe.– The clasping bellflower–Campanula perfoliata from the heart shaped leaves clasping the stalk an interesting flower–

The Convolvulus Sepium Large Bindweed–make a fresh morning impression as of dews & purity– The Adder's tongue Arethusa a delicate pink flower.

How different is day from day! Yesterday the air was filled with a thick fog-like haze so that the sun did not once shine with ardor but every thing was so tempered under this thin veil that it was a luxury merely to be out doors– You were less out for it. The shadows of the apple trees even early in the afternoon were remarkably distinct The landscape wore a classical smoothness– Every object was as in picture with a glass over it. I saw some hills on this side the river looking from Conantum on which the grass being of a yellow tinge, though the sun did not shine out on them they had the appearance of being shone upon peculiarly.– It was merely an unusual yellow tint of the grass. The mere surface of water was an object for the eye to linger on.

The panicled cornel a low shrub in blossom by wall sides now.

I thought that one peculiarity of my "Week" was its *hypaethral* character–to use an epithet applied to those Egyptian temples which are open to the heavens above–*under the ether*– I thought that it had little of the atmosphere of the house about–but might wholly have been written, as in fact it was to a considerable extent–out of doors. It was only at a late period in writing it, as it happened, that I used any phrases implying that I lived in a house, or lead a *domestic* life. I trust it does not smell of the study & library–even of the Poets attic, as of the fields & woods.– that it is a hypaethral or unroofed book– lying open under the *ether*–& permeated by it. Open to all weathers –not easy to be kept on a shelf.

The potatoes are beginning to blossom

Riding to survey a woodlot yesterday I observed that a dog accompanied the wagon– Having tied the horse at the last house and entered the woods, I saw no more of the dog while there;–but when riding back to the village I saw the dog again running by the wagon–and in answer to my inquiry was told that the horse & wagon were hired & that the dog always accompanied the horse. I queried whether it might happen that a dog would accompany the wagon if a strange horse were put into it–whether he would ever attach himself to an inanimate object. Methinks the driver though a stranger as it were added intellect to the mere animality of the horse and the dog not making very nice distinctions yielded respect to the horse and equipage as if it were human If the horse were to trot off alone without wagon or driver—I think it doubtful if the dog would follow—if with the wagon then the chances of his following would be increased—but if with a driver though a stranger I have found by experience that he would follow.

At a distance in the meadow I hear still at long intervals the hurried commencement of the bobolink's strain the bird just dashing into song—which is as suddenly checked as it were by the warder of the seasons—and the strain is left incomplete forever. Like human beings they are inspired to sing only for a short season.

That little roadside—pealike blossomed blue flower is interesting to me. The mulleins are just blossoming.

The voice of the crickets heard at noon from deep in the grass allies day to night— It is unaffected by sun & moon. It is a midnight sound heard at noon—a midday sound heard at mid night.

I observed some mulleins growing on the western slope of the sandy railroad embankment—in as warm a place as can easily be found—where the heat was reflected from the sand oppressively at 3 o clock P M this hot day— Yet the green & living leaves felt rather cool than other-wise to the hand—but the dead ones at the root were quite warm. The living plant thus preserves a cool temperature in the hottest exposure. as if it kept a cellar below from which cooling liquors were drawn up.

Yarrow is now in full bloom. & elder—and a small many-head white daisy like a small white weed. The epilobium too is out.

The night warbler sings the same strain at noon. The song-sparrow still occasionally reminds me of spring.

I observe that the high water in the ponds—which have been rising for a year—has killed most of the pitch pines & alders which it had planted & merely watered at its edge during the years of dryness — But now it comes to undo its own work.

How aweful is the least unquestionable meanness—when we cannot deny that we have been guilty of it— There seems to be no bounds to our unworthiness

June 30th

Haying has commenced. I see the farmers in distant fields cocking their hay—now at six o'clock. The day has been so oppressively warm that some workmen have laid by at noon—and the haymakers are mowing now in the early twilight.

The blue flag iris versicolor enlivens the meadow— The lark sings at sundown off in the meadow. It is a note which belongs to a new England summer evening. Though so late I hear the summer hum of a bee in the grass—as I am on my way to the river behind Hubbards to bathe. After hoeing in a dusty garden all this warm afternoon—so warm that the baker says he never knew the like & expects to find his horses dead in the stable when he gets home—it is very grateful to wend ones way at evening to some pure & cool stream & bathe therein.

The cranberry is now in blossom. Their fresh shoots have run a foot or two over the surface.

I have noticed an abundance of poison sumack this season It is now in blossom In some instance it has the size & form of a healthy peach tree.

The cuccoo is faintly heard from a neighboring grove. Now that it is beginning to be dark, as I am crossing a pasture I hear a happy cricket-like—shrill little lay—from a sparrow either in the grass or else on that distant tree—as if it were the vibrations of a watch spring—its vespers. The tree primrose which was so abundant in one field last Saturday is now all gone.

The cattle on Bear Garden Hill seen through the twilight look monstrously large. I find abounding in the meadows the adder's tongue Arethusa & occasionally with it the Cymbidium tuberosum of the same tint. The obtuse Galium Hypericum perforatum is a delicate vine-like plant with a minute white blossom in the same places. The St John's wort has blossomed. The OEnothera pumila or Dwarf tree primrose a neat yellow flower abounds in the meadows. which the careless would mistake at a distance for buttercups The white white buds of the clethra (alder leaved) rise above their recent shoots— The narrow leaved cotton grass spots the meadow with white seeming like loose down, its stems are so slight.— The carrot growing wild which I observed by the rail road is now blossoming with its dishing blossom— I found by the rail-road ¼ mile from the road some common Garden catch-fly the pink flower growing wild. Angelica is now in blossom—with its large umbels. Swamp rose— fugacious petalled. The Prinos or winter-berry budded with white clustered berry-like flower-buds is a pretty contrast to itself in the winter—waxlike. While bathing I plucked the common floating plant like a small yellow lily—the Yellow-Water-Ranunculus—R. multifidus. What I suppose is the Aster Miser—Small flowered Aster a small many-headed white weed has now for a week been in bloom—

a humble weed, but one of the earliest of the asters. The umbelled
Thesium, a simple white flower on the edge of the woods.
Erysimum officinale, Hedge mustard with its yellow flowers.

I first observed about 10 days ago that the fresh shoots of the fir
balsam—abies balsamifera—found under the tree wilted, or plucked &
kept in the pocket or in the house a few days—emit the fragrance of
strawberries, only it is somewhat more aromatic & spicy. It was to
me a very remarkable fragrance to be emitted by a pine. A very rich
delicious aromactic—spicy—fragrance which, if the fresh & living
shoots emitted they would be still more to be sought after.

Saw a brood of young partridges yesterday a little larger than
robins

July 2nd

It is a fresh cool summer morning— From the road at N Barretts
on my way to P. Blood's at 8½ A M. the Great Meadows have a
slight bluish misty tinge in part; elsewhere a sort of hoary sheen—like
a fine downiness—inconceivably fine & silvery far away—the light
reflected from the grass blades—a sea of grass hoary with light—the
counterpart of the frost in spring As yet no mower has profaned it—
scarcely a foot-step since the waters left it.

Miles of waving grass adorning the surface of the earth.

Last night—a sultry night—which compelled to leave all windows
open, I heard two travellers talking aloud—was roused out of my
sleep by their loud day-like & somewhat unearthly discourse at
perchance 1 o'clock— From the country whiling away the night
with loud discourse— I heard the words Theodore Parker &
Wendell Phillips loudly spoken—& so did half a dozen of my
neighbors who also were awakened such is fame It affected like
Dante talking of the men of this world in the internal regions— If
the traveller had called my own name I should equally have thought
it an unearthly personage which it would take me some hours into
day-light to realize.

My genius hinted before I fairly awoke—Improve your time.
What is the night that a traveller's voice should sound so hollow in
it! That a man speaking aloud in the night—speaking in regions
under the earth should utter the words Theodore Parker? A
Traveller! I love his title A Traveller is to be reverenced as such—
His profession is the best symbol of our life Going from—toward—
It is the history of every one of us. I am interested in those that
travel in the night.

It takes but little distance to make the hills & even the meadows

look blue today— That principle which gives the air an azure color
is more abundant.

To-day the milk-weed is blossoming— Some of the raspberries
are ripe—the most innocent & simple of fruits—the purest & most
etherial. Cherries are ripe—strawberries in the gardens have passed
their prime

Many large trees—especially elms about a house are a surer
indication of old family distinction & worth—than any evidence of
wealth. Any evidence of care bestowed on these trees—secures the
traveller's respect as for a nobler husbandry than the raising of corn
& potatoes.

I passed a regular country door-yard this forenoon. the unpainted
one story house—long & low with projecting stoop—a deep grass plot
unfenced for yard—hens & chickens scratching amid the chip dirt
about the door— This last the main feature relics of wood-piles—sites
of the wooden towers—

The night shade has bloomed & the Prinos or winter-berry.

Jly 5th

The vetch like flower by the Marlboro Road the Tephrosia
Virginica is in blossom with mixed red & yellowish blossoms.

Also the White fine flowered Jersey Tea Ceanothus
Americana— And by the side of wood paths the humble cow-wheat
Apocynum &c

The blue flower by the road side, slender but pretty spike is the
Pale lobelia L. Palida.

The reddish blossoms of the umbelled winter-green P. umbellata—
are now in perfection & are exceedingly beautiful.

Also the white sweet scented flowers of the P. Rotundifolia.

It is a remarkably cool clear breezy atmosphere today— One
would say there were were fewer flowers just now than there have
been and are to be. The earliest small fruits are just beginning to be
ripe—the raspberry thimbleberry blueberry &c—we have no longer
the blossoms of those which must ripen their fruits in early autumn.

I am interested in these fields in the woods where the potatoe
is cultivated growing in the light dry sandy soil free from weeds—
now in blossom the slight vine not crowded in the hill. I think they
do not promise many potatoes though mealy & wholesome like
nuts. Many fields have now received their last hoeing & the farmers
work seems to be soon over with them. It is pleasing to consider
man's cultivating this plant thus assiduously—without reference to any

crop it may yield him, as if he were to cultivate Johns wort in like manner. What influences does he receive from this long intercourse.

The flowers of the umbelled Pyrola or common winter-green are really very handsome now—dangling red from their little umbels like jewelry— Especially the unexpanded buds with their red calyx leaves against the white globe of petals.

There is a handsome wood path on the east side of White pond— The shadows of the pine stems & branches falling across the patch which is perfectly red with pine needles—make a very handsome carpet. Here is a small road runing north & south along the edge of the wood which would be a good place to walk by moonlight.

The calamint grows by the lane beyond seven-star lane—now in blossom.

As we come over Hubbards Bridge between 5 & 6 pm the sun getting low—a cool wind blowing up the valley—we sit awhile on the rails which are destined for the new railing. The light on the Indian hills is very soft & glorious—giving the idea of the most wonderful fertility— The most barren hills are gilded like waving grainfields— What a paradise to sail by! The cliffs and woods up the stream are nearer and have more shadow & actuality about them— This retired bridge is a favorite spot with me. I have witnessed many a fair sunset from it.

July 6th Sunday

I walked by night last moon & saw and saw its disk reflected in Walden Pond—the broken disk, now here now there, a pure & memorable flame unearthly bright—like a cucullo of a water-bug.— Ah! but that first faint tinge of moonlight on the gap!—a silvery light from the east before day had departed in the west.

What an immeasurable interval there is between the first tinge of moonlight which we detect—lighting with mysterious silvery poetic light the western slopes—like a paler grass—and the last wave of day light on the eastern slopes. It is wonderful how our senses ever span so vast an interval how from being aware of the one we become aware of the other. And now the night wind blows—from where? What gave it birth? It suggests an interval equal to that in between the most distant periods recorded in History— The silver eye is not more distant from the golden—than moonlight is from sunlight. I am looking into the west where the red clouds still indicate the course of departing day— I turn & see the silent spiritual—contemplative moonlight shedding the softest imaginable light on the western slopes of the hills—as if after a thousand years of polishing their surfaces were just beginning to be bright—a pale whitish lustre—already the crickets chirp to the moon a different strain—& the night-wind rustles the leaves of the wood. A different dynasty has commenced. Moonlight like day-light is more valuable for what it suggests than for what it actually is. It is a long past season of which I dream. And the season is perchance because it is a more sacred and glorious season to which I instantly refer all glorious actions in past time. Let a nobler landscape present itself let a purer air blow—& I locate all the worthies of the world. Ah there is the mysterious light which for some hours has illustrated Asia and the scene of Alexander's victories now at length after two or 3 hours spent in surmounting the billows of the atlantic come to shine on America.

There on that illustrated sandbank was revealed an antiquity beside which Ninevah is young. Such a light as sufficed for the earliest ages. From what star has it arrived on this planet? At midday I see the full moon shining in the sky— What if in some vales only its light is reflected! What if there are some spirits which walk in its light alone still? Who separate the moonlight from the sun-light & are shined on by the former only! I passed from Dynasty to dynasty—from one age of the world to another age of the world—from Jove perchance back to Saturn. What river of Lethe was there to run between? I bad farewell to that light sitting in the west & turned to salute the new light rising in the east.

There is some advantage in being the humblest cheapest least dignified man in the village—so that the very stable boys shall damn-you. Methinks I enjoy that advantage to an unusual extent. There is many a coarsely well meaning fellow, who knows only the skin of me who addresses me familiarly by my christian name— I get the whole good of him & lose nothing myself. There is "Sam" the jailor—whom I never call Sam however, who exclaimed last evening "Thoreau, are you going up the street pretty soon?— Well, just take a couple of these hand bills along & drop on in at Hoar's Piazza and one at Holbrooks, & I'll do as much for you another time." I am not above being used, aye abused, sometimes.

The red clover heads are now turned black— They no longer impart that rosaceous tinge to the meadows & fertile fields. It is but a short time that their rich bloom lasts.

The white is black or withering also. White weed still looks white in the fields— Blue-eyed grass is now rarely seen. The grass & in the fields and meadows is not so fresh & fair as it was a fortnight ago—it is drier & riper & ready for the mowers— Now June is past.

June is the month for grass & flowers— Now grass is turning to hay & flowers to fruits. Already I gather ripe blueberries on the hills.

The red-topped grass is in its prime tinging the fields with red.

It is a free flowing wind—with wet clouds in the sky though the sun shines. The distant hills look unusually near in this atmosphere. Acton M. houses seen to stand on the side of some hills, Nagog or Nashoba—beyond, as never before Nobscot looks like a high pasture in the sun light not far off.

From time to time I hear a few drops of rain falling on the leaves, but none is felt & the sun does not cease to shine— All serious showers go-round me & get out of my way.

The clasping harebell is certainly a pretty flower and so is the Tephrosia. The Poke has blossomed & the Indigo weed—

July 7th

The intimations of the night are divine methinks. men might meet in the morning & report the news of the night.— What divine suggestions have been made to them I find that I carry with me into the day often some such hint derived from the gods Such impulses to purity—to heroism—to literary effort even as are never day-born.

One of those morning's which usher in no day—but rather an endless morning—a protracted auroral season—tor clouds prolong the twilight the livelong day—

And now that there is an interregnum in the blossoming of the flowers so is there in the singing of the birds— The golden robin is rarely heard—& the bobolink &c.

I rejoice when in a dream I have loved virtue & nobleness.

Where is Grecian History? It is when in the morning I recall the intimations of the night.

July 7th

The moon is now more than half full. When I come through the village at 10 o'clock this cold night—cold as in May—the heavy shadows of the elms covering the ground with their rich tracery impress me as if men had got so much more than they had bargained for—not only trees to stand in the air, but to checquer the ground with their shadows— At night they lie along the earth. They tower—they arch—they droop over the streets like chandeliers of darkness. In my walk the other afternoon I saw the sun shining into the depths of a thick pine wood, checkering the ground like like moonlight—and illuminating the lichen-covered bark of a large white-pine, from which it was reflected Through the surrounding thicket as from another sun–;   This was so deep in the woods that you would have said no sun could penetrate thither.

I have been tonight with Anthony Wright to look through Perez Bloods Telescope a 2nd time. A dozen of *his* Bloods neighbors were swept along in the stream of our curiosity. One who lived half a mile this side said that Blood had been down that way within a day or two with his terrestrial or day glass looking into the eastern horizon the hills of Billerica Burlington–and Woburn–   I was amused to see what sort of respect this man with a telescope had obtained from his neighbors–something akin to that which savages award to civilized men–though in this case the interval between the parties was very slight. Mr Blood with his scull cap on his short figure–his north European figure made me think of Tycho Brahe– He did not invite us into his house this cool evening–men nor women–   Nor did he ever before to my knowledge

I am still contented to see the stars with my naked eye   Mr Wright asked him what his instrument cost   He answered–"Well, that is something I dont like to tell. (stuttering or hesitating in his speech a little, as usual)   It is a very proper question however"– "Yes," said I, "and you think that you have given a very proper answer."

Returning my companion Wright the sexton told me how dusty he found it digging a grave that afternoon for one who had been a pupil of mine–for two feet he said, notwithstanding the rain, he found the soil as dry as ashes.

With a certain wariness, but not without a slight shudder at the danger oftentimes, I perceive how near I had come to admitting into my mind the details of some trivial affair, as a case at court–   And I am astonished to observe how willing men are to lumber their minds with such rubbish–to permit idle rumors tales incidents even of an insignificant kind–to intrude upon what should be the sacred ground of the thoughts   Shall the temple of our thought be a public arena where the most trivial affair of the market & the gossip of the teatable is discussed–a dusty noisy trivial place–or shall it be a quarter of heaven itself–a place consecrated to the service of the gods–a hypaethral temple. I find it so difficult to dispose of the few facts which to me are significant that I hesitate to burden my mind with the most insignificant which only a divine mind could illustrate. Such is for the most part the news–in newspapers & conversation. It is important to preserve the mind's chastity in this respect   Think of admitting the details of a single case at the

criminal court into the mind—to stalk profanely through its very
sanctum sanctorum for an hour—aye for many hours——to make a
very bar-room of your mind's inmost apartment—as if for a moment
the dust of the street had occupied you—aye the very street itself
with all its travel passed through your very mind of minds—your
thoughts shrine—with all its filth & bustle— Would it not be an
intellectual suicide? By all manner of boards & traps threatening the
extreme penalty of the divine law excluding trespassers from these
grounds it behoves us to preserve the purity & sanctity of the mind.
It is so hard to forget what it is worse than useless to remember. If I
am to be a channel or thorough—I prefer that it be of the mountain
springs—& not the town sewers— The Parnassian streams There is
inspiration—the divine gossip which comes to the ear of the attentive
mind—from the Courts of Heaven—there is the profane & stale
revelation of the barroom & the police Court. The same ear is fitted
to receive both communications—only the character of the individual
determines to which source chiefly it shall be open & to which
closed. I believe that the mind can be profaned by the habit of
attending to trivial things so that all our thoughts shall be tinged
with triviality. They shall be dusty as stones in the street— Our very
minds shall be paved and macadamized as it were—its foundation
broken into fragments for the wheels of travel to roll over. If we
have thus desecrated ourselves the remedy will be by circumspection
—& wariness by our aspiration & devotion to consecrate ourselves—to
make a fane of the mind. I think that we should treat ourselves as
innocent & ingenuous children whose guardians we are—be careful
what objects & what subjects we thrust on its attention
     Even the facts of science may dust the mind by their dryness—
unless they are in a sense effaced each morning or rather rendered
fertile by the dews of fresh & living truth. Every thought that passes
through the mind helps to wear & tear it & to deepen the ruts
which as in the streets of Pompeii evince how much it has been
used. How many things there are concerning which we might well
deliberate whether we had better know them. Routine—
conventionality manners &c &c—how insensibly and undue attention
to these dissipates & impoverishes the mind—robs it of its simplicity
& strength emasculates it. Knowledge does not come to us by details
but by lieferungs from the gods. What else is it to wash & purify
ourselves? Conventionalities are as bad as impurities. Only thought
which is expressed by the mind in repose as it were lying on its back
& contemplating the heaven's—is adequately & fully expressed—

What are side long—transient passing half views? The writer expressing his thought—must be as well seated as the astronomer contemplating the heavens—he must not occupy a constrained position. The facts the experience we are well poised upon—! Which secures our whole attention!

The senses of children are unprofaned their whole body is one sense—they take a physical pleasure in riding on a rail—they love to teter—so does the unviolated—the unsophisticated mind derive an inexpressable pleasure from the simplest exercise of thoughts.

I can express adequately only the thought which I *love* to express. — All the faculties in repose but the one you are using—the whole energy concentrated in that.

Be ever so little distracted—your thoughts so little confused— Your engagements so few—your attention so free your existence so mundane—that in all places & in all hours you can hear the sound of crickets in those seasons when they are to be heard. It is a mark of serenity & health of mind when a person hears this sound much—in streets of cities as well as in fields. Some ears never hear this sound—are called deaf. Is it not because they have so long attended to other sounds?

Tuesday July 8th 1851.

Walked along the clam-shell bank after sundown.— a cloudy sky. The heads of the grass in the pasture behind Dennis' have a reddish cast, but another grass with a lighter colored stem & leaves on the higher parts of the field gives a yellowish tinge to those parts as if they reflected a misty sunlight. Even much later in the night these light spots were distinguishable. I am struck by the cool juicy pickled cucumber green of the potatoe fields now— How lusty these vines look. The pasture naturally exhibits at this season no such living green as the cultivated fields.

I perceive that flower of the lowlands now with a peculiar leaf—and conspicuous white umbels?

Here are mulleins covering a field (the Clam shell field) where 3 years were none noticeable—but a smooth uninterrupted pasture sod. 2 years ago it was ploughed for the first time for many years & Millet & corn & potatoes planted—and now *where the millet grew* these mulleins have sprung up. Who can write the history of these fields? The millet does not perpetuate itself, but the few seeds of the mullein which perchance were brought here with it, are still multiplying the race.

The thick heads of the yellow dock warn me of the lapse of time.

Here are some rich rye-fields waving over all the land—their heads
nodding in the evening breeze with an apparently alternating motion
—i.e. they do not all bend at once by ranks but separately & hence
this agreeable alternation How rich a sight this cereal fruit—now
yellow for the cradle—flavus— It is an impenetrable phalanx— I
walk for half a mile beside the Macedons looking in vain for an
opening— There is no Arnold Winkelried to gather these spear-
heads upon his breast & make an opening for me— This is food for
man; the earth labors not in vain—it is bearing its burden. The
yellow waving rustling rye extends far up & over the hills on either
side leaving only a narrow and dark passage at the bottom of a deep
ravine. How rankly it has grown!—how it hastes to maturity! I
discover that there is such a goddess as Ceres. The long grain fields
which you must respect—must go round—occupying the ground like
an army. The small trees & shrubs seen dimly in its midst are
overwhelmed by the grain as by an inundation— Indistinct forms of
bushes—green leaves mixed with the yellow stalks. There are certain
crops which give me the idea of bounty—of the *Alma* Natura— I
mean the grains. Potatoes do not so fill the lap of earth. This rye
excludes everything else & takes possession of the soil. The farmer
says next year I will raise a crop of rye. & he proceeds to clear
away the brush—& either plows it, or if it is too uneven or stoney—
burns & harrows it only—& scatters the seed with faith— And all
winter the earth keeps his secret—unless it did leak out somewhat in
the fall, and in the spring this early green on the hill sides betrays
him. When I see this luxuriant crop spreading far and wide in spite
of rock & bushes and unevenness of ground, I can not help thinking
that it must have been unexpected by the farmer himself—& regarded
by him as a lucky accident for which to thank fortune.— This to
reward a transient faith—the gods had given. As if he must have
forgotten that he did it until he saw the waving grain inviting his
sickle. A kind of pin-a-fore to Nature.

July 9th

When I got out of the cars at Porter's Cambridge this morning—I
was pleased to see the handsome blue flowers of the Succory or
Endive Cichorium intybus—which reminded me that within the hour
I had been whirled into a new botanical region. They must be
extremely rare, if they occur at all in Concord. This weed is
handsomer than most garden flowers. Saw there also the Cucubalus
behen or Bladder Campion. also The Autumnal dandelion Apargia
Autumnalis.

Visited the Observatory. Bond said they were cataloguing the stars

at Washington? or trying to. They do not at Cambridge of no use
with their force. Have not force enough now to make mag. obs.
When I asked if an observer with the small telescope could find
employment—he said "O yes—there was employment enough for
observation with the naked eye—observing the changes in the
brilliancy of stars &c &c—if they could only get some good
observers.— One is glad to hear that the naked eye still retains some
importance in the estimation of astronomers.

Coming out of town—willingly as usual—when I saw that reach of
Charles River just above the Depot—the fair still water this cloudy
evening suggesting the way to eternal peace & beauty—whence it
flows—the placid lake-like fresh water so unlike the salt brine—
affected me not a little— I was reminded of the way in which
Wordsworth so coldly speaks of some natural visions or scenes
"giving him pleasure". This is perhaps the first vision of elysium on
this rout from Boston.

And just then I saw an encampment of Penobscots—their
wigwams appearing above the rail road fence—they too looking up
the river as they sat on the ground & enjoying the scene. What can
be more impressive than to look up a noble river just at evening—
one perchance which you have never explored—& behold its placid
waters reflecting the woods—& sky lapsing inaudibly toward the
ocean—to behold as a lake—but know it as a river—tempting the
beholder to explore it—& his own destiny at once. haunt of
waterfowl——this was above the factories—all that I saw That water
could never have flowed under a factory—how *then* could it have
reflected the sky?

July 10th

A gorgeous sunset after rain with horizontal bars of clouds red
sashes to the western window—barry clouds hanging like a curtain
over the window of the west—damask. First there is a low arch of
the storm clouds in the west under which
is seen the clearer fairrer serener—sky—and
more distant sunset clouds and under all on
the horizon's edge heavier massive dark clouds not to be
distinguished from the *mts.* How many times I have seen this kind of
sunset—the most gorgeous sight in nature. From the hill behind
Minots I see the birds flying against this red sky the sun having set—
one looks like a bat. Now between two stupendous *mts* of the low
stratum under the evening red—clothed in slightly rosaceous amber
light—through a magnificent gorge far far away—as perchance may

occur in pictures of the Spanish Coast viewed from the
mediterranean I see a city—the eternal city of the west—the phantom
city—in whose streets no traveller has trod—over whose pavements
the horses of the sun have already hurried. Some Salamanca of the
imagination. But it lasts only for a moment—for now the changing
light has wrought such changes in it that I see the resemblance no
longer.

A softer amber sky than in any picture. The swallows are
improving this short day—twittering as they fly, & the huckleberry
bird repeats his jingling strain—& the song-sparrow more honest than
most.

I am always struck by the centrality of the observer's position. He
always stands fronting the middle of the arch—& does not suspect at
first that a thousand observers on a thousand hill's behold the sunset
sky from equally favorable positions.

And now I turn & observe the dark masses of the trees in the east
—not green but black while the sun was setting in the west the trees
were rising in the east.

I perceive that the low stratum of dark clouds under the red sky
all slips one way—and to a remarkable degree presents the appearance
of the but ends of cannons slanted toward the sky—thus

Such uniformity on a large scale is unexpected & pleasant to detect—
evincing the simplicity of the laws of their formation. Uniformity in
the shapes of clouds of a single stratum is always to be detected—the
same wind shaping clouds of the like consistency and in like
positions. No doubt an experienced observer could discover the
states of the upper atmosphere by studying the forms & characters of
the clouds.

I traced the distinct form of the cannon in 7 instances stretching
over the whole length of the cloud many a mile in the horizon.

And the night-hawk dashes past in the twilight with mottled?
wing within a rod of me.

Friday July 11th

At 7¼ PM with W.E.C go forth to see the moon the glimpses
of the moon— We think she is not quite full— we can detect a
little flatness on the eastern side. Shall we wear thick coats? The day
has been warm enough, but how cool will the night be? It is not

sultry as the last night. As a general rule, it is best to wear your thickest coat even in a July night. Which way shall we walk? North west—that we may see the moon returning— But on that side the river prevents our walking in the fields—and on other accounts that direction is not so attractive. We go toward Bear Garden Hill. The sun is setting. The meadow sweet has bloomed. These dry hills & pastures are the places to walk by moon light— The moon is silvery still—not yet inaugurated. The tree tops are seen against the amber west— Methinks I see the outlines of one spruce among them—distinguishable afar. My thoughts expand & flourish most on this barren hill where in the twilight I see the moss spreading in rings & prevailing over the short thin grass carpeting the earth—adding a few inches of green to its circle annually while it dies within. As we round the sandy promontory we try the sand & rocks with our hands—the sand is cool on the surface but warmer a few inches beneath—though the contrast is not so great as it was in May. The larger rocks are perceptibly warm. I pluck the blossom of the milk-weed in the twilight & find how sweet it smells. The white blossoms of the Jersey tea dot the hill side—with the yarrow everywhere. Some woods are black as clouds—if we knew not they were green by day, they would appear blacker still.

When we sit we hear the mosquitoes hum. The woodland paths are not the same by night as by day—if they are a little grown up the eye cannot find them—but must give the reins to the feet as the traveller to his horse—so we went through the aspens at the base of the cliffs—their round leaves reflecting the lingering twilight on the one side the waxing moon light on the other—always the path was unexpectedly open. Now we are getting into moon light. We see it reflected from particular stumps in the depths of the darkest woods, and from the stems of trees, as if it selected what to shine on.— a silvery light. It is a light of course which we have had all day but which we have not appreciated— And proves how remarkable a lesser light can be when a greater has departed. Here simply & naturally the moon presides— Tis true she was eclipsed by the sun—but now she acquires an almost equal respect & worship by reflecting & representing him—with some new quality perchance added to his light—showing how original the disciple may be—who still in mid-day is seen though pale & cloud-like beside his master. Such is a worthy disciple— In his masters presence he still is seen & preserves a distinct existence—& in his absence he reflects & represents him—not without adding some new quality to his light—

not servile & never rival— As the master withdraws himself the disciple who was a pale cloud before begins to emit a silvery light— acquiring at last a tinge of golden as the darkness deepens, but not enough to scorch the seeds which have been planted or to dry up the fertilising dews which are falling. Passing now near Well meadow head toward Bakers orchard— The sweet fern & Indigo weed fill the path up to ones middle wetting us with dews so high The leaves are shining & flowing— We wade through the luxuriant vegetation seeing no bottom— Looking back toward the cliffs some dead trees in the horizon high on the rocks make a wild New Hampshire prospect. There is the faintest possible mist over the pond holes, where the frogs are eructating—like the falling of huge drops—the bursting of mephitic air bubbles rising from the bottom—a sort of blubbering Such conversation as I *have* heard between men.— a belching conversation expressing a sympathy of stomachs & abdomens. The peculiar appearance of the Indigo weed, its misty massiveness is striking.

In Baker's Orchard the thick grass looks like a sea of mowing in this weird moonlight—a bottomless sea of grass— our feet must be imaginative—must know the earth in imagination only as well as our heads. We sit on the fence, & where it is broken & interupted the fallen & slanting rails are lost in the grass (really thin & wiry) as in water. We ever see our tracks a long way behind, where we have brushed off the dew. The clouds are peculiarly wispy wispy tonight some what like fine flames—not massed and dark nor downy—not thick but slight thin wisps of mist— I hear the sound of Heywood's brook falling into Fair Haven Pond—inexpressibly refreshing to my senses—it seems to flow through my very bones.— I hear it with insatiable thirst— It allays some sandy heat in me— It affects my circulations—methinks my arteries have sympathy with it What is it I hear but the pure water falls within me in the circulation of my blood—the streams that fall into my heart?— what mists do I ever see but such as hang over—& rise from my blood— The sound of this gurgling water—running thus by night as by day—falls on all my dashes—fills all my buckets—overflows my float boards—turns all the machinery of my nature makes me a flume—a sluice way to the springs of nature— Thus I am washed thus I drink—& quench my thirst. Where the streams fall into the lake if they are only a few inches more elevated all walkers may hear— On the high path through Bakers wood I see or rather feel the Tephrosia— Now we come out into the open pasture. And under those woods of elm &

button wood where still no light is seen—repose a family of human
beings By night there is less to distinguish this locality from the
woods & meadows we have threaded.

We might go very near to Farm houses covered with ornamental
trees & standing on a high road, thinking that were in the most
retired woods & fields still. Having yielded to sleep man is a less
obtrusive inhabitant of nature. Now having reached the dry pastures
again—we are surrounded by a flood of moon light— The dim cart
path over the wood curves gracefully through the Pitch-pines, ever
to some more fairy-like spot. The rails in the fences shine like
silver—

We know not whether we are sitting on the ruins of a wall—or
the materials which are to compose a new one. I see half-a mile off
a phosphorescent arc on the hill side where Bartletts cliff reflects the
moon light. Going by the shanty I smell the excrements of its
inhabitants which I had never smelt before. And now at half past 10
o'clock I hear the cockrils crow in Hubbard's barns.— and morning
is already anticipated. It is the feathered wakeful thought in us that
anticipates the following day. This sound is wonderfully exhilirating
at all times. These birds are worth far more to me for their crowing
& cackling—than for their drumsticks & eggs. How singular the
connexion of the hen with man, that she leaves her eggs in his barns
always—she is a domestic fowl though still a little shyish of him— I
cannot looking at the whole as an experiment still and wondering
that in each case it succeeds. There is no doubt at last but hens may
be kept—they will put there eggs in your barn—by a tacit agreement
— They will not wander far from your yard.

July 12th 8 PM Now at least the moon is full—and I walk alone
—which is best by night, if not by day always. Your companion must
sympathize with the present mood. The conversation must be
located where the walkers are & vary exactly with the scene &
events & the contour of the ground. Farewell to those who will talk
of nature unnaturally—whose presence are an interuption. I know but
one with whom I can walk. I might as well be sitting in a bar room
with them as walk and talk with most— We are never side by side
in our thoughts—& we cannot bear each other's silence— Indeed we
cannot be silent— We are forever breaking silence, that is all, and
mending nothing. How can they keep together who are going
different ways!

I start a sparrow from her 3 eggs in the grass where she had
settled for the night. The earliest corn is beginning to show its tassels

now & I scent it as I walk—its peculiar dry scent. (This afternoon I gathered ripe blackberies & felt as if the autumn had commenced) Now perchance many sounds & sights only remind me that they once said something to me, and are so by association interesting. I go forth to be reminded of a previous state of existence, if perchance any memento of it is to be met with hereabouts. I have no doubt that nature preserves her integrity. Nature is in as rude health as when Homer sang. We may at least by our sympathies be well. I see a skunk on bare garden hill stealing noiselessly away from me, while the moon shines over the pitch pines which send long shadows down the hill— Now looking back I see it shining on the S side of farm houses & barns with a weird light—for I pass here half an hour later than last night. I smell the huckleberry bushes. I hear a human voice some laborer singing after his days toil—which I do not often hear—loud it must be for it is far away—methinks I should know it for a white man's voice—some strains have the melody of an instrument. Now I hear the sound of a bugle in the "Corner" reminding me of Poetic Wars, a few flourishes & the bugler has gone to rest. At the foot of the Cliff hill I hear the sound of the clock striking nine as distinctly as within a quarter of a mile usually though there is no wind. The moonlight is more perfect than last night—hardly a cloud in the sky—only a few fleecy ones—there is more serenity & more light— I hear that sort of throttled or chuckling note as of a bird flying high—now from this side then from that. Methinks when I turn my head I see Wachusett from the side of the hill. I smell the butter & eggs as I walk. I am startled by the rapid transit of some wild animal across my path a rabbit or a fox—or you hardly know if it be not a bird. Looking down from the cliffs the leaves of the tree tops shine more than ever by day—here & there a lightning bug shows his greenish light over the tops of the trees— As I return through the orchard a foolish robin bursts away from his perch unnaturally—with the habits of man. The air is remarkably still and unobjectionable on the hill top & the whole world below is covered as with a gossamer blanket of moonlight— It is just about as yellow as a blanket. It is a great dimly burnished shield with darker blotches on its surface. You have lost some light, it is true, but you have got this simple & magnificent stillness, brooding like genius.

July 13th

Observed yesterday while surveying near Gordon's a bittern flying over near Gordons with moderate flight and outstretched neck its

breast bone sticking out sharp like the bone in the throats of some
persons.— Its anatomy exposed. The evergreen is very handsome in
the woods now—rising somewhat spirally in a round tower of 5 or 6
stories surmounted by a long bud. Looking across the river to
Conantum from the open plains—I think how the history of the hills
would read—since they have been pastured by cows—if every plowing
& mowing & sowing & chopping were recorded. I hear 4 PM a
pigeon wood pecker on a dead pine near by uttering a harsh and
scolding scream, spying me—the chewink jingles on the tops of the
bushes—and the rush sparrow—the vireo—& oven bird at a distance—&
a robin sings superior to all and a barking dog has started something
on the opposite side of the river—and now the wood thrush surpasses
them all— These plains are covered with shrub oaks—birches—aspens
—hickories, mingled with sweet fern & brakes & huckleberry bushes
& epilobium now in bloom—& much fine grass. The Hellebore by
the brooksides has now fallen over though it is not broken off—
The cows now repose & chew the cud under the shadow of a tree—
or crop the grass in the shade along the side of the woods, and
when you approach to observe them they mind you just enough. I
turn up the Juniper repens & see the lighter color of its leaves on
the under sides & its berries with three petal like divisions in one
end. The sweet scented life everlasting is budded.

This might be called the hayer's or hay-maker's moon, for I
perceive that when the day has been oppressively warm the
haymakers rest at noon & resume their mowing after sunset,
sometimes quite into evening.

July 14th

Passing over the Great Fields (where I have been surveying a
road) this forenoon where were some early turnips—the county
Commissioners pluck & pared them with their knives and ate them.
I too tried hard to chew a mouthful of raw-turnip and realize the
life of cows & oxen—it might be a useful habit in extremities—
These events in the revolution of the seasons— These are things
which travellers will do. How many men have tasted a raw turnip—!
how few have eaten a whole one? Some bovine appetites. Fodder
for men. For like reasons we sometimes eat sorrel & say we love it,
that we may return the hospitality of nature by exhibiting a good
appetite.

The citizen looks sharp to see if there is any dogwood or Poison
Sumac in the swamp before he enters.

If I take the same walk by moonlight an hour later or earlier in the evening it is as good as a different one. I love the night for its novelty; it is less prophaned than the day.

The creaking of the crickets seems at the very foundation of all sound. At last I cannot tell it from a ringing in my ears. It is a sound from within not without You cannot dispose of it by listening to it. When I am stilled I hear it. It reminds me that I am a denizen of the earth.

Wednesday July 16th

Methinks my present experience is nothing my past experience is all in all. I think that no experience which I have today comes up to or is comparable with the experiences of my boyhood— And not only this is true—but as far back as I can remember I have unconsciously referred to the experience of a previous state of existence. "Our life is a forgetting" &c

Formerly methought nature developed as I developed and grew up with me. My life was extacy. In youth before I lost any of my senses—I can remember that I was all alive—and inhabited my body with inexpressible satisfaction, both its weariness & its refreshment were sweet to me. This earth was the most glorious musical instrument, and I was audience to its strains. To have such sweet impressions made on us—such extacies begotten of the breezes. I can remember how I was astonished. I said to myself—I said to others— There comes into my mind or soul an indescribable infinite all absorbing divine heavenly pleasure, a sense of elevation & expansion —and have had nought to do with it. I perceive that I am dealt with by superior powers This is a pleasure, a joy, an existence which I have not procured myself— I speak as a witness on the stand and tell what I have perceived The morning and the evening were sweet to me, and I lead a life aloof from society of men. I wondered if a mortal had ever known what I knew. I looked in books for some recognition of a kindred experience—but strange to say, I found none. Indeed I was slow to discover that other men had had this experience—for it had been possible to read books & to associate with men on other grounds.

The maker of me was improving me. When I detected this interference I was profoundly moved. For years I marched as to a music in comparison with which the military music of the streets is noise & discord. I was daily intoxicated and yet no man could call me intemperate. With all your science can you tell how it is—& whence it is, that light comes into the soul?

———

Set out at 3 Pm for Nine Acre Corner bridge via Hubbards
bridge & Conantum—returning via dashing brook—rear of Bakers &
railroad at 6½ Pm. The song sparrow—the most familiar & New
England bird—is heard in fields and pastures—setting this midsummer
day to music—as if it were the music of a mossy rail or fence post, a
little stream of song cooling—ripling through the noon—the usually
unseen songster—usually unheard like the cricket it is so common—
Like the poet's song unheard by most men whose ears are stopped
with business. Though perchance it sang on the fence before the
farmer's house this morning for an hour. There are little strains of
poetry in our annuals. Berries are just beginning to ripen—and
children are planning expeditions after them— They are important as
introducing children to the fields & woods—and as wild fruits of
which much account is made. During the berry season the Schools
have a vacation and many little fingers are busy picking these small
fruits— It is ever a pastime not a drudgery. I remember how glad I
was when I was kept from school a half a day to pick huckleberries
on a neighboring hill all by myself to make a pudding for the family
dinner. Ah, they got nothing but the pudding—but I got invaluable
experience beside— A half a day of liberty like that—was like the
promise of life eternal. It was emancipation in New England. Oh
what a day was there my country-man. I see the yellow butterflies
now gathered in fleets in the road—& on the flowers of the
milkweed Asclepias pulchra by the roadside, a really handsome
flower. Also the smaller butterfly with reddish wings—& a larger
black or steel blue with wings spotted red on edge and one of equall
size reddish copper-colored—now you may see a boy stealing after
one hat in hand. The earliest corn begins to tassel out, and my
neighbor has put his hand in the hill some days ago and abstracted
some new potatoes as big as nuts—then covered up again—now they
will need or will get no more weeding. The lark sings in the
meadow—the very essence of the afternoon is in his strain. This is a
New England sound—but the cricket is heard under all sounds. Still
the cars come & go with the regularity of nature—of the sun &
moon (If a hen puts her eggs elsewhere than in the barns—in woods
or among rocks—she is said to *steal* her nest!) The twittering of
swallows is in the air reminding me of water— The meadow sweet
is now in bloom & the yarrow prevails by all road-sides— I see the
hard-hack too, homely but dear plant—just opening its red clustered
flowers The small aster too now abounds Aster miser—and the tall
butter cup still. After wading through a swamp the other day with

my shoes in my hand I wiped my feet with Sassafras leaves which
reminded me of some Arabian practices   The bruised leaves
perfuming the air—and by their softness being adapted to this
purpose. The tree primrose or Scabish still is seen over the fence.
The red wings & crow blackbirds are heard chattering on the trees—
& the cowtroopials are accompanying the cows in the pastures for
the sake of the insects they scare up. Oftentimes the thoughtless
sportsman has lodged his charge of shot in the cow's legs or body in
his eagerness to obtain the birds. St Johns wort one of the first of
yellow flowers begins to shine along the road side—the mullein for
some time past. I see a farmer cradling his rye John Potter— Fields
are partly mown some English grass on the higher parts of the
meadow next to the road. The farmers work comes not all at once.
In haying time—there is a cessation from other labors to a
considerable extent— Planting is done & hoeing mainly—only some
turnip-seed is to be scattered amid the corn. I hear the kingbird
twittering or chattering like a stout-chested swallow. The prunella
sends back a blue ray from under my feet as I walk—the pale lobelia
too. The plaintive spring-restoring peep of a blue-bird is occasionally
heard. I met loads of hay on the road—which the oxen draw
indifferently—swaggering in their gate as if it were not fodder for
them. Methinks they should testify sometimes that they are working
for themselves. The white-weed is turning black. Grapes are half
grown and lead the mind forward to autumn. It is an air this
afternoon that makes you indifferent to all things—perfect summer—
but with a comfortable breeziness—you know not heat nor cold—
What season of the year is this? The balls of the button bush are half
formed with its fine glossy red stemmed leaf atoning for its
nakedness in the spring.

My eye ranges over green fields of oats—for which there is a
demand then somewhere. The wild-rose peeps from amid the alders
& other shrubs by the roadside— The elder blow fills the air with its
scent. The angelica with its large umbels is gone to seed. On it I
find one of those slow-moving green worms with rings spotted
black & yellow—like an East Indian production. What if these grew
as large as elephants— The honest & truly fair is more modestly
colored— Notwithstanding the drifting clouds you fear no rain today
As you walk you smell some sweet herbage but detect not what it is
— Hay is sticking to the willows & the alders on the causeway, &
the bridge is sprinkled with it— The hemlock Cicuta Am. displays

its white umbels now— The yellow lilies reign in the river— The
painted tortoises drop off the willow stumps as you go over the
bridge— The river is now so low that you can see its bottom shined
on by the sun—& travellers stop to look at fishes as they go over—
leaning on the rails. The pickerel weed—sends up its heavenly blue.
The color of the cows on Fair Haven Hill—how fair a contrast to
the hill-side—how striking & wholesome their clean brick red— when
were they painted? How carelessly the eye rests on them or passes
them by as things of course.

The tansey is budded— The Devils needles seem to rest in air
over the water. There is nothing New English about them. Now at
4 Pm I hear the Pewee in the woods & the Cuccoo reminds me of
some silence among the birds I had not noticed— The vireo (redeyed?) sings like a robin at even incessantly. for I have now turned
into Conants woods. The oven bird helps fill some pauses. The
poison sumack shows its green berries now unconscious of guilt.
The heart leaved loosestrife—Lysimachia Ciliata is seen in in low
open woods— The breeze displays the white under sides of the oak
leaves & gives a fresh & flowing look to the woods. The river is a
dark blue winding stripe amid the green of the meadow What is
the color of the world.— Green mixed with yellowish & reddish for
hills & ripe grass—& darker green for trees & forests—blue spotted
with dark & white for sky & clouds—& dark blue for water. Beyond
the old house I hear the squirrel chirp in the wall like a sparrow so
Nature merges her creations into one. I am refreshed by the view of
Nobscot and the South-western vales from Conantum seething with
the blue element— Here comes a small bird with a ricochet flight &
a faint twittering note like a messenger from Elysium. The rush-
sparrow jingles her small change—pure silver, on the counter of the
pasture. From far I see the rye stacked up. A few dead trees impart
the effect of wildness to the landscape—though it is a feature rare in
an old settled country.

Methinks this is the first of dog-days. The air in the distance has a
peculiar blue mistiness or furnace-like look—though, as I have said it
is not sultry yet— It is not the season for distant views— Mountains
are not *clearly* blue now— The air is the opposite to what it is in
october & november. You are not inclined to travel. It is a world of
orchards & small fruits now—& you can stay at home if the well has
cool water in it. The black thimble berry is an honest homely berry
now drying up as usual— I used to have a pleasant time stringing
them on herds grass stems tracing the wall sides for them. It is

pleasant to walk through these elevated fields—terraced upon the side
of the hill so that the eye of the walker looks off into the blue
cauldron of the air at his own level.

Here the haymakers have just gone to tea—(at 5 o'clock the
farmers hour—before the afternoon is end—while he still thinks much
work may still be done before night.— He does not wait till he is
strongly reminded of the night   In the distance some burdened
fields are black with haycocks. Some thoughtless & cruel sports man
has killed 22 young partridges not much bigger than robins, against
the laws of Massachusetts & humanity. At the Corner bridge the
white lilies are budded. Green apples are now so large as to remind
me of codling & the autumn again. The season of fruits is arrived.
The dog's bane has a pretty delicate bell-like flower — The jersey
tea abounds. I see the the marks of the scythes in the fields showing
the breadth of each swath the mowers cut. Cool springs are now a
desideratum. The geranium still hangs on. Even the creeping vines
love the brooks & I see where one slender one has struggled down
& dangles into the current which rocks it to & fro. Filberts are
formed & you may get the berry stains out of your hands with their
husks, if you have any— Night shade is in blossom. Came thro the
pine plains behind James Bakers—where late was open pasture now
open pitch pine woods—only here and there the grass has given place
to a carpet of pine needles   These are among our pleasantest woods
—open—level—with blackberry vines interspersed & flowers, as ladies
slippers earlier—& pinks On the outskirts each tree has room
enough & now I hear the wood thrush from the shade who loves
these pine woods as well as I.— I pass by walden's scolloped shore.
The epilobium reflects a pink gleam up the vales & down the hills—
The chewink jingles on a bushes top— Why will the Irishman drink
of a puddle by the railroad instead of digging a well how shiftless—
what death in life. He cannot be said to live who does not get pure
water. The milkweeds or silkweeds are rich flowers now in blossom
— The Asclepias syriaca or Common Milk weed its buds fly open
at a touch—but handsomer much is Asclepias Pulchra or water
silkweed—the thin green bark of this last & indeed of the other is so
strong that a man cannot break a small strip of it by fair means. It
contains a mass of fine silken fibers arranged side by side like the
strings of a fiddle bow & may be bent short without weakening it.

What more glorious condition of being can we imagine than
from impure to be becoming pure. It is almost desirable to be

impure that we may be the subjects of this improvement. That I am
innocent to myself. That I love & reverence my life! That I am
better fitted for a lofty society today than I was yesterday to make
my life a sacrament— What is nature without this lofty tumbling
May I treat myself with more & more respect & tenderness— May I
not forget that I am impure & vicious May I not cease to love
purity. May I go to my slumbers as expecting to arise to a new &
more perfect day.

    May I so live and refine my life as fitting myself for a society ever
higher than I actually enjoy. May I treat myself tenderly as I would
treat the most innocent child whom I love—may I treat children &
my friends as my newly discovered self— Let me forever go in
search of myself— Never for a moment think that I have found
myself. Be as a stranger to myself never a familiar—seeking
acquaintance still. May I be to myself as one is to me whom I love—
a dear & cherished object— What temple what fane what sacred
place can there be but the innermost part of my own being? The
possibility of my own improvement, that is to be cherished. As I
regard myself so I am. O my dear friends I have not forgotten you
I will know you tomorrow. I associate you with my ideal self. I had
ceased to have faith in myself. I thought I was grown up & become
what I was intended to be. But it is earliest spring with me. In
relation to virtue & innocence the oldest man is in the beginning
spring & vernal season of life. It is the love of virtue makes us young
ever— That is the fountain of youth— The very aspiration after the
perfect. I love & worship myself with a love which absorbs my love
for the world. The lecturer suggested to me that I might become
better than I am—was it not a good lecture then? May I dream not
that I shunned vice— May I dream that I loved & practiced virtue.

July 18th

    It is a test question affecting the youth of a person— Have you
knowledge of the morning? Do you sympathise with that season of
nature? Are you abroad early—brushing the dews aside—? If the sun
rises on you slumbering— If you do not hear the morning cock-
crow, if you do not witness the blushes of Aurora if you are not
acquainted with venus as the morning star what relation have you to
wisdom & purity. You have then forgotten your creator in the days
of your youth. Your shutters were darkened till noon!— You rose
with a sick-head ache! In the morning sing—as do the birds. What of
those birds which should slumber on their perches till the sun was
an hour high—! What kind of fowl would they be & new kind of

bats & owls—hedge sparrows or larks! then took a dish of tea or hot coffee before they began to sing!

I might have added to the list of July 16th   The Aralia hispida Bristling aralia—   The heart-leaved Loosestrife Lysimachia ciliata— Also the upright loose strife L. racemosa with a rounded terminal raceme. The Tufted Vetch Vicia cracca. Sweet gale fruit now green.

I first heard the locust sing so dry & piercing by the side of the pine woods in the heat of the day.

July 19th

Here I am 34 years old, and yet my life is almost wholly unexpanded. How much is in the germ! There is such an interval between my ideal and the actual in many instances that I may say I am unborn. There is the instinct for society—but no society. Life is not long enough for one success. Within another 34 years that miracle can hardly take place. Methinks my seasons revolve more slowly than those of nature, I am differently timed. I am—contented. This rapid revolution of nature even of nature in me—why should it hurry me. Let a man step to the music which he hears however measured. Is it important that I should mature as soon as an apple tree? Ye, as soon as an oak? May not my life in nature, in proportion as it is supernatural, be only the spring & infantile portion of my spirit's life shall I turn my spring to summer? May I not sacrifice a hasty & petty completeness here to entireness there? If my curve is large—why bend it to a smaller circle? My spirits unfolding observes not the pace of nature. The society which I was made for is not here, shall I then substitute for the anticipation of that this poor reality. I would have the unmixed expectation of that than this reality.

If life is a waiting—so be it. I will not be shipwrecked on a vain reality. What were any reality which I can substitute. Shall I with pains erect a heaven of blue glass over myself though when it is done I shall be sure to gaze still on the true etherial heaven—far above as if the former were not that still distant sky oer arching that blue expressive eye of heaven. I am enamored of the blue eyed arch of heaven

I did not *make* this demand for a more thorough sympathy. This is not my idiosyncrasy or disease. He that made the demand will answer the demand.

My blood flows as slowly as the waves of my native Musketaquid —yet they reach the ocean sooner perchance than those of the Nashua.

Already the golden-rod is budded, but I can make no haste for that.

July 19th 2 Pm

The weather is warm & dry—& many leaves curl. There is a threatening cloud in the S W. The farmers dare not spread their hay. It remains cocked in the fields. As you walk in the woods now a days the flies striking against your hat sound like rain drops. The stump or root fences on the Corner road remind me of fossil remains of mastodons &c exhumbed and bleached in sun & rain. To day I met with the first orange flower of autumn— What means this doubly torrid—this Bengal tint— Yellow took sun enough—but this is the fruit of a dogday sun. The year has but just produced it. Here is the Canada thistle in bloom visited by butterflies & bees The butterflies have swarmed within these few days especially about the milkweed's. The swamp pink still fills the air with its perfume in swamps & by the causeways—though it is far gone. The wild rose still scatters its petals over the leaves of neighboring plants. The wild morning glory or bind-weed with its delicate red & white blossoms— I remember it ever as a goblet full of purest morning air & sparkling with dew. showing the dew point—winding round itself for want of other support— It grows by the Hubbard bridge causeway near the Angelica. The cherry birds are making their seringo sound as they flit past. They soon find out the locality of the cherry trees. And beyond the bridge there is a golden rod partially blossomed. Yesterday it was spring & to-morrow it will be autumn— Where is the summer then? First came the St Johns wort & now the golden rod to admonish us. I hear too a cricket amid these stones under the blackbery vines—singing as in the fall. Ripe blackberries are multiplying. I see the red-spotted berries of the small solomons seal in my path. I notice in the decayed end of an oak post that the silver grain is not decayed—but remains sound in thin flakes alternating with the decayed portions, & giving the whole a honey-combed look.— Such an object supramundane—as even a swallow may descend to light on—a dry mullein stalk for instance—— I see that hens too follow the cows feeding near the house like the cowtroopial—& for the same object. They cannot so well scare up insects for themselves. This is the dog the cowbird uses to start its insect game

I see yellow butterflies in pairs pursuing each other—a rod or two into the air & now as he had bethought himself of the danger of being devoured by a passing birds he descends with a zig zag flight

to the earth & the other follows. The black hucklberries are now so
thick among the green ones that they no longer incur suspicion of
being worm eaten. When formerly I was looking about to see what
I could do for a living—some sad experience in comforming to the
wishes of friends being fresh in my mind to tax my ingenuity—I
thought often & seriously of picking huckleberries—that surely I
could do, and its small profits might suffice. So little capital it
required—so little distraction from my wonted thoughts I foolishly
thought— While my acquaintances went unhesitatingly into trade or
the professions I thought of this occupation as most like theirs.
ranging the hills all summer to pick the berries which came in my
way which I might carelessly dispose of—so to keep the flocks of
king Admetus— My greatest skill has been to want but little. I also
dreammed that I might gather the wild herbs—or carry evergreens to
such villagers as love to be reminded of the woods & so find my
living got.

But I have since learned that trade curses everything it handles.
& though you *trade* in messages from heaven—the whole curse of
trade attaches to the business.

The wind rises more & more The river & the pond are blacker
than the threatening cloud in the south— The thunder mutters in
the distance— The surface of the water is slightly rippled— Where
the pads grow is a light green border— The woods roar. Small
white clouds are hurrying across the dark blue ground of the storm—
which rests on all the woods of the South horizon But still no rain
now for some hours as if the clouds were dissipated as fast as they
reached this atmosphere.

The barberry's fruit hangs yellowish green— What pretty covers
the thick bush makes so large & wide & drooping. The Fringilla
juncorum sings still in spite of the coming tempest which perchance
only threatens

The wood chuck is a good native of the soils. The distant hills
side & the grain fields & pastures are spotted yellow or white with
his recent burrows—and the small mounds remain for many years
Here where the clover has lately been cut, see what a yellow mound
is brought to light!

Heavily hangs the Common Yellow lily Lilium Canadense in
the meadows— In the thick alder copses by the causeway side
I find the Lysimachia hybrida. Here is the Lactuca Sanguinea
with its runcinate leaves—tall-stem & pale crimson ray. And
that green stemmed one higher than my head resembled

the last in its leaves—is perchance the "tall lettuce or Fire weed. Can that fine white flowered meadow plant with the leaf be a Thalictrum?

July 20th Sunday Morn.

A thunder shower in the night. Thunder near at hand though louder is a more trivial & earthly sound than at a distance—likened to sounds of men. The clap which waked me last night was as if some one was moving lumber in an upper apartment—some vast hollow hall tumbling it down & dragging it over the floor, and ever & anon the lightning filled the damp air with light like some vast glow worm in the fields of ether—opening its wings

The river too steadily yields its crop In louring days it is remarkable how many villagers resort to it. It is of more worth than many gardens— I meet one late in the afternoon going to the river with his basket on his arm & his pole in hand—not ambitious to catch pickerel this time, but he thinks he may perhaps get a mess of small fish. These kind of values are real & important—though but little appreciated—& he is not a wise legislator who underrates them and allows the bridge to be built low so as to prevent the passage of small boats. The town is but little conscious how much interest it has in the river—& might vote it away anyday thoughtlessly. There is always to be seen either some unshaven wading man—an old mower of the river meadows familiar with water—vibrating his long pole over the lagoons of the off shore pads—or else some solitary fisher in a boat behind the willows—like a moat in the sunbeams reflecting the light & who can tell how many a mess of river fish is daily cooked in the town. They are an important article of food to many a poor family.

Some are poets some are not—as in relation to getting a living so to getting a wife. As their ideals of life vary—so do their ideals of love.

4 PM Annursnack The under sides of the leaves exposed by the breeze give a light blueish tinge to the woods as I look down on them. Looking at the woods west of this hill there is a grateful dark shade under their eastern sides where they meet the meadows—their cool night side—a triangular segment of night to which the sun has set. The mts look like waves on a blue ocean tossed up by a stiff gale. The rhexia Virginica is in bloom

July 21st 8 AM

The forenoon is fuller of light. The butterflies on the flowers look like other & frequently larger flowers themselves. Now I yearn

for one of those old meandering dry uninhabited roads which lead
away from towns—which lead us away from temptation, which
conduct to the outside of earth—over its uppermost crust—where you
may forget in what country you are travelling—where no farmer can
complain that you are treading down his grass—no gentleman who
has recently constructed a seat in the country that you are trespassing
—on which you can go off at half cock—and waive adieu to the
village—along which you may travel like a pilgrim—going nowhither.
Where travellers are not too often to be met. Where my spirit is free
—where the walls & fences are not cared for—where your head is
more in heaven than your feet are on earth—which have long
reaches—where you can see the approaching traveller half a mile off
and be prepared for him —not so luxuriant a soil as to attract men—
some root and stump fences which do not need attention— Where
travellers have no occasion to stop—but pass along and leave you to
your thoughts— Where it makes no odds which way you face
whether you are going or coming—whether it is morning or evening
—mid noon or mid-night— Where earth is cheap enough by being
public. Where you can walk and think with least obstruction—there
being nothing to measure progress by. Where you can pace when
your breast is full and cherish your moodiness. Where you are not in
false relations with men—are not dining nor conversing with them.
By which you may go to the uttermost parts of the earth— It is
wide enough—wide as the thoughts it allows to visit you. Sometimes it is some particular half dozen rods which I wish to find
myself pacing over—as where certain airs blow then my life will
come to me methinks like a hunter I walk in wait for it. When I
am against this bare promontory of a hucklebery hill then forsooth
my thoughts will expand. Is it some influence as a vapor which
exhales from the ground, or something in the gales which blow
there or in all things there brought together agreeably to my spirit?
The walls must not be too high imprisoning me—but low with
numerous—gaps— The trees must not be too numerous nor the hills
too near bounding the view—nor the soil too rich attracting the
attention to the earth— It must simply be the way and the life. A
way that was never known to be repaired nor to need repair within
the memory of the oldest inhabitant— I cannot walk habitually in
those ways that are liable to be repaired, for sure it was the devil
only that wore them—never by the heel of thinkers (of thought)
were they worn—the zephyrs could repair that damage. The
saunterer wears out no road—even though he travel on it—&
therefore should pay no highway tax—he may be taxed to construct a

higher way than men travel. A way which no geese defile nor hiss
along it—but only some times their wild brethren fly far overhead—
which the king bird & the swallow twitter over—& the song sparrow
sings on its rails. where the small red butterfly is at home on the
yarrow—& no boys threaten it with imprisoning hat. There I can
walk & stalk & pace & plod— Which no body but Jonas Potter
travels beside me—where no cow but his is tempted to linger for the
herbage by its side— Where the guide board is fallen & now the
hand points to heaven significantly—to a sudbury & Marlborough in
the skies. That's a road I can travel thats the particular sudbury I am
bound for 6 miles an hour or 2 as you please— And few there be
that enter thereon. There I can walk and recover the lost child that I
am without any ringing of a bell— Where there was nothing ever
discovered to detain a traveller but all went through about their
business— Where I never passed the time of day with any—
indifferent to me were the arbitrary divisions of time— Where
Tullus Hostilius might have disappeared—at any rate has never been
seen The road to the corner—the ninety & nine acres that you go
through to get there I would rather see it again though I saw it this
morning, than Gray's churchyard. The road whence you may hear a
stake driver—a whipporwill—a quail in a mid summer day—a yes a
quail comes nearest to the gum C bird heard there— Where it
would not be sport for a sportsman to go.— (and the may weed
looks up in my face—not there) the pale lobelia & the Canada Snap
Dragon rather. a little hard hack & meadow sweet peeps over the
fence—nothing more serious to obstruct the view— And thimble
berries are the food of thought—before the droubt along by the
walls.

It is they who go to Brighton & to market that wear out the
roads—& they should pay all the tax—the deliberate pace of a thinker
never made a road the worse for travelling on. There I have
freedom in my thought & in my soul am free— Excepting the
omnipresent butcher with his calf cart—followed by a distracted &
anxious cow—

Be it known that in Concord where the first forcible resistance to
British aggression was made in the year 1775 they chop up the
young calves & give them to the hens to make them lay—it being
considered the cheapest & most profitable food for them—& they sell
the milk to Boston.

On the promenade deck of the world—an outside passenger—
The inattentive ever strange baker—whom no weather detains that

does not bake his bread in this hemisphere—and therefore it is dry
before it gets here— Ah there is a road where you might advertise
to fly—& make no preparations till the time comes where your
wings will sprout if anywhere. where your feet are not confined to
earth. An airy head makes light walking.

Where I am not confined & baulked by the sight of distant farm
houses which I have not gone past. In roads the obstructions are not
under my feet—I care not for rough ground or wet even—but they
are in my vision & in the thoughts or associations which I am
compelled to entertain I must be fancy free— I must feel that wet
or dry high or low it is the genuine surface of the planet & not a
little chip dirt or a compost heap—or made land or redeemed. Where
I can sit by the wall side and not be peered at by any old ladies
going a shopping—not have to bow to one whom I may have seen
in my youth—at least not more than once— I am engaged and
cannot be polite.

Did you ever hear of such a thing as a man sitting in the road—&
then have four eyes levelled at you. Have we any more right
sometimes to look at one than to point a revolver at him—it might
go off—& so perchance we might *see* him—which would be equally
fatal—if it *should* ever happen—though perhaps it never has.—

A thinker's weight is in his thought not in his tread—when he
thinks freely his body weighs nothing. He cannot tread down your
grass farmers.

I thought to walk this forenoon instead of this afternoon—for I
have not been in the fields & woods much of late except when
surveying—but the least affair of that kind is as if you had black veil
drawn over your face which shut out nature as that eccentric &
melancholy minister whom I have heard of. It may be the fairest day
in all the year & you shall not know it—one little chore to do—one
little commission to fulfil—one message to carry would spoil heaven
itself. Least of all is the lover *engaged*! And all you get is your dollars

To go forth before the heat is intolerable and see what is the
difference between forenoon & afternoon. It seems there is a little
more coolness in the air; there is still some dew even on this short
grass in the shade of the walls & woods—and a feeling of vigor the
walker has. There are few sounds but the slight twittering of
swallows & the *springy* note of the sparrow in the grass or trees—& a
lark in the meadow (now at 8 AM) and the cricket under all to ally
the hour to night. Day is in fact about as still as night. draw the
veil of night over this landscape and these sounds would not disturb

nor be inconsistent for their loudness with the night. It is a
difference of white & black. Nature is in a white sleep. It threatens
to be a hot day & the haymakers are whetting their scythes in the
fields where they have been out since 4 o'clock. When I have seen
them in the twilight commencing their labors, I have been impressed
as if it were last night. There is something ghastly about such very
early labor. I cannot detect the whole & characteristic difference
between this and afternoon—though it is positive & decided enough—
as my instincts know.

By two o'clock it will be warmer & hazier obscuring the mts, &
the leaves will curl—& the dust will rise more readily. Every herb is
fresher now—has recovered from yesterdays drought— The cooler air
of night still lingers in the fields as by night the warm air of day.
The noon is perchance the time to stay in the house.

There is no glory so bright but the veil of business can hide it
effectually With most men life is postponed to some trivial business
& so therefore is heaven. Men think foolishly they may abuse &
misspend life as they please and when they get to heaven turn over a
new leaf.

I see the track of a bare human foot in the dusty road, the toes &
muscles all faithfully imprinted— Such a sight is so rare that it affects
me with surprise as the foot print on the shore of Juan Fernandez
did Crusoe— It is equally rare here I am affected as if some Indian
or South Sea Islander had been along—some man who had a foot. I
am slow to be convinced that any of my neighbors—the judge on
the bench—the parson in the pulpit might have made that or some
thing like it however irregular. It is pleasant as it is to see the tracks
of cows & deer & birds. I am brought so much nearer to the tracker
—when again I think of the sole of my own foot—than when I
behold that of his shoe merely, or am introduced to him & converse
with him in the usual way.

Men are very generally spoiled by being so civil and well
disposed. You can have no profitable conversation with them they
are so conciliatory—determined to agree with you. They exhibit such
long suffering & kindness in a short interview. I would meet with
some provoking strangeness. So that we may be guest and host &
refresh one another. It is possible for a man wholly to disappear &
be merged in his manners. The thousand and one gentlemen whom
I meet I meet despairingly & but to part from them for I am not
cheered by the hope of any rudeness from them. A cross man a
coarse man an ecentric man a silent—a man who does not drill well

of him there is some hope. Your gentlemen, they are all alike They
utter their opinions as if it was not a man that uttered them. It is
"just as you please"–they are indifferent to everything– They will
talk with you for nothing. The interesting man will rather avoid–
and it is a rare chance if you get so far as talk with him. The
laborers whom I know–the loafers–fishers & hunters–I can spin
yarns with profitably for it is hands off they are they & I am I still–
they do not come to me & quarter themselves on me for an day or
an hour to be treated politely–they do not cast themselves on me for
entertainment–they do not approach me with a flag of truce. They
do not go out of themselves to meet me. I am never electrified by
my gentleman–he is not an electric eeel, but one of the common
kind that slip through your hands however hard you clutch them &
leave them covered with slime.

He is a man every inch of him–is worth a groom–

To eat berries on the dry pastures of Conantum as if they were
the food of thought–dry as itself. Berries are now thick enough to
pick. 9 A M on Conantum

A quarter of a mile is distance enough to make the atmosphere
look blue now. This is never the case in spring or early summer. It
was fit that I should see an Indigo bird here concerned about its
young–a perfect imbodiment of the darkest blue that ever fills the
vallies at this season– The meadow grass reflecting the light has a
bluish cast also.

Remember thy creator in the days of thy youth. i.e. Lay up a
store of natural influences–sing while you may before the evil days
come–he that hath ears let him hear–see–hear–smell–taste–&c while
these senses are fresh & pure

There is always a kind of fine Æolian harp music to be heard in
the air I hear now as it were the mellow sound of distant horns in
the hollow mansions of the upper air–a sound to make all men
divinely insane that hear it–far away over head subsiding into my
ear. to ears that are expanded what a harp this world is! The
occupied ear thinks that beyond the cricket no sound can be heard–
but there is an immortal melody that may be heard morning noon
and night by ears that can attend & from time to time this man or
that hears it–having ears that were made for music. To hear this the
hard hack & the meadow sweet *aspire* They are thus beautifully
painted because they are tinged in the lower stratum of that melody.

I eat these berries as simply & naturally as thoughts come to my
mind.

Never yet did I chance to sit in a house—except my own house in the woods—and hear a wood thrush sing—would it not be well to sit in such a chamber—within sound of the finest songster of the grove?

The quail—invisible—whistles—& who attends

10 A M— The white lily has opened how could it stand these heats—it has pantingly opened—and now lies stretched out by its too-long stem on the surface of the shrunken river. The air grows more & more blue.— making pretty effects when one wood is seen from another through a little interval. Some pigeons here are resting in the thickest of the white pines during the heat of the day—migrating no doubt. They are unwilling to move for me. Flies buz and rain about my hat—& the dead twigs & leaves of the White pine which the choppers have left here exhale a dry & almost sickening scent. A cuccoo chuckles half throtled on a neighboring tree—& now flying into the pine scares out a pigeon which flies with its handsome tail spread dashes this side and that between the trees helplessly like a ship carrying too much sail in midst of a small creek some great amiral.— having no room to manoeuvre— A fluttering flight.

The *mts* can scarcely be seen for the blue haze only Wachusett and the near ones.

The thorny apple bush on Conantum has lately sent up branches from its top resolved to become a tree, & these spreading (and bearing fruit) the whole has the form of a vast hour-glass.— The lower part being the most dense by far you would say the sand had run out.

I now return through Conants leafy woods by the spring—whose floor is sprinkled with sun-light—low trees which yet effectually shade you

The dusty may weed now blooms by the roadside one of the humblest flowers.

The rough hawkweed too by the damp roadside—resembling in its flower the autumnal dandelion— That was probably the verbena hastata or com. blue vervain which I found the other day by Walden Pond

The Antirrhinum Canadense Can. snap dragon in the Corner road. And the ragged Orchis on Conantum.

8½ PM

The streets of the village are much more interesting to me at this hour of a summer evening than by day. Neighbors and also farmers come ashopping after their day's haying are chatting in the streets and I hear the sound of many musical instruments and of singing from various houses. For a short hour or two the inhabitants are sensibly employed.

The evening is devoted to poetry such as the villagers can appreciate.

How rare to meet with a farmer who is a man of sentiment Yet there was one Gen. Joshua Buttrick who died the other day—who is said to have lived in his sentiments. He used to say that the smell of burning powder excited him.

It is said that Mirabeau took to highway robbery "to ascertain what degree of resolution was necessary in order to place one's self in formal opposition to the most sacred laws of society." He declared that "a soldier who fights in the ranks does not require half so much courage as a footpad."——"honor and religion have never stood in the way of a well considered & a firm resolve. Tell me, Du Saillant, when you lead your regiment into the heat of battle, to conquer a province to which he whom you call your master has no right whatever, do you consider that you are performing a better action than mine, in stopping your friend on the king's highway, and demanding his purse?"

"I obey without reasoning," replied the count.

"And I reason without obeying, when obedience appears to me to be contrary to reason,"—rejoined Mirabeau. Harpers New Month. vol 1st p 648 from Cham. Ed.— Journal

This was good & manly as the world goes— And yet it was desperate— A saner man would have found opportunities enough to put himself in formal opposition to the most sacred laws of society and so test his resolution in the natural course of events without violating the laws of his own nature. It is not for a man to *put himself* in such an attitude to society—but to *maintain* himself in whatever attitude he find himself through obedience to the laws of his being. which will never be one of opposition to a just government. Cut the leather only where the shoe pinches— Let us not have a rabid virtue that will be revenged on society—that falls on it not like the morning dew but like the fervid noonday sun to wither it.

July 22nd

The season of morning fogs has arrived I think it is connected with dog days Perhaps it is owing to the greater contrast between the night & the day—the nights being nearly as cold while the days

are warmer? Before I rise from my couch I see the ambrosial fog
stretched over the river draping the trees— It is the summers vapor
bath—what purity in the color— It is almost musical; it is positively
fragrant. How faery like it has visited our fields. I am struck by its
firm outlines as distinct as a pillow's edge about the height of my
house—a great crescent over the course of the river from SW to NE.

5½ Am Already some parts of the river are bare— It goes off in
a body down the river before this air—and does not rise into the
heavens— It retreats & I do not see how it is dissipated. This slight
thin vapor which is left to curl over the surface of the still dark
water still as glass—seems not be the same things—of a different
quality.

I hear the cockrils crow through it—and the rich crow of young
roosters—that sound indicative of the bravest rudest health—hoarse
without cold—hoarse with a rude health That crow is all nature
compelling—famine & pestilence flee before it— These are our fairest
days which are born in a fog

I saw the tall lettuce yesterday Lactucca elongata—whose top or
main shoot had been broken off—& it had put up various stems—
with entire & lanceolate—not runcinate leaves as usual—thus making
what some botanists have called a variety—β. linearis— So I have
met with some Geniuses who having met with some such accident
maiming them—have been developed in some such *monstrous* &
partial though original way. They were original in being less than
themselves.

Yes your leaf is peculiar—and some would make of you a distinct
variety—but to me you appear like the puny result of an accident &
misfortune—for you have lost your main shoot—and the leaves which
would have grown runcinate are small & lanceolate.

The last sunday afternoon I smelled the clear pork frying for a
farmer's supper 30 rods off (what a sunday supper!) the windows
being opens—& could imagine the *clear* tea without milk which
usually accompanies it

Now the catonine tails are seen in the impenetrable meadows &
the tall green rush is perfecting its tufts. The spotted Polygonum P.
Persicaria by the roadside

I scare up a wood-cock from some moist place at mid day—

The Pewee & Kingbird are killing bees perched on a post or a
dead twig.

I bathe me in the river— I lie down where it is shallow—amid
the weeds over its sandy bottom *but* it seems shrunken & parched—

I find it difficult to get *wet* through— I would fain be the channel of
a *mt* brook. I bathe & in a few hours I bathe again not remembering
that I was wetted before. When I come to the river I take off my
clothes & carry them over then bathe & wash off the mud &
continue my walk.

There was a singular charm for me in those French names more
than in the things themselves The name of Italian & Grecian cities
villages & natural features are not more poetic to me than the names
of those humble Canadian villages—to be told by a habitant when I
asked the name of a village in sight that is St Fereole or St Anne's
But I was quite taken off my feet when running back to inquire
what river we were crossing—and thinking for a long time he said la
Riviere d'Ocean it flashed upon me at last that it was la rivière du
chien the la rivière so often repeated in the

{One leaf missing}

There was so much grace and sentiment & refinement in the names
how could they be coarse who took them so often on their lips—St
Anne's St Joseph's the holy Annes the holy Joseph's. Next to the
Indian the French missionary & voyageur & Catholic habitant have
named the natural features of the land— The *prairie*—the voyageur—
Or does every man think his neighbor is the richer & more
fortunate man his neighbor's fields the richest.

It needed only a little outlandishness in the names a little foreign
accent a few more vowels in the words—to make me locate all my
ideals at once— How prepared we are for another world than this—
We are no sooner over the line of the states—than we expect to see
men leading poetic lives—nothing so natural that is the presumption—
the names of the mountains & the streams & the villages reel with
the intoxication of poetry Longoeil Chambly—Barthillon? Montilly?

Where there were books only—to find realities of course we assign
to the place the idea which the written history or poem suggested
Quebec of course is never seen for what it simply is to practical eyes
—but as the local habitation of those thoughts & visions which we
have derived from reading of Wolfe & Montcalm Montgomery &
Arnold—— It is hard to make me attend to the geology of Cape
diamond—or the botany of the Plains of Abraham. How glad we are
to find that there is another race of men—for they may be more
successful & fortunate than we.

Canada is not a place for rail-roads to terminate in or for
criminals to run to.

Wednesday July 23d

I remember the last moon shining through a creamy atmosphere—. with a tear in the eye of nature—& her tresses dishevelled & drooping. Sliding up the sky—the glistening air —the leaves shining with dew—pulsating upward—an atmosphere unworn unprophaned by day. What self healing in nature—swept by the dews.

For some weeks pasts the road sides & the dry & trivial fields have been covered with the field trefoil—trifolium arvense now in bloom.

8 AM

A comfortable breeze blowing. Methinks I can write better in the afternoon, for the novelty of it—if I should go abroad this morning— My genius makes distinctions which my understanding can not—and which my senses do not report. If I should reverse the usual, go forth & saunter in the fields all the forenoon then sit down in my chamber in the afternoon which it is so unusual for me to do—it would be like a new season to me & the novelty of it inspire me. The wind has fairly blown me out doors—the elements were so lively & active—& I so sympathized with them that I could not sit while the wind went by. And I am reminded that we should especially improve the summer to live out of doors— When we may so easily it behoves us to break up this custom of sitting in the house. for it is but a custom—and I am not sure that it has the sanction of common sense. A man no sooner gets up than he sits down again. Fowls leave their perch in the morning & beasts their lairs—unless they are such as go abroad only by night— The cockril does not take up a new perch *in the barn*—& he is the imbodiment of health & common sense. Is the literary man to live always or chiefly sitting in a chamber—through which Nature enters by a window only? What is the use of the summer?

You must walk so gently as to hear the finest sounds—the faculties being in repose— Your mind must not perspire True, out of doors my thought is commonly drowned as it were & shrunken pressed down by stupendous piles of light etherial influences—for the pressure of the atmosphere is still 15 lbs to a square inch— I can do little more than preserve the equilibrium & resist the pressure of the atmosphere— I can only nod like the rye-heads in the breeze.— I expand more surely in my chamber—as far as expression goes, as if that pressure were taken off.— but here outdoors is the place to store up influences

The swallows twitter is the sound of the lapsing waves of the air—

or when they break & burst—as his wings represent the ripple—he has more air in his bones than other birds—his feet are defective—the fish of the air—his note is the voice of the air— As fishes may hear the sound of waves lapsing on the surface—& see the outlines of the ripples so we hear the note & see the flight of swallows

The influences which make for one walk more than another & one day more than another—one much more etherial than terrestrial. It is the quality of the air much more than the quality of the ground that concerns the walker cheers or depresses him. What he may find in the air, not what he may find on the ground.

On such a road (the Corner) I walk securely—seeing far and wide on both sides—as if I were flanked by light infantry on the hills, to rout the provincials as the brittish marched into Concord, while my grenadier thoughts keep the main road That is my light armed & wandering thoughts scour the neighboring fields—& so I know if the coast is clear. With what a breadth of van I advance—I am not bounded by the walls— I think more than the road full.

While I am abroad the ovipositors plant their seeds in me I am fly blown with thought—& go home to hatch—& brood over them.

I was too discursive & rambling in my thought for the chamber & must go where the wind blows on me walking

A little brook crossing the road (the Corner road) a few inches depth of transparent water rippling over yellow sand & pebbles—the pure blood of nature how miraculously crystal like—how exquisite fine and subtle & liquid this element—which an imperceptible inclination in the channel causes to flow thus surely & swiftly— How obedient to its instinct—to the faintest suggestion of the hills—if inclined but a hairs breadth it is in a torrent haste to obey. & all the revolutions of the planet Nature is so exquisitely adjusted—& the attraction of the stars, do not disturb this equipoise—but the rills still flow the same way—& the water levels are not disturbed.

We are not so much like debauchees as in the afternoon.

The mind is subject to moods as the shadows of clouds pass over the earth— Pay not too much heed to them— Let not the traveller stop for them— They consist with the fairest weather. By the mood of my mind I suddenly felt dissuaded from continuing my walk—but I observed at the same instant that the shadow of a cloud was passing one spot on which I stood—though it was of small extent— which if it had no connexion with my mood at any rate suggested how transient & little to be regarded that mood was— I kept on & In a moment the sun shone on my walk within & without.

The button bush in blossom—the tobacco pipe in damp woods—
Certain localities only a few rods square in the fields & on the hills—
some times the other side of a wall—attract me—as if they had been
the scene of pleasure in another state of existence

But this habit of close observation— In Humboldt—Darwin &
others. Is it to be kept up long—this science— Do not tread on the
heels of your experience Be impressed without making a minute of
it. Poetry puts an interval between the impression & the expression—
waits till the seed germinates naturally.

July 24th

5 Am

The street & fields betray the drought & look more parched than
at noon they look as I feel languid & thin and feeling my nerves.
The potatoes & the elms & the herbage by the road side—though
there is a slight dew—seem to rise out of an arid & thirsty soil into a
the atmosphere of a furnace slightly cooled down— The leaves of
the elms are yellow.— Ah! now I see what the noon *was* & what it
may be again. The effects of drought are never more apparent than
at dawn. Nature is like a hen panting with open mouth in the grass.

Friday July 25th 1851

Started for Clark's Island at 7 A M. At 9 Am took the Hingham
boat and was landed at Hull. There was a pleasure party on board,
apparently boys & girls belonging to the South end going to
Hingham. There was a large proportion of ill-dressed and ill-
mannered boys—of Irish extraction— A sad sight to behold Little
boys of 12 years prematurely old sucking cigars I felt that if I were
their mothers I should whip them & send them to bed. Such
children should be deallt with as for stealing or impurity. The
opening of this valve for the safety of the city! Oh what a wretched
resource! What right have parents to beget—to bring up & attempt to
educate children in a city— I thought of infanticide among the
orientals with complacency— I seemed to hear infant Voices lisp—
"give us a fair chance parents." There is no such squalidness in the
country— You would have said that they must all have come from
the house of correction and the farm-school—but such a company do
the boys in Boston Streets make. The birds have more care for their
young—where they place their nests— What are a city's charities—?
She could be charitable perchance if she had a resting place without
herself. A true culture is more possible to the savage than to the boy
of average intellect born of average parents in a great city— I believe
that they perish miserably. How can they be kept clean physically or

morally? It is folly to attempt to educate children within a city—the first step must be to remove them out of it.

It seemed a groping & helpless philanthropy—that I heard of.

I heard a boy telling the story of Nix's Mate to some girls as we passed that spot—how he said "If I am guilty this island will remain, but if I am innocent it will be washed away—& now it is all washed away" this was a simple & strong expression of feeling suitable to the occasion by which he committed the evidence of his innocence to the dumb-isle— Such as the boy could appreciate—a proper sailors legend—and I was reminded that it is the illiterate and unimaginative class that seizes on & transmits the legends in which the more cultivated delight. No fastidious poet dwelling in Boston had tampered with it—no narrow poet—but broad mankind Sailors from all ports sailing by. They sitting on the deck were the literary academy that sat upon its periods.

On the beach at Hull, and afterwards all along the shore to Plymouth—I saw the Datura—the variety (red stemmed) methinks, which some call tatula *instead* of stramonium— I felt as if I was on the highway of the world at sight of this cosmopolite & veteran traveller It told of commerce & sailors yarns without end. It grows luxuriantly in sand & gravel. This Capt. Cook among plants— This norse man or sea pirate—Vikingrs King of the bays—the beaches. It is not an innocent plant— It suggests commerce with its attendant vices.

Saw a public House where I landed at Hull made like some barns which I have seen of boards with a cleet nailed over the cracks, without clapboards or paint— Evidently very simple & cheap—yet neat & convenient as well as airy. It interested me—as the New House at Long Island did not—as it brought the luxury & comfort of the sea shore within reach of the less wealthy— It was such an exhibition of good sense as I was not prepared for and do not remember to have seen before. Ascended to the top of the hill where is the old French Fort with the well said to be 90 feet deep now covered. I saw some horses standing on the very top of the ramparts the highest part of Hull, where there was hardly room to turn round—for the sake of the breeze. It was excessively warm, and their instincts—or their experience perchance guided them as surely to the summit as it did me. Here is the Telegraph 9 miles from Boston whose state House was just visible—moveable signs on a pole with holes in them for the passage of the wind. A man about the Telegraph Station thought it the highest point in the harbor—said

they could tell the kind of vessel 30 miles off—the no at mast head
10 or 12 miles—name on hull 6 or 7 miles. They can see furthest in
the fall. There is a mist summer and winter when the contrast bet.
the temperature of the sea & the air is greatest. I did not see why
this Hill should not be fortified as well as George's Island, it being
higher & also commanding the main channel— However an enemy
could go by all the forts in the dark—as Wolfe did at Quebec They
are bungling contrivances. Here the bank is rapidly washing away—
on every side in Boston Harbor— The evidences of the wasting
away of the islands are so obvious and striking that they appear to be
wasting faster than they are— You will sometimes see a springing
hill showing by the interrupted arch of its surface against the sky
how much space must have occupied where there is now water as at
Pt Allerton—what Botanists call premorse _____ Hull looks as
if it had been two islands since connected by a beach—
I was struck by the gracefully curving & fantastic shore
of a small island (Hog I.) inside of Hull—where every
thing seemed to be gently lapsing into futurity as if the
inhabitants should bear a ripple for device on their coat of arms—a
wave passing over them with the Datura growing on
their shores— The wrecks of isles fancifully arranged
into a new shore. To see the sea nibbling thus
voraciously at the continents.— A man at the Telegraph told me of
a White oak pole 1½ ft in diam. 40 feet high & 4 feet or more in
the rock at Minots ledge with 4 guys—which stoood only one year—
— Stone piled up cob fashion near same place stood 8 years. Hull
pretty good land but bare of trees only a few cherries for the most
part & mostly uncultivated being owned by few. I heard the voices
of men shouting aboard a vessel half a mile from the shore which
sounded as if they were in a barn in the country—they being
between the sails. It was not a sea sound. It was a purely rural
sound.

Man needs to know but little more than a lobster in order to
catch him in his traps.

Here were many lobster traps on the shore. The beds of dry
seaweed or eel grass on the beach reminds me of narrow shavings
On the farther hill in Hull I saw a field full of Canada thistles close
up to the fences on all sides while beyond them there was none So
much for these fields having been subjected to diff. culture. So a
diff. culture in the case of men brings in diff. weeds. Weeds come in
with the seeds—though perhaps much more in the manure. Each
kind of culture will introduce its own weeds.

It is not necessary to keep step with your companion as some endeavor to do.

They told me at Hull that they burned the *stem* of the kelp chiefly for potash— Chemistry is not a splitting hairs when you have got half a dozen raw Irishmen in the laboratory.

As I walked on the beach (Nantasket) panting with thirst a man pointed to a white spot on the side of a distant hill (Strawberry Hill he called it) which rose from the gravelly beach, and said that there was a pure and cold and unfailing spring—and I could not help admiring that in this town of Hull of which I had heard but now for the first time saw a single spring should appear to me and should be of so much value. I found Hull indeed but there was also a spring on that parched unsheltered shore—the spring, though I did not visit it, made the deepest impression on my mind. Hull the place of the spring & of the well. This is what the traveller would remember. All that he remembered of Rome was a spring on the Capitoline Hill!

{Two-thirds page missing}

rocks and the perfectly clean & rich looking rockweed—greatly enhance the pleasure of bathing here— It is the most perfect sea shore I have seen. The rockweed falls over you like the *tresses* of mermaids—& you see the propriety of that epithet— You cannot swim among these weeds and pull yourself up by them without thinking of mermen & mermaids. I found the

{Two-thirds page missing}

water & fresh if you taste high enough up are all convenient to bathe your extremities in.— The barnacles on the rocks which make a whitish strip a few feet in width just above the weeds remind me of some vegetable growth which I have seen—surrounded by a circle of Calyx-like or petal-like shells ⊗ like some buds or seed vessels. They too clinging to the rocks like the weeds. Lying along the seams of the rock like buttons on a waistcoat. I saw in Cohasset— separated from the sea only by a narrow beach a very large & handsome but shallow lake, of at least 400 acres—with five rockly islets in it—which the sea had tossed over the beach in the great storm in the spring and after the alewives had passed in to it— stopped up its outlet and now the alewives were dying by thousands —& the inhabitants apprehended a pestilence as the water evaporated. The water was very foul.

The rockweed is considered the best for manure. I saw them

drying the Irish moss in quantities at Jerusalem village in Cohasset—
It is said to be used for sizing calico. Finding myself on the edge of
a thunder storm I stopped a few moments at the Rock House in
Cohasset close to the shore. There was scarcely rain enough to wet
one & no wind. I was therefore surprised to hear afterward through
a young man who had just returned from Liverpool that there was a
severe squawl at Quarantine ground only 7 or 8 miles north-west of
me such as he had not experienced for 3 years—which sunke several
boats & caused some vessels to drag their anchors & come near
going ashore.— Proving that the gust which struck the water there
must have been of very limited breadth for I was or might have
been overlooking the spot & felt no wind. This Rocky shore is
called Pleasant cove on large maps—on the map of Cohasset alone
the name seems to be confined to the cove where I first saw the
wreck of the St John alone.

Brush island opposite this with a hut on it—not permanently
inhabited— It takes but little soil to tempt men to inhabit such
places. I saw here the Am. Holly Ilex Opaca which is not found
further north than Mass. but S & west— The yellow gerardia in the
woods.

July 26th at Cohasset

Called on Capt. Snow who remembered hearing fishermen say
that they "fitted out at Thoreau's"—remembered him. He had
commanded a packet bet. Boston or New York & England—spoke
of the wave which he sometimes met on the Atlantic coming against
the wind & which indicated that the wind was blowing from an
opposite quarter at a distance— The undulation travelling faster than
the wind. They see Cape Cod loom here— Thought the Bay bet.
here & Cape Ann 30 fathom deep—bet here & Cape Cod 60 or 70
fathoms. The "Annual of Sci. Discovery—" for 1851 says quoting a
Mr A. G. Findley "waves travel very great distances, and are often
raised by distant hurricanes, having been felt simultaneously at St.
Helena & Ascension, though 600 miles apart, and it is probable that
ground swells often originate at the Cape of Good Hope, 3000 miles
distant."

Sailors tell of tide-rips Some are thought to be occasioned by
earthquakes

The Ocean at Cohasset did not look as if any were ever
shipwrecked in it—not a vestige of a wreck left— It was not grand &
sublime now but beautiful The water held in the little hollows of
the rocks on the receding of the tide is so crystal-pure that you
cannot believe it salt. but wish to drink it

The architect of a Minot rock light house might profitably spend a day studying the worn rocks of Cohasset shore & learn the power of the waves— See what kind of sand the sea is using to grind them down.

A fine delicate sea weed which some properly enough call sea-green.   Saw here the stag horn or velvet sumack Rhus typhinum so called from form of young branches—a size larger than the Rhus glabrum common with us.— The Plantago Maritima or Sea Plantain properly named—I guessed its name before I knew what it was called by botanists. The Am. Sea Rocket—Bunias edentula I suppose it was that I saw the succulent plant with much cut leaves & small pinkish? flowers.

Sunday 27 walked from Cohasset to Duxbury & sailed thence to Clark's Island. Visited the large Tupelo Tree Nyssa multiflora in Scituate whose rounded & open top like some umbelliferous plants I could see from Mr Sewal's—the tree which Geo Emerson went 25 miles to see— Called sometimes Snag tree & swamp Hornbeam also Pepperidge & Gumtree. Hard to split— We have it in Concord. Cardinal flower in bloom. Scit. meeting houses on very high ground—the principal one a landmark for sailors saw the buckthorn which is naturalized. one of Marshfield meet. houses on the height of land on my road   The country generally descends westerly toward the sources of Taunton river.— After taking the road by Webster's beyond South Marshfield I walked a long way at noon hot & thirsty before I could find a suitable place to sit & eat my dinner—a place where the shade & the sward pleased me. At length I was obliged to put up with a small shade close to the ruts where the only stream I had seen for some time crossed the road. Here also numerous robins came to cool & wash themselves & to drink. They stood in the water up to their bellies from time to time wetting their wings & tails & also ducking their heads & sprinkling the water over themselves—then they sat on a fence near by to dry. Then a goldfinch came & did the same accompanied by the less brilliant female. These birds evidently enjoyed their bath greatly.— & it seemed indispensable to them.

A neighbor of Websters told me that he had hard onto 1600 acres & was still buying more—a farm & factory within the year—cultivated 150 acres— I saw 12 acres of potatoes together—the same of rye & wheat & more methinks of buck wheat. 15 or 16 men Irish mostly at 10 dollars a month doing the work of 50 with a yankee overseer long a resident of Marshfield named Wright. Would eat only the produce of his farm during the few weeks he was at home—brown bread & butter—& milk—& sent out for a pig's cheek to eat with his greens—ate only what grew on his farm but drank more than ran on his farm

Took refuge from the rain at a Mr Stetsons in Duxbury—told me an anecdote which he heard Charles Emerson tell of meeting Webster at a splendid house of ill fame in Washington where he (Emerson) had gone unwittingly to call on a lady whose acquaintance he had formed in the stage. Mr Webster coming into the room unexpectedly—& patting him on the shoulder remarks "This is no place for young men like you" I forgot to say that I passed the Winslow House now belonging to Webster— This land was granted to the family in 1637.

Sailed with tavern keeper Windsor who was going out mackreling. 7 men stripping up their clothes each bearing an arm full of wood & one some new potatoes walked to the boats then shoved them out a dozen rods over the mud—then rowed half a mile to the schooner of 43 tons. They expected be gone about a week & to begin to fish perhaps the next morning—fresh mackerel which they carried to Boston. Had 4 dories & commonly fished from them. Else they fished on the starboard side aft where their lines hung ready with the old baits on 2 to a man I had the experience of going on a mackerel cruise.

They went aboard their schooner in a leisurely way this Sunday evening with a fair but very slight wind— The sun now setting clear & shining on the vessel after several thunder showers. I was struck by the small quantity of supplies which they appeared to take. We climbed aboard and there we were in a mackerel schooner— The baits were not dry on the hooks. Windsor cast overboard the foul juice of mackerels mixed with rain water which remained in his trough. There was the mill in which to grind up the mackerel for bait—& the trough to hold it & the long handled dipper to cast it overboard with. and already in the harbor we saw the surface rippled with schools of small mackerel. They proceeded leisurely to weigh anchor—& then to raise their two sails— There was one passenger going for health or amusement—who had been to California. I had the experience of going a mackereling—though I was landed on an island before we got out of the harbor. They expected to commence fishing the next morning. It had been a very warm day with frequent thunder showers— I had walked from Cohasset to Duxbury—& had walked about the latter town to find a passage to Clarks Island about 3 miles distant. But no boat could stir

they said at that state of the tide. The tide was down & boats were
left high & dry At length I was directed to Windsors tavern where
perchance I might find some mackerel fishers who were going to sail
that night to be ready for fishing in the morning—& as they would
pass near the island they would take me. I found it so Windsor
himself was going— I told him he was the very man for me—but I
must wait an hour— So I ate supper with them— Then one after
another of his crew was seen straggling to the shore—for the most
part in high boots—some made of India rubber—some with their
pants stripped up—there were 7 for this schooner beside a passenger
& myself The leisurely manner in which they proceeded struck me.
I had taken off my shoes & stockings & prepared to wade. Each of
the 7 took an armful of pine wood & walked with it to the 2 boats
which lay at high water mark in the mud—then they resolved that
each should bring one more armful & that would be enough. They
had already got a barrel of water and had some more in the
schooner—also a bucket of new potatoes. Then dividing into two
parties we pulled & shoved the boats a dozen rods over the mud &
water till they floated—then rowed half a mile or more over the
shallow water to the little schooner & climbed aboard— many seals
had their heads out— We gathered about the helmsman and talked
about the compass which was affected by the iron in the vessel,
&c &c

Clark's Island Sunday night

On Friday night Dec 8th o.s. the Pilgrims exploring in the shallop
landed on Clark's Island (so called from the Master's mate of the
May Flower) where they spent 3 nights & kept their first sabbath.
On Monday or the 11th o.s. they landed on the rock. This island
contains about 86 acres and was once covered with red cedars which
were sold at Boston for gate posts— I saw a few left—one 2 ft in
diameter at the ground—which was probably standing when the
pilgrims came. Ed. Watson who could remember them nearly fifty
years—had observed but little change in them. Hutchinson calls this
one of the best islands in Mass. Bay. The Town kept it at first as a
sacred place—but finally sold it in 1690 to Sam. Lucas, Elkanah
Watson, & Geo. Morton. Saw a Stag's horn Sumach 5 or 6 inches
in diameter and 18 ft high— Here was the Marsh golden rod
Solidago laevigata—not yet in blossom—a small bluish flower in the
marshes which they called rosemary—a kind of Chenopodium which
appeared distinct from the common—and a short oval leaved set
looking plant which I suppose is Glaux Maritima sea milkwort or

Saltwort. Scates-eggs called in England Scate-barrows from their form on the sand. The old cedars were flat-topped spreading the stratum of the wind drawn out—

Monday morn 28th

Sailed the Gurnet. which runs down seven miles into the bay from Marshfield. Heard the *peep* of the *beach bird*—saw some ring-necks in company with peeps. They told of eagles which had flown low over the island lately— went by Saquish.— Gathered a basket full of Irish-moss bleached on the beach. Saw a field full of pink-blossomed potatoes at the light house—remarkably luxuriant & full of blossoms—also some French barley. Old fort & barracks by light house. Visited lobster houses or huts there where they use lobsters to catch bait for lobsters Saw on the shanties signs from ships as "Justice Story" & "Margueritta". To obtain bait is sometimes the main thing.— Samphire which they pickle—also a kind of prickly samphire which I suppose is Salt-wort or Salsola Caroliniana. Well at C. Island 27¾ ft deep. Cut the rock weed on the rocks at low tide once in 2 or 3 years—very valuable more than they have time to save.

Uncle Ned told of a man who went off fishing from back of Welfleet in calm weather & with great difficulty got ashore through the surf. Those in the other boat who had landed were unwilling to take the responsibility of telling them when to pull for shore—the one who had the helm was inexperienced. They were swamped at once— So treacherous is this shore—before the wind comes perchance the sea may run so as to upset & drown you on the shore. At first they thought to pull for Provincetown but night was coming on & that was distant many a long mile. Their case was a desperate one—when they came near the shore & saw the terrific breakers that intervened they were deterred. They were thoroughly frightened.

Were troubled with skunks on this Island—they must have come over on the ice. Foxes they had seen—had killed one woodchuck—even a large *mud-turtle*—which they *conjectured some bird must have* dropped muskrats they had seen & killed 2 raccoons once. I went a clamming just before night. this the clam-digger— Borrowed of uncle Bill (Watson) in his schooner home The clams nearly a foot deep—but I broke many in digging said not to be good now—but we found them good eaten fresh. No sale for them now—fetch 25 cts a bucket in their season. Barry caught squids as bait for bass. We found many dead clams—the shells full of sand—called sand clams— By a new clam law any one can dig clams here. Brown's Island so called—a shoal off the Gurnet thought to have been an isle once—a dangerous place. Saw here fences the posts set in cross sleepers ⟨diagram⟩ made to be removed in winter.

The finest music in a menagerie its wildest strains have something in them akin to the cries of the tigers & leopards around in their native forests— Those strains are not unfitted to the assemblage of wild beasts— They express to my ear what the Tigers stripes & the leopards spots express to my eye—& the they appear to grin with satisfaction at the sound. That nature has any place at all for music is very good.

Tuesday 29th

A NE wind with rain—but the sea is the wilder for it. I heard the surf roar on the Gurnet the night—which as uncle Ned & Freeman said showed that the wind would work round east and we should have rainy weather— It was the wave reaching the shore before the wind. The ocean was heaped up somewhere to the eastward and this roar was occasioned by its effort to preserve its equilibrium. The rut of the sea In the afternoon I sailed to Plymouth 3 miles notwithstanding the drizzling rain or "drisk" as Uncle Ned called it. We passed round the head of Plymouth beach which is 3 miles long — I did not know till afterward that I had landed where the Pilgrims did & passed over the rock on Hedges Wharf— Returning we had more wind & tacking to do. Saw many seals together on a flat. Singular that these strange animals should be so abundant here & yet the man who lives a few miles inland never hear of them. To him there is no report of the sea—though he may read the Plymouth paper. The Boston papers do not tell us that they have seals in the Harbor. The inhabitants of Plymouth do not seem to be aware of it — I always think of seals in connexion with Esquimaux or some other outlandish people—not in connexion with those who live on the shores of Boston & Plymouth harbors.— Yet from their windows they may daily see a family seals—the seal phoca vitulinus— collected on a flat or sporting in the waves I saw one dashing through the waves just ahead of our boat going to join his companions on the bar—as strange to me as the merman. No less wild essentially than when the Pilgrims came is this Harbor. It being low tide we landed on a flat which makes out from Clark's Island to while away the time—(not being able to get quite up yet— I found numerous *large* holes of the sea clam in this sand—(no small clams)

and dug them out easily & rapidly with my hands—could have got a
large quantity in a short time. but here they do not eat them—
think they will make you sick. They were not so deep in the sand
not more than 4 or 5 inches I saw where one had squirted full ten
feet before the wind. as appeared by the marks of the drops on
the sand— Some small ones I found not more than ¼ inch in
length— (Le Barron brought me round clam or qua–hog alive with
a very thick   shell & not so nearly an isosceles triangle
as the Sea   clam—more like this with a protuberance
on the back—the sea clam

A small narrow clam   which they called the bank clam—
also crab cases handsomely spotted—small crabs always in a cockle
shell if not in a case of his own.— A cockle as large as my fist—
muscles small ones empty shells, an extensive bank where they had
died—occasionally a large deep sea muscles which some kelp had
brought-up. We caught some sand eels 7 or eight inches long—
Ammodytes tobianus according to Storer & not the A. lancea of
Yarrell though the size of the last comes nearer. They were in the
shallow pools left on the sand (the flat was here pure naked
yellowish sand) & quickly buried them selves when pursued.— They
are used as bait for basse. Found some sand circles or sand paper-
like top of a stone jug cut off with a large nose.— said to be made
by the foot of the large cockle which has some glutinous matter on
it. The nidus of the animal of natica cells with eggs in sand. A circle
of sand about as thick as thick pasteboard It reminded me of the
cadisworm cases. Scate-barrows &c &c. I observed the shell of a sea-
clam one valve of which was filled exactly even full with sand—
evenly as if it had been heaped & then scraped off as when men
measure by the peck— This was a fresher one of the myriad sand
clams—& it suggested to me how the stone clams which I had seen
on Cape Cod might have been formed— Perchance a clam shell was
the mould in which they were cast—& a slight hardening of the level
surface—before the whole is turned to stone causes them to split in
two. The sand was full of stone clams in the mould. I saw the kelp
attached to stones half as big as my head which it had transported. I
do not think I ever saw the kelp in situ—also attached to a deep-sea
muscle. The kelp is like a broad ruffled belt— The middle portion is
thicker & flat—the edges for 2 or 3 inches thinner & fuller so that it
is frilled or ruffled—as if the edges had been hammered. The

extremity is generally worn & ragged from the lashing of the waves.
It is the prototype of a fringed belt. Uncle Ned said that the cows
ate it. We saw in the shallow water a long *round* green grass 6 or 8
feet long clogging up the channel. Round grass I think they called
it. We caught a lobster as you might catch a mud turtle in the
country—in the shallow water—pushing him ashore with the paddle—
Taking hold of his tail to avoid being bitten. They are obliged to
put wooden plugs or wedges beside their claws to prevent their
tearing each other to pieces. All weeds are bleached on the beach.
This sailing on salt water was something new to me. The boat is
such a living creature— Even this clumsy one sailing within 5 points
of the wind. The sail boat is an admirable invention by which you
compel the wind to transport you even against itself— It is easier to
guide than a horse—the slightest pressure on the tiller suffices. I think
the inventor must have been greatly surprised as well as delighted
at the success of his experiment. It is so contrary to expectation—as if
the elements were disposed to favor you. This deep unfordable sea—
but this wind ever blowing over it to transport you. At 10 PM—it
was perfectly fair & bright starlight.

Wednesday 30th

The house here stands within a grove of balm of gileads—horse-
chestnuts—cherries apples & plums—&c Uncle bill who lives in his
schooner—not turned up Numidian fashion but anchored in the mud
—whom I meant to call on yesterday morn—lo! had run over to
"The Pines" last evening—fearing an easterly storm. He out rode the
great gale in the spring alone in the harbor dashing about— He goes
after rockweed—lighters vessels & saves wrecks— Now I see him
lying in the mud over at the Pines in the horizon, which place he
cannot leave if he will till flood tide—but he will not it seems. This
waiting for the tide is a singular feature in the life by the shore. In
leaving your boat today you must always have reference to what you
are going to do the next day. A frequent answer is "Well, you cant
start for two hours yet." It is something new to a landsman & at
first he is not disposed to wait. I saw some heaps of shells left by the
Indians near the N end of the Island. They were a rod in diameter
& a foot or more high in the middle—& covered with a shorter &
greener grass than the surrounding field. found one imperfect
arrowhead. At 10 AM sailed to Websters—past Powder point in
Duxbury—we could see his land from the island. I was steersman and
learned the meaning of some nautical phrases—"luff" to keep the
boat close to the wind till the sails begin to flap. "bear-away" to

put the sail more at right angles with the wind. A "close-haul"
when the sails are brought & belayed nearly or quite in a line with
the vessel.

On the marshes we saw patches of a "*black* grass" A large field of
wheat at Websters—half a dozen acres at least—many appletrees—3
thorned accacias—tulip trees—cranberry experiment sea weed spread
under his tomatoes— Wild geese with black & gray heads & necks—
not so heavy & clumsy as the tame Bremens— Large noisy Hong-
kong geese. handsome calves. (3000? acres of marsh) Talked with
Websters nearest neighbor Capt. Hewit whose small farm he
surrounds & endeavors in vain to buy. A fair specimen of a retired
Yankee sea Captain turned farmer—proud of the quantity of carrots
he had raised on a small patch. It was better husbandry than
Websters. He told a story of his buying a cargo for his owners at St
Petersburg just as Peace was declared in the last war. These men are
not so remarkable for anything as the quality of hardness. The very
fixidness & rigidity of their jaws & necks express a sort of admantine
hardness. This is what they have learned by contact with the
elements. The man who does not grow rigid with years &
experience! Where is he? What avails it to grow hard merely—the
harder you are the more brittle really—like the bones of the old—
How much rarer & better to grow mellow— A sort of stone fruit
the man bears commonly—a bare stone it is without any sweet and
mellow pericarp around it. It is like the peach which has dried to
the stone as the season advanced—it is dwindled to a dry stone with
its almond. In presence of one of these hard men I think "how
brittle, how easily you would crack—what a poor & lame conclusion.
I can think of nothing but a stone in his head. Truly genial men do
not grow. It is the result of despair this attitude of resistance. They
behave like men already driven to the wall. Notwithstanding that
the speaker trembles with infirmity while he speaks (his hand on the
spade—) it is such a trembling as betrays a stony nature. His hand
trembles so that the full glass of cider which he prizes to a drop will
have lost half its contents before it reaches his lips—as if a tempest
had arisen in it. Hopelessly hard. But there is another view of him.
He is somebody. He has an opinion to express if you will wait to
hear him.— A certain manliness & refreshing resistance is in him.
He generally makes Webster a call. but Webster does not want to
see you more than 20 minutes. It does not take him long to say all
he had got to say. He had not seen him to speak to him since he
had come home this time. he had sent him over a couple of fine

cod the night before.— Such a man as Hewit sees not finely but coarsely. The eagle given by Lawrence on the hill in the buckwheat field.

Thursday 31st

Those same round shells scutella parma (placenta)? on the sand as at Cape Cod the live ones reddish the dead white— Went off early this morning with Uncle Ned to catch basse with the small fish I had found on the sand the night before— 2 of his neighbor Albert Watson's boys were there—not James the oldest—but Edward the sailor & Mortimer—(or Mort—) in their boat They killed some striped basse Labrax lineatus with paddles in a shallow creek in the sand—& caught some lobsters. I remarked that the sea shore was singularly clean for notwithstanding the spattering of the water & mud & squirting of the clams & wading to & fro the boat my best black pants retained no stains nor dirt as they would acquire from walking in the country. I caught a bass with a young (haik? (pirchance) trailing 30 feet behind while Uncle Ned paddled.— They catch them in England with a "trawl-net" sometimes they weigh 75 lbs here

At 11 AM set sail to Plymouth. We went somewhat out of a direct course to take advantage of the tide which was coming in. Saw the site of the first house which was burned—on Leyden Street walked up the same.—parallel with the Town Brook. Hill from which Billington Sea was discovered hardly a mile from the shore on Watsons grounds. Watsons Hill where treaty was made across brook South of Burying Hill At Watsons— The Oriental Plane— Abies Douglasii— Jingo tree q. v. on Common.—a foreign hardhack—Eng. oak—dark colored small leaf—Spanish chestnut. Chinese arbor-vitae— Norway spruce like our fir balsam— A new kind of fir balsam— Black eagle one of the good cherries— fuchsias in hot house— Earth bank covered with cement.

Mr Thomas Russel—who cannot be 70—at whose house on Leyden st. I took tea & spent the evening—told me that he remembered to have seen Ebeneezer Cobb a nat. of Plymouth who died in Kingston in 1801 aged 107 who remembered to have had personal knowledge of Peregrine White saw him an old man riding on horse back—(he lived to be 83)— White was born at Cape Cod harbor before the Pilgrims got to Plymouth— C. Sturgis's mother told me the same of herself at the same time. She remembered Cobb sitting in an arm chair like the one she herself occupied with his

silver locks falling about his shoulders twirling one thumb over the
other— Russell told me that he once bought some *primitive*
woodland in P. which was sold at auction the bigest Pitch pines 2 ft
diameter—for *8 shillings* an acre— If he had bought enough it would
have been a pasture. There is still forest in this town which the axe
has not touched says Geo. Bradford. According to Thatchers Hist. of
P. there were 11,662 acres of woodland in '31. or 20 miles square.
Pilgrims first saw Bil. sea about Jan 1st—visited it Jan 8th.

The oldest stone in the Plymouth Burying ground 1681 (Coles?
hill where those who died the first winter were buried—said to have
been levelled & sown to conceal loss from Indians.) Oldest on our
hill 1677 In Mrs Plympton's Garden on Leyden st. running down
to Town Brook. Saw an abundance of pears—gathered excellent
June-eating apples—saw a large lilack about 8 inches diameter—
Methinks a soil may improve when at length it has shaded itself with
vegetation.

Wm S Russel the Registrer at the Court House showed the
oldest Town records. for all are preserved—on 1st page a plan of
Leyden st dated Dec. 1620—with names of settlers. They have a great
many folios. The writing plain. Saw the charter granted by the
Plymouth Company to the Pilgrims signed by Warwick date 1629 &
the box in which it was brought over with the seal.

Pilgrim Hall— They used to crack off pieces of the Forefathers
Rock for visitors with a cold chisel till the town forebade it. The
stone remaining at wharf is about 7 ft square. Saw 2 old arm chairs
that came over in the May flower.— the large picture by Sargent.—
Standish's sword.— gun barrel with which Philip was killed——mug
& pocket-book of Clark the mate— Iron pot of Standish.— Old
pipe tongs. Ind relics a flayer ⟨figure⟩ a pot or mortar of a
kind of fire proof stone very ⟨figure⟩ hard——only 7 or 8 inches
long. A Commission from ⟨figure⟩ Cromwell to Winslow? —his
signature torn off. They talk of a monument on the rock. The
burying hill 165 ft high. Manomet 394 ft high by state map. Saw
more pears at Washburn's garden. No graves of Pilgrims.

Seaweed generally used along shore— Saw the Prinos Glaber
inkberry at Bil. sea. Sandy plain with oaks of various kinds cut in
less than 20 yrs— No communication with Sandwich— P end of
world 50 miles thither by rail road— Old. Colony road
poor property. Nothing saves P. but the rock. Fern-leaved beach—

Saw the King crab Limulus polyphemus—horshoe & saucepan fish
—at the island covered with sea green & buried in the sand—for
concealment.

In P. the Convolvulus arvensis—small Bindweed.

left at 9 AM Aug. 1st

After Kingston—came Plympton Halifax & Hanson all level with frequent cedar swamps especially the last—also in Weymouth.

Desor & Cabot think the jelly-fish (oceania tubulosa are buds from a polyp of Genus Lyncoryne.) Desor accounting for suspended moisture or fogs over sand banks (or shoals) says the heat being abstracted by radiation the moisture is condensed in form of fog.

Lieut Walsh lost his lead & wire when 34,200 or more than 6 statute miles had run out perpendicularly.

I could make a list of things ill managed— We Yankees do not deserve our fame. viz:

I went to a menagerie the other day. The proprietors had taken wonderful pains to collect rare and interesting animals from all parts of the world. And then placed by them—a few stupid and ignorant fellows who knew little or nothing about the animals & were unwilling even to communicate the little they knew. You catch a rare creature interesting to all mankind & then place the first biped that comes along with but a grain more reason in him to exhibit & describe the former— At the expense of Millions this rare quadruped from the sun is obtained, and then Jack Halyard or Tom Coach Whip is hired to explain it. Why all this pains taken to catch in Africa—and no pains taken to exhibit in America? Not a cage was labelled— There was nobody to tell us how or where the animals were caught—or what they were— Probably the proprietors themselves do not know—or what their habits are— But hardly had we been ushered into the presence of this choice this admirable collection—than a ring was formed for Master Jack & the poney. Were they *animals* then who had caught and exhibited these—& who had come to see these? Would it not be worth the while to learn something? to have some information imparted?

The absurdity of importing the behemoth & then instead of somebody appearing tell which it is—to have to *while away the time*— though your curiosity is growing desperate—to learn one fact about the creature—to have Jack and the poney introduced!!!

Why I expected to see some descendant of Cuviers there to improve this opportunity for a lecture on Nat. Hist.

That is what they should do make this an—occasion for communicating some solid information—that would be fun alive that would be a sunny day—a sun day in one's existence not a secular day

of shetland ponies—not jack and his poney & a tintimmara of musical
instruments—and a man with his head in the lions mouth. I go not
there to see a man hug a lion—or fondle a tiger—but to learn how he
is related to the wild beast— There'll be All-fool days enough
without our creating any intentionally. The presumption is that men
wish to behave like reasonable creatures—that they do not need and
are not seeking relaxation—that they are not dissipated. Let it be a
travelling zoological garden—with a travelling professor to accompany
it— At present foolishly the professor goes alone with his poor
painted illustrations of animated— While the menagerie takes
another road without its professor only its keepers.

I see June & co or Van Amberg & Co—are engaged in a
pecuniary speculation in which certain wild beasts are used as the
counters

Cuvier & co are engaged in giving a course of lectures on Nat.
History. Now why could they not put head & means together for
the benefit of mankind—and still get their living. The present
institution is imperfect precisely because its object is to enrich Van
amburg & co—& their low aim unfits them for rendering any more
valuable service—but no doubt the most valuable course would also
be the most valuable in a pecuniary sense— No doubt a low self
interest is a better motive force to these enterprises than no interest
at all but a high self interest—which consists with the greatest
advantage of all would be a better still.

Item 2nd Why have we not a decent pocket map of the State of
Mass? There is the large map why is it not cut into half a dozen
sheets & folded into a small cover for the pocket? Are there no
travellers to use it? Well to tell the truth there are but few, & that's
the reason why. Men go by rail road—& state maps hanging in bar
rooms are small enough— The state has been admirably surveyed at
a great cost—and yet Dearborne's Pocket map is the best one—we
have!

Aug 4th

Now the hard-hack & meadow sweet reign—the former one of
our handsomest flowers I think—the mayweed too dusty by the road
side—& in the fields I scent the sweet scented life everlasting which
is half expanded. The grass is withered by the drought— The
potatoes begin generally to flat down— The corn is tasselled out its
crosses show in all fields above the blades. The turnips are growing
in its midst.

As my eye rested on the blossom of the meadow-sweet in a

hedge I heard the note of an autumnal cricket—& was penetrated with the sense of autumn—was it sound? or was it form? or was it scent?, or was it flavor? It is now the royal month of August. When I hear this sound I am as dry as the rye which is every where cut & housed—though I am drunk with the seasons wine.

The farmer is the most inoffensive of men with his barns & cattle & poultry & grain & grass— I like the smell of his hay well enough —though as grass it may be in my way.

The Yellow Bethlehem star still—& the yellow Gerardia—And a bluish "savory leaved aster"

Aug 5th

7½ P.M. Moon half full.

I sit beside Hubbards grove.— a few level red bars above the horizon—a dark irregular bank beneath—with a streak of read sky below on the horizon's edge. This will describe many a sunset. It is 8 o clock—the farmer has driven in his cows & is cutting an arm full of green corn fodder for them. Another is still patching the roof of his barn making his hammer heard afar in the twilight as if—he took a satisfaction in his elevated work—sitting astride the ridge—which he wished to prolong. The robin utters a sort of cackling note as if he had learned the ways of man. The air is still— I hear the voices of loud talking boys in the early twilight it must be a mile off. The swallows go over with a watery twittering.

When the moon is on the increase & half full it is already in mid heavens at sunset—so that there is no marked twilight intervening— I hear the whipporwill at a distance—but they are few of late.

It is almost dark. I hear the voices of berry-pickers coming homeward from Bear garden. Why do they go home, as it were defeated by the approaching night? Did it never occur to them to stay over night? The wind now rising from over Bear Garden Hill falls gently on my ear & delivers its message the same that I have heard passing over bare & stoney *mt* tops— So uncontaminated & untamed is the wind. The air that has swept over caucasus & the sands of Arabia comes to breathe on New England fields. The dogs bark they are not as much stiller as man. They are on the alert suspecting the approach of foes. The darkness perchance affects them —makes them mad & wild— The mosquitoes hum about me. I distinguish the modest moon light on my paper As the twilight deepens and the moonlight is more & more bright—I begin to distinguish myself who I am & where—as my walls contract I become more collected & composed & sensible of my own existence

–as when a lamp is brought into a dark apartment & I see who the
company are. With the coolness & the mild silvery light I recover
some sanity–my thoughts are more distinct moderated & tempered–
Reflection is more possible while the day goes by. The intense light
of the sun unfits me for meditation makes me wander in my
thought–my life is too diffuse & dissipated–routine succeeds &
prevails over us–the trivial has greater power then & most at noon
day the most trivial hour of the 24. I am sobered by the moon light
  – I bethink myself– It is like a cup of cold water to a thirsty man.
The moonlight is more favorable to meditation than sun-light.

  The sun lights this world from with out shines in at a window–
but the moon is like a lamp within an apartment. It shines for us.
The stars themselves make a more visible & hence a nearer & more
domestic roof at night– Nature broods us–and has not left our
germs of thought to be hatched by the sun.

  We feel her heat & see her body darkening over us. Our
thoughts are not dissipated but come back to us like an echo.

  The different kinds of moonlight are infinite. This is not a night
for contrasts of light & shade–but a faint diffused light in which
there is light enough to travel and that is all

  A road (the Corner road) that passes over the Height of land–
between earth & heaven–separating those streams which flow
earthward from those which flow heavenward–

  Ah what a poor dry compilation is the Annual of Scientific
Discovery. I trust that observations are made during the year which
are not chronicled there. That some mortal may have caught a
glimpse of Nature in some corner of the earth during the year–1851.
One sentence of Perennial poetry would make me forget–would
atone for volumes of mere science. The astronomer is as blind to the
significant phenomena–or the significance of phenomena as the
wood-sawyer who wears glasses to defend his eyes from sawdust–
The question is not what you look at–but how you look & whether
you see.

  I hear now from Bear Garden Hill– I rarely walk by moonlight
without hearing the sound of a flute or a horn or a human voice–
It is a performer I never see by day–should not recognise him if
pointed out–but you may hear his performance in every horizon–
He plays but one strain and goes to bed early–but I know by the
character of that single strain that he is deeply dissatisfied with the
manner in which he spends his day. He is a slave who is purchasing
his freedom. He is apollo watching the flocks of Admetus on every

hill—& this strain he plays every evening to remind him of his heavenly descent— It is all that saves him—his one redeeming trait— It is a reminiscence—he loves to remember his youth— He is sprung of a noble family— He is highly related I have no doubt—was tenderly nurtured in his infancy.— poor hind as he is—that noble strain he utters instead of any jewel on his finger or prescious locket pasted to his breast—or purple garments that came with him— The elements recognize him & echo his strain— Ah the dogs know him their master—though lords & ladies—rich men & learned know him not— He is the son of a rich man—of a famous man who served his country well—he has heard his sire's stories— I thought of the time when he would discover his parentage—obtain his inheritance—& sing a strain suited to the morning hour. He cherishes hopes.

The distant lamps in the farm house look like fires. The trees & clouds are seen at a distance reflected in the river as by day. I see Fair Haven Pond from the Cliffs—as it were through a slight mist—it is the wildest scenery imaginable—a Lake of the woods I just remembered the wildness of St Anne's—that's the ultima Thule of wildness to me. I never see the man by day who plays that claironet.

What an entertainment for the traveller—this incessant motion apparently of the moon traversing the clouds whether you sit or stand it is always preparing new developments for you— It is event enough for simple minds.

You all alone the moon all alone overcoming with incessant victory whole squadrons of clouds above the forests & the lakes & rivers & the mountains— You cannot always calculate which one the moon will undertake next.

I see a solitary firefly over the woods

The moon wading through clouds—though she is eclipsed by this one I see her shining on a more distant but lower one. The entrance into Hubbards wood above the spring coming from the hill is like the entrance to a cave but when you are within—there are some streaks of light on the edge of the path.

All these leaves so still none whispering no birds in motion— how can I be else than still & thoughtful?

Aug 6th

The motions of circus horses are not so expressive of music—do not harmonize so well with a strain of music as those of animals of the cat kind— An Italian has just carried a hand-organ through the village— I hear it even at walden wood—it is as if a cheeta had skulked howling through the streets of the village with knotted tail.

Neglected gardens are full of Flea-bane? now not yet in blossom.
Thoroughwort has opened—& golden-rod is gradually opening the
smooth sumac shows its red fruit The berries of the bristly aralia are
turning dark— The wild holly's scarlet fruit is seen & the red dwarf
chock cherry Cerasus is (Prunus Obovata— After how few steps—
how little exertion—the student stands in pine woods above the
solomon's seal & the cow wheat—in a place still unaccountably
strange & wild to him—& to all civilization. This so easy & so
common—though our literature implies that it is rare—we in the
country make no report of the seals & sharks in our neighborhood
to those in the city We send them only our huckle berries not free
wild thoughts.

Why does not man sleep all day as well as all night—it seems so
very natural & easy—for what is he awake.

A man must generally get away some hundreds or thousands of
miles from home before he can be said to begin his travels— Why
not begin his travels at home—! Would he have to go far or look
very closely to discover novelties. The traveller who in this sense
pursues his travels at home, has the advantage at any rate of a long
residence in the country to make his observations correct &
profitable. Now the American goes to England while the
Englishman comes to America in order to describe the country—
No doubt there some advantages in this kind of mutual criticism—
But might there not be invented a better way of coming at the truth
than this scratch-my back & I'll scratch your's method? Would not
the American for instance who had himself perchance travelled in
England & elsewhere—make the most profitable & accurate traveller
in his own country. How often it happens that the travellers
principal distinction is that he is one who knows less about a
country than a native. Now if he should begin with all the
knowledge of a native—& add thereto the knowledge of a traveller—
Both natives & foreigners would be obliged to read his book. & the
world would be absolutely benefitted It takes a man of genius to
travel in his own country—in his native village—to make any progress
between his door & his gate. But such a traveller will make the
distances which Hanno & Marco Polo—& Cook & Ledyard went
over ridiculous.

So worthy a traveller as Wm Bartram heads his first chapter with
the words "The author sets sail from Philadelphia, and arrives at
Charleston, from whence he begins his travels."

I am perchance most & most profitably interested in the things

which I already know a little about—a mere & utter novelty is a
mere monstrosity to me. I am interested to see the yellow pine
which we have not in Concord though Michaux says it grows in
Mass—. or the English Oak having heard of the royal oak—& having
oaks ourselves Or the oriental Plane having often heard of it—&
being well acquainted with its sister the occidental plane—but the
new Chinese flower whose cousin I do not happen to know I pass
by with indifference. I do not know that I am very fond of novelty.
I wish to get a clearer notion of what I have already some inkling.

These Italian boys with their hand-organs remind me of the
keepers of wild beasts in menageries—whose whole art consists in
stirring up their beasts from time to time with a pole. I am
reminded of bright flowers & glancing birds & striped pards of the
jungle— these delicious harmonies tear me to pieces while they
charm me—the tigir's musical smile.

How some inventions have spread—some brought to perfection by
the most enlightened nations have been surely & rapidly
communicated to the most savage— The gun for instance How
soon after the settlement of America were comparitively remote
Indian tribes—most of whose members had never seen a white man
supplied with guns— The gun is invented by the civilized man &
the savage in remote wildernesses on the other side of the globe
throws away his bow & arrows & takes up this arm. Bartram
travelling in the S states bet 70—& 80 describes the warriors as so
many gun-men.

Ah, yes even here in concord horizon Apollo is at work for King
Admetus— Who is King Admetus? It is Business with his four prime
ministers Trade & Commerce—& Manufactures & Agriculture. And
this is what makes Mythology true & interesting to us

Aug 8th 7½ PM

To Conantum— The moon has not yet quite filled her horns— I
perceive why we so often remark a dark cloud in the west at and
after sunset— It is because it is almost directly between us' and the
sun & hence we see the dark side and moreover it is much darker
than it other-wise would be because of the little light reflected from
the earth at that hour. The same cloud at mid day & over head
might not attract attention. There is a pure amber sky beneath the
present bank—thus framed off from the rest of the heavens—which
with the outlines of small dead elms seen against it—I hardly know
far or near—make picture enough.

Men will travel far to see less interesting sights than this. Turning

away from the sun we get this enchanting view as when a man
looks at the landscape with inverted head. Under shadow of the dark
cloud which I have described the cricket begins his strain—his
ubiquitous strain. Is there a fall-cricket distinct from the species we
hear in spring & summer?

I smell the cornfield over the brook a dozen rods off—& it
reminds me of the green corn feasts of the Indians. The evening
train comes rolling in—but none of the passengers jumping out in
such haste attend to the beautiful fresh picture which nature has
unrolled in the west—& surmounted with that dark frame. The
circular platter of the carrots blossom is now perfect.

Might not this be called the invalid's moon on account of the
warmth of the nights? The principal employments of the farmers
now seems to be getting their meadow hay. & cradling some
oats &c.

The light from the western sky is stronger still than that of the
moon—and when I hold up my hand the west side is lighted while
the side toward the moon is comparatively dark.——— But now that
I have put this dark wood (Hubbards's) between me and the west—I
see the moon light plainly on my paper— I am even startled by it—
One star too, is it Venus?, I see in the west Starlight—! that would
be a good way to mark the hour if we were precise. Hubbards
brook— How much the beauty of the moon is enhanced by being
seen shining between two trees—or even by the neighborhood of
clouds! I hear the clock striking eight faintly. I smell the late shorn
meadows

One will lose no music by not attending the oratorios & operas.
The really inspiring melodies are cheap & universal—& are as audible
to the poor man's son as to the rich mans. Listening to the
harmonies of the universe is not allied to dissipation. My neighbors
have gone to the vestry to hear "Ned Kendal" the bugler tonight,
but I am come forth to the hills to hear my bugler in the horizon—
I can forego the seeming advantages of cities without misgiving. No
heavenly strain is lost to the ear that is fitted to hear it for want of
money—or opportunity. I am convinced that for instrumental music
All Vienna cannot serve me more than the Italian boy who seeks my
door with his organ.

And now I strike the road at the causeway— It is hard & I hear
the sound of my steps a sound which should never be heard—for it
draws down my thoughts. It is more like the treadmill exercise. The
fireflies are not so numerous as they have been. There is no dew as

yet. The planks & railing of Hubbards bridge are removed. I walk over on the string pieces resting in the middle until the moon comes out of a cloud that I may see my path—for between the next piers the string pieces also are removed & there is only a rather narrow plank—let down 3 or 4 feet.— I essay to cross it—but it springs a little & I mistrust myself—whether I shall not plunge into the river. Some demonic genius seems to be warning me. Attempt not the passage—you will surely be drowned— It is very real that I am thus affected— Yet I am fully aware of the absurdity of minding such suggestions— I put out my foot but I am checked as if that power had laid a hand on my breast & chilled me back—never the less I cross—stooping at first—& gain the other side.— (I make the most of it—on account of the admonition—but it was nothing to remark on— I returned the same way 2 hours later & made nothing of it) It is easy to see how by yielding to such feelings as this men would recreate all reestablish all the superstitions of antiquity. It is best that reason should govern us and not these blind intimations—in which we exalt our fears into a genius.

On Conantum I sit awhile in the shade of the woods & look out on the moonlit fields— White rocks are more remarkable than by day.

The air is warmer than the rocks now. It is perfectly warm & I am tempted to stay out all night & observe each phenomenon of the night until day dawns. But if I should do so, I should not wonder if the town were raised to hunt me up. Sitting on the door step of Conant-house—at 9 o clock I hear a pear drop—how few of all the apples that fall do we hear fall.

I could lie out here on this pinnacle rock all night without cold— I hear a horse *sneeze*? from time to time in his pasture— He sees me & knows me to be a man—though I do not see him.

To lie here on your back with nothing between your eye & the stars—nothing but space—they your nearest neighbors on that side—be they strange or be they tame—be they other worlds or merely ornaments to this— Who could ever go to sleep under these circumstances. I hear the 9 o clock bell ringing in Bedford—an unexpectedly musical sound that of a bell in the horizon always is— Pleasantly sounds the voice of one village to another. It is sweet as it is rare. Since I sat here a bright star has gone behind the stem of a tree—proving that my machine is moving— I hear a solitary whipporwill—& a bull frog on the river fewer sounds than in spring. The grey cliffs across the river are plain to be seen— And now the

star appears on the other side of the tree—& I must go— Still no
dew up here I see 3 scythes hanging on an apple tree— There is the
wild apple tree where hangs the forgotten scythe.— the rock where
the shoe was left.

The woods & the separate trees cast longer shadows than by day—
for the moon goes lower in her course at this season. Some dew at
last in the meadow. As I recross the string pieces of the bridge—I see
the water bugs swimming briskly in the moonlight. I scent the
Roman Wormwood in the Potatoe fields.

Sat Aug 9th tansy now in bloom and the fresh white clethra—
Among the pines & birches I hear the invisible Locust as I am going
to the pond to bathe I see a black cloud in the Northern horizon—
& hear the muttering of thunder & make haste— Before I have
bathed and dressed the gusts which preceed the tempest are heard
roaring in the woods & the first black gusty clouds have reached my
zenith Hastening toward town I am overtaken by the rain at the
edge of the wood and take refuge under the thickest leaves where
not a drop reaches me & at the end of half an hour the renewed
singing of the birds—alone advertises me that the rain has ceased and
it is only the dripping from the leaves which I hear in the woods. It
was a splendid sunset that day—a celestial light on all the land so that
all people went to their doors & windows to look on the grass and
leaves & buildings & the sky—and it was equally glorious in whatever
quarter you looked—a sort of fulgor as of stereotyped lightning filled
the air. Of which this is my solution. We were in the westernmost
edge of the shower at the moment the sun was setting—& its rays
shone through the cloud & the falling rain. We were in fact in a
rainbow & it was here its arch rested on the earth. At a little
distance we should have seen all the colors—

The Oenothera biennis along the rail road now Do the cars
disperse seeds? The Trichostema dichotoma is quite beautiful now in
the cool of the morning. The Epilobium in the woods still. Now
the earliest apples begin to be ripe—but none are so good to eat as
some to smell. Some gnarly apple which I pick up in the road
reminds me by its fragrance of all the wealth of Pomona.

Tuesday Aug. 12th

1½ AM. Full moon Arose and went to the river and bathed,
stepping very carefully not to disturb the household and still carefully
in the street not to disturb the neighbors. I did not walk naturally &
freely till I had got over the wall. Then to Hubbards bridge at 2 AM
— There was a whipporwill in the road just beyond Godwins which

flew up & lighted on the fence & kept alighting on the fence within
a rod of me & circling round me with a slight squeak as if
inquisitive about me. I do not remember what I observed or
thought in coming hither. The traveller's whole employment is to
calculate what cloud will obscure the moon and what she will
triumph over— In the after midnight hours the traveller's sole
companion is the moon— All his thoughts are centered in her She
is waging continual war with the clouds in his behalf What cloud
will enter the lists with her next this employs his thoughts—and
when she enters on a clear field of great extent in the heavens &
shines unobstructedly he is glad. And when she has fought her way
through all the squadrons of her foes—& rides majestic in a clear sky—
he cheerfully & confidently pursues his way—& rejoices in his heart.
But if he sees that she has many new clouds to contend with he
pursues his way moodily as one disappointed & aggrieved—he resents
it as an injury to himself. It is his employment to watch the moon
the companion & guide of his journey wading through clouds—and
calculate what one is destined to shut out her cheering light.

He traces her course now almost completely obscured—through
the ranks of her foes and calculates where she will issue from them.
He is disappointed & saddened when he sees that she has many
clouds to contend with. Sitting on the sleepers of Hubbards bridge
which is being repaired now 3 o clock AM I hear a cock crow.
How admirably adapted to the dawn is that sound.— as if made by
the first rays of light rending the darkness—the creaking of the sun's
axle heard already over the eastern hills.

Though man's life is trivial & handselled nature is holy & heroic.
With what infinite faith & promise & moderation begins each new
day. It is only a little after 3 o clock and already there is evidence of
morning in the sky. He rejoices when the moon comes forth from
the squadrons of the clouds unscathed and there are no more any
obstructions in her path. And the cricket also seems to express joy in
his song. It does not concern men who are asleep in their beds, but
it is very important to the traveller whether the moons shines bright
& unobstructed or is obscured by clouds. It is not easy to realize the
serene joy of all the earth when the moon commences to shine
unobstructedly unless you have often been a traveller by night.

The traveller also resents it if the wind rises & rustles the leaves—
or ripples the water and increases the coolness at such an hour. A
solitary horse in his pasture was scared by the sudden sight of me an
apparition to him standing still in the moonlight & moved about

inspecting with alarm—but I spoke & he heard the sound of my voice, he was at once reassured & expressed his pleasure by wagging his stump of a tail. though still half a dozen rods off— How wholesom the taste of huckleberries, when now by moon light I feel for them amid the bushes.

And now the first signs of morning attract the traveller's attention, and he cannot help rejoicing, and the moon begins gradually to fade from his recollection. The wind rises & rustles the copses (The sand is cool on the surface but warm 2 or 3 inches beneath & the rocks are quite warm to the hand, so that he sits on them or leans against them for warmth though indeed it is not cold elsewhere) As I walk along the side of Fair Haven Hill I see a ripple on the river—& now the moon has gone behind a large & black mass of clouds, and I realize that I may not see her again in her glory this night—that perchance ere she rises from this obscurity the sun will have risen, & she will appear but as a cloud herself—& sink unnoticed into the west (being a little after full (a day?)) As yet no sounds of awakening men—only the more frequent crowing of cocks still standing on their perches in the barns. The milkmen are the earliest risers, though I see no lanthorn's carried to their barns in the distance—preparing to carry the milk of cows in their tin cans for men's breakfasts even for those who dwell in distant cities. In the twilight now by the light of the stars alone, the moon being concealed they are pressing the bounteous streams from full udders into their milk pails & the sound of the streaming milk is all that breaks the sacred stillness of the dawn—distributing their milk to such as have no cows. I perceive no mosquitoes now are they vespertinal like the singing of the whippoorwill. I see the light of the obscured moon reflected from the river brightly—with what mild emphasis nature marks the spot—so bright & serene a sheen that does not more contrast with the night. 4 AM. It adds a charm—a dignity, a glory—to the earth to see the light of the moon reflected from her streams. There are but us three the moon—the earth which wears this jewel (the moons reflection) in her crown—& myself. Now there has come round the cliffs (on which I sit) all unobserved & mingled with the dusky sky of night—a lighter—and more etherial living blue— whispering of the sun still far far away behind the horizon— From the summit of our atmosphere perchance he may already be seen by soaring spirits that inhabit those thin upper regions & they communicate the glorious intelligence to us lower ones. (Not without sadness and compassion I reflect that I shall not see the

moon again in her glory.) The real *divine* the heavenly blue—the Jove
containing air it is I see through this dusky lower stratum. The sun
gilding the summits of the air. The arteries of light flow over all the
sky. (Not far from four still in the night I heard a night-hawk
squeak & *boom* high in the air—as I sat on the cliff— What is said
about this being less of a night bird than the whippoorwill is perhaps
to be questioned. For neither do I remember to have heard the
whipporwill *sing* at 12 o'clock—though I met one sitting & flying
between 2 & 3 this morning— I believe that both may be heard at
midnight—though very rarely.)

Now at *very earliest* dawn the night hawk booms & the
whippoorwill sings. Returning down the hill by the path to where
the woods cut off I see the signs of the day—the morning red
There is the lurid morning star soon to be blotted out by a
cloud

There is an early redness in the east which I was not prepared for
changing to amber or saffron—with clouds beneath in the horizon
and also above this clear streak—

The birds utter a few languid & yawning notes as if they had not
left their perches—so sensible to light to wake so soon— A faint
peeping sound from I know not what kind—a slight innocent half
awake sound—like the sounds which a quiet house wife makes in the
earliest dawn. I hear a wood-thrush even now long before sunrise as
in the heat of the day. & the peewee & the catbird—& the vireo-
redeyed?

I do not hear—or do not mind perchance the crickets now. Now
whippoorwills commence to sing in earnest considerably *after* the
wood thrush— The wood-thrush that beautiful singer inviting the
day once more to enter his pine woods. (So you may hear the
woodthrush & whippoorwill at the same time.) Now go by two
whippoorwills in haste seeking some coverts from the eye day. And
the bats are flying about on the edge of the wood improving the last
moments of their day—in catching insects. The moon appears at
length—not yet as a cloud—but with a frozen light ominous of her
fate. The early cars sound like a wind in the woods— The chewinks
make a business now of waking each other up with their low
"yorrick" in the neighboring low copse The sun would have
shown before but for the cloud. Now on his rising not the clear sky
but—the—cheeks of the clouds high & wide are tinged with red
which like the sky before turns gradually to saffron—& then to the
white light of day.

The nettle leaved vervain Verbena Urticifolia by road side at
Emerson's.

What we have called hemp answers best to urtica dioica large
stinging nettle? Now the great sunflower's golden disk is
seen

The days for some time have been sensibly shorter—there is time
for music in the evening

I see polygonums in blossom by road side—white & red.

A Eupatoreum from Hubbard bridge causeway—answers to E.
Purpureum—except in these doubtful points that the former has 4
leaves in a whorl—is unequally serrate, the stem is *nearly* filled with a
thin pith—the corymb is not merely terminal—florrets 8 & 9.

Differs from verticillatum—in the stem being not solid—and I
perceive no diff— bet calyx & corolla in color if I know what the
two are.

It may be one of the intermediate varieties referred to.

Friday Aug 15th

Hypericum Canadense Canadian St Johns Wort distinguished by
its red capsules. The petals shine under the microscope as if they had
a golden dew on them.

Cnicus pumilus pasture thistle— How many insects a single one
attracts. While you sit by it bee after bee will visit it & busy himself
probing for honey & loading himself with pollen regardless of your
over shadowing presence. He sees its purple flower from afar—and
that use there is in its color.

Oxalis stricta upright wood sorrel the little yellow ternate leaved
flower in pastures & cornfields

Sagittaria Sagittifolia or arrowhead It has very little root that I
can find to cut.

Campanula crinoides var, 2nd Slender Bell flower vinelike like a
Galium. by brook side in Depot field.

Impatiens noli me tangere or touch me not—with its dangling
yellow pitchers or horns of plenty—which I have seen for a month
by damp causeway thickets but the whole plant was so tender and
drooped so soon I could not get it home.

Mimulus ringens or monkey flower by

{One leaf missing}

May I love & revere myself above all the Gods that men have
ever invented.— may I never let the vestal fire go out in my
recesses—

Aug. 16

Agrimonia Eupatoria small flowered (yellow) plant with hispid fruit 2 or 3 feet high turnpike at Tuttles peatmead. Hemp—Cannabis sativa said by Gray to have been introduced not named by Bigelow— is it not a native?

It is true man can and does live by preying on other animals, but this is a miserable way of sustaining himself—and he will be regarded as a benefactor of his race—along with Prometheus & Christ—who shall teach men to live on a more innocent & wholesome diet. Is it not already acknowledged to be a reproach that man is a carnivorous animal?

Aug 17th

For a day or two it has been quite cool—a coolness that was felt even when sitting by an open window in a thin coat on the west side of the house in the morning—& you naturally sought the sun at that hour— The coolness concentrated your thought however— As I could not command a sunny window I went abroad on the morning of the 15th and lay in the sun in the fields in my thin coat though it was rather cool even there. I feel as if this coolness would do me good. If it only makes my life more pensive why should pensiveness be akin to sadness. There is a certain fertile sadness which I would not avoid but rather earnestly seek— It is positively joyful to me— It saves my life from being trivial. My life flows with a deeper current—no longer as a shallow & brawling stream parched & shrunken by the summer heats— This coolness comes to condense the dews & clear the atmosphere. The stillness seems more deep & significant—each sound seems to come from out a greater thoughtfulness in nature—as if nature had acquired some character & mind—the cricket—the gurgling—stream—the rushing wind amid the trees—all speak to me soberly yet encouragingly of the steady onward progress of the universe— My heart leaps into my mouth at the sound of the wind in the woods— I whose life was but yesterday so desultory & shallow—suddenly recover my spirits—my spirituality through my hearing— I see a goldfinch go twittering through the still louring day and am reminded of the peeping flocks which will soon herald the thoughtful season— Ah! if I could so live that there should be no desultory moment in all my life! That in the trivial season when small fruits are ripe my fruits might be ripe also that I could watch nature always with my moods! That in each season when some part of nature especially flourishes—then a corresponding part of me may not fail to flourish Ah, I would walk I would sit &

sleep with natural piety— What if I could pray aloud or to myself as
I went along by the brooksides a cheerful prayer like the birds! For
joy I could embrace the earth— I shall delight to be buried in it.
And then to think of those I love among men—who will know that
I love them though I tell them not. I sometimes feels as if I were
rewarded merely for expecting better hours— I did not despair of
worthier moods—and now I have occasion to be grateful for the
flood of life that is flowing over me. I am not so poor— I can smell
the ripening apples—the very rills are deep—the autumnal flowers the
trichostema dichotoma—not only its bright blue flower above the
sand but its strong wormwood scent which belongs to the season
feed my spirit—endear the earth to me—make me value myself &
rejoice— The quivering of pigeons' wings—reminds me of the tough
fibre of the air which they rend. I thank you God. I do not deserve
anything I am unworthy of the least regard & yet I am made to
rejoice. I am impure & worthless—& yet the world is gilded for my
delight & holidays are prepared for me—& my path is strewn with
flowers But I cannot thank the Giver— I cannot even whisper my
thanks to those human friends I have. It seems to me that I am
more rewarded for my expectations than for anything I do or can
do. Ah I would not tread on a cricket in whose song is such a
revelation—so soothing & cheering to my ear. O keep my senses
pure! And why should I speak to my friends? for how rarely is it
that I am I—and are they, then, they? We will meet then far away.
The seeds of the summer are getting dry & falling from a thousand
nodding heads. If I did not know you through thick & thin how
should I know you at all? Ah the very brooks seem fuller of
reflections than they were—ah such provoking sybilline sentences
they are——the shallowest is all at once unfathomable— how can that
depth be fathomed when a man may see himself reflected— The rill
I stopped to drink at I drink in more than I expected— I satisfy—&
still provoke the thirst of thirsts— Nut Meadow brook where it
crosses the road beyond Jenny Dugans that was. I do not drink in
vain I mark that brook as if I had swallowed a water snake—that
would live in my stomack— I have swallowed something worth the
while— The days is not what it was before I stooped to drink. Ah I
shall hear from that draught—it is not in vain that I have drunk.— I
have drank an arrow-head. It flows from where all fountains rise.

How many ova have I swallowed—who knows what will be
hatched within me? There were some seeds of thought methinks
floating in that water which are expanding in me— The man must

not drink of the running streams the living waters—who is not
prepared to have all nature reborn in him—to suckle monsters— The
snake in my stomack lifts his head to my mouth at the sound of
running water. When was it that I swallowed a snake. I have got rid
of the snake in my stomack. I drank at stagnant waters once. That
accounts for it. I caught him by the throat & drew him out & had a
well day after all. Is there not such a thing as getting rid of the snake
which you swallowed when young? When thoughtless you stooped
& drank at stagnant waters—which has worried you in your waking
hours & in your sleep ever since & appropriated the life that was
yours. Will he not ascend into your mouth at the sound of running
water— Then catch him boldly by the head & draw him out
though you may think his tail be curled about your vitals.

The farmers are just finishing their meadow haying (today is
sunday)— Those who have early potatoes may be digging them or
doing any other job which the haying has obliged them to postpone
— For six weeks or more this has been the farmer's work to shave
the surface of the fields & meadows clean. This is done all over the
country—the razor is passed over these parts of nature's face the
country over— A 13th labor which methinks would have broken
the backs of Hercules would have given him a memorable sweat—
accomplished with what sweating of scythes & early & late— I
chance know one young man who has lost his life in this seasons
campaingn by over doing— In haying time some men take double
wages & they are engaged long before in the spring. To shave all the
fields & meadows of New England clean— If men did this but once
& not every year—we should never hear the last of that labor—it
would be more famous in each farmers case than Buonaparte's road
over the Simplon. It has no other bulletin but the truthful farmer's
almanac— Ask them where scythe snathes are made & sold & rifles
too if it is not a real labor. In its very weapons & its passes it has the
semblance of war. Mexico was won with less exertion & less true
valor than are required to do one season's haying in New England—
The former work was done by those who played truant and ran
away from the latter.

Those Mexican's were mown down more easily than the
summer's crop of grass in many a farmer's fields.

Is there not some work in New England men. This haying is no
work for marines nor for deserters—nor for U S troops so called nor
for Westpoint cadets—it would wilt them & they would desert. Have
they not deserted?— every field is a battle field to the mower—a

pitched battle too—and whole winrows of dead have covered it in
the course of the season. Early & late the farmer has gone forth with
his formidable scythe—weapon of time—Times weapon—& fought the
ground inch by inch— It is the summer's enterprise. And if we were
a more poetic people horns would be blowed to celebrate its
completion—there might be a hay maker's day— New Englands
peaceful battles— At Bunker Hill there were some who stood at the
rail fence & behind the winrows of new mown hay— They have
not yet quitted the field. They stand there still—they have not
retreated.

The polygala sanguinea caducous polygala in damp ground with
red or purple heads—

The dandelion still blossoms & the lupine still belated. I have
been to Tarbels swamp by the 2nd division this afternoon & to the
Marlboro road It has promised rain all day—cloudy & still & rather
cool—from time to time a few drops gently spitting but no shower
The landscape wears a sober autumnal look— I hear a drop or two
on my hat— I wear a thick coat— The birds seem to know that it
will not rain just yet. The swallows skim low over the pastures
twittering as they fly near me with forked tail dashing near me as if I
scared up insects for them. I see where a squirrel has been eating
hazel nuts on a stump.

Tarbel's swamp is mainly composed of low & even but dense
beds of Andromeda caliculata or dwarf Andromeda which bears the
early flower in the spring— Here & there mingled with it is the
Andromeda polifolia or Water Andromeda? Also pitch pines birches—
hardhack & the common alder Alnus serrulata—and in separate &
lower beds the cranberry—& probably the Rhodora Canadensis
might be found.

The lead colored berries of the viburnum dentatum now— Cow
Wheat & indigo weed still in bloom by the dry woodpath side. &
Norway cinquefoil. I detected a wild apple on the Marlboro road by
its fragrance—in the thick woods—small stems 4 inches in diameter
falling over or leaning like rays on every side—a clean white fruit—the
ripest yellowish—a pleasant acid—the fruit covered the ground. It is
unusual to meet with an early apple thus wild in the thickest woods.
It seemed admirable to me. One of the noblest of fruits. With green
specks under the skin

Prenanthes Alba white flowering P. with its strange halbert &
variously shaped leaves.

Neottia

& Hypericum

I hear the rain (11 PM) distilling upon the ground—wetting the grass & leaves— The melons needed it— Their leaves were curled & their fruit stinted.

I am less somnolent for the cool season. I wake to a perennial day. The hayer's work is done, but I hear no boasting—no firing of guns nor ringing of bells. He celebrates it by going about the work he had postponed. "till after haying." If all this steadiness & valor were spent upon some still worthier enterprise!!

All men's employments—all trades & professions in some of their aspects are attractive— Hence the boy resolved to be a minister & make cider—not thinking boy as he was how little fun there was in being a minister—willing to purchase that pleasure at any price— When I saw the carpenters the other day repairing Hubbards bridge their bench on the new platform they had laid over the water in the sun & air with no railing yet to obstruct the view I was almost ready to resolve that I would be a carpenter & work on bridges— To secure a pleasant place to work— One of the men had a fish line cast round a sleeper which he looked at from time to time.

—John Potter told me that those root fences on the Corner road were at least 60 or 70 yrs old.— I see a solitary Goldfinch now & then.

Hieracium Marianum or scabrum $\left.\right\}$ Marlboro road.
     "   Kalmii or Canadense
Leontodon Autumnale passim

Aug 18th

It plainly makes men sad to think. Hence *pensiveness* is akin to sadness.

Some dogs I have noticed have a propensity to worry cows—they go off by themselves to distant pastures & ever and anon like four legged devils they worry the cows—full of the devil. They are so full of the devil they know not what to do. I come to interfere between the cows & their tormentors. Ah I grieve to see the devils escape so easily by their swift limbs imps of mischief— They are the dog state of those boys who pull down hand bills in the streets. Their next migration perchance will be into such dogs as these—ignoble fate. The dog whose office it should be to guard the herd turned its tormentor. Some courageous cow endeavoring in vain to toss the nimble devil.

Those soldiers in the Champ de Mars at Montreal convinced me that I had arrived in a foreign country under a different government

—where many are under the control of one. Such perfect drill could
never be in a republic Yet it had the effect on us as when the
keeper shows his animals claws— It was the English leopard showing
his claws. The Royal something or other— I have no doubt that
soldiers well drilled as a class are peculiarly destitute of originality &
independence. The men were dressed above their condition had the
bearing of gentlemen without a corresponding intellectual culture.

The Irish was a familiar element—but the Scotch a novel one—the
St Andrew's Church was prominent—& sometimes I was reminded
of Edinburg—indeed much more than of London—

Warburton remarked soon after landing at Quebec—that
Everything was cheap in that country but men— My thought when
observing how the wooden pavements were sawed by hand in the
streets instead of by machinery because labor was cheap——how
cheap men are here.

It is evident that a private man is not worth so much in Canada
as in the U. S. & if that is the bulk of a man's property i.e. the
being private & peculiar he had better stay here— An Englishman
methinks, not to speak of other nations—habitually regards himself
merely as a constituent part of the English nation—he holds a
recognized place as such—he is a member of the Royal regiment of
Englishmen. & he is proud of his nation— But an American cares
very little about such & greater of freedom & independence are
possible to him. He is nearer to the primitive condition of man—
Government lets him alone & he lets government alone.

I often thought of the tories & refugees who settled in Canada at
the revolution— These English were to a considerable extent their
descendants—

Quebec began to be fortified in a more regular manner in 1690

The most modern fortifications have an air of antiquity about
them—they have the aspect of ruins in better or worse repair—ruins
kept in repair from the day they were built though they were
completed yesterday—because they are not in a true sense the work
of this age. I couple them with the dismantled spanish forts to be
found in so many parts of the world—they carry me back to the
middle ages—. & the siege of Jerusalem & St Jean D'acre—& the
days of the Buccaniers Such works are not consistent with the
development of the intellect. Huge stone structures of all kinds—both
by their creation & their influence rather oppress the intellect than
set it free A little thought will dismantle them as fast as they are
built. They are a bungling contrivance— It is an institution as rotten

as the church— The soldiers—the sentinel with his musket beside a man with his umbrella is spectral. There is not sufficient reason for his existence— My friend there with a bullet resting on half an ounce of powder—does he think that he needs that argument in conversing with me? Of what use this fortification to look at it from the soldiers point of view— General Wolfe sailed by it with impunity—& took the town of Quebec—without experiencing any hindrance from its fortifications. How often do we have to read that the enemy occupied a position which commanded the old. & so the post was evacuated.

How impossible it is to give that soldier a good education—without first making him virtually a deserter.

It is as if I were to come to a country Village surrounded with palisadoes in the old Indian style—interesting as a relic of antiquity & barbarism. A fortified town is a man cased in the heavy armor of antiquity & a horse load of broad swords & small arms slung to him. endeavoring to go about his business.

The idea seemed to be that sometime the inhabitants of Canada might wish to govern themselves and this was to hinder— But the inhabitants of California succeed well without any such establishment. There would be the same sense in a man's wearing a breast plate all his days for fear somebody should fire a bullet at his vitals. The English in Canada—seem to be everywhere prepared & preparing for war in the U S they are prepared for anything—they may even be the aggressors—

This is a ruin kept in a remarkably good repair—there are some 800 or 1000 men there to exhibit it. One regiment goes bare-legged to increase the attraction— If you wish to study the muscles of the legs about the knee repair to Quebec.

Aug 19th

Clematis Virginiana—Calamint—Lycopus Europeus water horehound

This is a world where there are flowers. Now at 5 AM the fog which in the west looks like a wreath of hard rolled cotton batting—is rapidly dispersing. The echo of the railroad whistle is heard the horizon round—the gravel train is starting out. The farmers are cradling oats in some places. For some days past I have noticed a *red* maple or two about the pond though we have had no frost. The grass is very wet with dew this morning.

The way in which men cling to old institutions after the life has departed out of them & out of themselves reminds me of those monkies which cling by their tails—aye whose tails contract about the limbs—even the dead limbs of the forest and they hang suspended beyond the hunters reach long after they are dead It is of no use to argue with such men They have not an apprehensive intellect but merely as it were a prehensile tail. Their intellect possesses merely the quality of a prehensile tail. The tail itself contracts around the dead limb even after they themselves are dead—and not till corruption takes place do they fall.

The black howling monkey, or Caraya—according to Azara it is extremely dif. to get at them for "When mortally wounded they coil the tail round a branch, and hang by it with the head downwards for days after death, and until, in fact, decomposition begins to take effect."— The commenting Naturalist says "a singular peculiarity of this organ is to contract at its extremity of its own accord as soon as it is extended to its full length." I relinquish argument, I wait for decomposition to take place, for the subject is dead. as I value the hide for museums. They say "though you've got my soul, you shan't have my carcass."

PM to Marlboro Road via Clamshell Hill—Jenny Dugan's—Round Pond Canoe Birch road (Dea Dakins) & White Pond.—

How many things concur to keep a man at home, to prevent his yielding to his inclination to wander. If I would extend my walk a hundred miles I must carry a tent on my back for shelter at night or in the rain, or at least I must carry a thick coat to be prepared for a change in the weather. So that it requires some resolution as well as energy and foresight to undertake the simplest journey. Man does not travel as easily as the birds migrate— He is not everywhere at home like flies. When I think how many things I can conveniently carry, I am wont to think it most convenient to stay at home. My home then to a certain extent is the place where I keep my thick-coat & my tent & some books which I can not carry. Where next I can depend upon meeting some friends— And where finally I even I have established myself in business— But this last in my case is the least important qualification of a home.

The poet must be continually watching the moods of his mind as the astronomer watches the aspects of the heavens. What might we not expect from a long life faithfully spent in this wise—the humblest observer would see some stars shoot.— A faithful description as by a disinterested person of the thoughts which visited a certain mind in 3 score years & 10 as when one reports the number & character of the vehicles which pass a particular point. As travellers go round the

world and report natural objects & phenomena—so faithfully let
another stay at home & report the phenomena of his own life.
Catalogue stars—those thoughts whose orbits are as rarely calculated
as comets It matters not whether they visit my mind or yours—
whether the meteor falls in my field or in yours—only that it came
from heaven. (I am not concerned to express that kind of truth
which nature has expressed. Who knows but I may suggest some
things to her. Time was when she was indebted to such suggestions
from another quarter—as her present advancement shows. I deal with
the truths that recommend themselves to me please me—not those
merely which any system has voted to accept.) A meteorological
journal of the mind— You shall observe what occurs in your
latitude, I in mine.

Some institutions—most institutions, indeed, have had a divine
origin. But of most that we see prevailing in society nothing but the
form, the shell, is left—the life is extinct—and there is nothing divine
in them. Then the reformer arises inspired to reinstitute life—& what
ever he does or causes to be done is a reestablishment of that same
or a similar divineness. But some who never knew the significance
of these instincts—are by a sort of false instinct found clinging to the
shells. Those who have no knowledge of the divine appoint
themselves defenders of the divine—as champions of the church &c
I have been astonished to observe how long some audiences can
endure to hear a man speak on a subject which he knows nothing
about—as religion for instance—when one who has no ear for music
might with the same propriety take up the time of a musical
assembly with putting through his opinions on music. This young
man who is the main pillar of some divine institution—does he know
what he has undertaken. If the saints were to come again on earth
would they be likely to stay at his house—would they meet with his
approbation even? Ne sutor ultra crepidam. They who merely have
a talent for affairs—are forward to express their opinions—

A Roman soldier sits there to decide upon the righteousness of
Christ— The world does not long endure such blunders—though
they are made every day. The weak-brained & pusilanimous farmers
would fain abide by the the institutions of their fathers. their
argument is they have not long to live, and for that little space let
them not be disturbed in their slumbers—blessed are the peace
makers—let this cup pass from me &c

How vain it is to sit down to write when you have not stood up
to live! Methinks that the moment my legs begin to move my

thoughts begin to flow—as if I had given vent to the stream at the lower end & consequently new fountains flowed into it at the upper. A thousand rills which have their rise in the sources of thought—burst forth & fertilise my brain. ` you need to increase the draught below—as the owners of meadows on C. river say of the Billerica Dam. Only while we are in action is the circulation perfect. The writing which consists with habitual sitting is mechanical wooden dull to read.

The grass in the high pastures is almost as dry as hay— The seasons do not cease a moment to revolve and therefore nature rests no longer at her culminating point than at any other. If you are not out at the right instant the summer may go by & you not see it. How much of the year is spring & fall—how little can be called summer! The grass is no sooner grown than it begins to wither— How much nature herself suffers from drought! It seems quite as much as she can do to produce these crops

The most inattentive walker can see how the science of geology took its rise. The inland hills & promontories betray the action of water on their rounded sides as plainly as if the work were completed yesterday. He sees it with but half an eye as he walks & forgets his thought again. Also the level plains & more recent meadows & marine shells found on the tops of hills— The Geologist painfully & elaborately follows out these suggestions—& hence his fine spun theories.

The gold finch—though solitary is now one of the commonest birds in the air.

What if a man were earnestly & wisely to set about recollecting & preserving the thoughts which he has had! How many perchance are now irrecoverable!— Calling in his neighbors to aid him.

I do not like to hear the name of particular states given to birds & flowers which are found in all equally— Maryland yellow throat &c &c The Canadenses & virginicas may be suffered to pass for the most part for there is historical reason at least for them Canada is the peculiar country of some & the northern limit of many more plants And Virginia which was originally the name for all the Atlantic shore has some right to stand for the south.

The fruit of the sweet gale by nut-meadow brook is of a yellowish green now & has not yet its greasy feel.

The little red streaked & dotted excrescences on—the shrub oaks I find as yet no name for.

Now for the pretty red capsules or pods of the Hypericum Canadense

White golden rod is budded along the Marlboro Road

Chicadees & jays never fail— The cricket's is a note which does not attract you to itself. It is not easy to find one

I fear that the character of my knowledge is from year to year becoming more distinct & scientific— That in exchange for views as wide as heaven's cope I am being narrowed down to the field of the microscope— I see details not wholes nor the shadow of the whole. I count some parts, & say 'I know'. The cricket's chirp now fills the air in dry fields near pine woods.

Gathered our first watermelon today. By the Marl. Road I notice the richly veined leaves of the Neottia pubescens or veined Neottia Rattle-snake plantain. I like this last name very well though it might not be easy to convince a quibbler or proser of its fitness. We want some name to express the mystic wildness of its rich leaves. Such work as men imitate in their embroidery—unaccountably agreeable to the eye—as if it answered its end only when it met the eye of man—a reticulated leaf—visible only on one side—little strings which make one pause in the woods—take captive the eye.

Here is a bee's or wasp's nest in the sandy mouldering bank by the road side—4 inches in diameter—as if made of scales of striped brown paper. It is singular if indeed man first made paper & then discovered its resemblance to the work of the wasps & did not derive the hint from them.

Canoe birches by road to Dakins'—Cuticle stripped off—inner bark dead & scaling off—new (inner) bark formed

The solomans seals are fruited now with finely red-dotted berries

There was one original name well given *Buster* Kendal. The fragrance of the clethra fills the air by water sides. In the hollows where in winter is a pond the grass is short thick & green still—and here & there are tufts pulled up as if by the mouth of cows.

Small rough sunflower by side of road between Canoe birch & white pond. Helianthus divaricatus.

Lespedeza capitata, shrubby Lespedeza White pond road &

Marl. road

"   Polystachya, Hairy   "   Corner Road beyond

Hub's Bridge.

Aug 20th

2 PM. To Lees bridge via Hubbards wood Potters field—Conantum—returning by Abel Minot's House—Clematis brook—Baker's Pine plain & rail road.

I hear a cricket in the depot field—walk a rod or two and find the note proceeds from near a rock— Partly under a rock between it &

the roots of the grass he lies concealed—for I pull away the withered grass with my hands—uttering his night-like creak with a vibratory motion of his wings & flattering himself that it is night because he has shut out the day— He was a black fellow nearly an inch long with two long slender feelers They plainly avoid the light & hide their heads in the grass—at any rate they regard this as the evening of the year— They are remarkable secret & unobserved considering how much noise they make— Every milkman has heard them all his life—it is the sound that fills his ears as he drives along—but what one has ever got off his cart to go in search of one? I see smaller ones moving stealthily about whose note I do not know Who ever distinguished their various notes? which fill the crevices in each others song— It would be a curious ear indeed that distinguished the species of the crickets which it heard—& traced even the earth song home each part to its particular performer I am afraid to be so knowing. They are shy as birds, these little bodies, Those nearest me continually cease their song as I walk so that the singers are always a rod distant—& I cannot easily detect one— It is difficult moreover to judge correctly whence the sound proceeds. Perhaps this wariness is necessary to save them from insectevorous birds—which would other wise speedily find out so loud a singer— They are somewhat protected by the universalness of the sound each ones song being merged and lost in the general concert—as if it were the creaking of earth's axle. They are very numerous in oats & other grain which conceals them & yet affords a clear passage— I never knew any drought or sickness so to prevail as to quench the song of the crickets—it fails not in its season night or day.

The lobelia inflata Ind. Tobacco meets me at every turn— At first I suspect some new bluish flower in the grass, but stooping see the inflated pods—tasting one such herb convinces me that there *are* such things as drugs—which may either kill or cure

The rhexia Virginica is a showy flower at present.

How copious & precise the botanical language to describe the leaves, as well as the other parts of a plant. Botany is worth studying if only for the precision of its terms—to learn the value of words & of system. It is wonderful how much pains has been taken to describe a flowers leaf—, compared for instance with the care that is taken in describing a psychological fact. Suppose as much ingenuity (perhaps it would be needless) in in making a language to express the sentiments, We are armed with language adequate to describe each leaf in the field.— or at least to distinguish it from each other—but not to describe a human character—with equally wonderful indistinctness & confusion we describe men— The precision and copiousness of botanical language applied to the description of moral qualities!

The neottia or ladies tresses behind Garfields house. The Golden robin is now a rare bird to see. Here are the small lively tasting blackberries. so small they are not commonly eaten. The grass hoppers seem no drier than the grass. In Lee's field are two kinds of plantain— Is the common one found there?

The willow reach by Lees bridge has been stripped for powder— none escapes. This morning hearing a cart I looked out & saw Geo. Dugan going by with a horse load of his willow—toward Acton powder mills—which I had seen in piles by the turnpike. Every traveller has just as particular an errand which I might likewise chance to be privy to. Now that I am at the extremity of my walk I see a threatening cloud blowing up from the south—which however methinks will not compel me to make haste.

Apios tuberosa or Glycine apios Ground nut

The Prenanthes now takes the place of the Lactucas which are gone to seed— In the dry ditch near Abel Minots house that was I see cardinal flowers—with their red artillery, reminding me of soldiers —red men war—& blood shed. Some are 4½ feet high.

Thy sins shall be as scarlet—is it my sins that I see? It shows how far a little color can go for the flower is not large yet it makes itself seen from a far—& so answers the purpose for which it was colored completely. It is remarkable for its intensely brilliant scarlet color— You are slow to concede to it a high rank among flowers—but ever and anon as you turn your eyes away—it dazzles you & you pluck it. scutellaria lateriflora side flowering skull cap here This brook deserves to be called Clematis Brook (though that name is too often applied) for the clematis is very abundant running over the alders & other bushes on its brink.

Where the brook issues from the pond the night shade grows profusely spreading 5 or 6 feet each way with its red berries now ripe— It grows too at the upper end of the pond.— But if it is the button bush that grows in the now low water—it should rather be called the button bush pond. Now the tall rush is in its prime on the shore here—& the clematis abounds by this pond also.

I came out by the leafy columned elm—under Mt Misery—where the trees stood up one above another higher & higher immeasurably far to my imagination—as on the side of a New Hampshire Mountain.

On the pitch pine plain at first the pines are far apart—with—a

wiry grass between & golden rod & hard hack & St Johns-wort &
black-berry vines—each tree nearly keeping down the grass for a
space about itself—meditating to make a forest floor. & here & there
younger pines are springing up.— Further in you come to moss
covered patches dry deep white moss—or almost bare mould—half
covered with pine needles— Thus begins the future forest floor.

The sites of the shanties that once stood by the railroad in
Lincoln when the Irish built it, the still remaining hollow square
mounds of earth which formed their embankments reminding me
are to me instead of barrows & druidical monuments & other ruins.
It is a sufficient antiquity to me since they were built their material
being earth.

—Now the canada thistle & the mullein crown their tops— I see
the stones which made their simple chimneys still left one upon
another at one end—which were surmounted with barrels to eek
them out—& clean boiled beef bones & old shoes are strewn about.
Otherwise it is a clean ruin & nothing is left but a mound—as in the
grave yard.

Sium lineare a kind of water parsnip whose blossom resembles the
Cicuta maculata The flowers of the blue vervain have now nearly
reached the summit of their spikes.

A traveller who looks at things with an impartial eye may see
what the oldest inhabitant has not observed.

Aug 21st 1851

To a great extent the feudal system still prevails there (in Canada)
and I saw that I should be a bad citizen—that any man who thought
for himself and was only reasonably independent would naturally be
a rebel. You could not read or hear of their laws without seeing that
it was a legislating for a few & not for all. That certainly is the best
government where the inhabitants are least often reminded of the
government. Where a man cannot be a poet even without danger of
his being made poet laureat—where he cannot be healthily neglected
—& grow up a man, and not an Englishman merely.— Where it is
the most natural thing in the world for a government that does not
understand you, to let you alone! Oh—what a government were
there my countrymen! It is a government that English one—& most
other European ones that cannot afford to be forgotten—as you
would naturally forget them—that cannot let you go alone, having
learned to walk— It appears to me that a true Englishman can only
speculate within bounds—he has to pay his respects to so many things
that before he knows it he has paid all he is worth. The principle

respect in which our government is more tolerable is in the fact that
there is so much less of government with us. In the States it is only
once in a dog's age that a man needs remember his government—but
here he is reminded of it every day.— Government parades itself
before you. It is in no sense the servant but the master.

What a faculty must that be which can paint the most barren
landscape and humblest life in glorious colors It is pure &
invigorated senses reacting on a sound & strong imagination. Is not
that the poets case? The intellect of most men is barren. They
neither fertilize nor are fertilized. It is the mariage of the soul with
nature that makes the intellect fruitful—that gives birth to
imagination. When we were dead & dry as the high-way some sense
which has been healthily fed will put us in relation with nature in
sympathy with her—some grains of fertilizing pollen floating in the
air fall on us—& suddenly the sky is all one rain bow—is full of music
& fragrance & flavor— The man of intellect only the prosaic man is
a barren & staminiferous flower the poet is a fertile & perfect flower
Men are such confirmed arithmeticians & slaves of business that I
cannot easily find a blank book that has not a red line or a blue one
for the dollars and cents, or some such purpose.

As is a man's intellectual character, is not such his physical after
all? Can you not infer from knowing the intellectual characters of
two which is most tenacious of life & will live the longest? Which is
the toughest—which has most brute strength—which the most passive
endurance— Methinks I could to some extent infer these things.

1 PM Round Flints Pond via RR—my old field—Goose Pond—
Wharf rock—Cedar Hill—Smiths and so back.

Bigelow speaking of the spikes of the blue vervain (verbena
hastata) says "The flowering commences at their base and is long in
reaching their summit." I perceive that only one circle of buds about
half a dozen blossoms at a time, and there are about 30 circles in the
space of 3 inches—while the next circle of buds above at the same
time shows the blue. Thus this triumphant blossoming circle travels
upward driving the remaining buds off into space— I think it was
the 16th of July when I first noticed them and now they are all
within about half an inch of the top of the spikes— Yet the
blossoms have got no nearer the top on long spikes which had many
buds than on short ones only an inch long— Perhaps the blossoming
commenced enough earlier on the long ones to make up for the
difference in length. It is very pleasant to measure the progress of the

season by this & similar clocks— So you get not the absolute time
but the true time of the season.

The prevailing conspicuous flowers at present are. The early
golden-rods—Tansy—The Life-everlastings—fleabane though not for its
flower Yarrow (rather dry)—hardhack & meadow sweet (both getting
dry also may-weed) Eupatorium purpureum—Scabish—Clethra
(—really a fine sweet scented and this year particularly fair & fresh
flower—some unexpanded buds at top tinged with red)—Rhexia
Virginica—Thoroughwort—Polygala sanguinea—Prunella & Dogsbane—
(getting stale) &c &c Touch-me-not (less observed) Canada Snap-
Dragon by roadside (not conspicuous)

The purple Gerardia now—horse mint or mentha borealis—
veronica scutellata marsh speedwell.— ranunculas acris—Tall
Crowfoot still— Mowing to some extent improves the landscape to
the eye of the walker. The aftermath—so fresh & green begins now
to recall the spring to my mind—

In some fields fresh clover heads appear. This is certainly better
than fields of lodged & withered grass.

I find ground nuts by the RR causeway ¾ inch long by ⅓ inch.
The epilobium still.

Cow wheat—melampyrum Americanum still flourish as much if
not more than ever—& shrubby looking helps cover the ground
where the wood has recently been cut off—like huckleberry bushes.

There is some advantage intellectually & spiritually in taking wide
views with the bodily eye & not pursuing an occupation which
holds the body prone— There is some advantage perhaps in
attending to the general features of the landscape over studying the
particular plants & animals which inhabit it. A man may walk abroad
& no more see the sky than if he walked under a shed. The poet is
more in the air than the naturalist though they may walk side by
side.— Granted that you are out of door—but what if the outer door
is open, if the inner door is shut. You must walk sometimes
perfectly free—not prying nor inquisitive—not bent upon seeing
things— Throw away a whole day for a single expansion. a single
inspiration of air—

Any anomaly in vegetation makes nature seem more real &
present in her working—as the various red & yellow excrescences on
young oaks— I am affected as if it were a different Nature that
produced them. As if a poet were born—who had designs in his
head.

It is remarkable that animals are often obviously manifestly related
to the plants which they feed upon or live among—as catterpillars—

butterflies—tree toads—partridges—chewinks—& this afternoon I
noticed a yellow spider on a golden rod—   As if every condition
might have its expression in some form of animated being. Spear
leaved golden rod in path to NE of Flints Pond.

Hieracium Paniculatum a very delicate & slender hawkweed—   I
have now found all the hawkweeds. Singular these genera of plants—
plants manifestly related yet distinct   They suggest a history to
Nature—a Natural *history* in a new sense.

At wharf rock found water lobelia in blossom—   I saw some
smilax vines in the swamp which were connected with trees ten feet
above the ground whereon they grew & 4 or 5 feet above the
surrounding bushes—   This slender vine which cannot stand erect
how did it establish that connexion—   Have the trees & shrubs by
which it once climbed been cut down? Or perchance do the young
& flexible shoots blow up in high winds & fix themselves? On
Cedar Hill S side Pond I still hear the locust though it has been so
much colder for the last week. It is quite hazy in the west—though
comparitively clean in other directions. The barberry bushes with
their drooping wreathes of fruit now turning red—bushed up with
some other shrub or tree.

Aug 22nd

I found last winter that it was expected that I would give some
account of canada because I had *visited* it and because many of them
had & so felt interested in the subject—visited it as the bullet visits
the wall at which it is fired & from which it rebounds as quickly &
flattened (somewhat damaged perchance)—   Yes a certain man
contracted to take 1500 live Yankees through Canada—at a certain
rate & within a certain time—   It did not matter to him what the
commodity was   If only it were dilivered to him according to
agreement at the right place & time—and rightly ticketed—so much in
bulk—wet or dry on deck or in the hold—at the option of the carrier
how to stow the cargo & not always right side up—   In the mean
while it was understood that the freight was not to be willfully &
intentionally debarred from seeing the country if it had eyes—   It was
understood that there would be a country to be seen on either side—
though that was a secret advantage which the contractors seemed not
to be aware of—

I fear that I have not got much to say not having seen much—for
the very rapidity of the motion had a tendency to keep my eye lids
closed—   What I got by going to Canada was a cold and not till I
get a fever shall I appreciate it.

It is the fault of some excellent writers—De Quincy's first

impressions on seeing London suggest it to me—that they express
themselves with too great fullness & detail. They give the most
faithful natural & living account of their sensations mental & physical
—but they lack moderation and sententiousness—they do not affect us
by an inefficual earnesst and a reserve of meaning—like a stutterer—
they say all they mean. Their sentences are not concentrated and
nutty. Sentences which suggest far more than they say, which have
an atmosphere about them—which do not merely report an old but
make a new impression— Sentences which suggest as many things
and are as durable as a Roman Acqueduct To frame these that is
the *art* of writing. Sentences which are expensive towards which so
many volumes—so much life went—which lie like boulders on the
page—up & down or across. Not mere repetition but creation.
Which a man might sell his grounds & castle to build. If De Quincy
had suggested each of his pages in a sentence & passed on it would
have been far more excellent writing.— His style is no where
kinked and knotted up into something hard & significant which you
could swallow like a diamond without digesting.

Aug 23d Sat.

To walden to bathe at 5½ AM Traces of the heavy rains in the
night The sand and gravel are beaten hard by them. 3 or 4
showers in succession. But the grass is not so wet as after an ordinary
dew. The verbena hastata at the pond has reached the top of its
spike—a little in advance of what I noticed yesterday—only one or
two flowers are adhering. At the commencement of my walk I saw
no traces of fog. but after detected fogs over particular meadows &
high up some brooks' valleys—and far in the deep cut the wood fog
1st muskmelon this morning—

I rarely pass the shanty in the woods, where human beings are
lodged literally no better than pigs in a stye little children—a grown
man & his wife—& an aged Grandmother—living this squalid life
squatting on the ground—but I wonder if it can be indeed true that
little Julia Ruyaden calls this place home comes here to rest at night
—& for her daily food—in whom ladies & gentlemen in the village
take an interest— Of what significance are charity & alms houses?
That there they live unmolested! in one sense so many degrees
below the alms house! beneath charity. It is admirable— Nature
against alms houses. A certain wealth of nature not poverty it
suggests— Not to identify health & contentment aye and
independence with the possession of this world's goods. It is not
wise to waste compassion on them.

As I go through the deep cut I hear one or two early humble bees come out on the damp sandy bank—whose low hum sounds like distant horns from far in the horizon over the woods. It was long before I detected the bees that made it.— So far away musical it sounded like the shepherds in some distant eastern vale greeting the king of day.

The farmers now carry—those who have got them—their early potatoes & onions to market—starting away early in the morning or at midnight. I see them returning in the afternoon with the empty barrels.

Perchance the copious rain of last night will trouble those who had not been so provident as to get their hay from the Great Meadows where it is often lost.

PM—walk to Anursnack & back over Stone B

I sometimes reproach myself because I do not find anything attractive in certain more trivial employments of men—that I skip men so commonly & their affairs—the professions and the trades—do not elevate them at least in my thought and get some material for poetry out of them directly. I will not avoid then to go by where these men are repairing the Stone Bridge—see if I cannot see poetry in that—if that will not yield me a reflection. It is narrow to be confined to woods & fields and grand aspects of nature only.— The greatest & wisest will still be related to men. Why not see men standing in the sun & casting a shadow—even as trees—may not some light be reflected from them as from the stems of trees— I will try to enjoy them as animals at least. They are perhaps better animals than men. Do not neglect to speak of men's low life and affairs with sympathy—though you ever so speak as to suggest a contrast between them & the ideal & divine— You may be excused if you are always pathetic—but do not refuse to recognize.

Resolve to read no book—to take no walk—to undertake no enterprise but such as you can endure to give an account of to yourself Live thus deliberately for the most part.

When I stopped to gather some blueberries by the roadside this afternoon I heard the shrilling of a cricket or a grasshopper close to me quite clear almost like a bell—a clear ring—incessant not intermittent like the song of the black fellow I caught the other day —and not suggesting the night, but belonging to day— It was long before I could find him though all the while within a foot or two— I did not know whether to seaarch amid the grass & stones or amid the leaves. At last by accident I saw him, he shrilling all the while

under an alder leaf 2 feet from the ground—a slender green fellow
with long feelers & transparent wings. When he shrilled his wings
which opened on each other in the form of a heart perpendicularly
to his body like the wings of fairies   vibrated swiftly on each
other. The apparently wingless female as I thought was
near.

We experience pleasure when an elevated field or even road in
which we may be walking—holds its level toward the horizon at a
tangent to the earth—is not convex with the earths surface—but an
absolute level—

On or under E side of Annursnack Epilobium coloratum colored
willow herb (near the spring.) Also Polygonum sagitatum Scratch
grass.

The Price Farm Road—one of those everlasting roads—which the
sun delights to shine along in an August afternoon—playing truant—
Which seem to stretch themselves with terrene jest as the weary
traveller journeys— Where there are three white sandy furrows, two
for the wheels & one between them for the horse—with endless
green grass borders between—& room on each side for huckleberries
& birches.— where the walls indulge in peaks—not always parallel to
the ruts—& golden rod yellows all the path— Which some elms
began to fringe once but left off in despair it was so long. From no
point on which can you be said to be at any definite distance from a
town.

I associate the beauty of Quebec with the steel-like and
flashing air.

Our little river reaches are not to be forgotten. I noticed that seen
northward on the Assabet from the cause-way bridge near the 2nd
stone bridge. There was man in a boat in the sun just disappearing
in the distance round a bend. lifting high his Arms & dipping his
paddle—as if he were a vision bound to land of the blessed.— far off
as in picture. When I see Concord to purpose—I see it as if it were
not real but painted, and what wonder if I do not speak to *thee*. I
saw a snake by the roadside & touched him with my foot to see if
he were alive—he had a toad in his jaws which he was preparing to
swallow with his jaws distended to 3 times his width—but he
relinquished his prey in haste & fled—& I thought as the toad
jumped leisurely away with his slime covered hind quarters glistening
in the sun—as if I his deliverer wished to interrupt his meditations—
with out a shriek or fainting—I thought what a healthy indifference
he manifested. Is not this the broad earth still—he said.

Aug 24th

Mollugo verticillata carpet weed flat whorl-leaved weed in gardens with small white flowers— Portulaca oleracea Purslane with its yellow blossoms—Chelone Glabra I have seen the small mulleins as big as a ninepence in the fields for a day or two.

The weather is warmer again after a week or more of cool days— There is greater average warmth—but not such intolerable heat as in July— The nights especially are more equalbly warm now even when the day has been comparatively rather cool. There are few days now—fewer than in July, when you cannot lie at your length on the grass— You have now forgotten winter & its fashions & have learned new summer fashions. Your life may be out of doors now mainly.

Rattle snake grass is ripe. The pods of the Asclepias pulchra stand up pointedly like slender vases—on a salver—Those of the Asclepias Syriaca hang down. The interregnum in the blossoming of flowers being *well* over Many small flowers blossom now in the low grounds having just reached their sumner— It is now dry enough—& they feel the heat their tenderness required. The Autumnal flowers Golden rods—Asters & Johnswort though they have made demonstrations have not yet commenced to reign. The tansy is already getting stale it is perhaps the first conspicuous yellow flower that passes from the stage

In Hubbard's swamp where the blue berries—Dangle berries & especially the Pyrus or chokeberries were so abundant last summer— there is now perhaps not one (unless a blueberry) to to be found. Where the choke-berries held on all last winter—the black & the red.

The Comm skull-cap Scutellaria Galericulata quite a handsome & middling large blue flower— Lobelia pallida still— Pointed Cleavers or Clivers Galium asprellum.

Is that the naked Viburnum so common with its white—red—then purple berries?—in Hubbards mead.

Did I find the Dwarf Tree Primrose in Hubbards' meadow today? Stachys aspera Hedge Nettle or Woundwort a rather handsome purplish flower—

The Capsules of the Iris versicolor or blue flag are now ready for humming. Elder berries are ripe

Monday Aug 25th 1851

What the little regular rounded light blue flower in Heywood
Brook which I make Class V—ord 1

Also the small purplish flower growing on the mud in Hubbard's
meadow perchance C. XIV with one pistil.

What the bean vine in the garden   Class 8 ord 1

I do not find the name of the large white polygonum of the river
Was it the filiform ranunculus which I found on Hubbards shore?

Hypericum Virginicum mixed yellow & purple

The black rough fruit of the skunk-Cabbage—though green within
—barely rising above the level of the ground—   You see where it has
been cut in two by the mowers in the meadows.

Polygonum Amphibium red—in river—   Lysimachia
Hybrida still. Checquer berry in bloom $\bigcup$ —blue-eyed grass still.

Rhus Copallinum Mt or Dwarf sumach   I now know all of the
Rhus genus in Bigelow—we have all but the Staghorn in Concord.
What a miserable name has the Gratiola aurea hedge hyssop? Whose
hedge does it grow by pray in this part of the world.

Aug 26th

A cool and even piercing wind blows today—making all shrubs to
bow & trees to wave—such as we could not have had in July—   I
speak not of its coolness but its strength & steadiness.

The wind & the coldness increased as the day advanced—and
finally the wind went down with the sun. I was compelled to put
on an extra coat for my walk. The ground is strewn with wind falls
and much fruit will consequently be lost—

The wind roars amid the pines like the surf. You can hardly hear
the crickets for the din—or the cars—   I think the last must be
considerably delayed when their course is against it. Indeed it is
difficult to enjoy a quiet Thought. You sympathise too much with
the commotion and restlessness of the elements. Such a blowing
stirring bustling day—what does it mean? All light things decamp—
straws and loose leaves change their places. Such a blowing day is no
doubt indispensable in the economy of nature. The whole country is
a sea shore & the wind is the surf that breaks on it. It shows the
white & silvery under sides of the leaves. Do plants & trees need to
be thus tried & twisted? Is it a first intimation to the sap to cease to
ascend—to thicken their stems?—   The Gerardia Pedicularis bushy
Gerardia—I find on the White pond road

I perceive that some farmers are cutting turf now—   They require

the driest season of the year. There is something agreeable to my
thoughts in thus burning a part of the earth—the stock of fuel is so
inexhaustible— Nature looks not mean & niggardly. Is not he a rich
man who owns a peat meadow? It is to enjoy the luxury of wealth.
It must be a luxury to sit around the fire in winter days & nights &
burn these dry slices of the meadow which contain roots of all herbs
you dry & burn the very earth itself.— It is a fact kindred with salt
licks The meadow is strown with the fresh bars—bearing the marks
of the fork & the turf cutter is wheeling them out with his barrow.
To sit & see the world aglow & try to imagine how it would seem
to have it so destroyed.

Aug 27th

I see the volumes of smoke—not quite the blaze from burning
brush as I suppose far in the western horizon. I believe it is at this
season of the year chiefly that you see this sight. It is always a
question with some whether it is not a fire in the woods or some
building. It is an interesting feature in the scenery—at this season.
The farmers simple enterprises. The vervain which I examined by
the R.R. the other day.— has still ¼ inch to the top of its spikes
Hawkweed Groundsel, Senecio Hieracifolius (fireweed)— Rubrus
Sempervirens Evergreen Raspberry the small low blackberry is now
in fruit. The medeola Virginica Cucumber root the whorl leaved
plant is now in green fruit— Polygala cruciata Cross leaved Polygala
in the mead. between Trillium Woods & RR.. This is rare & new
to me. It has a very sweet but as it were intermittent fragrance
as of checker berry & Mayflowers combined. The handsome calyx
leaves—

Aug 28th

The pretty little blue flower in the Heywood Brook—Class V
ord 1 corolla about ⅛ of inch in diam—with 5 rounded segments. Stamens & pistils shorter than corolla. Calyx with 5 acute
segments & acute sinuses. Leaves not opposite lanceolate spatulate,
blunt somewhat hairy on upper side with a mid-rib only sessile—
flowers in a loose raceme on rather long pedicels Whole plant
decumbent curving upward. Wet ground. Said to be like the Forget-
me-not.

Raphanus Raphanistrum or Wild Radish. in meadows.

I find 3 or 4 ordinary laborors to day putting up the necessary
outdoor fixtures for a magnetic telegraph from Boston to Burlington.
They carry along a basket full of simple implements—like travelling
tinkers—and with a little rude soddering & twisting and straightening

of wires the work is done. It is a work which seems to admit of the greatest latitude of ignorance and bungling—and as if you might set your hired man with the poorest head and hands to building a magnetic telegraph. All great inventions stoop too low to succeed—for the understanding is but little above the feet—they preserve so low a tone—they are simple almost to coarseness & commonplaceness. (Somebody had told them what he wanted and sent them forth with a coil of wire to make a magnetic Telegraph—

It seems not so wonderful an invention as a common cart or a plow.

Evening—

A new moon visible in the east—how unexpectedly it always appears! You easily lose it in the sky. The whipporwill sings—but not so commonly as in spring. The bats are active. The poet is a man who lives at last by watching his moods. An old poet comes at last to watch his moods as narrowly as a cat does a mouse.

I omit the unusual—the hurricanes & earthquakes & describe the common. This has the greatest charm—and is the true theme of poetry. You may have the extraordinary, if you will let me have the ordinary. Give me the obscure life—the cottage of the poor & humble—the work days of the world—the barren fields—the smallest share of all things but poetic perception. Give me but the eyes to see the things which you possess.

Aug 29th

Though it is early—my neighbor's hens have strayed far into the fog toward the river. I find a wasp in my window which already appears to be taking refuge from winter & unspeakable fate.

Those who first built it coming from old France with the memory & tradition of feudal days & customs weighing on them were unquestionably behind their age—and those who now inhabit it & repair it are behind their anscestors— It is as if the inhabitants of Boston should go down to Fort Independence—or the inhabitants of New York should go over to Castle William to live. I rubbed my eyes to be sure that I was in the 19th century. That would be a good place to read Froissart's Chronicles I thought.

It is a specimen of the old world in the new. It is such a reminiscence of the middle ages as one of Scott's Novels. Those old Chevaliers thought they could transplant the feudal system to America. It has been set out but it has not thriven.

Might I not walk a little further—till I hear new crickets Till their creak has acquired some novelty—as if they were a new species —whose habitat I had reached.

The Air is filled with mist—yet a transparent mist—a principle in it you might call *flavor* which ripens fruits. This haziness seems to confine & concentrate the sun light as if you lived in a halo. It is august

A flock of 44 young turkies with their old half a mile from a house on Conantum by the river— The old faintly gobbling the half grown young peeping. Turkey-men!

Gerardia Glauca Tall G. one flower only left—also Corydalis Glauca—

Sat Aug 30th

I perceive in the Norway Cinquefoil—Potentilla Norvegica—now nearly out of blossom that the alternate 5 leaves of the calyx are closing over the seeds to protect them. This evidence of forethought, this simple *reflection* in a double sense of the term, in this flower is affecting to me—as if it said to me Even I am doing my appointed work in this world faithfully. Not even do I however obscurely I may grow among the other loftier & more famous plants—shirk my work—humble weed as I am— Not even when I have blossomed and have lost my painted petals & am preparing to die down to its root do I forget to fall with my arms around my babe—that the infant may be found preserved in the arms of the frozen mother. That thus all the Norway Cinqefoils in the world had curled back their calyx leaves their warm Cloaks, when now their flowering season has past—over their progeny—from the time they were created. There is one door closed, of the closing Year— Nature ordered this bending back of the calyx leaves—& every year since this plant was created her order has been faithfully obeyed.— & this plant acts not an obscure—but essential part in the revolution of the seasons. I am not ashamed to be contemporary with the Norway Cinquefoil May I perform my part as well!— There is so much done toward closing up the years accounts.— It is as good as if I saw the great globe go round. It is as if I saw the Janus doors of the year closing. The fall of each humblest flower marks the annual period of some phase of human life.. experience. I can be said to note the flowers fall only when I see in it the symbol of my own change.— When I experience this then the flower appears to me.

Drosera rotundifolia in Moores new field ditch— The viola pedata & the houstonia now— What is the peculiarity of these flowers that *they* blossom again. Is it merely because they blossomed so early in the spring—& now are ready for a new spring? They impress me as so much more native or naturalized here.

We love to see nature fruitful in whatever kind— It assures us of

her vigor and that she may equally bring forth the fruits which we
prize. I love to see the acorns plenty—even on the shrub oaks—aye
and the night shade berries—. I love to see the potatoe balls
numerous & large as I go through a field,—the plant thus as it were
bearing fruit at both ends—saying ever & anon—not only these tubers
I offer you for the present—but if you will have new varieties (if
these do not satisfy you—) plant these seeds.— What abundance what
luxuriance what bounty— The potatoe balls which are worthless to
the farmer—combine to make the general impression of the years
fruitfulness. It is as cheering to me as the rapid increase of the
population of New York.

Aug 31st 51

Proserpinaca Palustris Spear leaved Proserpinaca. Mermaid weed—
(This in Hubbards Grove on my way to Conantum)— A hornets?
nest in a rather tall huckleberry bush—the stem projecting through
it—the leaves spreding over it—how these fellows avail themselves
of the vegetables! They kept arriving the great fellows but I never
saw whence they came but only heard the buzz just at the entrance.— (with whitish abdomens.) at length after I had stood
before the nest 5 minutes during which time they had taken no
notice of me—two seemed to be consulting at the entrance &
then one made a threatening dash at me and returned to the nest. I
took the hint & retired. They spoke as plainly as man could have
done.

I see that the farmers have begun to top their corn.

examined my old friend the Green locust? shrilling on an alder
leaf.

What relation does the fall dandelion bear to the spring
dandelion. There is a rank scent of tansy now on some roads—
disagreeable to many people—from being associated in their minds
with funerals where it is sometimes put into the Coffin & about the
corpse. I have not observed much St John's wort yet.

Galium triflorum 3 flowered cleavers in Conant's Spring swamp—
also fever-bush there now budded for next year— Tobacco pipe
Monotropa uniflora in Spring swamp path— I came out of the thick
dark swampy wood as from night into day—having forgotten the
daylight— I was surprised to see how bright it was. I had light
enough—methought—and here was an afternoon sun illumining all
the landscape. It was a surprise to me to see how much brighter an
ordinary afternoon is than the light which penetrates a thick
wood..

One of these drooping clusters of potatoe balls would be as good a symbol or emblem of the years fertility as anything—better surely than a bunch of grapes. Fruit of the strong soil—containing potash? The vintage is come—the olive is ripe

> I come to pluck your berries harsh & crude;
> And with forc'd fingers rude,
> Shatter your leaves before the mellowing year;

Why not for my coat of arms for device a drooping cluster of potatoe balls.— in a *potatoe* field.

What right has a New England poet to sing of wine who never saw a vineyard—who obtains his liquor from the grocers who would not dare if he could tell him what it is composed of A Yankee singing in praise of wine!—it is not sour grapes in this case, it is sweet grapes—the more inaccessible they are the sweeter they are. It seemed to me that the year had nothing so much to brag of as these potatoe balls Do they not concern New Englanders a thousand times more than all her grapes? In Moores new field they grow—cultivated with the bog hoe manured with ashes—& Sphagnum how they take to the virgin soil. Shannon tells me that he took a piece of bog land of Augustus Haden—cleared—turned up the stumps & roots & burned it over making a coat of ashes 6 inches deep then planted potatoes. He never put a hoe to it till he went to dig them—then between 8 o clock A M & 5 PM he and another man dug and housed 75 bushels apieece!!

Cohush—now in fruit—ivory white berries lipped *now* with black on stout red pedicels—Actaea alba. Collinsonia Canadensis Horseweed. I had discovered this singular flower there new to me And having a botany by me looked it out— What a surprise & disappointment—what an insult & impertinence—to my curiosity & expectation to have given me the name "horseweed."

Cohush Swamp is about 20 rods by 3 or 4— Among rarer plants it contains The basswood—the black (as well as white) ash—the fever bush—the Cohush—the—Collinsonia—not to mention—Sassafras—Poison Sumach ivy—agrimony—Arum Triphyllum—(Sweet Viburnum? in hedges near by) Ground nut—touch me not as high as your head & Eupatorium purpureum 8 ft $^{8}/_{12}$ high—with a large convex corymb — (hemispherical) of many stories 14 inches wide—width of plant from tip of leaf to tip of leaf 2 feet—diameter of stalk 1 inch at ground—leaves 7 in a whorl.— (Some) rare rare plants seem to love certain

localities, as if the original Conant had been a botanist & endeavored
to form an arboretum. A natural aboretum?

The handsome sweet viburnum berries now red on one cheek.

It was the filiform Crowfoot Ranunculus filiformis that I saw by
the river side the other day & today. The flowers of the nettle
leaved vervain are now near the ends of the spikes like the blue.

Sium Latifolium Water parsnep Tupelo cliff. also Conium
Maculatum.

Utricularia inflata whorled bladderwort floating on the water at
same place

Gentiana Saponaria budded

Gerardia flava at Conants Grove.

Half an hour before sunset I was at Tupelo Cliff—when looking
up from my botanizing (I had been examining the Ranunculus
filiformis—the Conium Maculatum—the sium latifolium—& the obtuse
galium on the muddy shore—) I saw the seal of evening on the river.
There was a quiet beauty in the landscape at that hour which my
senses were prepared to appreciate.

The sun going down on the west side that hand being already in
shadow for the most part—but his rays lighting up the water and the
willows & pads even more than before. His rays then fell at right
angles on their stems. I sitting on the old brown geologic rocks their
feet submerged and covered with weedy moss (Utricularia roots?)
sometimes their tops are submerged. The cardinal flowers standing
by me. The trivialness of the day is past— The greater stillness—the
serenity of the air—its coolness & transparency the mistiness being
condensed—are favorable to thought. (The pensive eve.) The
coolness of evening comes to condense the haze of noon & make
the air transparent and the outline of objects firm & distinct. &
chaste (chaste eve) Even as I am made more vigorous by my bath—
am more *continent* of thought After bathing even at noon day a man
realizes a morning or evening life. When I have walked all day in
vain under the torrid sun—and the world has been all trivial as well
field & wood as highway—then at eve the sun goes down westward—
& the wind goes down with it—& the dews begin to purify the air
& make it transparent and the lakes & rivers acquire a glassy stillness
—reflecting the skies—the reflex of the day— I too am at the top of
my condition for perceiving beauty— Thus long after feeding the
diviner faculties begin to be fed—to feel their oats their nutriment—
and are not oppressed by the belly's load. It is abstinence from
loading the belly anew until the brain and divine faculties have felt

their vigor—not till some hours does the my food invigorate my
brain—ascendeth into the brain— We practice at this hour an
involuntary abstinence— We are comparative chaste & temperate as
Eve herself—the nutriment is just reaching the brain. Every sound is
music now. The grating of some distant boat which a man is
launching on the rocky bottom—though here is no man nor
inhabited house—nor even cultivated field in sight—this is heard with
such distinctness that I listen with pleasure as if it was music. The
attractive point is that line where the water meets the land.— not
distinct but known to exist. The willows are not the less interesting
because of their nakedness below. How rich like what we love to
read of South American primitive forests is the scenery of this river—
What luxuriance of weeds— What depth of mud along its sides!
These old antehistoric—geologic—antediluvian rocks—which only
primitive wading birds are worthy to tread— The seasons which we
seem to *live* in anticipation of is arrived—the water indeed reflects
heaven because my mind does—such is its own serenity—its
transparency & stillness.

   With what sober joy I stand to let the water drip from me & feel
my fresh vigor—who have been bathing in the same tub which the
musk rat uses—— Such a medicated bath as only nature furnishes. A
fish leaps & the dimple he makes is observed now. How ample &
generous was nature My inheritance is not narrow Here is no
other this evening— Those resorts which I most love & frequent
numerous & vast as they are,—are as it were given up to me.—. as
much as if I were an autocrat or owner of the world—and by my
edicts excluded men from my territories.— Perchance there is some
advantage here not enjoyed in older countries. There are said to be
2000 inhabitants in Concord & yet I find such ample space & verge
—even—miles of walking every day in which I do not meet nor see a
human being—and often not very recent traces of them— So much
of man as their is in your mind there will be in your eye—
Methinks that for a great part of the time as much as it is possible I
walk as one possessing the advantages of human Culture—fresh from
society of men—but turned loose into the woods the only man in
nature—walking & meditating to a great extent as if man & his
customs & institutions was not.— The catbird or the jay is sure of
the whole of your ear now—each noise is like a stain on pure glass.
The rivers now—these great blue subterranean heavens reflecting the
supernal skies & red-tinted clouds.

   A fly or (gnat)? will often buzz round you & persecute you like

an imp. How much of implike pestering character they express! (I
hear a boy driving home his cows) What unanimity between the
water & the sky—one only a little denser element than the other.
The grossest part of heaven— Think of a mirror on so large a scale!
Standing on distant hills you see the heavens reflected the evening
sky in some low lake or river in the valley—as perfectly as in any
mirror they could be— Does it not prove how intimate heaven is
with earth?

We commonly sacrifice to supper this *serene*—& sacred hour—our
customs turn the hour of *sunset* to a trivial time as at the meeting of
two roads—one coming from the noon the other leading to the night
— It might be if our repasts were taken out of doors in view of the
sunset & the rising stars If there were two persons whose pulses beat
together—if men cared for the κοσμος or *beauty* of the world. If
men were *social* in a high & rare sence If they associated on high
levels. If we took in with our tea a draught of the transparent dew
freighted evening air—if with our bread & butter we took a slice of
the red western sky— If the smoking—steaming urn was the vapor
on a thousand Lakes & rivers & meads—

The air of the valleys at this hour is the distilled essence of all
those fragrances which during the day have been filling and have
been dispersed in the atmosphere the fine fragrances perchance
which have floated in the upper atmospheres—has settled to these
low vales!

I talked of buying Conantum once—but for want of money—we
did not come to terms— But I have farmed it in my own fashion
every year since.

I have no objection to giving the name of some Naturalists—men
of flowers to plants—if by their lives they have identified themselves
with them. There may be a few Kalmias— But it must be done very
sparingly or rather discriminatingly— And no man's name be used
who has not been such a lover of flowers—that the flowers
themselves may be supposed thus to reciprocate his love.

Sep. 1st

Mikania scandens with its purplish white flowers now covering
the button bushes and willows by the side of the stream.

Bidens Chrysanthemoides Large flowered Bidens edge of River—
Various colorored Polygonums standing high among the bushes &
weeds by river side—white & reddish—& red.

Is not disease the rule of existence? There is not a lily pad floating
on the river but has has been riddled by insects— Almost every

shrub and tree has its gall—oftentimes esteemed its chief ornament—
and hardly to be distinguished from the fruit. If misery loves
company—misery has company enough— Now at midsummer find
me a perfect leaf—or fruit.

The fruit of the trilliums is very handsome I found some a
month ago a singular *red*—angular cased pulp drooping with the old
anthers surrounding it ¾ inch in diam. —and now there is
another kind a dense crowded cluster of many ovoid berries
—turning from green to scarlet or bright brick color— Then there is
the mottled fruit of the clustered Solomons seal—and also the
greenish with blue meat fruit of the Convallaria Multiflora dangling
from the axils of the leaves

I suspect that the common wild bean vine of the gardens must be
the Polygonum Convolvulus or Black bindweed. though I do not
find the 3 styles.

Found a Utricularia on the North branch without leaves but
slight sheathes 7 or 8 flowered upright 6 or 8 inches high where the
water had gone down rooted yellow.— with racemed *pedicels about
½ inch* long—no bladders nor inflated leaves.

Then there is the small floating marry gold or sun flower of the
river—corolla spreading but little ⅞ inch—petals 8 ribbed yellow
obovate lanceolate blunt rounded ⅝ inch long tubular at base—stand
at ang of 45° / Calyx double outer 5 leaves green & spreading
inner 8 leaves close to petals & yellowish at tips. Calyx half as long
as corolla—florets more than half as long as corolla—5 stamens & one
pistil in a yellow cup with 5 lanceolate segments— Compound
flower—though stamens are not *decidedly* united by their anthers.
Pistil rising above stamens divided in two at top & curling over each
way, Stem 3 to 5 feet long—hollow & cellular—⅛ to ⅒ inch
diameter upper or emersed 2 or 3 sets of leaves crosswise opposite
lanceolate broad at base—fringe serrate—clasping sub-connate The
rest immersed opposite—capillaceo —multipartite forming a dark
cylindrical mass in shallow parts of rivers—covered with small fish ova
or perchance bladders?

Sep. 2nd 51

The dense fog came into my chamber early this morning
freighted with light & woke me. It was no doubt lighter at that
hour than if there had been no fog.

Not till after several months does an infant find its hands— And
it may be seen looking at them with astonishment holding them up
to the light—and so also it finds its toes. How many faculties there

are which we have never found! Some men methinks have found only their hands & feet—at least I have seen some who appeared never to have found their heads but used them only instinctively—as the negro who buts with his—or the water carrier—who makes a pack horse of his. They have but partially found their heads.

We cannot write well or truly but what we write with gusto. The body the senses must conspire with the spirit— Expression is the act of the whole man. that our speech may be vascular— The intellect is powerless to express thought without the aid of the heart & liver and of every member— Often I feel that my head stands out too dry—when it should be immersed. A writer a man writing is the scribe of all nature—he is the corn & the grass & the atmosphere writing. It is always essential that we love to do what we are doing—do it with a heart. The maturity of the mind however may perchance consist consist with a certain dryness.

There are flowers of thought & there are leaves of thought—most of our thoughts are merely leaves—to which the thread of thought is the stem.

What affinity is it brings the goldfinch to the sunflower—both yellow—to pick its seeds. Whatever things I perceive with my entire man—those let me record—and it will be poetry. The sounds which I hear with the consent & coincidence of all my senses these are significant & musical— At least they only are heard.

In a day or two the first message will be conveyed or transmitted over the magnetic telegraph through this town—as a thought traverses space—and no citizen of the town shall be aware of it. The atmosphere is full of telegraphs equally unobserved. We are not confined to Morses or Houses or Bain's line—

Raise some sun flowers to attract the goldfinches to feed them as well as your hens. What a broad & loaded bounteously filled platter of food is presented this bon vivant!

Here is one of those thick fogs which last well into the day. While the farmer is concerned about the crops which his fields bear, I will be concerned about the fertility of my human farm— I will watch the winds & the rains as they affect the crop of thought.— the crop of crops ripe thoughts—which glow & rustle—& fill the air with fragrance—for centuries— Is it a drought—how long since we had a rain—what is the state of the springs? Are the low springs high?

I now begin to pluck wild apples—

The difference is not great between some fruits in which the worm is always present and those gall fruits which were produced by the insect.

Old Cato says well—*patrem familias vendacem, non emacem esse opportet*— These Latin terminations express better than any English that I know the greediness as it were & tenacity of purpose with which the husbandman & householder is required to be a seller & not a buyer   with mastiff like tenacity these *lipped* words which like the lips of moose & browsing creatures gather in the herbage & twigs with a certain greed. This termination *cious* adds force to a word like the lips of browsing creatures which greedily collect what the jaw holds——as in the word tenacious the first half represents the jaw which holds the last the lips which collect— It can only be pronounced by a certain opening & protruding of the lips so avaricious— These words express the sense of their simple roots with the addition as it were of a certain lip greediness. hence capacious & capacity—emacity When these expressive words are used the hearer gets something to chew upon. To be a seller with the tenacity & firmness & of the jaws which hold & the greediness of the lips which collect. The audacious man not only dares—but he greedily collects more danger to dare. The avaricious man not only desires & satisfies his desire—but he collects ever new browse in anticipation of his ever springing desires—what is luscious is especially tasted by the lips.

The mastiff mouthed are tenacious. To be a seller with mastiff-mouthed tenacity of purpose—with moose-lipped greediness— To be edacious & voracius is to be not nibbling & swallowing merely—but eating & swallowing while the lips are greedily collecting more food.

There is a reptile in the throat of the greedy man always thirsting & famishing— It is not his own natural hunger & thirst which he satisfies.

The more we know about the ancients the more we find that they were like the moderns. When I read Mar. Cato De Re Rustica a small treatise or Farmer's Manual of those days fresh from the field of Roman life—all reeking with & redolent of the life of those days—containing more indirect history than any of the histories of Rome of direct—all of that time but that time— *Here* is a simple direct pertinent word addressed to the Romans— And where are *the Romans*? Rome and the Romans are commonly a piece of Rhetoric — As if New England had disappeared poetically and there were left —Buel's Farmers Companion or the letters of Solon Robinson—or a volume of extracts from the New England Farmer— Though the

Romans are no more but a fable and an ornament of Rhetoric—We
have here their New England Farmer the very manual those Roman
farmers read—speaking as if they were to hear—it—its voice not
silenced As if Rome were still the mistress of the world— As fresh
as a dripping dishcloth from a Roman kitchen.— As when you
overhaul the correspondence of a man who died 50 years ago—with
like surprise—& feelings you overhaul the manuscripts of of the
Roman Nation— There exist certain old papers manuscripts—either
the originals or faithful & trustworthy old copies of the originals
which were left by the Roman people. They have gone their way—
but these old papers of all sorts remain. Among them there are some
farm journals—or Farm books—just such a collection of Diary &
memorandum—as when the cow-calved—& the dimensions with a
plan of the barn—& How much paid to Joe Farrar for work done on
the farm &c &c as you might find in an old farmers pocketbook
today.

Indeed the farmer's was pretty much the same routine then as
now.

Cato says "Sterquilinium magnum stude ut habeas. Stercus sedulo
conserva, cum exportabis purgato et comminuito. Per autumnum
evehito."— Study to have a great dungheap. Carefully preserve your
dung, when you carry it out make clean work of it and break it up
fine. Carry it out during the autumn.— Just such directions as you
find in the Farmer's almanac today. It reminds me of what I see
going on in our fields every autumn. As if the Farmers of Concord
were obeying Cato's directions. And Cato but repeated the maxims
of a remote antiquity. Nothing can be more homely & suggestive of
the every day life of the Roman agriculturalists—thus supplying the
very deficiencies in what is commonly called Roman history—i.e.
revealing to us the actual life of the Romans——the how they got
their living and what they did from day to day.

They planted rapa raphanos milium and panicum in low foggy
land "ager nebulosus"

I see the farmer now i.e. I shall in Autumn on every side carting
out his manure & sedulously making his compost heap—or scattering
it over his grass ground and breaking it up with a mallet—and it
reminds me of Cato's advice.— He died 150 years before Christ.
Before Christianity was heard of this was done. A Roman family
appears to have had a great supply of tubs & kettles.

A fire in the sitting room today— Walk in the afternoon by
Walden Road & RR. to Minn's Place & round it to RR & home.

The first coolness is welcome so serious & fertile of thought. My skin contracts & I become more continent. Carried umbrellas— It mizzling. As in the night now in the rain I smell the fragrance of the woods. The Prunella leaves have turned a delicate claret or lake color—by the road side. I am interested in these revolutions as much as in those of kingdoms— Is there not tragedy enough in the autumn?

Walden seems to be going down at last— The pines are dead and leaning red & half upset about its shore. Thus by its rising once in 25 years perchance it keeps an open shore—as if the ice had heaved them over. Found the succory at Minn's Bridge on R R—& beyond. Query— May not this & the Tree Primrose and other plants be distributed from Boston on the rays of the Railroads—the seeds mixing with the grains & all kinds of dirt & being blown from the passing freight cars?

The feathery tailed fruit of the fertile flowers of the Clematis conspicuous now.

The shorne meadows looked—of a living green as we came home at eve even greener than in spring—the "foenum cordum" the aftermath "sicilimenta de prato" the 2nd mowings of the meadow. this reminds me of—in Cato

Sep. 3d

Why was there never a Poem on the cricket? Its creak seems to me to be one of the most prominent & obvious facts in the world.— & the least heeded. In the report of a man's contemplations I look to see somewhat answering to this sound.

When I sat on Lee's Cliff the other day (aug 29th) I saw a man working with a horse in a field by the river—carting dirt. & the horse & his relation to him struck me as very remarkable. There was the horse a mere animated machine—though his tail was brushing off the flies—his whole existence subordinated to the man's—with no tradition perhaps no instinct in him of independence & freedom—of a time when he was wild & free completely humanized. No compact made with him that he should have the saturday afternoons or the Sundays—or any holidays— His independence never recognized— It being now quite forgotten both by men & by horses that the horse was ever free— For I am not aware that there are any wild horses not descended from tame ones— Assisting that man to pull down that bank & spread it over the meadow— Only keeping off the flies with his tail & stamping & catching a mouthful of grass or leaves from time to time on his own account.— all the rest for man. It seemed hardly worth while that he should be *animated* for this. It was plain that the man was not educating the horse—not trying to develop his nature—but merely getting work out of him. That mass of animated matter seemed more completely the servant of man than any inanimate. For slaves have their holidays—a heaven is conceded to them but to the horse none Now & forever he is mans slave. The more I considered the more the man seemed akin to the horse—only his was the stronger will of the two. for a little further on I saw an Irishman shovelling—who evidently was as much tamed as the horse. He had stipulated that to a certain extent his independence be recognized & yet really he was but little more independent.— I had always instinctively regarded the horse as a free people somewhere. living wild—whatever has not come under the sway of man is wild— In this sense original & independent men are wild—not tamed & broken by society. Now for my part I have such a respect for the horse's nature as would tempt me to let him alone. — not to interfere with him—his walks—his diet—his loves— But by mankind he is treated simply as if he was an engine which must have rest & is sensible of pain. Suppose that every squirrel were made to turn a coffee mill! Suppose that the gazelles were made to draw milk carts?

There he was with his tail cut off because it was in the way or to suit the taste of his owner—his mane trimmed & his feet shod with iron that he might wear longer. What is a horse but an animal that has lost its liberty—what is it but a system of Slavery—& do you not thus by *insensible* & unimportant degrees come to human slavery?— has lost its liberty—& has man got any more liberty himself for having robbed the horse—or has he lost just as much of his own—& become more like the horse he has robbed— Is not the other end of the bridle in this case too coiled round his own neck? There he stood with his oblong square figure (his tailed being cut off) seen against the water—. brushing off the flies with his tail & stamping, braced back while the man was filling the cart.

It is a very remarkable and significant fact that though no man is quite well or healthy—yet every one believes practically that health is the rule & disease the exception— And each invalid is wont to think himself in a minority— And to postpone some what of endeavor to another state of existence— But it may be some encouragement to men to know that in this respect they stand on the same platform—that disease is in fact the *rule* of our terrestrial life —and the prophecy of a *celestial* life. Where is the coward who despairs because he is sick—? Every one may live either the life of

Achilles or of Nestor. Seen in this light our life with all its diseases
will look healthy—and in one sense the more healthy as it is the
more diseased— Disease is not the accident of the individual nor
even of the generation but of life itself. In some form & to some
degree or other it is one of the permanent conditions of life— It is
nevertheless a cheering fact that men affirm health unanimously &
esteem themselves miserable failures. Here was no blunder. They
gave us life on exactly these conditions—and methinks we shall live it
with more heart when we perceive clearly that these are the terms
on which we have it. Life is a warfare a struggle—and the diseaseses
of the body answer to the troubles and defeats of the spirit. Man
begins by quarrelling with the animal in him & the result is
immediate dis-ease. In proportion as the spirit is the more ambitious
and persevering—the more obstacles it will meet with. It is as a seer
that man asserts his disease to be exceptional.

2 PM To Hubbards swimming place & Grove in rain—

As I went under the new telegraph wire I heard it vibrating like a
harp high over head.— it was as the sound of a far off glorious life a
supernal life which came down to us.— and vibrated the lattice
work of this life of ours.

The melons & the apples seem at once to feed my brain.

Here comes a laborer from his dinner to resume his work at
clearing out a ditch not withstanding the rain—for as Cato says—per
ferias potuisse fossas veteres tergeri in the holidays old ditches might
have been cleared out.— This is what the pater familias will see if
the Steward has looked after—

The ivy leaves are turning red— Fall dandelions stand thick in the
meadows.

How much the Roman must have been indebted to his
agriculture dealing with the earth its clods & stubble its dust & mire
— Their farmer consuls were their glory—& they well knew the
farm to be the nursery of soldiers. Read Cato to see what kind of
legs the Romans stood on.

—The leaves of the hardhack are somewhat appressed clothing the
stem and showing their downy under sides like white waving wands.
Is it peculiar to the season or the rain—or the plant.

Walk often in drizzly weather for then the small weeds (especially
if they stand on bare ground—) covered with rain drops like beads—
appear more beautiful than ever. The hypericums for instance. They
are equally beautiful when covered with dew—fresh & adorned
almost spirited away in a robe of dew drops.

Some farmers have begun to thresh & winnow. their oats

Identified spotted spurge Euphorbia Maculata apparently out of blossom— Shepherd's purse & Chickweed—

As for walking the inhabitants of large English towns are confined almost exclusively to their parks & to the high ways—the few foot-paths in their vicinities "are gradually vanishing" says Wilkinson "under the encroachments of the proprietors."

He proposes that the peoples right to them be asserted & defended—& that they be kept in a passable state at the public expense— "This" says he "would be easily done by means of asphalt laid upon a good foundation"!!! So much for walking and the prospects of walking in the neighborhood of English large towns.

Think of a man—he may be a genius of some kind—being confined to a high way & a park for his world to range in— I should die from mere nervousness at the thought of such confinement. I should hesitate before I were born if those terms were revealed to me. Fenced in forever by those green barriers of fields—where gentlemen are seated! Can they be said to be inhabitants of this globe. Will they be content to inhabit heaven thus partially?

Sep. 4th

8 A M. A clear & Pleasant day after the rain. Start for Boons Pond in Stow with C. Every sight & sound was the more interesting for the clear atmosphere. When you are starting away—leaving your more familiar fields for a little adventure like a walk—you look at every object with a travellers or at least with historical eyes—you pause on the first bridge.— where an ordinary walk hardly commences, & begin to observe & moralize like a traveller— It is worthe the while to see your native Village thus sometimes—as if you were a traveller passing through it—commenting on your neighbors as strangers.

We stood thus on woods bridge the first bridge in the capacity of Pilgrims & strangers to its familiarity, giving it one more chance with us—though our townsmen who passed may not have perceived it.

There was a pretty good sized pickerel poised over the sandy bottom close to the shore—& motionless as a shadow— It is wonderful how they resist the slight current of our river. & remain thus stationary for hours. He no doubt saw us plainly on the bridge. In the sunny water—his whole form distinct & his shadow—motionless as the steel trap which does not spring till the fox's foot has touched it.

John Hosmer's dog sprang up, ran out, & growled at us—and in his eye I seemed to see the eye of his master. I have no doubt but that as is the master such in course of time tend to become his herds & flocks as well as dogs— One man's oxen will be clever & solid—anothers mischievous—another's mangy—in each case like their respective owners. No doubt man impresses his own character on the beasts which he tames & employs they are not only humanized—but they acquire his particular human nature. How much oxen are like farmers generally, and cows like farmers' wives! and young steers & heifers like farmers boys & girls! The farmer acts on the ox & the ox reacts on the farmer— They do not meet half way it is true—but they do meet at a distance from the centre of each—proportionate to each ones intellectual power. The farmer is oxlike in his thought in his walk—in his strength, in his trustworthiness—in his taste.

Hosmers man was cutting his millet—& his buckwheat already lay in *red* piles in the field.

The first picture we noticed was where the road turned among the pitch pines & showed the Hadley house with the high wooded hill behind with dew & sun on it—the gracefully winding road path—& a more distant horizon on the right of the house

Just beyond on the left it was pleasant walking where the road was shaded by a high hill—as it can be only in the morning. Even in the morning that additional coolness & early dawn like feeling of a more sacred and earlier season are agreeable.

The lane in front of Tarbel's house which is but little worne & appears to lead no where though it has so wide & all ingulfing an opening—suggested—that such things might be contrived for effect in laying out grounds— (Only those things are sure to have the greatest & best effect, which like this were not contrived for the sake of effect). An opened path which would suggest walking & adventuring on it—the going to some place strange & far away. It would make you think of or imagine distant places & spaces greater than the estate.

It was pleasant looking back just beyond—to see a heavy shadow (made by some high birches) reaching quite across the road. Light & shadow are sufficient contrast & furnish sufficient excitement when we are well.

Now we were passing the vale of Brown & Tarbel —a sunshiney mead pastured by cattle—& sparkling with dew—the sound of crows and swallows heard in the air—and leafy columned elms seen here & there. shining with dew The morning freshness & unworldliness of

that domain! The vale of Tempe and of Arcadey is not farther off—
than are the conscious lives of men from their opportunities— Our
life is as far from answering to its scenery as we are distant from
Tempe & arcadia. That is to say they are far away because we are far
from living natural lives. How absurd it would be to insist on the
vale of Tempe in particular—when we have such vales as we have.

In the Marlborough road in the woods I saw a purple streak like
a stain on the red pine leaves & sand under my feet—which I was
surprised to find was made by a dense mass of purple fleas—
somewhat like snow fleas—a faint purple stain as if some purple dye
had been spilt.

What is that slender pink flower that I find in the Marlborough
road—smaller than a snap Dragon—?

The slender stems of grass which hang over the ruts & horses
path in this little frequented road are so laden with dew that I am
compelled to hold a bush before me to shake it off.

The jays scream on the right & left—& are seen flying further off
as we go by.

We drink in the meadow at 2nd Division Brook—then sit awhile
to watch its yellowish pebbles & the cress? in it & other weeds The
ripples cover its surface like a network & are faithfully reflected on
the bottom. In some places the sun reflected from ripples on a flat
stone looks like a golden comb— The whole brook seems as busy as
a loom—it is a woof & warp of ripples—fairy fingers are throwing the
shuttle at every step—& the long waving brook is the fine product.
The water is wonderfully clear.

To have a hut here & a foot path to the brook. For roads I think
that a poet cannot tolerate more than a foot-path through the fields—
That is wide enough & for purposes of winged poesy suffices. It is
not for the muse to speak of cart-paths. I would fain travel by a
foot-path round the world. I do not ask the railroads of commerce—
not even the cartpaths of the farmer. Pray what other path would
you have than a foot-path?— what else should wear a path? This is
the track of man alone—what more suggestive to the pensive walker?
One walks in a wheel track with less emotion—he is at a greater
distance from man—but this footpath—was perchance worne by the
bare feet of human beings & he cannot but think with interest of
them. The grapes though their leaves are withering and falling are
yet too sour to eat.

In the summer we lay up a stock of experiences for the winter.
as the squirrel of nuts. Something for conversation in winter

evenings. I love to think then of the more distant walks I took in summer.

At the Powder mills—the carbonic acid gass in the road from the building where they were making charcoal made us cough for 20 or 30 rods

Saw some grey squirrels whirling their cylinder by the roadside. How fitted that cylinder to this animals— A squirrel is easily taught to turn his cylinder—might be a saying frequently applicable. And as they turned one leaped over or dodged under another most gracefully & unexpectedly with interweaving motions— It was the circus & menagerie combined   So human they were exhibiting themselves.

In the marlboro Road, I forgot to say we brushed the Polygonum articulatum with its spikes of reddish white flowers a slender & tender plant which loves the middle of dry & sandy not much travelled roads— To find that the very atoms bloom—that there are flowers we rudely brush against which only the microscope reveals!!

It is wise to write on many subjects to try many themes that so you may find the right & inspiring one. Be greedy of occasions to express your thought. Improve the opportunity to draw analogies. There are innumerable avenues to a perception of the truth. Improve the suggestion of each object however humble—however slight & transient the provocation—what else is there to be improved? Who knows what opportunities he may neglect. It is not in vain that the mind turns aside this way or that. Follow its leading —apply it whither it inclines to go. Probe the universe in a myriad points. Be avaricious of these impulses. You must try a thousand themes before you find the right one—as nature makes a thousand acorns to get one oak. He is a wise man & experienced who has taken many views— To whom stones & plants & animals and a myriad objects have each suggested something—contributed something.

And now methinks this wider wood-path is not bad—for it admits of society more conveniently— 2 can walk side by side in it in the ruts aye and one more in the horse track— The Indian walked in single file more solitary—not side by side chatting as he went. The woodman's cart & sled make just the path two walkers want through the wood. by 2nd Div. Brook

Beyond the Powder Mills we watched some fat oxen—elephantine —behemoths—one Rufus Hosmer eyed with the long lash & projecting eye-ball

Now past the Paper mills—by the westernmost road east of the river—the first new ground w'eve reached.

Not only the Prunella turns *lake* but the hypericum virginicum in the hollows by the road side—a handsome blush. A part of the autumnal tints. ripe leaves Leaves acquire red blood. Red colors touch our blood, & excite us as well as cows & geese.

And now we leave the road & go through the woods & swamps toward Boon's pond—crossing two or three roads & by Potter's House in Stow. still on East of river. The fruit of the Pyrola rotundifolia in The damp woods.

Larch trees in stow about the houses. Beyond Potters we struck in to the extensive wooded plain where the ponds are found in Stow—sudbury & Marlboro. Part of it called Boon's Plain— Boon said to have lived on or under Baileys Hill at west of pond— Killed by Indians between Boon & Whites Pond as he was driving his oxcart— The oxen ran off to Marlboro Garrison house. His remains have been searched for. A sandy plain a large level tract. The pond shores handsome enough—but water shallow & muddy looking. Well wooded shores. The maples begin to show red about it— Much fished— Saw a load of sunflowers in a farmers Such is the destiny of this large coarse flower the farmers gather it like pumpkins

Returned by RR.—down the Assabet. A potatoe field yellow with wild radish— But no good place to bathe for 3 miles— Knights new dam has so raised the river. A permanent freshet as it were— The fluviatile trees standing dead for fish hawk perches & the water stagnant for weeds to grow in—

You have only to dam up a running stream—to give it the aspect of a dead stream—& to some degree restore its primitive wild appearance. Tracts made inaccessible to man & at the same time more fertile. Some speculator comes & dams up the stream flow & low the water stands over all meadows making impassible morasses & dead trees for fish hawks a wild stagnant fenny country—the last gasp of wildness before it yields to the civilization of the factory. To cheer the eyes of the factory people & educate them. It makes a little wilderness above the factories.

The woodbine now begins to hang red about the maples & other trees.

As I look back up the stream from the near the bridge (I suppose on the road from Potters' house to stow) I on the RR. I saw the ripples sparkling in the sun—reminding me of the sparkling icy fleets which I saw last winter—and I saw how one corresponded to the other—ice waves to water ones—the erect ice flakes were the waves stereotyped. It was the same sight—the reflection of the sun sparkling from a myriad slanting surfaces at a distance—a rippled water surface or a crystalized frozen one.

Here crossed the river & climbed the high hills on the west side. The walnut trees conformed in their branches to the slope of the hill ⟨sketch⟩ —being just as high from the ground on the upper side as ⟨sketch⟩ on the lower.

On all sides now I see & smell the withering leaves of brush that has been cut to clear the land— I see some blackened tracts which have been burnt over It is remarkable, for it is rare to see the surface of the earth black. And in the horizon I can see the smokes of several fires. The farmers improve this season which is the dryest— their haying being done & their harvest not begun to do these jobs— burn brush—build walls—dig ditches cut turf. This is what I find them doing all over the country now—also topping corn & digging potatoes.

Saw quite a flock for the first time of Gold finches.

On the high round hills in the east & S E of Stow— Perchance they are called the Assabet Hills—rising directly from the river—they are the highest I know rising thus. The rounded hills of Stow. A hill & valley country. Very different from Concord.

It had been a warm day, especially warm to the head. I do not perspire as in the early summer—but am sensible of the ripening heat —more as if by contact. Suddenly the wind changed to east & the atmosphere grew more & more hazy & thick on that side obstructing the view while it was yet clear in the west. I thought it was the result of the cooler air from over the sea—meeting & condensing the vapor in the warm air of the land— That was the haze or thin dry fog—which some call smoke.

It gradually moved westward & affected the prospect on that side somewhat. It was a very thin fog invading all the east. I felt the cool air air from the ocean & it was very refreshing I opened my bosom & my mouth to inhale it. very delicious & invigorating.

We sat on the top of those hills looking down on the new brick ice house.

Where there are several hills near together you can not determine at once which is the highest. whether the one you are on or the next. So when great men are assembled—each yields an uncertain respect to the other—as if it were not certain whose crown rose highest.

Under the nut trees on these hills the the grass is short & green as if grazed close by cattle who had stood there for shade–making a distinct circular yard. Yet as there is no dung–& the form corresponds so closely to the tree–I doubt it that can be the cause.

On hill side N of river above Powder Mills the Pycnanthemum Incanum Mountain Mint (Calamint) & the Lespedeza violacea.

Saw what I thought a small red dog in the road–which cantered along over the bridge this side the Powder mills–& then turned into the woods. This decided me–this turning into the woods–that it was a fox. The dog of the woods The dog that is more at home in the woods than in the roads & fields. I do not often see a dog turning into the woods.

Some large white? oak acorns this side the last named bridge. A few oaks stand in the pastures still great ornaments. I do not see any young ones springing up to supply their places. Will there be any a hundred years hence. These are the remnants of the primitive wood methinks. We are a young people & have not learned by experience the consequence of cutting off the forest. One day they will be planted methinks. & nature reinstated to some extent.

I love to see the yellow knots & their lengthened stain on the dry unpainted Pitch-pine boards on barns & other buildings The Dugan house for instance– The indestructible yellow fat–it fats my eyes to see it–worthy for art to imitate.– telling of branches in the forest once.

Sep 5th No doubt like plants we are fed through the atmosphere & the varying atmospheres of various seasons of the year feed us variously. How often we are sensible of being thus fed & invigorated! And all nature contributes to this aerial diet its food of finest quality. Methinks that in the fragrance of the fruits I get a finer flavor and in beauty (which is appreciated by sight–the taste & smell of the eye–) a finer still. As Wilkinson says "The physical man himself is the builded aroma of the world. This, then, at least, is the office of the lungs–to drink the atmosphere with the planet dissolved in it."––"what is the import of *change of air*, and how each pair of lungs has a *native air* under some one dome of the sky."

Wilkinson's book to some extent realizes what I have dreamed of a reeturn to the primitive analogical & derivative senses of words– His ability to trace analogies often leads him to a truer word than more remarkable writers have found.– As when in his chapter on the human skin he describes the papillary cutis as "an encampment of small conical tents coextensive with the surface of the body"– The faith he puts in old & current expressions as having sprung from an instinct wiser than science—& safely to be trusted if they can be interpreted.

The man of science discovers no world for the mind of man with all its faculties to inhabit— Wilkinson finds a *home* for the imagination—& it is no longer out cast & homeless. All perception of truth is the detection of an analogy.— we reason from our hands to our head.

It is remarkable that Kalm says in 1748 (being in Philadelphia)— "Coals have not yet been found in Pensylvania; but people pretend to have seen them higher up in the country among the natives. Many people however agree that they are met with in great quantity more to the north, near Cape Breton"

As we grow old we live more coarsely—we relax a little in our disciplines—and cease to obey our finest instincts. We are more careless about our diet & our chastity. But we should be fastidious to the extreme of Sanity. All wisdom is the reward of a discipline conscious or unconscious.

By Moonlight at Potters field toward Bear Garden Hill 8 PM. The Whippoorwills sing.

Cultivate reverence It is as if you were so much more respectable yourself. By the quality of a man's writing—by the elevation of its tone you may measure his self-respect.

How shall a man continue his culture after manhood?

Moonlight on Fair Haven Pond seen from the Cliffs. A sheeny lake in the midst of a boundless forest— The windy surf sounding freshly & wildly in the single pine behind you— The silence of hushed wolves in the wilderness & as you fancy moose looking off from the shore of the lake. The stars of poetry & history—& unexplored nature looking down on the scene. This is my world now with a dull whitish mark curving northward through the forest marking the outlet to the lake. Fair Haven by moonlight lies there like a lake in the Maine Wilderness in the midst of a primitive forest untrodden by man. This light & this hour takes the civilization all out of the landscape— Even in villages dogs bay the moon, in forests like this we listen to hear wolves howl to Cynthia.

Even at this hour in the evening—the crickets chirp the small birds peep—the wind roars in the wood—as if it were just before dawn— The moonlight seems to linger as if it were giving way to the light of coming day.

The landscape seen from the slightest elevation by moonlight—is

seen remotely & flattened as it were into mere light & shade open
field & forest—like the surface of the earrth seen from the top of a
mountain.

How much excited we are how much recruited by a great many
particular fragrances— A field of ripening corn now at night—that
has been topped with the stalks stacked up to dry—an inexpressibly
dry rich sweet ripening scent. I feel as if I were an ear of ripening
corn myself. Is not the whole air then a compound of such odors
undistinguishable? Drying corn stalks in a field what an herb-garden—

Sep 6th

The other afternoon I met Sam. H   walking on the RR.
between the Depot & the back Road. It was something quite novel
to see him there—though the RR there is only a short thoroughfare
to the Public road— It then occured to me that I had never met
Mr. H on the railroad though he walks every day—& moreover that
it would be quite impossible for him to walk on the railroad—such a
formalist as he is—such straight jackets we weave for ourselves— He
could do nothing that was not sanctioned by the longest use of men
—and as men had voted in all their assemblies from the first to travel
on the Public way—he would confine himself to that— It would no
doubt seem to him very improper—not to say undignified to walk on
the railroad—& then is it not forbidden by the Rail-road
corporations? I was sure he could not keep the railroad but was
merely using the thoroughfare here which a thousand pioneers
had prepared for him. I stood to see what he would do. He turned
off the rails directly on to the Back road & pursued his
walk.

A passing train will never meet him on the R R. causeway. How
much of the life of certain men *goes* to sustain—to make respected—
the institutions of society. They are the ones who pay the heaviest
tax. Here are certain valuable institutions which can only be
sustained by a wonderful strain which appears all to come upon
certain spartans who volunteer— Certain men are always to be
found—especially the children of our present institutions—who are
born with an instinct to preserve them— They are in effect
supported by a fund which society possesses for that end—or they
receive a pension & their life *seems* to be a sine-cure—but it is not.
The unwritten laws are the most stringent. They are required to
wear a certain dress. What an array of gentlemen whose sole
employment—& it is no sinecure, is to support their dignity & with
it the dignity of so many indispensable institutions!

The use of many vegetables—wild plants for food which botanists relate—such as Kalm at Cap aux oyes on the St Lawrence—viz the sea plantain—sea-rocket sweet gale &c &c making us feel the poorer at first because we never use them—really advertise us of our superior riches—& show to what extremities men have been driven in times of scarcity— No people that fare as well as we will grub these weeds out of the seashore

2 P M

To Hapgoods in Acton direct returning via Strawberry Hill & Smith's Road—

The ripening grapes begin to fill the air with their fragrance.

The vervain will hardly do for a clock—for I perceive that some later & smaller specimens have not much more than begun to blossom— While most have done. Saw a tall pear tree by the roadside beyond Harris' in front of Hapgoods— Saw the lambkill Kalmia Angustifolia in blossom a few fresh blossoms at *the ends* of the fresh twigs—on strawberry Hill. beautiful bright flowers. Apparently a new spring with it. While seed vessels apparently of this year hung dry below— From Strawberry Hill the first but a very slight glimpse of Nagog Pond by standing upon the wall. That is enough to relate of a hill methinks that its elevation gives you the first sight of some distant lake.

The horizon is remarkably blue with mist this afternoon—looking from this hill over Acton— Successive valleys filled with blue mist appear & divided by darker lines of wooded hills. The shadows of the elms are deepened—as if the whole atmosphere was permeated by floods of ether— Anursnac never looked so well as now seen from this hill The ether gives a velvet softness to the whole landscape— The hills float in it. A blue veil is drawn over the earth.

The elecampane Inula Helenium with its broad leaves wrinkled underneath and the remains of sun-flower-like blossoms in front of Nathan Brooks' Acton & near J. H. Wheeler's.

Prenanthes alba This Gray calls Nabalus alba White lettuce or Rattlesnake root.—

Also I *seem?* to have found Nabalus Fraseri or Lion's foot

Every morning for a week there has been a fog which all disappeared by 7 or 8 oclock.

A large field of Sun flowers for hens now in full bloom at Temples surrounding the house—& now at 6 o clock faceing the east.

The larches in the front yards—both Scotch & American have turned red. Their fall has come.

Sep. 7th

We sometimes experience a mere fulness of life, which does not find any channels to flow into. We are stimulated but to no obvious purpose. I feel myself uncommonly prepared for *some* literary work, but I can select no work. I am prepared not so much for contemplation, as for force-ful expression. I am braced both physically and intellectually. It is not so much the music—as the marching to the music that I feel.

I feel that the juices of the fruits which I have eaten the melons & apples have ascended to my brain—& are stimulating it. They give me a heady force. Now I can write nervously. Carlyle's writing is for the most part of this character.

Miss Martineau's last book is not so bad as the timidity which fears its influence. As if the popularity of this or that book would be so fatal—& man would not still be man in the world. Nothing is so much to be feared as fear— Atheism may be popular with God himself.

What shall we say of these timid folk who carry the principle of thinking nothing & doing nothing and being nothing to such an extreme— As if in the absence of thought that vast yearning of their natures for something to fill the vacuum—made the least traditionary expression & shadow of a thought to be clung to with instinctive tenacity. They atone for their producing nothing by a brutish respect for something. They are as simple as oxen and as guiltless of thought & reflection.— their reflections are reflected from other minds. The creature of institutions—bigoted—& a conservatist——can say nothing hearty. he cannot meet life with life—but only with words. He rebuts you by avoiding you. He is shocked like a woman.

Our extatic states which appear to yield so little fruit, have this value at least—though in the seasons when our genius reigns we may be powerless for expression.— Yet in calmer seasons, when our talent is active, the memory of those rarer moods comes to color our picture & is the permanent paint pot as it were into which we dip our brush

Thus no life or experience goes unreported at last—but if it be not solid gold it is gold-leaf which gilds the furniture of the mind. It is an experience of infinite beauty—on which we unfailingly draw. Which enables us to exaggerate ever truly. Our moments of inspiration are not lost though we have no particular poems to show for them. For those experiences have left an indelible impression, and we are ever and anon reminded of them. Their truth subsides & in cooler moments we can use them as paint to gild & adorn our prose. When I despair to sing them I will remember that they will furnish me with paint with which to adorn & preserve the works of talent one day. They are like a pot of pure ether.

They lend the writer when the moment comes a certain superfluity of wealth—making his expression to overrun & float itself. It is the difference between our river now parched & dried up exposing its unsightly & weedy bottom—& the same when in the spring it covers all the meads with a chain of placid lakes, reflecting the forests & the skies.

We are receiving our portion of the Infinite. The *Art of life!* Was there ever anything memorable written upon it? By what disciplines to secure the most life—with what care to watch our thoughts. To observe not what transpires, in the street—but in the mind. & heart of me! I do not remember any page which will tell me how to spend this afternoon. I do not so much wish to know how to economize time—as how to spend it—by what means to grow rich. That the day may not have—been in vain.

What if one moon has come & gone with its world of poetry—its weird teachings—its oracular suggestions— So divine a creature—freighted with hints for me, and I not use her. One moon gone by unnoticed!!

Suppose you attend to the hints to the suggestions which the moon makes for one month—commonly in vain—will they not be very diffirent from any thing in literature or religion or philosophy. The scenery, when it is truly seen reacts on the life of the seer. How to live— How to get the most life! as if you were to teach the young hunter how to entrap his game. How to extract its honey from the flower of the world. That is my every day business. I am as busy as a bee about it. I ramble over all fields on that errand and am never so happy as when I feel myself heavy with honey & wax. I am like a bee searching the livelong day for the sweets of nature. Do I not impregnate & intermix the flowers produce rare & finer varieties by transfering my eyes from one to another? I do as naturally & as joyfully with my own humming music—seek honey all the day. With what honied thought any experience yields me I take a bee line to my cell. It is with flowers I would deal. Where is the flower there is the honey—which is perchance the nectareous portion

of the fruit—there is to be the fruit—& no doubt flowers are thus
colored & painted—to attract & guide the bee. So by the dawning or
radiance of beauty are we advertised where is the honey & the fruit
of thought of discourse & of action— We are first attracted by the
beauty of the flower, before we discover the honey which is a
foretaste of the future fruit. Did not the young Achilles (?) spend his
youth learning how to hunt? The art of spending a day. If it is
possible that we may be addressed—it behoves us to be attentive. If
by watching all day & all night—I may detect some trace of the
Ineffable—then will it not be worth the while to watch? Watch &
pray without ceasing—but not necessary in sadness—be of good cheer.
Those Jews were too sad: to another people a still deeper revelation
may suggest only joy. Dont I know what gladness is? Is it but the
reflex of sadness, its back side? In the Hebrew gladness I hear but
too distinctly still the sound of sadness retreating. Give me a gladness
which has never given place to sadness.

I am convinced that men are not well employed—that this is not
the way to spend a day. If by patience, if by watching I can secure
one new ray of light—can feel myself elevated for an instant upon
Pisgah—the world which was dead prose to me become living &
divine—shall I not watch ever—shall I not be a watchman henceforth?
— If by watching a whole year on the citys walls I may obtain a
communication from heaven, shall I not do well to shut up my shop
& turn a watchman? Can a youth—a man—do more wisely—than to
go where his life is to found? As if I had suffered that to be rumor—
which may be verified. We are surrounded by a rich & fertile
mystery— May we not probe it—pry into it—employ ourselves about
it—a little? To devote your life to the discovery of the divinity in
Nature or to the eating of oysters would they not be attended with
very different results?

I cannot *easily* buy a blank book to write thoughts in, they are all
ruled for dollars & cents.

If the wine which will nourish me grows on the surface of the
moon—I will do the best I can to go to the moon for it.

The discoveries which we make abroad are special and particular—
those which we make at home are general & significant. The further
off the nearer the surface. The nearer home the deeper. Go in search
of the springs of life—& you will get exercise enough. Think of a
man's swinging dumb bells for his health—when those springs are
bubbling in far off pastures unsought by him! The seeming necessity
of swinging dumbells proves that he has lost his way.

To watch for describe all the divine feautures which I detect in Nature.

My profession is to be always on the alert to find God in nature—to know his lurking places. To attend all the oratorios—the operas in nature.

The mind may perchance be persuaded to act—to energize—by the action and energy of the body. Any kind of liquid will fetch the pump.

We all have our states of fullness & of emptiness—but we overflow at different points. One overflows through the sensual outlets—another through his heart another through his head—& another perchance only through the higher part of his head or his poetic faculty— It depends on where each is tight & open. We can perchance thus direct our nutriment to those organs we specially use.

How happens it that there are few men so well employed—, so much to their minds, but that a little money—or fame—would by them off from their present pursuits!

7th still

To Conantum via fields Hubbards Grove & grain field To Tupelo cliff & Conantum and rturning over peak same way. 6. P M I hear no larks sing at evening as in the spring—nor robins. only a few distressed notes from the robin— In Hubbards grain field beyond the brook—now the the sun is down. The air is very still— There is a fine sound of crickets not loud The woods & single trees are heavier masses in the landscape than in the spring. Night has more allies. The heavy shadows of woods and trees are remarkable now. The meadows are green with their second crop. I hear only a tree toad or song sparrow singing as in spring at long intervals. The Roman wormwood is beginning to yellow-green my shoes.— intermingled with the blue-curls over the sand in this grain field. Perchance some poet likened this yellow dust to the ambrosia of the Gods. The birds are remarkably silent At the bridge perceive the bats are out. & the yet silvery moon not quite full is reflected in the water. The water is perfectly still—and there is a red tinge from the evening sky in it. The sky is singularly marked this evening. There are bars or rays of nebulous light springing from the western horizon where the sun has disappeared, and alternating with beautiful blue rays, by far more blue than any other portion of the sky these continue to diverge till they have reached the middle & then converge to the eastern horizon—making a symmetrical figure like the divisions of a muskmelon—not very bright yet distinct.—

though growing less & less bright toward the east. It was a quite remarkable phenomenon encompasing the heavens, as if you were to behold the divisions of a muskmelon thus alternately colored from within it. A proper vision—a colored mist. The most beautiful thing  in Nature is the sun reflected from a tear-ful cloud. These white and blue ribs embraced the earth. The two outer blues much the brightest & matching one another. You hear the hum of mosquitoes..

Going up the road. The sound of the crickets is now much more universal & loud. Now in the fields I see the white white streak of the neottia in the twilight— The whippoorwills sing far off. I smell burnt land somewhere. At Tupelo Cliff I hear the sound of singers on the river young men & women—which is unusual here—returning from their row. Man's voice thus uttered fits well the spaces— It fills Nature. And after all the singing of men is something far grander than any natural sound. It is wonderful that men do not oftener sing in the fields—by day & night. I bathe at the north side the cliff while the moon shines round the end of the rock— The opposite Cliff is reflected in the water. Then sit on the S side of the Cliff in the woods. One or two fireflies—could it be a glowworm— I thought I saw one or two in the air (—that is all in this walk) I hear a whippoorwill uttering a cluck of suspicion in my rear— He is suspicious & inquisitive. The river stretches off southward from me. I see the sheeny portions of its western shore interruptedly for a quarter of a mile—where the moon light is reflected from the pads.— a strong gleaming light while the water is lost in the obscurity.

I hear the sound from time to time of a leaping fish—or a frog—or a muskrat or turtle.— It is even warmer *methinks* than it was in August—& it is perfectly clear the air. I know not how it is that this universal cricket's creak should sound thus regularly intermittent—as if for the most part they fell in with one another & creaked in time— making a certain pulsing sound a sort of breathing or panting of all nature. You sit twenty feet above the still river—see the sheeny pads. & the moon & some bare tree tops in the distant horizon. Those bare tree tops add greatly to the wildness.

Lower down I see the moon in the water as bright as in the heavens—only the water bugs disturb its disk—and now I catch a faint glassy glare from the whole river surface which before was simply dark. This is set in a frame of double darkness on the east i.e. the reflected shore of woods & hills & the reality—the shadow & the substance bipartite answering to each. I see the northern lights over my shoulder to remind me of the Esquimaux & that they are still my contemporaries on this globe—that they too are taking their walks on another part of the planet.— in pursuit of seals perchance.

The stars are dimly reflected in the water— The path of water-bugs in the moon's rays is like ripples of light. It is only when you stand fronting the sun or moon that you see their light reflected in the water. I hear no frogs these nights—bull-frogs or others—as in the spring— It is not the season of sound.

At Conantum end—just under the wall From this point & at this height I do not perceive any bright or yellowish light on Fair Haven —but an oily & glass like smoothness on its southwestern bay— through a very slight mistiness. Two or three pines appear to stand in the moon lit air on this side of the pond—while the Enlightened portion of the water is bounded by the heavy reflection of the wood on the east It was so soft & velvety a light as contained a thousand placid days sweetly put to rest in the bosom of the water. So looked the north Twin Lake in the Maine woods. It reminds me of placid lakes in the mid-noon of Ind. Summer days—but yet more placid & civilized—suggesting a higher cultivation—which aeons of summer days have gone to make. Like a summer day seen far away. All the effects of sunlight—with a softer tone—and all this stillness of the water & the air superadded—& the witchery of the hour. What gods are they that require so fair a vase of gleaming water to their prospect in the midst of the wild woods by night? Else why this beauty allotted to night—a gem to sparkle in the zone of night. They are strange gods now out—methinks their names are not in any mythology— I can faintly trace its zigzag border of sheeny pads even here. If such is there to be seen in remotest wildernesses does it not suggest its own nymphs & wood Gods to enjoy it? As When at middle of the placid noon in Ind summer days all the surface of a lake is as one cobweb—gleaming in the sun which heaves gently to the passing zephyr— There was the lake—its glassy surface just distinguishable its sheeny shore of pads—with a few pines bathed in light on its hither shore just as in mid of a november day—except that this was the chaster light of the moon—the cooler—temperature of the night and these were the deep shades of night that fenced it round & imbosomed. It tells of a far away long passed civilization of an antiquity superior to time—unappreciable by time.

Is there such virtue in raking cranberries—that those men's industry whom I now see on the meadow—shall reprove my idleness? Can I not go over those same meadows after them & rake still more valuable fruits. Can I not rake with my mind? Can I not rake a thought perchance which shall be worth a bushel of cranber?—

A certain refinement & civilization in nature which increases with the wildness. The civilization that consists with wildness. The light that is in night. A smile as in a dream on the face of the sleeping lake. There is light enough to show what we see—what *night* has to exhibit—any more would obscure these objects. I am not advertised of any deficiency of light. The actual is fair as a vision or a dream. If ever we have attained to any nobleness—ever in our imagination & intentions—that will surely ennoble the features of nature for us that will clothe them with beauty. Of course no jeweller ever dealt with a gem so fair & suggestive as this actual lake. The scene it may be of so much noble & poetic life—& not merely adorn some monarch's crown.

It is remarkably still at this hour & season—no sound of bird or beast for the most part. This has none of the reputed noxious qualities of night.

On the Peak. The faint sounds of birds—dreaming aloud—in the night—the fresh cool air & sound of the wind rushing over the rocks —remind me of the tops of *mts*. That is all the earth is but the outside of the planet bordering on the hard eyed skyed—equally with drawn & near to heaven. is this pasture as the summit of the white *mts*— All the earth's surface like a mt top—for I see its relation to heaven as simply. & am not imposed upon by a difference of a few few feet in elevation.— In this faint light all fields are like a mossy rock—& remote from the cultivated plains of day. All is equally savage—equally solitary—& the dif. in elevation is felt to be unimportant. It is all one with caucasus the slightest hill pasture.

The bass wood had a singularly solid look & sharply defined—as by a web or film—as if its leaves covered it like scales—

Scared up a whippoorwill on the ground on the hill. Will not my townsmen consider me a benefactor if I conquer some realms from the night? If I can show them that there is some beauty awake while they are asleep.? If I add to the domains of poetry. If I report to the gazettes anything transpiring in our midst worthy of man's attention. I will say nothing now to the disparagement of Day, for he is not here to defend himself.

The northern lights now as I descend from the Conantum house have become a crescent of light crowned with short shooting flames —or the shadows of flames. for some times they are dark as well as white. There is scarcely any dew even in the low lands.

Now the fire in the north increases wonderfully—not shooting up so much as creeping along like a fire on the *mts* of the north seen afar in the night. The Hyperborean gods are burning brush, and it spread and all the hoes in heaven could'nt stop it. It spread from west to east over the crescent hill. Like a vast fiery worm it lay across the northern sky—broken into many pieces & each piece strives to advance itself worm like on its own muscles It has spread into the choicest woodlots of valhalla—now it shoots up like a single (solitary watch fire) or) burning bush—or where it ran up a pine tree like powder—& still it continues to gleam here & there like a fat stump in the burning & is reflected in the water. And now I see the gods by great exertions have got it under, & the stars have come out without fear in peace.

Though no birds sing, the crickets vibrate their shrill & stridulous cymbals especially on the alders of the causeway. Those minstrels especially engaged for night's quire.

It takes some time to wear off the trivial impression which the day has made—& thus the first hours of night are sometimes lost.

There were two hen hawks soared and circled for our entertainment when we were in the woods on that Boon Plain the other day—crossing each others orbits from time to time, alternating like the squirrels of the morning. Till alarmed by an imitation of a hawks shrill cry—they gradually inflated themselves made themselves more aerial and rose higher & higher into the heavens & were at length lost to sight— Yet all the while earnestly looking scanning the surface of the earth for a stray mouse or rabbit.

Sep 8th No fog this morning. Shall I not have words as fresh as my thought—? Shall I use any other man's word? A genuine thought or feeling can find expression for itself, if it have to invent hieroglyphics. It has the universe for type metal. It is for want of original thought that one man's style is like another's.

Certainly the voice of no bird or beast can be compared with that of man for true melody. All other sounds seem to be hushed as if their possessors were attending when the voice of man is heard in melody. The air gladly bears the burden It is infinitely significant. Man only sings in concert. The birds song is a mere interjectional shout of joy— Man's a glorious expression of the foundations of his joy—

Do not the song of birds & the fireflies go with the grass? While the grass is fresh the earth is in its vigor. The greenness of the grass is the best symptom or evidence of the earth's youth or health.

Perhaps it will be found that when the grass ceases to be fresh &
green or after June—the birds have ceased to sing—& that the fireflies
too no longer in *myriads* sparkle in the meadows— Perhaps a history
of the year would be a history of the grass—or of a leaf regarding the
grass blades as leaves—for it is equally true that the leaves soon loose
their freshness & soundness, & become the prey of insects & of
drought. Plants commonly soon cease to grow for the year unless
they may have a fall growth—which is a kind of 2nd spring. In the
feelings of the man too the year is already past & he looks forward
to the coming winter. His occasional rejuvenescence & faith in the
current time is like the aftermath a scanty crop. The enterprise
which he has not already undertaken—cannot be undertaken this
year. The period of youth is past. The year may be in its summer—in
its manhood, but it is no longer in the flower of its age— It is a
season of withering of dust & heat—a season of small fruits & trivial
experiences. Summer thus answers to manhood. But there is an
aftermath in early autumn—& some spring flowers bloom again—
followed by an Indian summer of finer atmosphere & of a pensive
beauty. May my life be not destitute of its Indian summer— A
season of fine & clear mild weather when I may prolong my
hunting before the winter comes. When I may once more lie on the
ground with faith as in spring—& even with more serene confidence
– And then I will drapery of summer about me & lie down to
pleasant dreams As one year passes into another through the
medium of winter—so does this our life pass into another through
the medium of death. De Quincey & Dickens have not moderation
enough—they never stutter—they flow too readily.

The tree primrose—& the dwarf—do—& epilobium still.. Locust is
heard. Aster amplexicaulis—beautiful blue purplish blue? about
twenty-four rayed. Utricularia vulgaris bladderwort. Dandelion &
houstonia.

Sep 9th 2 A M

The moon not quite full. To Conantum via road. There is a low
vapor in the meadows beyond the depot—dense & white though
scarcely higher than a man's head—concealing the stems of the trees.
I see that the oaks which are so dark & distinctly outlined, are
illumined by the moon on the opposite side. This as I go up the
back road. A few thin ineffectual clouds in the sky. I come out thus
into the moon-lit night—where men are not, as if into a scenery
anciently deserted by men. The life of men is like a dream It is 3000
years since night has had possession. Go forth and hear the crickets

chirp at midnight. Hear if their dynasty is not an ancient one and well founded. I feel the antiquity of the night—she surely repossesses her self of her realms as if her dynasty were uninterrupted or she had underlain the day. No sounds but the steady creaking of crickets and the occasional crowing of cocks.

I go by the farmers houses & barns standing there in the dim light under the trees, as if they lay at an immense distance or under a veil. The farmer & his oxen now all asleep. Not even a watch-dog awake. The human slumbers. There is less of man in the world.

The fog in the lowlands on the Corner road—is never still— It now advances & envelopes me as I stand to write these words—then clears away—with ever noiseless step— It covers the meadows like a web. I hear the clock strike 3 Now at the clayey bank. The light of orion's belt seems to show traces of the blue day through which it came to us— The sky at least is lighter on that side than in the west even about the moon. Even by night the sky is blue & not black for we see through the veil of night into the distant atmosphere of day. I see to the plains of the sun. Where the sun beams are revelling. The cricket's? song on the alders of the causeway not quite so loud at this hour as at evening. The moon is getting low. I hear a wagon cross on of the bridges leading into the town. I see the moon-light at this hour on a different side of objects. I smell the ripe apples many rods off beyond the bridge. A sultry night—a thin coat is enough.

On the first top of Conantum— I hear the farmer harnessing his horse and starting for the distant market, but no man harnesses himself, and starts for worthier enterprises.— One cock crow imbodies the whole story of the farmer's life. The moon is now sinking into clouds in the horizon— I see the glowworms deep in the grass by the brook side in midst of Conantum— The moon shines dun & red. A solitary Whippoorwill sings.

The clock strikes 4.

A few dogs bark—a few more wagons start for market—their faint rattling heard in the distance— I hear my owl without a name.— The murmur of the slow approaching freight-train—as far off perchance as Waltham & one early bird.

The round red moon disappearing in the west— I detect a whiteness in the east. Some dark massive clouds have come over from the west within the hour—as if attracted by the approaching sun —and have arranged themselves ray wise—about the eastern portal as if to bar his entrance. to obstruct his coming. They have moved

suddenly & almost unobservedly quite across the sky (which before
was clear–) from west to east. No trumpet was heard which
marshalled & advanced these dark masses of the west's forces thus
rapidly against the coming day. Column after colum the mighty west
sent forth across the sky–but all in vain.

The eastern horizon is now grown dun colored–showing where
the advanced guard of the night are already skirmishing with the van
guard of the sun–a lurid light tinging the atmosphere there–while a
dark columned cloud hangs imminent over the broad portal–
untouched by the glare. Some bird flies over making a noise like the
barking of a puppy. It is yet so dark that I have dropt my pencil and
cannot find it.

The sound of the cars is like that of a rushing wind, I thought at
first a morning wind was rising. And now (perchance at half past
four–) I hear the sound of some far off factory bell where perchance
I have never been– Arousing the operatives to their early labors. It
sounds very sweet here. It is very likely some factory which I have
never seen–in some valley which I have never visited–yet now I
hear this which is its only matin bell, sweet & inspiring as if it
summoned holy men & maids to worship and not factory girls &
men to resume their trivial toil. As if it were the summons of some
religious or even poetic community My first impresion is that it is
the matin bell of some holy community–who in a distant valley
dwell–a band of spiritual knights–thus sounding far and wide sweet
and sonorous, in harmony with their own morning thoughts–
What else could I suppose fitting this earth & hour.– Why should I
fear to tell that it is Knights factory-bell? And by its peals how many
men & maids are waked from peaceful slumbers to fragrant morning
thoughts. Some man of high resolve, devoted soul, has touched the
rope– A few melodious peals and all is still again

The whippoorwills now begin to sing in earnest about ½ hour
before sunrise–as if making haste to improve the short time that is
left them. As far as my observation goes they sing for several hours
in the early part of the night–are silent commonly at midnight–then
sing again just before sunrise. It grows more and more red in the
east–a fine grained red under the over hanging cloud–and lighter
too–& the threatening clouds are falling off to southward of the
sun's passage–shrunken & defeated leaving his path comparatively
clear.– The increased light shows more distinctly the river &
the fog.

5 o'clock.–

The light now reveals a thin film of vapor like a gossamer veil
cast over the lower hills beneath the Cliffs & stretching to the river—
thicker in the ravines—thinnest on the even slope. The distant
meadows towards the north beyond Conants Grove full of fog
appear like a vast lake out of which rise Anursnack & Ponkawtasset
like rounded islands. Nawshawtuct is a low & wooded isle—scarcely
seen above the waves— The heavens are now clear again. The
vapor which was confined to the river & meadows now rises &
creeps up the sides of the hills— I see it in transparent columns
advancing down the valley of the river from Fair Haven—& investing
some wooded or rocky promontory—before free.

  Anursnack is exactly like some round steep distant hill on the
opposite shore of a large lake (and Tabor on the other side)—with
here & there some low Brush Island in middle of the waves—(The
tops of some oaks or elms) O what a sail I could take if I had the
right kind of bark over to Anursnack for there she lies 4 miles from
land as sailors say. And all the farms & houses of Concord are at
bottom of that sea. So I forget them and my thought sails
triumphantly over them. As I looked down where the village of
Concord lay buried in fog—I thought of nothing but the surface of a
lake—a summer-sea over which to sail—no more than a voyager on
the Dead Sea who had not read the testament would think of
Sodom & Gomorrah once cities of the plain. I only wished to get
off to one of the low isles I saw in midst of the (It may have been
the top of Holbrooks elm) and spend the whole summer day there.

  Meanwhile the redness in the east had diminished & was less deep
(The fog over some meadows looked green.) I went down to
Tupelo cliff to bathe The redness had risen at length above the dark
cloud the sun approaching.

  And next the redness became a sort of yellowish or fawn colored
light & the sun now set fire to the edges of the broken cloud which
had hung over the horizon—& they glowed like burning turf.

Sep. 10th

  As I watch the groves on the meadow opposite our house—I see
how differently they look at different hours of the day i.e. in dif.
lights when the sun shines on them variously. In the morning
perchance they seem one blended mass of light greeen In the
afternoon distinct trees appear—separated by heavy shadows—& in
some places I can see quite through the grove.

  3 PM to the Cliffs & the Grape Cliff beyond— Hardhack &
meadow sweet are now all dry— I see the smoke of burning brush

in the west horizon this dry and sultry afternoon—& wish to look off
from some hill— It is a kind of work the farmer cannot do without
discovery— Sometimes I smell these smokes several miles off & by
the odor know it is not a burning building but withered leaves &
the rubbish of the woods & swamp. As I go through the woods I
see that the ferns have turned brown & give the woods an autumnal
look— The boiling spring is almost completely dry—nothing flows (I
mean without the shed) but there are many hornets & yellow wasps
apparently buzzing & circling about in jealousy of one another—
either drinking the stagnant water which is the most accessible this
dry parching day—or it may be collecting something from the slime.—
I think the former.

As I go up Fair Haven Hill I see some signs of the approaching
fall of the White pine—on some trees the old leaves are already
somewhat reddish though not enough to give the trees a
particolored look—& they come off easily on being touched. The old
leaves on the lower part of the twigs.

Some farmers are sowing their winter-rye?

I see the fields smoothly rolled—(I hear the locust still) I see
others ploughing steep rocky & bushy fields apparently for the same
purpose.— How beautiful the sprout land (burnt plain) seen from
the cliffs. No more cheering & inspiring sight than a young wood
springing up thus over a large tract—when you look down on it the
light green of the maples shaded off into the darker oaks—& here &
there a maple blushes quite red—enlivening the scene yet more.
Surely this earth is fit to be inhabited—& many enterprises may be
undertaken with hope where so many young plants are pushing up.
In the spring I burned over a hundred acres till the earth was sere
and black—& by mid-summer this space was clad in a fresher &
more luxuriant green than the surrounding even. Shall man then
despair? Is he not a sproutland too after never so many searings &
witherings? If you witness growth & luxuriance, it is all the same as
if you grew luxuriantly.

I see three smokes in Stow. One sends up dark volumes of
wreathed smoke as if from the mouth of Erebus. It is remarkably
what effects so thin & subtile a substance as smoke produces even at
a distance—dark & heavy & powerful as rocks at a distance. The
woodbine is red on the rocks. The poke is a very rich & striking
plant. Some which stand under the cliffs quite dazzeld—me with their
now purple stems gracefully drooping each way—their rich somewhat
yellowish purple veined leaves, their bright purple racemes—

peduncles & pedicels & calyx like petals from which the birds have
picked the berries—(these racemes with their petals now turned to
purple are more brilliant than anything of the kind) flower-buds—
flowers—ripe berries & dark purple ones & calyx like petals which
have lost their fruit all on the same plant— I love to see any redness
in the vegetation of the temperate zone It is the richest color. I
love to press these berries betwen my fingers & see their rich purple
wine staining my hand. It asks a bright sun on it to make it show to
best advantage & it must be seen at this season of the year— It
speaks to my blood— Every part of it is flower—such is its
superfluity of color—a feast of color— That is the richest flower
which most abounds in color— What need to taste the fruit to
drink the wine—to him who can thus taste & drink with his eyes?

Its boughs gracefully drooping offering repasts to the birds. It is
cardinal in its rank as in its color. Nature here is full of blood & heat
& luxuriance. What a triumph it appears in nature to have produced
& perfected such a plant. As if this were enough for a summer.

The downy seeds of the groundsel are taking their flight here—
The calyx has dismissed them & quite curled back—having done its
part.

Lespedeza sessiliflora or reticulated Lespedeza on the Cliffs now
out of bloom.

At the Grape cliff—the few bright red leaves of the tupelo contrast
with the polished green ones. The tupelos with drooping branches.

The grape vines over running & bending down the maples form
little arching bowers over the meadow 5 or 6 feet in diameter like
parasols held over the ladies of the harem. in the east. Cuscuta
Americana or dodder in blossom still. The desmodium paniculatum
of De Candolle & Gray (Hedysarum Paniculatum of L. & Big.)
Tick-trefoil—with still one blossom—by the path side up from the
meadow. The Rhomboidal joints of its loments adhere to my
Clothes. One of an interesting family that thus disperse themselves.

The oak ball of dirty drab now.

Sep. 11th

Every artizan learns positively something by his trade. Each craft is
familiar with a few simple well-known well established facts—not
requiring any genius to discover but mere use & familiarity. You
may go by the man at his work in the street every day of your life.—
& though he is there before you carrying into practice certain
essential information—you shall never be the wiser. Each trade is in
fact a craft a cunning a covering an ability—& its methods are the

result of a long experience. There sits a stone-mason splitting
Westford granite for fenceposts— Egypt has perchance taught New
England something in this matter— His hammer—his chisels, his
wedges—his shames? or half rounds—his iron spoon, I suspect that
these tools are hoary with age as with granite dust. He learns as
easily where the best granite comes from as he learns how to erect
that screen to keep off the sun. He knows that he can drill faster
into a large stone than a small one because there is less jar &
yielding. He deals in stone as the carpenter in lumber— In many of
his operations only the materials are different. His work is slow &
expensive. Nature is here hard to be overcome. He wears up one or
two drills in splitting a single stone. He must sharpen his tools
oftener than the carpenter He fights with granite. He knows the
temper of the rocks—he grows stoney himself—his tread is ponderous
& steady like the fall of a rock. And yet by patience & art he splits a
stone as surely as the carpenter or woodcutter a log. So much time
& perseverance will accomplish. One would say that mankind had
much less moral than physical energy—that every day you see men
following the trade of splitting rocks., who yet shrink from
undertaking apparently less arduous moral labors—the solving of
moral problems. See how surely he proceeds. He does not hesitate
to drill a dozen holes each one the labor of a day or two for a
savage—he carefully takes out the dust with his iron spoon—he inserts
his wedges one in each hole & protects the sides of the holes &
gives resistance to his wedges by thin pieces of half round iron (or
shames)—he marks the red line which he has drawn with his chisel—
carefully cutting it straight—& then how carefully he drives each
wedge in succession—fearful lest he should not have a good split.

   The habit of looking at men in the gross makes their lives have
less of human interest for us. But though there are crowds of
laborers before us—yet each one leads his little epic life each day.
There is the stone mason who methought was simply a stony man
that hammered stone from breakfast to dinner—& dinner to supper &
then went to his slumbers. But he I find is even a man like myself—
for he feels the heat of the sun & has raised some boards on a frame
to protect him. And now at midforenoon I see his wife & child
have come & brought him drink & meat for his lunch & to assuage
the stoniness of his labor—& sit to chat with him. There are many
rocks lying there for him to split from end to end and he will surely
do it—this only at the command of luxury since stone posts are
preferred to wood—but how many moral blocks are lying there in

every man's yard which he surely will not split nor earnestly endeavor to split.

There lie the blocks which will surely get split but here lie the blocks which will surely not get split— Do we say it is too hard for human faculties?— But does not the mason dull a basket-full of steel chisels in a day—& yet by sharpening them again & tempering them aright succeed? Moral effort—! difficulty to be overcome!!! Why men work in stone & sharpen their drills when they go home to dinner!

Why should Canada wild and unsettled as it is impress one as an older country than the states—except that her institutions are old. All things seem to contend there with a certain rust of antiquity—such as forms on old armor & iron guns. The rust of conventions and formalities. If the rust was not on the tinned roofs it was on the inhabitants.

2 P M to Hubbards meadow grove. The skunk cabbage's checkered fruit (spadix) one 3 inches long, all parts of the flower but the anthers left and enlarged.

Berdens cernua or Nodding Burr-Mary Gold like a small sunflower (with rays) in Heywood brook i.e. Beggar tick

Bidens Connata? without rays in Hubbards meadow— Blue eyed grass still— Drooping neottia very common

I see some yellow butterflies and others occasionally & singly only The Smilax berries are mostly turned dark I started a great bittern from the weeds at the swimming place.

It is very hot & dry weather. We have had no rain for a week & yet the pitcher plants have water in them.— Are they ever quite dry? Are they not replenished by the dews always—& being shaded by the grass saved from evaporation? What wells for the birds!

The White-red-purple berried bush in Hubbards meadow whose berries were fairest a fortnight ago—appears to be the Viburnum nudum or withe-rod

Our cornel (the common) with berries blue one side whitish the other appears to be either the C. sericea or C. Stolonifera of Gray i.e. the silky or the red-osier C. (*osier rouge*) though its leaves are neither silky nor downy nor rough. This and the last 4 or 5 nights have been perhaps the most sultry in the year thus far—

Sep 12th

Not till after 8 AM does the fog clear off so much that I see the sun shining in patches on Nawshawtuct. This is the season of fogs.

like knight like esquire When Benvenuto Cellini was attacked by the constables in Rome—His boy Cencio assisted him or at least stood by—& afterward related his masters exploits—"& as they asked him several times whether he had been afraid, he answered that they should propose the question to me, for he had been affected upon the occasion just in the same manner that I was."

Benvenuto Cellini relates in his Memoirs that during his confinement in the Castle of St Angelo in Rome he had a terrible dream or vision in which in which certain events were communicated to him which afterward came to pass—& he adds—"From the very moment that I beheld the phenomenon, there appeared (strange to relate!) a resplendent light over my head, which has displayed itself conspicuously to all that I have thought proper to show it to, but those were very few. This shining light is to be seen in the morning over my shadow till two o'clock in the afternoon, and it appears to the greatest advantage when the grass is moist with dew: it is likewise visible in the evening at sunset. This phenomenon I took notice of when I was at Paris, because the air is exceedingly clear in that climate, so that I could distinguish it there much plainer than in Italy, where mists are much more frequent; but I can still see it even here, and show it to others, though not to the same advantage as in France." This reminds me of the halo around my Shadow which I notice from the cause way in the morning—also by moonlight—as if in the case of a man of an excitable imagination this were basis enough for his superstition.

After I have spent the greater part of a night abroad in the moonlight I am obliged to sleep enough more the next night to make up for it—Endymionis somnum dormire—to sleep an Endymion sleep as the ancients expressed it. And there is something gained still by thus turning the day into night. Edymion is said to have obtained of Jupiter the privelege of sleeping as much as he would. Let no man be afraid of sleep—if his weariness comes of obeying his Genius. He who has spent the night with the gods sleeps more innocently by day than the sluggard who has spent the day with the satyrss sleeps by night. He who has travelled to fairy-land in the night—sleeps by day more innocently than he who is fatigued by the merely trivial labors of the day sleeps by night. That kind of life which sleeping we dream that we live awake—in our walks by night, we, waking, dream that we live, while our daily life appears as a dream.

2 P M To the Three Friends' Hill beyond Flints Pond—via RR. RWEs Wood Path S side Walden—Geo Heywood's Cleared Lot & Smith's orchards—return via E of Flints' P via Goose P & my old home to RR—

I go to Flints P. for the sake of the *Mt* view from the hill beyond looking over Concord. I have thought it the best especially in the winter which I can get in this neighborhood. It is worth the while to see the *Mts* in the horizon once a day. I have thus seen some earth which corresponds to my least earthly & trivial–to my most heaven-ward looking thoughts– The earth seen through an azure an etherial veil. They are the natural *temples* elevated brows of the earth–looking at which the thoughts of the beholder are naturally elevated and etherialized. I wish to see the earth through the medium of much air or heaven–for there is no paint like the air. *Mts* thus seen are worthy of worship. I go to Flints' Pond also to see a rippling lake & a reedy-island in its midst–Reed Island.

A man should feed his senses with the best that the land affords

At the entrance to the Deep Cut I heard the telegraph wire vibrating like an AEolian Harp. It reminded me suddenly–reservedly with a beautiful paucity of communication–even silently, such was its effect on my thoughts– It reminded me, I say, with a certain pathetic moderation–of what finer & deeper stirrings I was susceptible–which grandly set all argument & dispute aside–a triumphant though transient exhibition of the truth. It told me by the faintest imaginable strain–it told me by the finest strain that a human ear can hear–yet conclusively & past all refutation–that there were higher infinitely higher plains of life–which it behoved me never to forget. As I was entering the Dep Cut the wind which was conveying a message to me from heaven dropt it on the wire of the telegraph which it vibrated as it past. I instantly sat down on a stone at the foot of the telegraph pole–& attended to the communication. It merely said "Bear in mind, Child–& never for an instant forget–that there are higher plains infinitely higher plains of life than this thou art now travelling on. Know that the goal is distant & is upward and is worthy all your life's efforts to attain to." And then it ceased and though I sat some minutes longer I heard nothing more.

There is every variety & degree of inspiration from mere fullness of life to the most rapt mood. A human soul is played on even as this wire–which now vibrates slowly & gently so that the passer can hardly hear it & anon the sound swells & vibrates with such intensity as if it would rend the wire–as far as the elasticity & tension of the wire permits–and now it dies away and is silent–& though the breeze continues to sweep over it, no strain comes from it–& the traveller hearkens in vain. It is no small gain to have this wire stretched through Concord though there may be no Office here. Thus I make my own use of the telegraph–without consulting the

Directors—like the sparrows which I perceive use it extensively for a perch.

Shall I not go to this office to hear if there is any communication for me—as steadily as to the Post office in the village?

I can hardly believe that there is so great a diffirence between one year & another as my journal shows.

The 11th of this month last year the river was as high as it commonly is in the spring—over the causeway on the Corner Road. It is now quite low. Last year Oct 9th the huckleberries were fresh & abundant on Conantum— They are now already dried up.

We yearn to see the *Mts* daily—as the Israelites yearned for the Promised land—& we daily live the fate of Moses who only looked into the Promised land from Pisgah before he died.

On Monday the 15th instant I am going to perambulate the bounds of the town. As I am partial to across-lot routes, this appears to be a very proper duty for me to perform, for certainly no route can—well be chosen which shall be more across lot—since the roads in no case run round the town but ray out from its center, and my course will lie across each one. It is almost as if I had undertaken to walk round the town at the greatest distance from its centre & at the same time from the surrounding villages. There is no public house near the line.

It is a sort of reconnaisance of its frontiers authorized by the central government of the town—which will bring the surveyor in contact with whatever wild inhabitant or wilderness its territory embraces

This appears to be a very ancient custom. And I find that this word perambulation has exactly the same meaning that it has at present in Johnson & Walkers dictionary— A hundred years ago they went round the towns of this state every three years. And the old select men tell me that before the present split stones were set up in 1829, the bounds were marked by a heap of stones, and it was customary for each select man to add a stone to the heap.

Saw a pigeon place on Geo. Heywoods cleared lot—the six dead trees set up for the pigeons to alight on, and the brush-house close by to conceal the man. I was rather startled to find such a thing going now in Concord— The pigeons on the trees looked like fabulous birds with their long tails & their pointed breasts I could hardly believe they were alive & not some wooden birds used for decoys—they sat so still—and even When they moved their necks I thought it was the effect of art. As they were not catching them I approached & scared away a dozen birds who were perched on the trees and found that they were freshly baited there—though the net was carried away—perchance to some other bed. The smooth sandy bed was covered with buckwheat—wheat or rye—& acorns— sometimes they use corn shaved off the ear in its present state with a knife   There were left the sticks with which they fastened the necks—— As I stood there I heard a rushing sound & looking up saw a flock of 30 or 40 pigeons dashing toward the *trees*, who suddenly whirled on seeing me & circled round & made a new dash toward the bed as if they would fain alight if I had not been there— then steered off. I went into the bough-house & lay awhile looking through the leaves—hoping to see them come again & feed—but they did not while I stayed. This net & bed belongs to one Harrington of Weston as I hear— Several men still take pigeons in Concord every year. By a method methinks extremely old—and which I seem to have seen pictured in some old book of fables or symbols—& yet few in Concord know exactly how it is done. And yet it is all done for money & because the birds fetch a good price—just as the farmers raise corn & potatoes. I am always expecting that those engaged in such a pursuit will be somewhat less grovelling & mercenary than the regular trader or farmer, but I fear that it is not so.

Found a violet—apparently viola cucullata or hoodleaved violet in bloom in Bakers meadow beyond Pine Hill. Also the bidens cernua Nodding Burr-marygold with 5 petals—in same place. Went through the old cornfield on the hill side beyond now grown up to birches & hickories. Woods where you feel the old corn hills under your feet—for these not being disturbed or levelled in getting the crop like potatoe hills last an indefinite while—& by some they are called Indian corn fields—though I think erroniously not only from their position in rocky soil frequently—but because the squaws probably with their clam shells or thin stones or wooden hoes did not hill their corn more than many now recommend.

What we call woodbine is the vitis hederacea or Common creeper or American ivy.

When I got into the Lincoln road I perceived a singular sweet scent in the air—which I suspected arose from from some plant now in a peculiar state owing to the season, but though I smell everything around I could not detect it, but the more eagerly I smelled the further I seemed to be from finding it—but when I gave up the search—again it would be wafted to me— It was one of the sweet scents which go to make the autumn air—which fed my sense

of smell rarely & dilated my nostrils— I felt the better for it.
Methinks that I possess the sense of smell in greater perfection than
usual—& have the habit of smelling of every plant I pluck. How
autumnal is the scent of ripe grapes now by the roadside! From the
pondside hill I perceive that the forest leaves begin to look rather
rusty or brown. The pendulous drooping barberries are pretty well
reddened. I am glad when the berries look fair & plump. I love to
gaze at the low island in the Pond—at any island or inaccesible land.
The isle at which you look always seems fairer than the main-land
on which you stand.

I had already bathed in Walden as I passed, but now I forgot that
I had been wetted & wanted to embrace & mingle myself with the
water of Flints pond—this warm afternoon—to get wet inwardly &
deeply.

Found on the shore of the Pond that singular willow like herb in
blossom—though its petals were gone. It grows up 2 feet from a large
woody horizontal root & droops over to the sand again—meeting
which it puts out a myriad rootlets from the side of its stem—fastens
itself & curves upward again to the air——thus spanning or looping
itself along. The bark just above the ground thickens into a singular
cellular or spongey substance which at length appears to crack nearer
the earth giving that part of the plant a winged appearance & some
what 4 sided It appears to be the cellular tissue or what is
commonly called the green bark—& like-wise invests the root to a
great thickness—somewhat like a fungus & is of a fawn color The
Lythrum verticillatum or swamp Loosestrife—or Grass Poly—but I
think better named as in Dewey Swamp-willow herb— The Prinos
berries are pretty red.

Any redness like cardinal flowers or poke—or the evening sky or
Cheronaea excites us as a red flag does cows & turkies.

Sep 13th

RR causeway. before sunrise. Here is a morning after a warm
clear moon light night almost entirely without dew or fog. It has
been a little breezy through the night, it is true. But why so great a
dif. between this & other mornings of late? I can walk in any
direction in the fields without wetting my feet.

I see the same rays in the dun buff or fawn colored sky now just
20 minutes before sunrise—though they do not extend quite so far—as
at sundown the other night.— Why these rays? What is it divides
the light of the sun? It is thus divided by distant inequalities in the
surface of the earth, behind which the other parts are concealed—and
since the morning atmosphere is clearer they do not reach so far?

Some small island clouds are the first to look red. The cross-leaved polygala emits its fragrance as if at will. You are quite sure you smelled it and are ravished with its sweet fragrance, but now it has no smell. You must not hold it too near, but hold it on all sides and at all distances, & there will perchanc be wafted to you sooner or later a very sweet & penetrating fragrance— What it is like you cannot surely tell—for you do not enjoy it long enough nor in volume enough to compare it— It is very likely that you will not discover any fragrance— While you are rudely smelling at it—you can only remember that you once perceived it. But this & the caducous Polygala are now somewhat faded.

Now the sun is risen. The sky is almost perfectly clear this morning, not a cloud in the horizon. The morning is not pensive like the evening but joyous & youthful—& its blush is soon gone. It is unfallen day. The Bedford sunrise bell rings sweetly & musically at this hour, when there is no bustle in the village to drown it. Bedford deserves a vote of thanks from Concord for it. It is a great good at these still & sacred hours when towns can hear each other. It would be nought at noon.

Sep 14th

A great change in the weather from sultry to cold. from one thin coat to a thick coat or two thin ones. 2 Pm. To Cliffs. The dry grass yields a crisped sound to my foot. The white oak which appears to have made part of a hedge fence once—now standing in—Hubbards' fence near the Corner Road—where it stretches along horizontaly is (one of its arms, for it has one running each way) 2½ feet thick with a sprout growing perpendicularly out of it 18 inches in diameter. The corn stalks standing in stacks in long rows along the edges of the corn fields—reminds me of stacks of muskets

As soon as berries are gone grapes come. The chalices of the Rhexia Virginica Deer Grass or Meadow Beauty are literally littl reddish chalices now—though many still have petals. ⌒ little cream pitchers. The caducous polyagala in cool places is faded almost white. I see the river at the foot of Fair Haven Hill running up stream before the strong cooll wind which here strikes it from the North. The cold wind makes me shudder after my bath—before I get dressed.

Polyganum aviculare—Knot grass Goose grass or Door grass still in bloom.

Monday Sep 15

Ice in the pail under the pump—& quite a frost. Commenced perambulating the town-bounds. At 7½ AM rode in Co with A A

Kelsey & Mr Tolman to the bound between Acton & Concord near
Paul Dudley's. Mr Tolman told—a story of his wife walking in the
fields somewhere—& to keep the rain off throwing her gown over
her head & holding it in—her mouth—and so being poisoned about
her mouth—from the skirts of her dress having come in contact with
poisonous plants. At Dudleys, which house is handsomely situated
with 5 large elms in front, we met the Select men of Acton—Ivory
Keyes & Luther Conant. Here were 5 of us. It appeared that we
weighed—Tolman I think about 160—Conant 155—Keyes about 140—
Kelsey 130—myself 127. Tolman described the wall about or at
Forest Hill cemetery in Roxbury—as being made of stones upon
which they weere careful to preserve the moss, so that it cannot be
distinguished from a very old wall.

Found one intermediate boundstone near the Powder mill drying-
house on the Bank of the river. The workmen there wore shoes
without iron tacks— He said that the Kernel house was the most
dangerous—the Drying house next—the Press house next. One of the
Powder-mill buildings in Concord? All the intermediate bound-
stones are on the north sides of the different roads.— The potatoe
vines & the beans which were still green are now blackened &
flattened by the frost.

Sep. 16th 51

Met the Select men of Sudbury Moore and Haines— I trust that
towns will remember that they are supposed to be fairly represented
by their *select* men.

From the specimen which acton sent I should judge that the
inhabitants of that town were made up of a mixture of quiet
respectable & even gentlemanly farmer people, well to do in the
world, with a rather boisterous, coarse, and a little self willed class.
That the inhabitants of Sudbury are farmers almost exclusively—
exceedingly rough & countrified & more illiterate than usual, very
tenacious of their rights & dignities and difficult to deal with.

That the inhabitants of Lincoln yield sooner than usual to the
influence of the rising generation—and are a mixture of rather simple
but clever with a well informed & trustworthy people—that the
inhabitants of Bedford are mechanics who aspire to keep up with the
age—with some of the polish of society—mingled with substantial and
rather intelligent farmers.

Moore of Sudbury thinks the river would be still lower now if it
were not for the water in the reservoir pond in Hopkinton running
into it.

Sep. 17 '51

Perambulated the Lincoln line—

Was it the small rough sunflower which I saw this morning at the brook near Lees' bridge?

Saw at James Baker a Buttonwood tree with a swarm of bees now 3 years in it—but honey & all inaccessible. John W Farrar tells of sugar Maples behind Miles' in the Corner—

Did I see privet in the swamp at the Bedford stone near Giles' house? Swamp all dry now, could not wash my hands.

Sep 18th

Perambulated Bedford line

Sep 19th '51

Perambulated Carlisle line

Large flowered bidens or Beggar ticks or Burr-Marygold now abundant by river side. Found the bound-stones on Carlisle by the river—all or mostly tipped over by the ice & water like the pitch pines about Walden pond. Grapes very abundant along that line.

The soap-wort Gentian now— In an old pasture now grown up to birches & other trees—followed the cow paths to the old apple trees. Mr Isaiah Green of Carlisle who lives nearest to the Kibbe Place—can remember when there were 3 or 4 houses around him (he is nearly 80 years old & has always lived there & was born there) now he is quite retired—& the nearest road is scarcely used at all. He spoke of one old field, now grown up—which were going through, as the "hog-pasture", formerly. We found the meadows so dry that it was thought to be a good time to burn out the moss.

Sep. 20th

3 Pm. to Cliffs via Bear Hill. As I go through the fields endeavoring to recover my tone & sanity—& to perceive things truly & simply again, after having been perambulating the bounds of the town all the week, and dealing with the most common place and worldly minded men, and emphatically *trivial* things I feel as if I had committed suicide in a sense. I am again forcibly struck with the truth of the fable of Apollo serving king Admetus—its universal applicability. A fatal coarseness is the result of mixing in the trivial affairs of men. Though I have been associating even with the *select* men of this and the surrounding towns, I feel inexpressibly begrimmed, my pegasus has lost his wings, he has turned a reptile and gone on his belly. Such things are compatible only with a cheap and superficial life.

The poet must keep himself unstained and aloof. Let him

perambulate the bounds of Imagination's provinces the realms of
faery, and not the insignificant boundaries of towns. The excursions
of the imagination are so boundless—the limits of towns are so petty.

I scare up the great bittern in meadow by the Heywood Brook
near the ivy.— he rises buoyantly as he flies against the wind &
sweep south over the willow with outstretched neck surveying.

The ivy here is reddened. The dogwood or Poison sumack by
Hubbard's meadow is also turned redish. Here are late buttercups &
dwarf tree primroses still. Methinks there are not many Golden rods
this year. The river is remarkably low. There is a rod wide of bare
shore—beneath the Cliff Hill.

Last week was the warmest perhaps in the year. On Monday of
the present week—water was frozen in a pail under the pump. Yet
today I hear the locust sing as in August. This week we have had
most glorious autumnal weather—cool & cloudless bright days—filled
with the fragrance of ripe grapes—preceeded by frosty mornings All
tender herbs are flat in gardens & meadows— The cranberries too
are touched.

To day it is warmer—& hazier—& there is no doubt some smoke
in the air, from the burning of the turf & moss in low lands where
the smoke seen at sunset looks like a rising fog. I fear that the
autumnal tints will not be brilliant this season the frosts have
commenced so early.— Butter & eggs on Fair Haven. The Cleared
Plateau beneath the Cliff now covered with sprouts shows red, green
& yellow—tints like a rich rug.

I see ducks or teal flying silent swift & straight the wild creatures.
White pines on Fair Haven hill begin to look particolored with the
falling leaves—but not at a distance

Sep 21st Sunday.

It is remarkably dry weather— The neighbors' wells are failing—
The watering places for cattle in pastures though they have been
freshly scooped out are dry— People have to go far far for water to
drink—& then drink it warm. The river is so low that rocks which
are rarely seen show their black heads heads in mid channel. You see
the nests of the bream on the dry shore.

I perceive that many of the leaves of shrub-oaks and other bushes
have been killed by the severe frosts of last week, before they have
got ripe & acquired the tints of autumn and they now look as a fire
had run through them, dry & crispy & brown. So far from the frost
painting them, it has withered them— I notice new cabins of the
muskrats, in solitary swamps. The chestnut trees have suffered
severely from the drought, already their leaves look withered.

Moonlight is peculiarly favorable to reflection., It is a cold and dewy light in which the vapors of the day are condensed—and though the air is obscured by darkness it is more clear. Lunacy must be a cold excitement—not such insanity as a torrid sun on the brain would produce. In Rees Cyclopedia it is said—"The light of the moon, condensed by the best mirrors, produces no sensible heat upon the thermometer"

I see some cows on the new Wheeler's meadow which a man is trying to drive to ceartain green parts of the meadow next to the river to feed, the hill being dried up, but they seem disinclined & not to like the coarse grass there though it is green—. And now one cow is steering for the edge of the hill where is some greenness. I suppose that herds are attracted by a distant greenness, though it may be a mile or more off. I doubt if a man can drive his cows to that part of their pasture where is the best feed for them so soon as they will find it for themselves. The man tries in vain to drive them to the best part of the meadow—as soon as he is gone they seek their own parts—

The light of the moon sufficient though it is for the pensive walker and not disproportionate to the inner light we have is very inferior in quantity & intensity to that of the sun. The Cyclopedia says that Dr Hooke has calculated that "It would require 104.368 full moons to give a light and heat equal to that of the sun at noon." & Dr Smith says "the light of the full moon is but equal to a 90900dth part of the common light of the day, when the sun is hidden by a cloud."

But the moon is not to be judged alone by the quantity of light she sends us, but also by her influence on the earth. No thinker can afford to overlook the influence of the moon any more than the astronomer can. "The moon gravitates towards the earth, and the earth reciprocally towards the moon." This statement of the astronomer would be bald and meaningless, if it were not in fact a symbolical expression of the value of all lunar influence on man. Even the astronomer admits that "the notion of the moon's influence on terrestrial things was confirmed by her manifest effect upon the ocean" but is not the poet who walks by night conscious of a tide in his thought which is to be referred to lunar influence—in which the ocean within him overflows its shores & bathes the dry land. Has he not his spring tides & his neap-tides—the former sometimes combining with the winds of heaven to produce those memorable high-tides of the calender which leave their marks for ages?

Burritt in his Geography of the Heavens say "The quantity of light which we derive from the Moon when full, is at least 300 thousand times less than that of the Sun." This is Mons. Bouquer's inference as stated by La Place. Prof. Leslie makes it 150000 times less, older astronomers less still.

Rees says "It is remarkable, that the moon during the week in which she is full in harvest, rises sooner after sun-setting than she does in any other full moon week in the year. By doing so she affords an immediate supply of light after-sun-set, which is very beneficial to the farmers for reaping and gathering in the fruits of the earth; and therefore they distinguish this full moon from all the others in the year, by calling it the harvest-moon."

The retirement in which Green has lived for nearly eighty years in Carlisle is a retirement very different from & much greater than that in which the pioneer dwells at the west, for the latter dwells within sound of the surf of those billows of migration which are breaking on the shores around him or near him of the west—but those billows have long since sweept over the spot which Green inhabits & left him in the calm sea— There is somewhat exceedingly pathetic to think of in such a life as he must have lived—with no more to redeem it—such a life as an average Carlisle man may be supposed to live drawn out to 80 years—and he has died perchance and there is nothing but the mark of his cider-mill left. Here was the cider mill & there the orchard & there the hog-pasture—& so men lived & ate & drank and passed away.— like vermin. Their long life was mere duration. As respectable is the life of the woodchucks which perpetuate their race in the orchard still. That is the life of these *select-men*! spun out. They will be forgotten in a few years even by such as themselves like vermin. They will be known only like Kibbe, who is said to have been a large man who weighed 250—who had 5 or 6 heavy daughters who rode to concord Meeting house on horseback—taking turns they were so heavy that only one could ride at once. What then would redeem such a life? We only know that they ate & drank and built barns & died and were buried, and still perchance their toomb-stones cumber the ground. But if I could know that there was ever entertained over their cellar hole some divine thought which came as a messenger of the gods—that he who resided here acted once in his life from a noble impulse—rising superior to to his grovelling and penurious life—if only a single verse of poetry or of poetic prose had ever been written or spoken or conceived here beyond a doubt—I should not think it in vain that man had lived here.— It would to some extent be true then that God had lived here. That all his life he lived only as a farmer—as the most valuable stock only on a farm—& in no moments as a man!

Sep 22nd

To the Three Friends' Hill over Bear Hill. Yesterday & today the stronger winds of Autumn have begun to blow & the telegraph harp has sounded loudly. I heard it especially in the deep cut this afternoon. The tone varying with the tension of different parts of the wire. The sound proceeds from near the posts where the vibration is apparently more rapid. I put my ear to one of the posts, and it seemed to me as if every pore of the wood was filled with music, labored with the strain—as if every fibre was affected and being rearranged according to a new & more harmonious law—every swell and change or inflexion of tone pervaded & seemed to proceed from the wood the divine tree or wood—as if its very substance was transmuted—

What a recipe for preserving wood perchance—to keep it from rotting—to fill its pores with music!!

How this wild tree from the forest stripped of its bark and set up here rejoices to transmit this music

When no music proceeds from the wire—on applying my ear I hear the hum within the entrails of the wood—the oracular tree acquiring accumulating the prophetic fury.

The resounding wood! how much the ancients would have made of it!! To have a harp on so great a scale—girdling the very earth—& played on by the winds of every latitude & longitude—and that harp were as it were the manifest blessing of heaven on a work of man's— Shall we not add a 10th muse to the immortal nine? & that the invention thus divinely honored & distinguished—on which the muse has condescended to smile—is this magic medium of communication for mankind.

To read that the Ancients stretched a wire round the earth—attacching it to the trees of the forest—by which they sent messages by one named (Electricity father of Lightning—& Magnetism) swifter far than Mercury—the stern commands of war & news of peace—and that the winds caused this wire to vibrate so that it emitted a Harp like & Aeolian Music in all the lands through which it passed—as if to express the satisfaction of the Gods in this invention. Yet this is fact & we have yet attributed the invention to no God.

I am astonished to see how brown & sere the Groundsel or "fire weed" on hill side by Heywoods meadow—which has been touched

by frost—already is—as if it had died long months ago or a fire had
run through it. It is a very tender plant. Standing on Bear Hill in
Lincoln— The black birches (I think they are) now yellow on the
south side of Flints Pond on the hill side, look like flames. The
chestnut trees are brownish yellow—as well as green. It is a
beautifully clear and bracing air with just enough coolness full of the
memory of frosty mornings—through which all things are distinctly
seen & the fields look as smooth as velvet— The fragrance of grapes
is on the breeze & the red drooping barberries sparkle amid the
leaves. From the Hill on the S side of the Pond—the forests have a
singularly rounded & bowery look clothing the hills quite down to
the water's edge & leaving no shore; the Ponds are like drops of
dew amid and partly covering the leaves. So the great globe is
luxuriously crowded without margin.

The Utricularia cornuta or horned Utricularia on the sandy Pond-
shore not affected by the frost.

Sep 23d

Notwithstanding the fog—the fences this morning are covered
with so thick a frost that you can write your name anywhere with
your nail.

The partridge & the rabbit, they still are sure to thrive, like true
natives of the soil whatever revolutions occur. If the forest is cut off
many bushes spring up which afford them concealment, and they
become more numerous than ever.

The sumacs are among the reddest leaves at present. The
telegraph-harp sounds strongly today in the midst of the rain. I put
my ear to the trees and I hear it working terribly within & anon it
swells into a clear tone, which seems to concentrate in the core of
the tree—for all the sound seems to proceed from the wood. It is as
if you had entererd some world famous cathedral resounding to
some vast organ— The fibres of all things have their tension and are
strained like the strings of a lyre.. I feel the very ground tremble
under my feet as I stand near the post

This wire vibrates with great power as if it would strain & rend
the wood. What an aweful and fate-ful music it must be to the
worms in the wood—no better vermifuge were needed. No danger
that worms will attack this wood—such vibrating music would thrill
them to death. I scare up large flocks of sparrows in the garden—

Sep 24th

Returning over the Causeway from Flint's Pond the other
evening 22nd just at sunset I observed that while the west was of a

bright golden color under a bank of clouds—the sun just setting—and not a tinge of red was yet visible there, there was a distinct purple tinge in the nearer atmosphere, so that Anursnack Hill seen through it had an exceedingly rich empurpled look. It is rare that we perceive this purple tint in the air telling of the juice of the wild grape & poke-berries. The empurpled hills—methinks I have only noticed this in cooler weather.

Last night was exceedingly dark. I could not see the side walk in the street—but only felt it with my feet. I was obliged to whistle to warn travellers of my nearness & then I would suddenly find myself abreast of them without having seen anything or heard their footsteps. It was cloudy and rainy weather combined with the absence of the moon. So dark a night that if a farmer who had come in a shopping had spent but an hour after sunset in some shop he might find himself a prisoner in the village for the night. Thick darkness.

8 A M to Lees Bridge via Conantum   It is a cool and windy morning—and I have donned a thick coat for a walk. The wind is from the North so that the telegraph harp does not sound where I cross. This windy autumnal weather is very exciting & bracing clear & cold after the rain of yesterday—it having cleared off in the night. I see a small hawk—a pigeon? hawk over the Depot field which can hardly fly against the wind. At Hubbards Grove the wind roars loudly in the woods—   Grapes are ripe & already shrivelled by frost—barberries also—   It is Cattle-show day at Lowell.

Yesterday's wind and rain has strewn the ground with leaves, especially under the apple trees. Rain coming after frost seems to loosen the hold of the leaves making them rot off.

Saw a woodchuck disappearing in his hole. The river washes up stream before the wind, with white streaks of foam on its dark surface—diagonally to its course—showing the direction of the wind. Its surface reflecting the sun is dazzlingly bright. The outlines of the hills are remarkably distinct and firm & their surfaces bare & hard not clothed with a thick air. I notice one red tree—a red maple, against the green woodside in Conants meadow—   It is a far brighter red than the blossoms of any tree in summer—and more conspicuous. The huckleberry bushes on Conantum are all turned red.

What can be handsomer for a picture than our river scenery now! Take this view from the firsst Conantum Cliff. First this smoothly shorne meadow on the west side of the stream, with all the swathes distinct—   Sprinkled with apple trees casting heavy shadows—black as

ink, such as can be seen only in this clear air.– this strong light–
one cow wandering restlessly about in it and lowing.– Then the
blue river–scarcely darker than and not to be distinguished from the
sky–its waves driven sowthward or up stream by the wind–making
it appear to flow that way bordered by willows & button bushes.–
Then the narrow meadow beyond with varied lights & shades from
its waving grass which for some reason has not been cut this year.–
though so dry–now at length each grass blade bending south before
the wintery blast, as if bending for aid in that direction.– Then the
hill rising 60 feet to a terrace like plain–covered with shruboaks–
maples &c now variously tinted. clad all in a livery of gay colors–
every bush a feather in its cap. And further in the rear the wood
crowned Cliff some 200 feet high, where grey rocks here & there
project from amidst the bushes.– with its orchard on the slope. And
to the right of the cliff the distant Lincoln hills in the horizon. The
landscape so handsomely colored–the air so clear & wholesome–&
the surface of the earth is so pleasingly varied–that it seems rarely
fitted for the abode of man.

In Cohush swamp the sumac leaves have turned a very deep red,
but have not lost their fragrance. I notice wild apples growing
luxuriantly in the midst of the swamp–rising red over the colored
painted leaves of the sumac–& reminding me that they were ripened
& colored by the same influences–some green, some yellow, some
red, like the leaves.

Fell in with a man whose breath smelled of spirit which he had
drunk.– How could I but feel that it was his own spirit that I
smelt. Behind Miles' Darius Miles' that was–I asked an Irishman
how many potatoes he could dig in a day–wishing to know how
well they yielded– "Well, I dont keep any account", he answered,
"I scratch away, and let the day's work praise itself." Aye–there's the
difference between the Irishman and the Yankee–the Yankee keeps
an account. The simple honesty of the Irish pleases me. A sparrow-
hawk–hardly so big as a night-hawk flew over high above my head–
a pretty little graceful fellow too small & delicate to be rapacious.

Found a grove of young sugar maples Acer saccharinum–behind
what was Mile's– How silently & yet startlingly the existence of
these sugarmaples was revealed to me––which I had not thought
grew in my immediate neighborhood–when first I perceived the
entire edges of its leaves & their obtuse sinuses.

Such near hills as Nobscut & Nashoba have lost all their azure in
this clear air and plainly belong to earth. Give me clearness

nevertheless though my heavens be moved further off to pay for it.

I perceive from the hill behind Lees that much of the river meadow is not cut—though they have been very dry. The sun-sparkle on the river is dazzlingly bright in this atmosphere as it has not been perchance for many a month. It is so cold I am glad to sit behind the wall. Still the great bidens blooms by the causeway side beyond the bridge.

At Clematis Brook I perceive that the pods or follicles of the Asclepias Syriaca point upward—(did they before all point down?) They are already bursting. I release some seeds with the long fine silk attached—the fine threads fly apart open with a spring as soon as released—& then ray themselves out into a hemispherical form, each thread freeing itself from its neighbor & all reflecting prismatic tints. The seeds besides are winged, I let one go and it rises slowly & uncertainly at first now driven this way then that, by airs which I can not perceive—& I fear it will make shipwreck against the neighboring wood—but no, as it approaches it—it surely rises above it & then feeling the strong north wind it is borne off rapidly in the opposite direction—ever rising higher & higher—& tossing & heaved about with every commotion—till at a hundred feet in the air & 50 rods off steering south I loose sight of it   How many myriads go sailing away at this season over hill & meadow & river—to plant their race in new localities—on various tacks until the wind lulls—who can tell how many miles. And for this end these silken streamers have been perfecting all summer, snugly packed in this light chest—a perfect adaptation to this end—a prophecy of the fall & of future springs. Who could believe in prophecies of Daniel or of Miller that the world would end this summer while one Milkweed with faith matured its seeds!

The wings of the seed too plainly keep it steady and prevent its whirling round.—

On Mt Misery some very rich yellow leaves clear yellow of the Populus grandidentata. which still love to wag and tremble in my hands.— Also canoe-birches there.

The river & pond from the side of the sun looks comparatively dark. As I look over the country westward & north westward the prospect looks already bleak & wintry. The surface of the earth between the forests is no longer green but russet & hoary. You see distinctly 8 or 10 miles the russet earth—& even houses—and then its outline is distinctly traced against the further blue Mts—30 or 5 miles

distant.– You see distinctly perhaps to the height of land between
the Nashua & Concord–and then the convexity of the earth
conceals the further hills though high–& your vision leeaps a broad
valley at once to the Mts. Get home at noon

At sundown the wind has all gone down

Sep 25th

I was struck by the fitness of the expression chosen by the
Irishman yesterday–"I let the day's work praise itself" It was more
pertinent than a scholar could have selected. But the Irishman does
not trouble himself to inquire if the day's work has not reason to
blame itself.

Some men are excited by the smell of burning powder–but I
thought in my dream last night how much saner to be excited by
the smell of new bread..

I did not see but the seeds of the milkweed would be borne
many hundred miles–and those which were ripened in New
England might plant themselves in Pennsylvania. Packed in a little
oblong chest–armed with soft downy prickles & lined with a smooth
silky lining–lie some hundreds of pear shaped seeds or shaped like
the weight of steel-yards–the plumb? closely packed and filling the
follicle one or 2 hundred seeds–which have derived their nutriment
through a band of extremely fine silken threads attached by their
extremities to the core. At length when the seeds are matured &
cease to require nourishment from the plant–being weaned & the
pod with dryness & frost bursting–the extremities of the silken
threads detach them selves from the core & from being the conduits
of nutriment to the seed become the bouyant balloon which like
some spiders' webs bears the seeds to new & distant fields They
merely serve to buoy up the full fed seed.– far finer than the finest
thread. Think of the great variety of balloons which are buoyed up
by similar means. I am interested in the fate or success of every such
venture which the autumn sends forth.

I am astonished to find how much travellers both in the east and
west permit themselves to be imposed on by a name– That the
traveller in the east for instance presumes so great a difference
between one Asiatic and another because one bears the title of a
christian & the other not– At length he comes to a sect of
christians Armenians or Nestorians–& predicates of them a far
greater civilization–civility & humanity than of their neighbors–I
suspect not with much truth– At that distance & so impartially
viewed I see but little difference between a Christian & a

Mahometan—& so I perceive that European & American Christians so called are precisely like these heathenish Armenian & Nestorian Christians not christians of course in any true sense but one other heathenish sect in the west the difference between whose religion and that of the Mahometans is very slight & unimportant; Just such not Christians—but as it were heathenish Nestorian Christians are we Americans.

As if a Christian's dog were something better than a Mahometan's.— I perceive no triumphant superiority in the so called Christian over the so-called Mahometan. That nation is not Christian where the principles of humanity do not prevail, but the prejudices of race. I expect the Christian not to be superstitious—but to be distinguished by the clearness of his knowledge—the strength of his faith, the breadth of his humanity. A man of another race, an African for instance, comes to America to travel through it, & he meets with treatment exactly similar to that which the American meets with among the Turks—& Arabs—& Tartars— The traveller in both cases finds the religion to be a mere superstition & frenzy—or rabidness.

The season of flowers may be considered as past now that the frosts have come

Fires have become comfortable. The evenings are pretty long.

Sep. 25th

2 Pm to bathe in Hubbards Meadow thence to Cliffs—

It is beautiful weather—the air wonderfully clear & all objects bright & distinct. The air is of crystal purity. Both air & water are so transparent that the fisherman tries in vain to deceive the fish with his baits. Even our commonly muddy river looks clear today.. I find the water suddenly cold, and that the bathing days are over

I see numerous butterflies still yellow—& small red—though not in fleets. Examined the Hornets' nest near Hubbard's Grove—suspended from contiguous huckleberry bushes. The tops of the bushes appearing to grow out of it, little leafy sprigs, had a pleasing effect. an inverted cone 8 or 9 inches by 7 or 8 I found no hornets now buzzing about it. Its entrance appeared to have been enlarged—so I concluded it had been deserted—but looking nearer I discovered 2 or 3 dead hornets—men of war—in the entry way. Cutting off the bushes which sustained it I proceeded to open it with my knife. First there were half a dozen layers of waved brownish paper resting loosely on one another—occupying nearly an inch in thickness—for a covering. Within were the six-sided cells in 3 stories suspended from

the roof & from one another by one or two suspension rods only—
the lower story much smaller than the rest. And in what may be
called the attic garret of the structure were two live hornets
apparently partially benumed with cold, which in the sun seemed
rapidly recovering themselves, their faculties Most of the cells were
empty, but in some were young hornets still their heads projecting—
apparently still-born.— perhaps overtaken unexpectedly by cold
weather. These insects appear to be very sensible to cold. The inner
circles of cells were made of whitish—the outer of brown or greyish
paper. It was like a deserted castle of the Mohawks.— a few dead
ones at the entrance of their castle.—

I watched the seeds of the milk-weed rising higher & higher till
lost in the sky with as much interest as his friends did Mr Lauriat. I
brought home 2 of the pods which were already bursting open and
amused myself from day to day with releasing the seeds & watching
rise slowly into the heavens till they were lost to my eye. No doubt
the greater or less rapidity with which they rose would serve as a
natural barometer to test the condition of the air.

The hornets' nests not brown but grey two shades whitish & dark
—alternating on the outer layers or the covering—giving it a waved
appearance.

In these cooler—windier—crystal days the note of the jay sounds a
little more native— Standing on the Cliffs I see them flitting and
screaming from pine to pine beneath—displaying their gaudy blue
pinions. Hawks too I perceive sailing about in the clear air—looking
white against the green pines—like the seeds of the milk-weed. There
is almost always a pair of hawks. Their shrill-scream—that of the owls
& wolves are all related.

26th

Since I perambulated the bounds of the town I find that I have in
some degree confined myself——my vision and my walks—on
whatever side I look off I am reminded of the mean & narrow-
minded men whom I have lately met there— What can be uglier
than a country occupied by grovelling coarse & low-lived men—no
scenery will redeem it—what can be more beautiful than any scenery
inhabited by heroes!

Any landscape would be glorious to me, If I were assured that its
sky was arched over a single hero. Hornets hyaenas & Babboons are
not so great a curse to a country as men of a similar character. It is a
charmed circle which I have drawn around my abode—having
walked not with God but with the Devil. I am too well aware when

I have crossed this line. Most New England biographies & journals—John Adam's not excepted—affect me like opening of the tombs.

The prudent & reasonable farmers are already plowing against another year.

Sep 27th

Here is a cloudy day—& now the fisherman is out. Some tall many flowered blueish white asters are still abundant by the brook sides.

I never found a pitcher plant without an insect in it. The bristles about the nose of the pitcher all point inward, and insects which enter or fall in appear for this reason unable to get out again. It is some obstacle which our senses cannot appreciate.

We of Massachusetts boast a good deal of what we do for the education of our people—of our district-school system—& yet our district schools are as it were but infant schools—& we have no system for the education of the great mass who are grown up.— I have yet to learn that one cent is spent by this town—this political community called Concord directly to educate the great mass of its inhabitants who have long since left the district school.— for the Lyceum—important as it is comparatively—though absolutely trifling is supported by individuals— There are certain refining & civilizing influences as works of art—journals—& books & scientific instruments which this community is amply rich enough to purchase which would educate this village—elevate its tone of thought, & if it alone improved these opportunities easily make it the centre of civilization in the known world—put us on a level as to opportunities at once with London & Arcadia—and secure us a culture at once superior to both— Yet we spend 16000 dollars on a Town House a hall for our political meetings mainly and nothing to educate ourselves who are grown up. Pray is there nothing in the market—no advantages—no intellectual food worth buying? Have Paris & London & New York & Boston nothing to dispose of which this Village might buy & appropriate to its own use. Might not this great villager adorn his villa with a few pictures & statues—enrich himself with a choice library as available without being cumbrous as any in the world—with scientific instruments for such as have a taste to use them. Yet we are contented to be countrified—to be provincial. I am astonished to find that in this 19th century—in this land of free schools—we spend absolutely nothing as a town on our own education cultivation civilization. Each town like each individual has its own character—some more some less cultivated. I know many towns so mean spirited & benighted that it would be a disgrace to belong to them. I believe that some of our New England villages within 30 miles of Boston are as boorish & barbarous communities as there are on the face of the earth—and how much superior are the best of them? If London has any refinement any information to sell why should we not buy it? Would not the town of Carlisle do well to spend 16000 dollars on its own education at once—if it could only find a schoolmaster for itself— It has one man as I hear who takes the North-American Review—that will never Civilize them I fear— Why should not the town itself take the London & Edinburg Reviews—& put itself in communication with whatever sources of light & intelligence there are in the world?

Yet Carlisle is very little behind Concord in these respects— I do not know but it spends its proportional part on education. How happens it that the only libraries which the towns possess are the District school libraries—books for children only—or for readers who must needs be written down to— Why should they not have a library, if not so extensive yet of the same stamp & more select than the British museum? It is not that the town cannot well afford to buy these things—but it is unaspiring & ignorant of its own wants. It sells milk, but it only builds larger barns with the money which it gets for its milk. Undoubtedly every New England village is as able to surround itself with as many civilizing influences of this kind the members of the English nobility—& here there need be no peasantry. If the London Times is the best news-paper in the world why does not the village of Concord take it that its inhabitants may read it—& not the 2nd best. If the south sea explorers have at length got their story ready—& Congress has neglected to make it accessible to the people—why does not Concord purchase one for its grown up children.

Parrot in his "journey to Ararat" speaking of the difficulty of reaching it owing to the lateness of the season—says of the surrounding country.—"As early even as the month of June vegetable life becomes in a manner extinct, from the combined influence of the sun's rays, and the aridity of the atmosphere & soil: the plains & mountain sides, being destitute of both wood and water, have no covering but a scanty & burnt herbage, the roots of which are so rarely visited by a refreshing shower that the reparatory power of nature is all but lost, while the active animal kingdom seeks protection against the heat & drought either by burrowing in the earth, or retiring to the cool and inaccessible retreats in Caucasus and the mountains of Asia Minor."

This reminds me of what I have observed even in our own summers. With us too "vegetable life becomes in a manner extinct" —by the end of June & the beholder is impressed as if "the reparatory power of nature is? all but lost"

2 Pm Rowed down the river to Balls' Hill.

The maples by the river side look very green yet—have not begun to blush—nor are the leaves touched by frost. Not so on the uplands. The river is so low that off N Barrets shore some low islands are exposed covered with a green grass like mildew. There are all kinds of boats chained to trees & stumps by the riverside—some from Boston & the salt—but I think that none after all is so suitable and convenient as the simple flat bottomed & light boat that has long been made here by the farmers themselves. They are better adapted to the river than those made in Boston.

From Balls' Hill the Great meadows now smoothly shorn have a quite imposing appearance—so spacious & level— There is so little of this level land in our midst. There is a shadow on the sides of the hills surrounding—(a cloudy day) & where the meadow meets them it is darkest. The shadow deepens down the woody hills & is most distinctly dark where they meet the meadow line. Now the sun in the west is coming out & lights up the river a mile off so that it shines with a white light like a burnished silver mirror

The poplar tree seems quite important to the scene. The pastures are so dry that the cows have been turned on to the meadow, but they gradually devest it—all feeding one way— The patches of sunlight on the meadow look luridly yellow as if flames were traversing it. It is a day for fishermen. The farmers are gathering in their corn.

The Mikania scandens & the button bushes & the Pickerel weed are sere & flat with frost. We looked down the long reach toward Carlisle bridge— The river which is as low as ever still makes a more than respectable appearance here—& is of generous width. Rambled over the hills toward Tarbells. The huckleberry bushes appear to be unusually red this fall—reddening these hills— We scared a calf out of the meadow which ran like a ship tossed on the waves over the hills toward Tarbells. They run awkwardly—red oblong squares tossing up & down like a vessel in a storm—with great commotion. We fell into the path, printed by the feet of the calves—with no cows tracks. The note of the yellow hammer is heard from the edges of the fields. The soap-wort gentian looks like a flower prematurely killed by the frost. The soil of these fields look as yellowish white as the cornstalks themselves. Tarbells hip-roofed

house looked the picture of retirement—of cottage size under its
noble elm with its heap of apples before the door & the wood
coming up with-in a few rods—It being far off the road. The smoke
from his chimney so white & vaporlike like a winter scene. The
lower limbs of the Willows & maples & buttonbushes are covered
with the black & dry roots of the water-marygold & the ranunculi—
plants with filiform capillary rootlike-submerged leaves.

Sep 28th

A considerable part of the last two nights and yesterday—a steady
& rather warm rain such as we have not had for a long time. This
morning it is still completely overcast and drizzling a little. Flocks of
small birds apparently sparrows bobolinks or some bird of equal size
with a pencilled breast which makes a musical clucking—and piping
goldfinches are flitting about like leaves & hopping up on to the
bent grass stems in the garden, letting themselves down to the heavy
heads, either shaking or picking out a seed or two, then alighting to
pick it up. I am amused to see them hop up on to the slender
drooping grass stems then slide down or let them selves down as it
were foot over foot—. with great fluttering, till they can pick at the
head & release a few seeds then alight to pick them up. They seem
to prefer a coarse grass which grows like a weed in the garden
between the potatoe hills—also the amaranth.

It is an ill wind that blows nobody any good. They say that this
has been a good year to raise turkeys it has been so dry. So that we
shall have something to be thankful for.

Hugh Miller in his Old Red Sandstone—speaking of "the
consistency of style which obtains among the ichthyolites of this
formation" and the "microscopic beauty of these ancient fishes" says
—"The artist who sculptured the cherry-stone consigned it to a
cabinet, and placed a microscope beside it; the microscopic beauty of
these ancient fish was consigned to the twilight depths of a primeval
ocean. There is a feeling which at times grows upon the painter and
the statuary, as if the perception and love of the beautiful had been
sublimed into a kind of moral sense. Art comes to be pursued for its
own sake; the exquisite conception in the mind, or the elegant and
elaborate model, becomes all in all to the worker, and the dread of
criticism or the appetite of praise almost nothing. And thus, through,
the influence of a power somewhat akin to conscience, but whose
province is not the just and the good, but the fair, the refined, the
exquisite, have works prosecuted in solitude, and never intended for
the world, been found fraught with loveliness." The hesitation with

which this is said—to say nothing of its simplicity—betrays a latent infidelity more fatal far than that of the Vestiges of Creation which in another work this author endeavors to correct. He describes that as an exception which is in fact the rule. The supposed want of harmony between "the perception and love of the beautiful" and a delicate moral sense betrays what kind of beauty the writer has been conversant with. He speaks of his work becoming all in all to the worker his rising above the dread of criticism & the appetite of praise as if these were the very rare exceptions in a great artists life— & not the very definition of it.

2 Pm to Conantum

A warm, damp, mistling day—without much wind. The white pines in Hubbards' Grove have now a pretty distinct particolored look—green & yellow mottled—reminding me of some plants like the milkweed expanding with maturity & pushing off their downy seeds. They have a singularly soft look. For a week or ten days I have ceased to look for new flowers or carry my botany in my pocket. The fall dandelion is now very fresh and abundant in its prime.

I see where the squirrels have carried off the ears of corn more than twenty rods from the corn field into the woods. A little further on beyond Hubbards brook I saw a grey-squirrel with an ear of yellow corn a foot long sitting on the fence. 15 rods from the field. He dropped the corn but continued to sit on the rail where I could hardly see him, it being of the same color with himself—which I have no doubt he was well aware of—he next took to a red maple where his policy was to conceal himself behind the stem, hanging perfectly still there till I passed—his fur being exactly the color of the bark— When I struck the tree & tried to frighten him he knew better than to run to the next tree there being no continuous row by which he might escape, but he merely fled higher up and put so many leaves between us that it was difficult to discover him— When I threw up a stick to frighten him he disappeared entirely though I kept the best watch I could & stood close to the foot of the tree. They are wonderfully cunning.

The Eupatorium purpureum is early killed by frost—and stands now all dry and brown by the sides of other herbs like the golden rod and tansey which are quite green—& in blossom.

The rail-roads as much as anything appear to have unsettled the farmers. Our young Concord farmers & their young wives hearing this bustle about them—seeing the world all going by as it were— some daily to the cities about their business, some to California—

plainly cannot make up their minds to live the quiet retired old-
fashioned country-farmer's life— They are impatient if they live
more than a mile from a railroad. While all their neighbors are
rushing to the road—there are few who have character or bravery
enough to live off the road. He is too well aware what is going on
in the world not to wish to take some part in it. I was reminded of
this by meeting S Tutle in his wagon.

The pontederia—which apparently makes the mass of the weeds
by the side of the river,—is all dead and brown and has been for
some time—the year is over for it.

The mist is so thin that it is like haze or smoke in the air
imparting a softness to the landscape.

Sitting by the Spruce swamp in Conant's Grove, I am reminded
that this is a perfect day to visit the swamps, with its damp mistling,
mildewy air, so solemnly still. There are the spectre-like black spruce
hanging with esnea moss—and in the rear rise the dark green pines &
oaks on the hill side—touched here & their with livelier tints where a
maple or birch may stand—this so luxuriant vegetation standing heavy
dark sombre like mould in a cellar. The peculiar tops of the spruce
are seen against this.

I hear the barking of a red squirrel who is alarmed at something—
& a great scolding or ado among the jays—who make a great cry
about nothing. The swamp is bordered with the red-berried alder or
prinos & the button bush The balls of the last appear not half
grown this season probably on account of the drought.— & now
they are killed by frost.

This swamp contains beautiful specimens of the side-saddle flower
Sarracenia purpurea—better called Pitcher Plant— They ray out
around the dry-scape & flower which still remain, resting on rich
uneven beds of a coarse reddish moss through which the small
flowered andromeda puts up—presenting altogether a most rich &
luxuriant appearance to the eye. Though the moist is comparatively
dry—I cannot walk without upsetting the numerous pitchers which
are now full of water & so wetting my feet. I once accidently sat
down on such a bed of pitcher plants & found an uncommonly wet
seat where I expected a dry one. These leaves are of various colors
from Plain Green to a rich striped yellow or deep red. No plants are
more richly painted & streaked than the inside of the broad lips of
these Old Josselyn called this "Hollow-leaved Lavender" No other
plant methinks that we have is so remarkable & singular.

Here was a large hornets nest which when I went to take and

first knocked on it to see if any body was at home out came the whole swarm upon me lively enough— I do not know why they should linger longer than their fellows whom I saw the other day, unless because the swamp is warmer. They were all within & not working however.

I picked up two arrow-heads in the field beyond.

What honest homely—earth-loving unaspiring houses they used to live in. Take that on Conantum for instance—so low you can put your hand on the eaves behind— There are few whose pride could stoop to enter such a house to-day. & then the broad chimney built for comfort not for beauty—with no coping of bricks to catch the eye—no alto or basso relievo. The mist has now thickened into a fine rain & I retreat.

Sep 29th

Van der Donck says of the Water-beech [buttonwood] "This tree retains the leaves later than any other tree of the woods".

P m to Goose Pond via E Hosmers return by Walden.

Found Hosmer carting out manure from under his barn to make room for the winter. He said he was tired of farming—he was too old. Quoted Webster as saying that he had never eaten the bread of idleness for a single day—and thought that Lord Brougham might have said as much with truth while he was in the opposition,—but he did not know that he could say as much of himself. However—he did not wish to be idle—he merely wished to rest.

Looked on Walden from the hill with the sawed pine stump on the north side. Scared up 3 black ducks which rose with a great noise of their wings striking the water. The hills this fall are unusually red not only with the huckleberry—but the sumac & the blackberry vines

Walden plainly can never be spoiled by the wood-chopper—for do what you will to the shore there will still remain this crystal well.

The intense brilliancy of the red-ripe maples scattered here and there in the midst of the green oaks & hickories on its hilly shore is quite charming. They are unexpectedly & incredibly brilliant— especially on the western shore & close to the waters edge, where alternating with yellow birches & poplars & green oaks—they remind me of a line of soldiers red coats & riflemen in green mixed together.

The pine is one of the richest of trees to my eye—it stands like a great moss—a luxuriant mildew—the pumpkin pine—which the earth produces without effort.

The poet writes the history of his body. Query—Would not the cellular tissue of the Grass Poly—make good tinder? I find that when I light it it burns up slowly & entirely without blaze, like spunk.

Sep 30th

To Powder mills & set an intermediate boundstone on the new road there. Saw them making hoops for powder casks of alder & the sprouts of the white-birch which are red with whitish spots. How interesting it is to observe a particular use discovered in any material. I am pleased to find that the artizan has good reason for preferring one material to another for a particular purpose. I am pleased to learn that a man has detected any *use* in wood or stone or any material—or in other words its relation to man.

The white ash has got its autumnal mulberry hue— What is the autumnal tint of the black ash— The former contrasts strongly with the other shade trees on the village streeet—the elms & buttonwoods —at this season—looking almost black at the first glance— The diffirent characters of the trees appear at this season when their leaves so to speak are ripe than at any other—than in the winter for instance when they are little remarkable—& almost uniformly grey or brown or in the spring & and summer when they are undistinguishably green. Now a red maple—an ash—a white birch—a populus grandidentata &c is distinguished almost as far as they are visible. It is with leaves as with fruits & woods—& animals & men— when they are mature their different characters appear.

The sun has been obscured much of the day by passing clouds— but now at 5 Pm the sun comes out & by the very clear & brilliant light though the shadows begin to fall long from the trees, it is proved how remarkably clear or pure the atmosphere is— According to all accounts an hour of such a light would be something quite memorable in England.

As the wood of an old Cremona its very fibre perchance harmoniously transposed & educated to resound melody has brought a great price—so methinks these telegraph posts should bear a great price with musical instrument makers— It is prepared to be the material of harps for ages to come, as it were put a soak in & seasoning in music.

Saw a hornets nest on a tree over the road near the Powder Mills 30 or 40 feet high.

Even the pearl—like the beautiful galls on the oaks—is said to be the production of diseaseas or rather obstruction—the fish covering as with a tear some rough obstruction that has got into his shell.

Oct 1st 51

5 P m Just put a fugitive slave who has taken the name of Henry Williams into the cars for Canada. He escaped from Stafford County Virginia to Boston last October, has been in Shadracks place at the Cornhill Coffee-house—had been corresponding through an agent with his master who is his father about buying—himself—his master asking $600 but he having been able to raise only $500.— heard that there were writs out for two Williamses fugitives—and was informed by his fellow servants & employer that Augerhole Burns & others of the police had called for him when he was out. Accordingly fled to Concord last night on foot—bringing a letter to our family from Mr Lovejoy of Cambridge—& another which Garrison had formerly given him on another occasion.

He lodged with us & waited in the house till funds were collected with which to forward him. Intended to despatch him at noon through to Burlington—but when I went to buy his ticket saw one at the Depot who looked & behaved so much like a Boston policeman, that I did not venture that time.

An intelligent and very well behaved man—a mullatto.

There is art to be used not only in selecting wood for a withe but in using it. Birch withes are twisted, I suppose in order that the fibres may be less abruptly bent—or is it only by accident that they are twisted?

The slave said he could guide himself by many other stars than the north star whose rising & setting he knew— They steered for the north star even when it had got round and appeared to them to be in the south. They frequently followed the telegraph when there was no railroad. The slaves bring many superstitions from Africa. The fugitives sometimes superstitiously carry a turf in their hats thinking that their success depends on it.

These days when the trees have put on their autumnal tints are the gala days of the year—when the very foliage of trees is colored like a blossom— It is a proper time for a yearly festival—an agricultural show.

Candlelight To Conantum— The moon not quite half full. The twilight is much shorter now than a month ago, probably as the atmosphere is clearer and there is less to reflect the light. The air is cool & the ground also feels cold under my feet as if the grass were wet with dew which is not yet the case. I go through Wheelers cornfield in the twilight, where the stalks are bleached almost white— and his tops are still stacked along the edge of the field. The moon

is not far up above the southwestern horizon. Looking west at this
hour the earth is an unvaried undistinguishable black in contrast with
the twilight sky. It is as if you were walking in night up to your
chin. There is no wind stirring. An oak tree in Hubbard's pasture
stands absolutely motionless and dark against the sky. The crickets
sound farther off or fainter at this season as if they had gone deeper
into the sod to avoid the cold. There are no crickets heard on the
alders on the causeway. The moon looks colder in the water. There
is a great change between this and my last moon light walk— I
experience a comfortable warmth when I approach the south side of
a dry wood—which keeps off the cooler air and also retains some of
the warmth of day. The voices of travellers in the road are heard afar
over the fields. even to Conantum house. The moon is too far west
to be seen reflected in the river at Tupelo cliff—but the stars are
reflected— The river is a dark mirror with bright points feebly
fluctuating— I smell the bruised horsemint which I cannot see while
I sit on the brown rocks by the shore. I see the glow-worm under
the damp cliff— No whippoorwills are heard tonight—and scarcely a
note of any other bird. At 8 o'clock the fogs have begun which
with the shining on them look like cobwebs or thin white veils
spread over the earth— They are the dreams or visions of the
meadow.

The second growth of the white-pine is probably softer & more
beautiful than the primitive forest ever afforded. The primitive forest
is more grand with its bare mossy stems and ragged branches, but
exhibits no such masses of green needles trembling in the light.

The elms are generally of a dirty or brownish yellow now

Oct 2nd

PM. Some of the white Pines on Fair Haven Hill have just
reached the acme of their fall;—others have almost entirely shed their
leaves, and they are scattered over the ground and the walls. The
same is the state of the Pitch pines. At the Cliffs I find the wasps
prolonging their short lives on the sunny rocks just as they
endeavored to do at my house in the woods. It is a little hazy as I
look into the west today. The shrub oaks on the terraced plain are
now almost uniformly of a deep red.

Sat Oct 4th

The emigrant had for weeks been tossing on the Atlantic &
perchance as long ascending the St Lawrence with contrary winds—
conversant as yet in the new world only with the dreary coast of
Newfondland & Labrador—& the comparatively wild shores of the

river below the Isle of Orleans. It is said that under these circumstances, the sudden apparition of Quebec on turning Point Levi—makes a memorable impression on the beholder.

Minot was telling me today that he used to know a man in Lincoln who had no floor to his barn but waited till the ground froze then swept it clean in his barn & threshed his grain on it

He also used to see men threshing their buck-wheat in the field where it grew—having just taken off the surface down to a hard pan.

Minot used the word *"gavel"* to describe a parcel of stalks cast on the ground to dry. His are good old English words and I am always sure to find them in the dictionary—though I never heard them before in my life.

I was admiring his corn stalks disposed about the barn to dry over or astride the braces & the timbers—of such a fresh clean & handsome green retaining their strength & nutritive properties so—unlike the gross & careless husbandry of speculating money-making farmers—. who suffer their stalks to remain out till they are dry & dingy & black as chips. Minot is perhaps the most poetical farmer who most realizes to me the poetry of the farmer's life—that I know. He does nothing (with haste and drudgery—) but as if he loved it. He makes the most of his labor and takes infinite satisfaction in every part of it. He is not looking forward to the sale of his crops—or any pecuniary profit, but he is paid by the constant satisfaction which his labor yields him. He has not too much land to trouble him—too much work to do—no hired man nor boy. but simply to amuse himself & live. He cares not so much to raise a large crop as to do his work well.

He knows every pin & nail in his barn. If another linter is to be floored he lets no hired man rob him of that amusement—but he goes slowly to the woods and at his leisure selects a pitch pine tree cuts it & hauls it or gets it hauled to the mill and so he knows the history of his barn-floor

Farming is an amusement which has lasted him longer than gunning or fishing— He is never in a hurry to get his garden planted & yet is always planted soon enough—& none in the town is kept so beautifully clean— He always prophecies a failure of the crops.— and yet is satisfied with what he gets. His barn-floor is fastened down with oak pins & he prefers them to iron spikes—which he says will rust & give way—

He handles & amuses himself with every ear of his corn crop as much as a child with its playthings & so his small crop goes a great

way. He might well cry if it were carried to market. The seed of
weeds is no longer in his soil.

He loves to walk in a swamp in windy weather & hear the wind
groan through the pines.

He keeps a cat in his barn to catch the mice. He indulges in no
luxury of food or dress or furniture—yet he is not penurious but
merely simple. If his sister dies before him he may have to go to the
alms house in his old age—yet he is not poor—for he does not want
riches.

He gets out of each manipulation in the farmers operations a fund
of entertainment which the speculating drudge hardly knows.

With never failing rhumatism & trembling hands—he seems yet to
enjoy perennial health. Though he never reads a book—since he has
finished the Naval Monument—he speaks the best of English

Sunday Oct 5th

I noticed on Friday Oct 3d that the Willows generally were green
& unchanged The red-maples varied from green through yellow to
bright red.

The black-cherry was green inclining to yellow

(I speak of such trees as I chanced to see) The apple trees green
but shedding their leaves like most of the trees

Elm a dingy yellow. White ash from green to dark purple or
Mulberry White-oak green inclining to yellow Tupelo reddish
yellow & red— Tree bushed about the head, limbs small & slanting
downward.

Some maples when ripe are yellow or whitish yellow—others
reddish yellow—others bright red—by the accident of the season or
position—the more or less light & sun—being on the edge or in the
midst of the wood— Just as the fruits are more or less deeply
colored.

Birches green & yellow. Swamp white oak a yellowish green—
Black ash—greenish yellow & now sered by frost— Bass sered
yellowish.

Color in the maturity of foliage is as variable & little characteristic
as naturalists have found it to be for distinguishing fishes &
quadrupeds &c.

Observed that the wood-chuck has two or more holes—a rod or
two apart— One or the front door—where the excavated sand is
heaped up—another not so easily discovered—very small round
without any sand about it being that by which he emerged—smaller
directly at the surface than beneath—on the principle by which a well

is dug making as small a hole as possible at the surface to prevent caving. About these holes is now seen their manure apparently composed chiefly of the remains of crickets which are seen crawling over the sand.

Saw a very fat woodchuck on a wall—evidently prepared to go into winter quarters.

Still purplish asters—& late golden rods—& fragrant life everlasting—& purple gerardia—great Bidens &c &c

The Dogwood by the Corner road has lost every leaf—its bunches of dry greenish berries hanging straight down from the bare stout twigs as if their peduncles were broken. It has assumed its winter aspect. A Mithridatic look

The Prinos berries are quite red.

The panicled hawkweed is one of those yellowish spherical or hemispherical fuzzy seeded plants—which you see about the wood-paths & fields at present—which however only a strong wind can blow far.—

Saw by the path-side beyond the Conant Spring that singular jelly like sort of Mushroom—which I saw last spring while surveying Whites farm—now red globular ¾ inch in diameter, covering the coarse moss by the ruts on the path side with jelly-covered seeds(?)

2 P M to the high open land between Batemans' Pond & the lime kiln.

It is a still cloudy afternoon rather cool As I go past Cheney's Boathouse—the river looks lighter than the sky— The butternuts have shed nearly all their leaves, and their nuts are seen black against the sky. The White oaks are turned a reddish brown in some valleys. The Norway cinquefoil and a smaller cinquefoil are still in blossom & also the late buttercup My companion remarked that the land (for the most part consisting of decayed orchards huckleberry pastures and forests) on both sides of the Old Carlisle road, uneven and undulating like the road appeared to be all in-motion like the traveller—travelling on with him. Found a wild russet apple very good—of peculiar form flattened at the poles. ↻ Some red maples have entirely lost their leaves— The black birch is straw colored.

The rocks in the high open pasture are peculiar & interesting to walk over—for though presenting broad & flat surfaces—the strata are perpendicular producing a grained & curled appeareance—this rocky crown like a hoary head covered with curly hair—or it is like walking over the edges of the leaves of a vast book. I wonder how these rocks were ever worn even thus smooth by the elements. The strata are remarkably serpentine or waving. It appears as if you were upon the axis of elevation geologically speaking. I do not remember any other pasture in Concord where the rocks are so remarkable for this.

What is that fleshy or knot-fleshy root which we found in the soil on the rocks by Bateman's pond—which looked so edible? All meadows and swamps have been remarkably dry this year & are still notwithstanding the few showers and rainy days. Witch hazel now in bloom I perceive the fragrance of ripe grapes in the air, and after a little search discover the ground covered with them where the frost has stripped the vines of leaves—still fresh & plump & perfectly ripe. The little conical burrs of the agrimony stick to my clothes. The pale lobelia still blooms freshly— The rough hawkweed—holds up its globes of yellowish fuzzy seeds as well as the panicled. The clouds have cleared away the sun come out & it is warmer & very pleasant. The declining sun falling on the willows &c below Mrs Ripleys & on the water—produces a rare soft light—such as I do not often see—a greenish yellow. The milk weed seeds are in the air. I see one in the river—which a minnow occasionally jostles. (stood near a small rabbit hardly half grown by the old carlisle road) I hear the red wing black-birds by the river side again as if it were a new spring. They appear to have come to bid farewell. The birds appear to depart with the coming of the frosts which kill the vegetation & directly or indirectly the insects on which they feed. The American bittern Ardea Minor flew across the river trailing his legs in the water scared up by us— This according to Peabody is the boomer—[stake driver] In their sluggish flight they can hardly keep their legs up. Wonder if they can soar

8 Pm to Cliffs

Moon ¾ full. The nights now are very still for there is hardly any noise of birds or of insects. The whippoorwill is not heard—nor the mosquito—only the occasional lisping of some sparrow. The moon gives not a creamy but white cold light—through which you can see far distinctly. About villages You hear the bark of dogs instead of the howl of wolves— When I descend into the valley by Wheelers grain field I find it quite cold. The sand slopes in the deep Cut gleam coldly as if covered with rime. As I go through the *Spring* woods I perceive a sweet dry scent from the underwoods like that of the fragrant life everlasting. I suppose it is that. To appreciate the moonlight you must stand in the shade & see where a few rods or a few feet distant it falls in between the trees. It is a "milder day" made for some inhabitants whom you do not see. The fairies are a

quiet gentle folk invented plainly to inhabit the moonlight. I
frequently see a light on the ground within thick & dark woods–
where all around is in shadow & haste forward expecting to find
some decayed & phosphorescent stump–but find it to be some clear
moon light that falls in between some crevice in the leaves. As
moonlight is to sunlight so are the fairies to men

Standing on the Cliffs no sound comes up from the woods. The
earth has gradually turned more northward–the birds have fled south
after the sun–& this impresses me as well by day or by night as a
deserted country–there is a down-like mist over the river and pond–
and there are no bright reflections of the moon or sheeniness from
the pond in consequence–all the light being absorbed by the
low fog.

Monday Oct 6th '51

12 M to Bedford line to set a stone by river on Bedford line. The
portion of the river between Bedford and Carlisle seen from a
distance in the road today as formerly has a singularly etherial
celestial, or elysian look. It is of a light sky-blue alternating with
smoother white streaks, where the surface reflects the light differently
–like a milk-pan full of the milk of Valhalla partially skimmed more
gloriously & heavenly fair & pure than the sky itself. It is something
more celestial than the sky above it. I never saw any water look so
celestial. I have often noticed it. I believe I have seen this reach
from the hill in the middle of Lincoln. We have names for the rivers
of hell but none for the rivers of heaven., unless the milky way be
one. It is such a smooth & shining blue–like a panoply of sky-blue
plates– Our dark & muddy river has such a tint in this case as I
might expect Walden or White Pond to exhibit if they could be
seen under similar circumstances–but Walden seen from Fair Haven
is if I remember–of a deep blue color tinged with green. Cerulian?
Such water as that river reach appears to me of quite incalculable
value, and the man who would blot that out of his prospect for a
sum of money does not otherwise than to sell heaven.

Geo. Thatcher, having searched an hour in vain this morning to
find a frog–caught a pickerel with a mullein leaf.

The White ash near our house which the other day was purple or
mulberry color is now much more red.

7½ PM to Fair Haven Pond by boat. the moon ⅘ full, not a
cloud in the sky. paddling all the way. The water perfectly still &
the air almost–the former gleaming like oil in the moonlight. with
the moon's disk reflected in it.

When we started saw some fishermen kindling their fire for

spearing by the river side. It was a lurid reddish blaze, contrasting
with the white light of the moon, with a dense volumes of black
smoke from the burning pitch pine roots, rolling upward in the
form of an inverted pyramid. The blaze reflected in the water almost
as distinct as the substance. It looked like tarring a ship on the shore
of the styx or Coceytus. For it is still and dark notwithstanding the
moon—and no sound but the crackling of the fire. The fishermen
can be seen only near at hand though their fire is visible far away
and then they appear as dusky fuliginous figures, half enveloped in
smoke, seen only by their enlightened sides—like devils they look—
clad in old coats to defend themselves from the fogs—one standing
up forward holding the spear ready to dart while the smoke &
flames are blown in his face—the other paddling the boat slowly &
silently along close to the shore with almost imperceptible motion.

The river appears indefinitely wide—there is a mist rising from the
water which increases the indefiniteness. A high bank or moon-lit
hill rises at a distance over the meadow on the bank—with its sandy
gullies & clam shells exposed where the Indians feasted— The shore
line though close is removed by the eye to the side of the hill— It is
at high water mark— It is continued till it meets the hill. Now the
fisherman's fire left behind acquires some thick rays in the distance
and becomes a star—as surely as sun light falling through an irregular
chink makes a round figure on the opposite wall so the blaze at a
distance appears a star. Such is the effect of the atmosphere. The
bright sheen of the moon is constantly travelling with us & is seen at
the same angle in front on the surface of the pads—and the reflection
of its disk in the rippled water by our boatside appears like bright
gold pieces falling on the river's counter.— This coin is incessantly
poured forth as from some unseen horn of plenty at our side

(I hear a lark singing this morn Oct 7th and yesterday saw them
in the meadows. Both larks & blackbirds are heard again now
occasionally seemingly after a short absence, as if come to bid
farewell)

I do not know but the weirdness of the gleaming oily surface is
enhanced by the thin fog. A few water bugs are seen glancing in our
course.

I shout like a farmer to his oxen—and instantly the woods on the
eastern shore take it up & the western hills a little up the stream,
and so it appears to rebound from one side the river valley to the
other till at length I hear a farmer call to his team far up as Fair
Haven bay whither we are bound.

We pass through reaches where there is no fog—perhaps where a little air is stirring— Our clothes are almost wet through with the mist—as if we sat in water. Some portions of the river are much warmer than others. In one instance it was warmer in the midst of the fog—than in a clear reach.

In the middle of the Pond we tried the echo again 1st the hill on the right took it up; then further up the stream on the left; and then after a long pause when we had almost given it up—and the longer expected the more in one sense unexpected & surprising it was we heard a farmer shout to his team in a distant valley far up on the opposite side of the stream much louder than the previous echo— and even after this we heard one shout faintly in some neighboring town. The 3d echo seemed more loud and distinct than the second. But why I asked do the echoes always travel up the stream—

I turned about and shouted again—and then I found that they all appeared equally to travel down the stream, or perchance I heard only those that did so.

As we rowed to Fair Havens eastern shore a moon-lit hill covered with shrub oaks—we could form no opinion of our progress toward it, not seeing the water line where it met the hill—until we saw the weeds & sandy shore & the tall bullrushes rising above the shallow water the the masts of large vessels in a haven. The moon was so high that the angle of excidence did not permit of our seeing her reflection in the pond.

As we paddled down the stream with our backs to the moon, we saw the reflection—of every wood & hill on both sides distinctly These answering reflections—shadow to substance,—impress the voyager with a sense of harmony & symmetry—as when you fold a blotted paper & produce a regular figure.— a dualism which nature loves. What you commonly see is but half. As we paddle up or down we see the cabins of muskrats faintly rising from amid the weeds—and the strong odor of musk is borne to us from particular parts of the shore. also the odor of a skunk is wafted from over the meadows or fields. The fog appears in some places gathered into a little pyramid or squad by itself—on the surface of the water. Where the shore is very low the actual & reflected trees appear to stand foot to foot—& it is but a line that separates them & the water & the sky almost flow into one another—& the shore seems to float. Home at 10.

Oct 7th

This morning the fog over the river & the brooks & meadows running into it has risen to the height of 40 or 50 feet.

{One-half page blank}

Oct 7th 51.

1 PM to river by boat to Corner Bridge A very still warm bright clear afternoon. Our boat so small and low that we are close to the water. The muskrats all the way are now building their houses— about ⅔ done. They are of an oval form ◯ (looking down on them) sloping upward from the smaller end by which the rat ascends —and composed of mouthfuls of Pontederia leaf stems (now dead) the capillaceous roots or leaves of the water marygold & other capillaceous leaved water plants.— flag-root—a plant which looks like a cock's tail or a peacocks feather in form—clam shells &c—sometimes rising from amidst the dead pontederia stems or the Button bushes— or the willows. The mouthfuls are disposed in layers successively smaller—forming a somewhat conical mound. Seen at this stage they show some art and a good deal of labor. We pulled one to pieces to examine the inside. There was a small cavity, which might hold 2 or 3 full grown muskrats just above the level of the water, quite wet and of course dark and narrow communicating immediately with a gallery under water. There were a few pieces of the white root of some water plant—perhaps a pontederia—or a lily root in it. There they dwell in close contiguity to the water itself—always in a wet apartment—in a wet coat never changed with immeasurable water in the cellar, through which is the only exit. They have reduced life to a lower scale than Diogenes. Certainly they do not fear cold—ague— or consumption. Think of bringing up a family in such a place— worse than a broad street cellar— But probably these are not their breeding places. The muskrat and the fresh water muscle are very native to our river— The Indian their human compere has departed. There is a settler whom our low lands and our bogs do not hurt.

One of the fishermen speared one last night. How long has the muskrat dined on muscles? The river Mud itself will have the ague as soon as he. What occasion has he for a dentist? Their unfinished rapidly rising nests look now like truncated cones They seem to be all building at once in different parts of the river and to have advanced equally far.

The weeds being dead & the weather cooler the water is more transparent. Now is the time to observe such weeds as have not been destroyed. The fishes are plainly seen. Saw a pickerel which had swallowd a smaller fish—with the tail projecting from his mouth. There is a dirty looking weed quite submerged with short densely crowded finely divided leaves, in dense masses atop like the tops of spruce trees, more slender below. The shores for a great width are occupied by the dead leaves and stems of the Pontederia which give the river a very wild look. There is a strong-scented green plant which looks like a fresh water sponge or coral—clumsy limbed like a dead tree. or a cactus. A long narrow grass like a freshwater eel grass.

The swamp white oak on the meadow which was blown down in the spring is still alive as if it had been supported by the sap in its trunk. The dirt still adheres to its roots which are of the color of an elephants skin.

I suppose it is the Nuphar Kalmiana which I find in blossom in deep water though its long stem 4 feet or more round & gradually tapering toward the root—with no leaves apparent make me doubt a little. Apparently 5 sepals—grenish & yellow without, yellow within 8 small petals—many stamens—stigma 8 rayed.—

Saw the ardea minor walking along the shore like a hen with long green legs—its pencilled throat is so like the reeds & shore amid which it holds its head erect to watch the passer that it is difficult to discern it. You can get very near it for it is unwilling to fly— preferring to hide amid the weeds. The lower parts of the willows & the button-bushes are black with the capillaceous leaves & stems of of the water marygold &c.

The saw edge of The rushes (common soft bulrush—juncus effusus I think it is) 2 to 4 ft high in dense fields along the shore in various stages of decay look like a level rainbow skirting the waters edge—& reflected in the water.— Though a single one or a few near at hand do not exhibit very marked or distinct colors. But a distance from a shore which is lined with them—the colors are very distinct—& produce a pleasing effect 1st next the water a few inches of pink then a faint narrow line or halo of yellowish—then a broad & lively green—the proper color of the rush—then a suny yellow—passing into the brown of the dead & seered tops— The different shades of different parts of the plant from the surface of the water to its tip— when you look at the edge of a large & dense field of them— produce 5 distinct horizontal & parrallel bars of different colors like a level rain bow—making a pleasing border to the river in a bright day like this. And occasionally the sun light from the rippled surface produced by our boat—reflected on them enhances the effect— The colors pass into each other so gradually and indefinitely as if it were the reflection of the sun falling on a mist.

The rounded hills beyond the clam shells look velvety smooth as we are floating down the stream—covered with the now red blackberry vines. The oaks look light against the sky, rising story above story. I see small whitish & pinkish polygonums along the waterside.

There is a great difference between this season and a month ago— as between one period of your life & another. A little frost is at the bottom of it.

It is a remarkable difference between night & day on the river— that there is no fog by day.

Wednesday Oct 8th

A slight wind now fills the air with elm leaves. The nights have been cool of late so that a fire has been comfortable, but the last was quite warm.

2 Pm to the Marlboro Road.

This day is very warm—yet not bright like the last, but hazy. Picked up an Ind. gouge on Dennis' Hill. The foliage has lost its very bright tints now—it is more dull—looks dry or as if burnt even— The very ground or grass is crisped with drought—and yields a crispy sound to my feet. The woods are brownish—reddish—yellowish merely—excepting of course the evergreens. It is so warm that I am obliged to take off my neck-handkerchief & laborers complain of the heat.

By the side of J. P. Browns grain field I picked up some white-oak acorns in the path by the woodside—which I found to be unexpectedly sweet & palateable, the bitterness being scarcely perceptible— To my taste they are quite as good as chestnuts. No wonder the first men lived on acorns Such as these are no mean food—such as they are represented to be. Their sweetness is like the sweetness of bread—and to have discovered this palatableness in this neglected nut—the whole world is to me the sweeter for it. I am related again to the first men What can be handsomer—wear better to the eye—than the color of the acorn like the leaves on which they fall—polished. or varnished.

To find that acorns are edible—it is a greater addition to ones stock of life than would be imagined. I should be at least equally pleased if I were to find that the grass tasted sweet and nutritious— It increases the number of my friends—it diminishes the number of my foes. How easily at this season I could feed myself in the woods! There is mast for me too—as well as for the pigeon—& the squirrel. This Dodonean fruit.

The Goldfinches are in the air. I hear a black bird also—and see a downy wood-pecker—& see & hear a hairy one. The seeds of the pasture thistle are not so buoyed up by their down as the milkweed.

In the forenoon commonly I see nature only through a window in the afternoon—my study or apartment in which I sit is a vale

The farmers are ditching—redeeming more meadow—getting corn—collecting their apples—threshing &c

I cannot but believe that acorns were intended to be the food of man—they are agreeable to the palate as the mother's milk to the babe. The sweet acorn tree is famous & well known to the boys. There can be no question respecting the wholesomeness of this diet.

This warm day is a godsend to the wasps. I see them buzzing about the broken windows of deserted buildings as Jenny Dugans—the yellow-knotted— I smell the dry leaves like hay from the woods — Some elms are already bare— The bass wood here is quite sere. The pines are still shedding their leaves. This brook by Jenny's is always a pleasant sight & sound to me. In the spring I saw the sucker here. It is remarkable through what narrow & shallow brooks a sucker will be seen to dart and a trout. I perceive that some white oaks are quite red—the black oaks are yellowish— I know not surely whether brighter red & more divided leaf is that of the red or the scarlet oak. The jointed polygonum in the Marlboro Road is an interesting flower—it is so late—so bright a red though inobvious.—from its minuteness—without leaves—above the sand. like sorrel. mixed with other minute flowers—& the empty chalices of the Trichostema— I saw one blue curl still adhering.

The puff balls are split open & rayed out on the sand like 5 or 10! fingers The milk weed seeds must be carried far for it is only when a strong wind is blowing that they are loosened from their pods. An arrowhead at the desert. Spergula Arvensis Corn-Spurrey (some call it tares) at the acorn tree— Filled my pockets with acorns. Found another gouge on Dennis' Hill. To have found two Ind. gouges and tasted sweet acorns—is it not enough for one afternoon?

The sun set red in haze visible 15 *ms* before setting & the moon rose in like manner at the same time.

This evening, I am obliged to sit with my door & window open—in a thin coat—which I have not done for 3 weeks at least.

A warm night like this at this season produces its effect on the village— The boys are heard at play in the street now at 9 'o'clock—in greater force & with more noise than usual. My neighbor has got out his flute— Therre is more fog than usual—the moon is full. The tops of the woods in the horizon seen above the fog look exactly like long low black clouds—the fog being the color of the sky.

Oct 9th 51

Heard 2 Screech owls in the night Boiled a quart of acorns for breakfast—but found them not so palateable as raw—having acquired a bitterish taste perchance from being boiled with the shells and skins, yet one would soon get accustomed to this.

The sound of fox-hounds in the woods heard now at 9 Am in the village—reminds me of mild winter mornings.

2 P M to Conantum In the maple woods the ground is strewn with new fallen leaves. I hear the green locust again on the alders of the causeway—but he is turned a straw color. The warm weather has revived them. All the acorns on the same tree are not equally sweet—They appear to dry sweet. From Conantum I see them getting hay from the meadow below the Cliffs. It must have been quite dry when cut. The black ash has lost its leaves & the white here is dry & brownish yellow—not having turned mulberry. I see half a dozen snakes in this walk green & striped (one very young striped one)—who appear to be out enjoying the sun. They appear to make the most of the last warm days of the year. The hills & plain on the opposite side of the river is covered with deep warm red leaves of shrub-oaks— On Lee's hill-side by the pond the old leaves of some pitch pines are almost of a golden Yellow hue seen in the sun light—a rich autumnal look. The green are as it were set in the yellow. The witch hazel here is in full blossom—on this magical hill-side—while its broad yellow leaves are falling—some bushes are completely bare of leaves, and leather-colored they strew the ground. It is an extremely interesting plant—October & November's child—and yet reminds me of the very earliest spring— Its blossoms smell like the spring—like the willow catkins—by their color as well as fragrance they belong to the saffron dawn of the year.— Suggesting amid all these signs of Autumn—falling leaves & frost—that the life of nature—by which she eternally flourishes, is untouched. It stands here in the shadow on the side of the hill while the sun-light from over the top of the hill lights up its topmost sprays & yellow blossoms. Its spray so jointed and angular is not to be mistaken for any other. I lie on my back with joy under its boughs. While its leaves fall—its blossoms spring. The autumn then is in deed a spring. All the year is a spring.

I see two blackbirds high over head going south, but I am going north in my thought with these hazel blossoms

It is a faery-place. This is a part of the immortality of the soul. When I was thinking that it bloomed too late for bees or other insects to extract honey from its flowers—that perchance they contained no honey—I saw a bee upon it. How important then to the bees this late blossoming plant.

The circling hawk steers himself through the air—like the skater—without a visible motion.

The hoary cinquefoil in blossom. A large sassafras tree behind Lee's 2 feet diam. at ground. As I return over the bridge I hear a song-sparrow singing on the willows exactly as in spring. I see a large sucker rise to the surface of the river. I hear the crickets singing loudly in the walls as they have not done (so loudly) for some weeks—while the sun is going down shorn of his rays by the haze.

There is a thick bed of leaves in the road under Hubbards elms.

This reminds me of Cato—as if the ancients made more use of nature—he says Stramenta si deerunt, frondem iligneam legito, eam substernito ovibus bubusque. If litter is wanting, gather the leaves of the holm oak and strew them under your sheep & oxen. In another place he says circum vias ulmos serito, et partim populos, uti frondem ovibus et bubus habeas. I suppose they were getting that dry meadow grass for litter. There is little or no use made by us of the leaves of trees—not even for beds—unless it be sometimes to rake them up in the woods & cast into hog-pens or compost heaps.

Cut a stout purple cane of poke weed.

Oct 10 '51

The air this morning is full of blue-birds—and again it is spring. There are many things to indicate the renewing of spring at this season. The blossoming of spring flowers—not to mention the witch-hazel—the notes of spring birds—the springing of grain & grass and other plants.

Ah I yearn toward thee my friend, but I have not confidence in thee. We do not believe in the same God. I am not thou— Thou art not I. We trust each other today but we distrust tomorrow. Even when I meet thee unexpectedly I part from thee with disappointment. Though I enjoy thee more than other men yet I am more disappointed with thee than with others. I know a noble man what is it hinders me from knowing him better? I know not how it is that our distrust our hate is stronger than our love. Here I have been on what the world would call friendly terms with one 14 years, have pleased my imagination sometimes with loving him—and yet our hate is stronger than our love. Why are we related—yet thus unsatisfactorily. We almost are a sore to one another.

Ah I am afraid because thy relations are not my relations. Because I have experienced that in some respects we are strange to one another—strange as some wild creature. Ever and anon there will come the consciousness to mar our love—that change the theme but a hair's breadth & we are tragically strange to one another. We do not know what hinders us from coming together. But when I consider what my friends relations & acquaintances are—what his tastes & habits—then the difference between us gets named. I see that all these friends & acquaintances & tastes & habits are indeed my friend's self. In the first place my friend is prouder than I am—& I am very proud perchance.

2 PM to Flints Pond It was the seed vessel of the Canada Snap Dragon in the Marlboro Road that I mistook for a new flower— This is still in bloom in the Deep Cut. The chickadee—sounding all alone now that birds are getting scarce reminds me of the winter in which it almost alone is heard.

How agreeable to the eye at this season the color of new fallen leaves (I am going through the young woods where the locusts grow near Goose Pond) sere & crisp. When freshly fallen with their forms & their veins still distinct they have a certain life in them still. The chestnut leaves now almost completely cover the ground under the trees lying up light & deep—so clean and wholesome—whether to look at or handle or smell—the tawny leaves, nature's color. They look as if they might all yield a wholesome tea— They are rustling down fast from the young chestnuts leaving their bare & blackish looking stems. You make a great noise now walking in the woods on account of the dry leaves—especially chestnut & oak—& maples that cover the ground. I wish that we might make more use of leaves than we do— We wait till they are reduced to virgin mould— Might we not fill beds with them—or use them for fodder or litter. After they have been flattened by the snow & rain they will be much less obvious. Now is the time to enjoy the dry leaves. Now all nature is a dried herb. full of yielding medicinal odors.

I love to hear of a preference given to one kind of leaves over another for beds. Some maples which a week ago were a mass of yellow foliage are now a fine grey smoke as it were. & their leaves cover the ground.

Plants have two states, certainly, the green & the dry—the Lespedeza & primrose heads &c &c— I look on these with interest as if they were newly blossoming plants

Going through Britton's clearing I find a black snake out enjoying the sun— I perceive his lustrous greenish blackness he holds up his head & threatens—then dashes off into the woods—making a great rustling among the leaves. This might be called snake-summer or snakes' week.

Our Irish Washwoman seeing me playing with the milkweed Seeds——said they filled beds with that down in her country.

The horned utricularia by Flints Pond still. There a gunner has built his bower to shoot ducks from, far out amid the rushes. The nightshade leaves have turned a very dark purple almost steel blue—lighter more like mulberry underneath—with light glossy viscid or sticky spots above as if covered with dew— I do not think of any other leaf of this color.

The delicate pinkish leaves of the Hypericum Virginicum about the shore of the pond. The yellow leaves of the Clethra mixed with the green.

The stones of Flints pond shore are comparatively flat, as the pond is flatter than Walden. The young trees & bushes—perhaps the birches particularly are covered now—with a small yellowish insect like a louse spotted with green above which cover the hat and clothes of him who goes through them. Now certainly is the season for rushes—for most other weeds being dead these are the more obvious along the shore of the ponds & rivers.

A very fair canoe birch near Flint's Pond.

The witch hazel loves a hill side with or without wood or shrubs. It is always pleasant to come upon it unexpectedly, as you are threading the woods in such places Methinks I attribute to its some elvish quality apart from its fame. It affects a hill side partially covered with young copsewood. I love to behold its *grey speckled stems.* The leaf first green then yellow for a short season then when it touches the ground tawny leather color. As I stood amid the witch hazels—near Flint's Pond—a flock of a dozen chicadees—came flitting & sing about me with great ado—a most cheering & enlivening sound. with incessant day-day-day—& a fine wiry strain between whiles—flitting ever nearer & nearer & nearer inquisitively—till the boldest was within 5 feet of me—then suddenly—their curiosity satiated they flit by degrees further away & disappear.— & I hear with regret their retreating day-day-days.

Saw a smooth Sumac beyond Cyrus Smiths very large.

The elms in the village have lost many of their leaves & their shadows by moonlight are not so heavy as last month.

Another warm night.

Sunday Oct 12th. 51

Yesterday after noon saw by the brookside above Emerson's the dwarf primrose in blossom—the norway Cinquefoil—& fall dandelions which are now drying up. the houstonia—buttercups—small golden-rods & various asters more or less purplish. The seeds of the bidens—without florets or beggar ticks with 4 barbed awns like hay-hooks now adhere to your clothes—so that you are all bristling with them Certainly they adhere to nothing so readily as to woolen cloth, as if in the creation of them the invention of woolen clothing by man had been foreseen. How tenacious of its purpose to spread and plant its race— By all methods nature secures this end whether by the balloon or parachute or hook or barbed spear like this—or mere lightness which the winds can waft. What are those seeds big as skunk cabbage seeds amid leafless stalks like Pontederia in the brooks —now bending their stems ready to plant themselves at the bottom?

The swamp pink buds begin to show

Black birds & larks are about. And the Flicker or Yellow hammer so beautifully spotted (in the hand) & the Goldfinches. I see a cow in the meadow with a new dropt calf by her side.

The anemone nemorosa in bloom & the Potentilla Sarmentosa or running cinquefoil which springs in April—now again springing.

I love very well this cloudy afternoon so sober—and favorable to reflection after so many bright ones—what if the clouds shut out the heavens provided they concentrate my thoughts and make a more celestial heaven below? I hear the crickets plainer—I wander less in my thoughts—am less dissipated.— am aware how shallow was the current of my thoughts before—deep streams are dark as if there were a cloud in their sky—shallow ones are bright & sparkling reflecting the sun from their bottoms— The very wind on my cheek seems more fraught with meaning.

Many maples around the edges of the meadows are now quite bare like smoke

I seem to be more constantly merged in nature—my intellectual life is more obedient to nature than formerly—but perchance less obedient to Spirit— I have less memorable seasons. I exact less of myself. I am getting used to my meanness—getting to accept my low estate— O if I could be discontented with myself! If I could feel anguish at each descent!

The sweet fern is losing its leaves— I see where a field of oats has been cradled by the railroad—alternate white & dark green stripes the width of a swathe running across the field— I find it arises from the stubble being bent a particular way by the cradle—as the the cradler advanced—and accordingly reflecting the light but one way—and if I look over the field from the other side—the first swaths will be dark & the latter white.

Minot shells all his corn by hand. He has got a box full ready for the mill. He will not winnow it for he says the chaff? makes it lie loose & dry faster. He tells me that Jacob Baker who raises as fair corn as anybody—gives all the corn of his own raising to his stock & buys the flat yellow corn of the South for bread—& yet the northern corn is worth the most per bushel

Minot did not like this kind of farming any better than I— Baker also buys a great quantity of "Shorts" below for his cows—to make more milk.

He remembers when a Prescott who lived where E. Hosmer does used to let his hogs run in the woods in the fall—and they grew quite fat on the acorns &c they found, but now there are few nuts & it is against the law.

He tells me of places in the woods which to his eyes are unchanged since he was a boy—as natural as life—he tells me then that in some respects he is still a boy. & yet the grey-squirrels were 10 then to 1 now. But for the most part he says the world is turned upside down.

P M To Cliffs

I hear Lincoln bell tolling for church At first I thought of the telegraph harp. Heard at a distance the sound of a bell acquires a certain vibratory hum, as it were from the air through which it passes—like a harp— All music is a harp music at length— As if the atmosphere were full of strings vibrating to this music. It is not the mere sound of the bell but the humming in the air that enchants me —just azure tint which much air or distance imparts delights the eye. It is not so much the object as the object clothed with an azure veil. All sound heard at a great distance thus tends to produce the same music—vibrating the strings of the universal lyre. There comes to me a melody which the air has strained.— which has conversed with every leaf and needle of the woods. It is by no means the sound of the bell as heard near at hand, and which at this distance I can plainly distinguish—but its vibrating echoes that portion of the sound which the elements take up and modulate. A sound which is very much much modified sifted and refined before it reaches my ear.

The echo is to some extent an independent sound—and therein is the magic and charm of it. It is not merely a repetition of my voice—but it is in some measure the voice of the wood.

A cloudy misty day with rain more or less steady— This gentle rain is fast loosening the leaves— I see them filling the air at the least puff—and it is also flattening down the layer which has already fallen. The pines on Fair Haven have shed nearly all their leaves— Butter & eggs still blooms—barrels of apples lie under the trees— The Smiths have carried their last load of peaches to market.

To day no part of the heavens is so clear & bright as Fair Haven Pond & the river. Though the air quite misty yet the island wood is distinctly reflected.

Ever & anon I see the mist thickening in the S— W— and concealing trees which were before seen, and revealing the direction and limits of the valleys—precursor of harder rain which soon passes again.

Minot calls the stakes-driver belcher-squelcher—says he has seen them when making the noise— They go slug-toot, slug-toot, slug-toot.

Told me of his hunting grey squirrels with old Colnel Brooks's hound. How the latter came into the yard one day—& he spoke to him—patted him—went into the house took down his gun marked London—thought he would go a squirrel hunting. Went over among the ledges—away from Brooks's for Tige had a dreadful strong voice and could be heard as far as a cannon—& he was plaguey afraid Brooks would hear him. How tige treed them on the oaks on the plain below the cliffs. He could tell by his bark when he had treed one—he never told a lie. How tige told him from a distance that he had got one—but when he came up he could see nothing—but still he knew that Tige never told a lie—and at length he saw his head, in a crotch high up in the top of a very tall oak—and though he did'nt expect to get him—he knocked him over.

Oct 13th

Drizzling misty showers still with a little misty sun shine at intervals. The trees have lost many of their leaves in the last 24 hours. The sun has got so low that it will do to let his rays in on the earth—the cattle do not need their shade now nor men. Warmth is more desirable now than shade

The alert and energetic man leads a more intellectual life in winter than in summer. In summer the animal and vegetable in him are perfected as in a torrid zone—he lives in his senses mainly— In

winter cold reason & not warm passion has her sway—he lives in
thought & reflection— He lives a more spiritual & less sensual life.

If he has passed a merely sensual summer—he passes his winter in
a torpid state like some reptils & other animals.

The mind of man in the two seasons is like the atmosphere of
summer compared with the atmosphere of winter. He depends more
on himself in winter—on his own resources—less on outward aid—
Insects it is true disappear for the most part—and those animals which
depend upon them but the nobler animals abide with man the
severity of winter. He migrates into his mind—to perpetual summer.
And to the healthy man the winter of his discontent never comes.

Mr Pratt told me that Jonas? Melven found a honey bee's nest
lately near Beck. Stow's swamp with 25 lbs of honey in it—in the
top a maple tree which was blown down—

There is now a large swarm in the meeting-house chimney—in a
flue not used. Many swarms have gone off that have not been heard
from.

Oct 14th

Down the R R. before sun rise A freight train in the Deep Cut.
the sun rising over the woods.— When the vapor from the engine
rose above the woods the level rays of the rising sun fell on it it
presented the same redness—morning red—inclining to saffron which
the clouds in the eastern horizon do.

There was but little wind this morning yet I heard the telegraph
harp—it does not require a strong wind to wake its strings—it depends
more on its direction & the tension of the wire apparently—a gentle
but steady breeze will often call forth its finest strains when a strong
but unsteady gale—blowing at the wrong angle withal fails to elicit
any melodious sound.

In the psychological world there are phenomena analogous to
what zoologists call *alternate reproduction* in which it requires several
generations unlike each other to produce the perfect animal— Some
men's lives are but an aspiration—a yearning toward a higher state—
and they are wholly misapprehended—until they are referred to or
traced through all their metamorphoses. We cannot pronounce upon
a man's intellectual & moral state until we forsee what
metamorphosis it is preparing him for.

It is said that "the working bees——are barren females. The
attributes of their sex——seem to consist only in their solicitude for
the welfare of the new generation, of which they are the natural
guardians, but not the parents." Agassiz & Gould. This phenomenon

is paralleled in man by maiden aunts & bachelor uncles who perform a similar function.

"The muskrat," according to Agassiz & Gould, "is found from the mouth of Mackenzie's River to Florida" It is moreover of a type peculiar to temperate America. He is a native american surely. He neither dies of Consumption in New England nor of Fever & ague at the south & west—thoroughly acclimated & naturalized.

"The hyenas, wild-boars, and rhinoceroses of the Cape of Good Hope, have no analogues on the American continent"— At the last menagerie I visited they told me that one of the hyenas came from S america!

There is something significant and interesting in the fact that the fauna of Europe and that of the United States are very similar—pointing to the fitness of this country for the settlement of Europeans.

They say "There are many species of animals whose numbers are daily diminishing, and whose extinction may be foreseen; as the Canada deer (Wapiti), the Ibex of the Alps, the Lämmergeyer, the bison, the beaver, the wild-turkey, &c." With these of course is to be associated the Indian.

They say that the house-fly has followed man in his migrations.

One would say that the Yankee belonged properly to the *northern* temperate Fauna—the region of the pines.

Wednesday Oct 15

8½ AM up the river in a boat to Pelham's Pond with W.E.C. (But first a neighbor sent in a girl to inquire if I knew where worm-seed grew otherwise called "Jerusalem oak"—(so said the recipe which she brought cut out of a newspaper) for her mistress' hen had the "gapes"— But I answered that this was a southern plant & knew not where it was to be had. Referred her to the poultry book.— Also the next proprietor commenced stoning & settling down the stone for a new well—an operation which I wished to witness—purely beautiful—simple & necessary. The stones laid on a wheel—and continuually added to above as it is settled down by digging under the wheel.— Also Godwin with a partridge & a stout mess of large pickerel—applied to me to dispose of a mud turtle which he had found moving the mud in a ditch. Some men will be in the way to see such movements.)

The muskrat houses appear now for the most part to be finished— Some it is true are still rising— They line the river all the way.

Some are as big as small hay cocks— The river is still quite low—
though a foot or more higher than when I was last on it— There is
quite a wind & the sky is full of flitting clouds—so that sky & water
are quite unlike that warm bright transparent day when I last sailed
on the river—when the surface was of such oily smoothness— You
could not now study the river bottom for the black waves & the
streaks of foam. When the sun shines brightest today—its pyramidal
shaped sheen (when for a short time we are looking up stream—for
we row) is dazzling & blinding— It is pleasant to hear the sound of
the waves & feel the surging of the boat—an inspiriting sound as if
you were bound on adventures It is delightful to be tossed about in
such a harmless storm.— & see the waves look so angry & black.
We see objects on shore, trees &c, much better from the boat—from
a low point of View—it brings them against the sky—into a novel
point of view at least— The other wise low on the meadows as well
as the hills is conspicuous. I perceive that the bullrushes are nibbled
along the shore as if they had been cut by a scythe—yet in such
positions as no mower could of reached—even outside the flags.
Probably the muskrat was the mower. In this cool sunlight Fair
Haven Hill shows to advantage Every rock & shrub—&
protuberance has justtice done it—the sun shining at angle on the hill
& giving each a shadow. The hills have a hard & distinct outline & I
see into their very texture. On Fair Haven I see the sun-lit light
green grass in the hollows where snow makes water sometimes—and
on the russet slopes. Cut three white pine boughs opposite Fair
Haven and set them up in the bow of our boat for a sail— It was
pleasant hear the water begin to ripple under the prow telling of our
easy progress we thus without a tack made the S side of Fair haven
—then threw our sails over board—and the moment after mistook
them for green bushes or weeds which had sprung from the bottom
unusually far from shore.— Then to hear the wind sough in your
sail—that is to be a sailor & hear a land sound. The grayish whitish
mikania all fuzzy covers the endless button bushes which are now
bare of leaves. Observed the verification of the scripture saying "as
the dog returns to his vomit?"? Our black pup sole passenger in the
stern, perhaps made sea-sick—vomited then cleaned the boat again
most faithfully—and with a bright eye—licking his chops & looking
round for more. We comment on the boats of different patterns—
dories? punts—bread troughs—flat irons &c &c which we pass—the
privailing our genuine dead-river boats—not to be matched by
Boston carpenters— One farmer blacksmith whome we know whose

boat we pass in Sudbury—has got a horse-shoe nailed about the
sculling hole;—keeps off the witches too?—. The water carriages of
various patterns & in various conditions—some for pleasure against
the gentlemans seat?—some for ducking—small & portable—some for
honest fishing broad & leaky but not cranky—some with spearing
fixtures—some stout & squareendsish for hay boats— One canal boat
or mudscow in the weeds not worth getting down the stream. like
some vast pike that could swallow all the rest.— proper craft for our
river— In some places in the meadows opposite Bound Rock the
river seemed to have come to an end it was so narrow suddenly.

After getting in sight of Sherman's bridge—counted 19 birches on
the right hand shore in one whirl.

Now commenced the remarkable meandering of the river—so that
we seemed for some to be now running up—then running down
parallel with a long low hill—tacking over the meadow in spite of
ourselves. Landed at Shermans bridge. An apple tree made scrubby
by being browsed by cows.— Through what early hardships it may
attain to bear a sweet fruit—no wonder it is provoked to grow thorns
at last to defend itself from such foes. The pup nibbles clams, or
plays with a bone no matter how dry— Thus the dog can be taken
on a river Voyage—but the cat cannot. she is too set in her ways.
Now again for the great meadows. What meandering—the Serpentine
our river should be called—what makes the river love to delay here?
Here come to study the law of meandering. We see the vast
meadow studded with haycocks—we suspect that we have got to visit
them all—it proves even so—now we run down one hay-cock—now
another.— The distance gained is frequently not more than a third
the distance gone Between Sherman's Br. & Causeway Br is about
1¾ mi in a straight line but we judged that we went more than 3
miles. Here the "pipes" (at first) line the shore—& muskrat houses
still. A duck (a loon?) sails within gun-shot—unwilling to fly— Also
a stake driver ardea minor rises with prominent breast or throat bone
—as if badly loaded his ship—now no button bushes line the stream—
the changeable? stream no rocks exist—the shores are lined with first
in the water still green polygonums then wide fields of dead
pontideria then great bulrushes—then various reeds sedges or tall
grasses—also dead Thalictrum? or is it cicuta? Just this side the
Causeway bridges a field like a tall corn-field of tall rustling reeds?
10 feet high with broadish leaves & large now seedy tufts—standing
amid the button bushes & great bulrushes. I remember to have seen
none elsewhere in this vicinity unless at Fresh Pond & are they not

straighter? Also just beyond the bridges very tall flags from 6 to 8 feet high leaves like the cat-tail but no tail what are they? We pass under 2 bridges above the causeway bridge. After passing under the first one of *these two* at the mouth of Larnum Brook—which is fed from Blandfords Pond—comes from Marlboro—thro Mill-vil.—& has a branch Hop Brook from S of Nobscot—we see Nobscot very handsome in a purplish atmosphere in the west over a *very* deep meadow which makes far up— A good way to skate to Nobscot or within a mile or two.— To see a distant hill from the surface of water over a low & very broad meadow—much better than to see it from another hill. This perhaps the most novel & so memorable prospect we got— Walked across half a mile to Pelham's Pond. whose waves were dashing quite grandly. A house near with two grand elms in front— I have seen other elms in Wayland. This pond a good point to skate to in Winter—when it is easily accessible—now we should have to draw our boat.—

On the return as in going we expended nearly as much time & labor in counteracting the boat's tendency to whirl round—it is so miserably built. Now & then aye—aye—almost an everlasting *now*—it will take the bits in its mouth and go round in spite of us though we row on one side only—for the wind fills the after part of the boat which is nearly out of water—& we therefore get along best & fastest when the wind is strong & dead ahead—that's the kind of wind we advertise to race with (or in) To row a boat thus all the day with an hour's intermission—making fishes of ourselves as it were—putting on these long fins—realizing the finny life—surely oars & paddles are but the fins which a man may use. The very pads stand perpendicular (on their edges) before this wind which appears to have worked more to the north—showing their red under sides. The muskrats have exposed the clam shells to us in heaps all along the shore—else most not know that a clam existed. If it were not for muskrats how little would the fisherman see or know of fresh water clam shells or clams! In the Great meadows again the loon? rises—and again alights—& a heron? too flies sluggishly away with vast wings—& small ducks which seem to have no tails—but their wings set quite aft — The crows ashore are making an ado perchance about some carrion. We taste some swamp-white oak acorns at the south end of Bound rock meadow— The sun sets when we are off Israel Rices— A few golden coppery clouds—intensely glowing like fishes in some molten metal of the sky——& then the small scattered clouds grow blue-black above—or one half—& reddish or pink the other half—&

after a short twilight the night sets in. The reflections of the stars in
the water are dim & elongated like the zodiacal light straight down
into the depths, but no mist rises tonight— We think it is pleasantest
to be on the water at this hour. We row across Fair Haven in the
thickening twilight & far below it steadily & without speaking.— As
the night draws on her vail the shores retreat—we only keep in the
middle of this low stream of light—we know not whether we float in
the air or in the lower regions. We seem to recede from the trees
on shore—or the island very slowly—& yet a few reaches make all our
voyage— Nature has divided it agreeably into reaches— It is
pleasant not to get home till after dark—to steer by the lights of the
villagers— The lamps in the houses twinkle now like stars—they
shine doubly bright. Rowed about 24 miles going & coming In a
straight line it would be 15½

Oct 16th

The new moon seen by day reminds me of a poet's cheese.
Surveying for Loring today. Saw the Indian ditch, so called. A plant
newly leaving out—a shrub look somewhat like shad blossom.— To
night the spearers are out again.

Oct 17th

Surveying for Loring. A severe frost this morn. which puts one
remove further from summer.

Oct 19th

The Indian? Ditch crosses the road beyond Lorings, running S 7½
W or within about 2½° of the true meridian. Accord. to Stephen
Hosmer's plan of Thomas Jones' woodland made in 1766 the ditch
where Derby & Loring bound on it—must be about 84 rods from
old town-line

To the northern voyager who does not see the sun for 3 months—
night is expanded into winter, & day into summer.

Observed today on the edge of a woodlot of Loring's where his
shrub oaks bounded on a neighbors small pitch pines, which grew
very close together, that the line of separation was remarkably
straight & distinct neither a shruboak nor a pine passing its limit—the
ground where the pines grew having apparently been cultivated so
far, and its edges defined by the plow.

A surveyor must be curious in studying the wounds of trees—to
distinguish a natural disease or scar from the "blazing" of an axe

?Has the aspen? poplar any more of a red heart than the other?
The powder man does not want the red hearted. Even this poor
wood has its use

Observed an oak—a red or black—at a pigeon place—whose top limbs were cut off perhaps a month ago; the leaves had dried a sort of snuff-yellow & rather glossy.

Oct 22nd

The pines, both white & pitch, have now shed their leaves. And the ground in the pine woods is strewn with the newly fallen needles.

The fragrant life everlasting is still fresh—& the Canada Snap Dragon still blooms bluely by the roadside.— The rain & dampness have given birth to a new crop of mushrooms. The small willow like shrub (sage willow? salix longirostris Mx) is shedding its small leaves which turn black in drying and cover the path.

Oct 23d

It is never too late to learn. I observed to-day the Irishman who helped me survey *twisting* the branch of a birch for a withe—& *before* he cut it off, also wishing to stick a tall smooth pole in the ground—cut a notch in the side of it by which to drive it with a hatchet

Oct 26th

I awoke this morning to infinite regret. In my dream I had been riding—but the horses bit the horses bit each other and occasioned endless trouble and anxiety & it was my employment to hold their heads apart. Next I sailed over the sea in a small vessel such as the Northmen used—as it were to the Bay of Funday & thence over land I sailed still over the shallows about the sources of rivers toward the deeper channel of a stream which emptied into the gulf beyond.

Again I was in my own small pleasure boat—learning to sail on the sea—& I raised my sail before my anchor which I dragged far into the sea— I saw the buttons which had come off the coats of drowned men—and suddenly I saw my dog—when I knew not that I had one—standing in the sea up to his chin to warm his legs which had been wet—which the cool wind numbed. And then I was walking in a meadow—where the dry Season permitted me to walk further than usual—& there I met Mr Alcott—& we fell to quoting & referring to grand & pleasing couplets & single lines which we had read in times past—and I quoted one which in my waking hours I have no knowledge of but in my dream it was familiar enough— I only know that those which I quoted expressed regret—and were like the following though they were not these—viz—

> "The short parenthesis of life was sweet"
> "The remembrance of youth is a sigh." &c

It had the word memory in it!! And then again the instant that I awoke methought I was a musical instrument—from which I heard a strain die out—a bugle—or a clarionet—or a flute—my body was the organ and channel of melody as a flute is of the music that is breathed through it. My flesh sounded & vibrated still to the strain—& my nerves were the chords of the lyre. I awoke therefore to an infinite regret—to find myself not the thoroughfare of glorious & world-stirring inspirations—but a scuttle full of dirt—such a thoroughfare only as the street & the kennel—where perchance the wind may sometimes draw forth a strain of music from a straw.

I can partly account for this. Last evening I was reading Laing's account of the Northmen—and though I did not write in my journal—I remember feeling a fertile regret—and deriving even an inexpressible satisfaction as it were from my ability to feel regret—which made that evening richer than those which had preceeded it.

I heard the last strain or flourish as I woke played on my body as the instrument. Such I knew I had been & might be again—and my regret arose from the consciousness how little like a musical instrument my body was now.

Oct 27th

This morning I wake and find it snowing & the ground covered with snow—quite unexpectedly—for last night it was rainy but not cold.

The obstacles which the heart meets with are like granite blocks which one alone can not move. She who was as the morning light to me, is now neither the morning star nor the evening star. We meet but to find each other further asunder, and the oftener we meet the more rapid our divergence. So a star of the first magnitude pales in the heavens, not from any fault in the observers eye nor from any fault in it self perchance, but because its progress in its own system has put a greater distance between

The night is oracular— What have been the intimations of the night? I ask. How have you passed the night? Good night!

My friend will be bold to conjecture, he will guess bravely at the significance of my words.

The cold numbs my fingers this morning. The strong northwest wind blows the damp snow along almost horizontally. The birds fly about as if seeking shelter

Perhaps it was the young of the purple finch that I saw sliding down the grass stems some weeks ago—or was it the white-throated finch? Winter with its *inwardness* is upon us. A man is constrained to sit down, and to think.

The ardea minor still with us— Saw a woodcock feeding probing the mud with its long bill under the RR bridge within 2 feet of me for a long time could not scare it far away— What a disproportionate length of bill.— It is a sort of badge they wear as a punishment for greediness in a former state.

The highest arch of the stone bridge is 6 feet 8 inches above the present surface of the water which I should think was more than a foot higher than it has been this summer—and is 4 inches below the long stone in the east abutment.

Oct 31st

The wild apples are now getting palateable. I find a few left on distant trees—which the farmer thinks it not worth his while to gather—he thinks that he has better in his barrels, but he is mistaken unless he has a walker's appetite & imagination—neither of which can he have. These apples cannot be too gnurly & rusty & crabbed (to look at)— The gnurliest will have some redeeming traits even to the eyes— You will discover some evening redness dashed or sprinkled—on some protuberance or in some cavity— It is rare that the summer lets an apple go without streaking or spotting it on some part of its sphere—though perchance one side may only seem to betray that it has once fallen in a brick yard—and the other have been bespattered from a roily ink bottle. The saunterer's apple not even the saunterer can eat in the house.— Some red stains it will have commemorating the mornings & evenings it has witnessed—some dark & rusty blotches in memory of the clouds, & foggy mildewy days that have passed over it—and a spacious field of green reflecting the general face of nature—green even as the fields— Or yellow its ground if it has a sunny flavor yellow as the harvests or russet as the hills. The noblest of fruits is the apple Let the most beautiful or swiftest have it.

The robins now fly in flocks.

NB (Sat—*Nov 1st*)

RWE says that Channing calls Stow 7 feet of sandstone with a spoonful of wit.

When R.W.E. had got his new barn built with substantial underpinning he looked at it privately & after informed me that he could not ascertain that they had *pinned* it down any where to the *underpinning*.

It is a rare qualification to be ably to state a fact simply & adequately. To digest some experience cleanly. To say yes and no with authority— To make a square edge. To conceive & suffer the truth to pass through us living & intact—even as a waterfowl an eel—

thus peopling new waters. First of all a man must see, before he can say.– Statements are made but partially– Things are said with reference to certain conventions or existing institutions.– not absolutely. A fact truly & absolutely stated is taken out of the region of commonsense and acquires a mythologic or universal significance. Say it & have done with it. Express it without expressing yourself. See not with the eye of science–which is barren–nor of youthful poetry which is impotent. But taste the world. & digest it. It would seem as if things got said but rarely & by chance– As you *see* so at length will you *say*. When facts are seen superficially they are seen as they lie in relation to certain institution's perchance. But I would have them expressed as more deeply seen with deeper references.– so that the hearer or reader cannot recognize them or apprehend their significance from the platform of common life–but it will be necessary that he be in a sense translated in order to understand them.

When the truth respecting *his* things shall naturally exhale from a man like the odor of the muskrat from the coat of the trapper. At first blush a man is not capable of reporting truth–he must be drenched & saturated with it first. What was *enthusiasm* in the young man must become *temperament* in the mature man. without excitement–heat or passion he will survey the world which excited the youth–& threw him off his balance. As all things are significant; so all words should be significant. It is a fault which attaches to the speaker to speak flippantly or superficially of anything. Of what use are words which do not move the hearer.– are not oracular & fateful?– A style in which the matter is all in all & the manner nothing at all.

In your thoughts no more than in your walks do you meet men– in moods I find such privacy as in dismal swamps & on mountain tops.

Man recognizes laws little enforced & he condescends to obey them. In the moment that he feels his superiority to them as compulsatory he as it were courteously reenacts them but to obey them.

This on my way to Conantum 2½ Pm It is a bright clear warm november day. I feel blessed. I love my life. I warm toward all nature.

The woods are now much more open than when I last observed them–the leaves have fallen & they let in light & I see the sky through them as through a crows wing in every direction. For the most part only the pines & oaks (white?) retain their leaves. At a distance accordingly the forest is green & reddish. The crickets now sound faintly & from very deep in the sod.

Minot says that G. M. Barret told him that Amos Baker told him that during Concord fight he went over behind the hill to the old Whittaker place (Sam Buttrick's) and stayed. Yet he was described as the only survivor of Concord Fight. Received a pension for running away?

Fall dandelions look bright still. The grass has got a new greenness in spots.

At this season there are stranger sparrows or finches about. The skunk cabbage is already pushing up again. The alders have lost their leaves & the willows except (the last) a few shrivelled ones.

It is a remarkable day for fine gossamer cob-webs. Here on the causeway as I walk toward the sun I perceive that the air is full of them streaming from off the willows & spanning the road—all stretching across the road—and yet I cannot see them in any other direction—and feel not one. It looks as if the birds would be incommoded. They have the effect of a shimmer in the air. This shimmer moving along them as they are waved by the wind gives the effect of a drifting storm of light. It is more like a fine snow storm which drifts athwart your path than anything else. What is the peculiar condition of the atmosphere to call forth this activity. If there were no sunshine I should never find out that they existed— I should not know that I was bursting a myriad barriers. Though you break them with your person you feel not one. Why should this day be so distinguished. The rain of night before last has raised the river at least 2 feet. And the meadows wear a late-fall look. The naked and weedy stems of the button bush are suddenly submerged— You no longer look for pickerel from the bridges— The shallow & shrunken shore is also submerged.

I see so far & distinctly my eyes seem to slide in this clear air— The river is peculiarly sky blue today—not dark as usual. It is all in the air— The cinque-foil on Conantum. Counted 125 crows in one straggling flock moving westward.

The red shruboak leaves abide on the hills.

The witch hazel blossoms have mostly lost their blossoms—perhaps on account of the snow. The ground wears its red carpet under the pines. The pitch pines show new buds at the end of their plumes— How long this?

Saw a canoe birch by road beyond the Abel Minot house,

distinguished it 30 rods off by the chalky whiteness of its limbs. It is
of a more unspotted transparent & perhaps pinkish white than the
common—has considerable branches—as well as white ones and its
branches do not droop & curl downward—like that—   There will be
some loose curls of bark about it. The common birch is *finely*
branched and has frequently a *snarly* head—the former is a more open
& free-growing tree. If at a distance you see the birch near its top
forking into two or more white limbs you may know it for a canoe
birch. You can tell where it has grown after the wood has turned to
mould by a small fragment of its bark still left—if it divides readily.—
The common birch is more covered with moss—has the aspect of
having grown more slowly & has many more branches

Sunday Nov 2nd

The muskrat housse are mostly covered by the rise of the river—
not a very unexpected one either. Old wells as well as walls must be
among the oldest monuments of civilized man here. How old may
be the most ancient well which men use today. Saw a canoe birch
beyond Nawshawtuct—growing out of the middle of a white pine
stump—which still showed the mark of the axe—16 inch diameter at
its bottom or 2 feet from the ground, or where it had first taken
root on the stump.

Nov. 4th

To Saw Mill Brook by Turnpike return by Walden. I see why
the checquerberry was so called—Mitchella repens (we call it falsely
Partridge berry) for its leaves variegated *chequer* the ground—now
mingled with red berries & partially covered with the fallen leaves of
the forest.

Saw-Mill-brook is peculiar among our brooks as a mountain
brook for a short distance it reminds me of runs I have seen in
N. H. A brawling little stream tumbling through a rocky wood—ever
down & down. Where the wood has been cleared it is almost
covered with the rubbish which the woodchoppers have left—the
fine tree tops which no one cared to make into faggots. It was quite
a discovery when I first came upon this brawling mountain stream in
Concord woods. Rising out of an obscure meadow in the woods,
for some 50 or 60 rods of its course.—   it is a brawling *mt* stream in
our quiet Concord woods—as much obstructed by rocks—rocks out
of all proportion to its tiny stream—as a brook can well be. And the
rocks are bared through out the wood on either side as if a torrent
had anciently swept through here—   So unlike the after character of
the stream—   Who would have thought that on tracing it up from

where it empties into the larger Mill brook in the open peat
meadows—it would conduct him to such a headlong & impetuous
youth—perchance it should be called a "force"— It suggests what
various moods may attach to the same character. Ah if I but knew
that some minds which flow so muddily in the lowland portion of
their course—where they cross the highways—tumbled thus
impetuously & musically mix themselves with the air in foam but a
little way back in the woods. That these dark and muddy pools
where only the pout & the leach are to be found—issued from pure
trout streams higher up—. That the man's thoughts ever flowed as
sparkling *mt* water, that trout there loved to glance through his
dimples.— where the witch hazel hangs over his stream.

This stream is here sometimes quite lost amid the rocks—which
appear as if they had been arched over it—but which it in fact it has
undermined and found its way beneath—and they have merely fallen
together arch wise as they were undermined. It is truly a raw &
gusty day & I hear a tree creak sharply like a bird—a phoebe— The
hypericums stand red or lake over the brook— The jays with their
scream are at home in the scenery. I see where trees have spread
themselves over the rocks in a scanty covering of soil—been
undermined by the brook—then blown over and as they fell lifted
and carried over with them all the soil together with considerable
rocks. So from time to time by these natural levers rocks are
removed from the middle of the stream to the shore. The slender
chestnuts maples elms & white ash trees which last are uncommonly
numerous here are now all bare of leaves—& a few small hemlocks
with their now thin but unmixed & fresh green foliage stand over &
cheer the stream & remind me of Winter—the snows which are to
come and drape them & contrast with their green—& the chickadees
that are to flit & lisp amid them.

Ah the beautiful tree the hemlock with its green canopy—under
which little grows—not exciting the cupidity of the carpenter—
Whose use most men have not discovered. I know of some
memorable ones worth walking many miles to see— These little
cheerful hemlocks—the lisp of chic-a-dees seems to come from them
now—each standing with its foot on the very edge of the stream—
reaching sometimes part way over its channel & here and there one
has lightly stepped across— These evergreens are plainly as much for
shelter for the birds as for anything else. The fallen leaves are so
thick they almost fill the bed of the stream & choke it. I hear the
runnel gurgling underground.— As if this puny rill had ever tossed

these rocks about! These storied rocks with their fine lichens—&
sometimes red stains as of Indian blood on them. There are a few
bright green ferns lying flat by the sides of the brook—but it is cold—
cold—withering to all else. A whitish lichen on the witch-hazel—rings
it here I glimpse the frizzled tail of a red squirrel with a chestnut in
its mouth on a white pine.

The ants appear to be gone into winter-quarters—here are two
bushels of fine gravel piled up in a cone—overpowering the grass—
which tells of a corresponding cavity.

Nov 6th

{Four-fifths page missing}

I had on my "bad-weather clothes" at Quebec like Olaf
Tryggvesson the Northman when he went to Thing in England

Nov 7th

   8 AM to Long Pond with W E C

{Four-fifths page missing}

tree to have near a house summer & winter Is it the same with
Potter's?

From there we looked over the lower lands westward to the
Jenkins' House & Wachuset—the latter today a very faint blue—
almost lost in the atmosphere— Entering Wayland— The sluggish
country town— C remarked that we might take the town if we had
a couple of oyster knives. We marvelled as usual at the queer
looking building which C thought must be an engine house but
which a boy told us was occupied as a shoe makers shop but was
built for a library. C. was much amused here by a bigger school boy
whom we saw on the comnon—one of those who stretch themselves
on the back seats & can chew up a whole newspaper into a spitball
to plaster the wall with when the master's back was turned—made
considerable fun of him and thought this the *event* of Wayland. Soon
got into a Country new to us in Wayland opposite to Pelham or
Hurd's Pond, going across lots. Cedar hills & valleys near the river.
A well placed farm house with great old chestnuts near—it. The
greatest collection of large chestnuts which I remember to have seen.
It is a tree full and well outlined at top—being bushy with short
twigs at top—a firm outline. Some long moraine-like hills covered
with cedars. with the hill country of Wayland on our left. The
white oaks still thick with leaves turned pinkish? From a pretty high
hill on the left of the road—after passing a very large field which was

being plowed—a glorious view of the meadows & Nobscot—now red or purplish with its shrub oaks in this air—& Wachuset here seen in perfection & Dudley P. first seen on the south. Dudley pond is revealed due South now at noon 12 by its sparkling water—on both sides its promontory—the sparkles are even like fireflies in a meadow — This is not far above the opening to Pelham Pond. Which also we fairly see The white pines now look uncommonly soft. Their foliage indeed is not so thick as it was—but the old leaves being fallen & none left which are a year old.— it is perchance more bright & fair. Dudley P. beyond the promontory appears to be revealed by such a mirage as the coin in a basin. The sun sparkles seen through the leafless woods on both sides this promontory.— over its neck are very large & innumerable when one goes out up flashes another like a meadow full of fireflies dancing sparkles— When we reach the Pond we find much beach wood just last winter cut down & still standing on its shores. Where young beaches have been cut off 4 feet from the ground to cord the wood against I see that that they have put out sprouts this summer in a dense bunch at its top—and also all those stumps which are clothed with short sprouts still covered with curled & crisped leaves are beaches. These large sparkles are magic lanterns by day light It is the game of go away Jack come again Gill—played by the Genius of the lake with the sun on his nail instead of a piece of paper—to amuse Nature's children with. Should it not be called Sparkle pond? Button wood trees are frequent about its shores—its handsome hilly shores.— This side cedars also on its pleasant hilly shores—and opposite dark dense hemlocks. Thus in the form of its shores & above all in the trees which prevail about it it is peculiar or at least unlike the concord ponds—& is exceedingly handsome— It has perhaps greater variety than any pond I know. Let it be called Peninsula Pond. never the less. The willow herb is there abundant with its arching stem & its calices or dried flowers still attached. No tree has so fair a bole & so handsome an *instep* as the beach. The lower leaves which are an orange? red hang on (dry) While the rest of the tree is bare.

Chased by an ox whom we escaped over a fence while he gored the trees in stead of us. the first time I was ever chased by his kind. It is a clear water without weeds— There is a handsomely sloping grassy shore on the west.

Close by we found Long Pond In Wayland Framingham & Natick—a great body of water—with singularly sandy shelving caving undermined banks.— and there we ate our luncheon— The Mayflower leaves we saw there & the viola pedata in blossom. We went down it a mile or two on the Eeast side thro the woods on its high bank & then dined looking far down to what seemed the Boston outlet (opposite to its natural outlet) where a solitary building stood on the shore. It is a wild & a stretching loch—where yachts might sail—Cochituate. It was not only larger but wilder & more novel than I had expected. In some respects unlike New England. I could hardly have told in what part of the world I was if I had been carried there blindfolded. Yet some features—at least the composition of the soil was familiar. The glorious sandy banks far & near caving and sliding—far sandy slopes ‾‾‾‾‾⟍   the forts of the land—where you see the naked flesh of   ⟍ New England her garment being blown aside like that of the priests of the Levites? when they ascend to the altar. Seen through this november sky these sands are dear to me—worth all the gold of California—suggesting Pactolus— While the Saxonville factory bell sounds o'er the woods. That sound perchance it is that whets my vision. The shore suggests the seashore —and 2 objects at a distance near the shore look like seals on a sand bar.— Dear to me to lie in—this sand—which will preserve the bones of a race for thousands of years. to come. And this is my home—my native soil, and I am a New Englander. Of thee o earth are my bone & sinew made—to thee o sun am I brother. It must be the largest lake in Middlesex. To this dust my body will gladly return as to its origin. Here have I my habitat. I am of thee.— Returned by the S side of Dudley P. which looked fairer than ever—though smaller.— now so still—the afternoon somewhat advanced Nobscot in the west —in a purplish light—& the scolloped peninsula before us—when we held our heads down this was thrown far off— This shore was crowded with a hemlock—which else where I do not remember to have seen so numerous. Outside the wood there are little rounded clumps of smaller ones about.

This P must have been dear to the Indians.

At Nonesuch P. in Natic—we saw a boulder some 32 feet square by 16 high—with a large rock leaning against it—under which we walked—forming a triangular frame through which we beheld the picture of the pond. How many white men & Indians have passed under it /⟍   Boulder Pond! Thence across lots by the Weston / ⫽⫽   elm to the bounds of Lincoln at the RR. Saw a delicate fringed purple flower—Gentiana Crinita between those Weston hills in a meadow & after on higher land.

C kept up an incessant strain of wit banter about my legs—which

were so springy & unweariable—declared I had got my double legs
on—that they were not cork but steel—that I should let myself to Van
Amburg—should have sent them to the World's fare &c &c wanted
to know if I could not carry my father Anchises The sun sets while
we are perched on a high rock in the North of Weston. It soon
grows finger cold— at Walden are three reflections of the bright full
(or nearly) moon. one moon—& 2 sheens further off.

Nov. 8th

The dark spruce tree at Sherman's—its vicinity the site for a house.
Ah those sun sparkles on Dudley P. in this november air what a
heaven to live in! Intensely brilliant as no artificial light I have seen—
like a dance of diamonds. Coarse mazes of a diamond dance seen
through the trees. All objects shine today—even the sportsmen seen
at a distance—as if a cavern were unroofed and its crystals gave
entertainment to the sun. This great see-saw of brilliants.— the
$ανηριθμον$ $γελασμα$. You look several inches into the sod.— The
cedarn hills. The squirrels that run across the road sport their tails
like banners— The grey squirrels in their cylinders are set out in the
sun.— When I saw the bare sand at Cochituate I felt my relation to
the soil.— these are *my* sands not yet run out. Not yet will the fates
turn the glass. This air have I title to taint—with my decay. In this
clean sand my bones will gladly lie. Like viola pedata I shall be ready
to bloom again here in my Indian summer days. Here ever springing
—never dying with perrennial root I stand.— for the winter of the
land is warm to me—while the flowers bloom again as in the spring—
shall I pine? When I see her sands exposed thrown up from beneath
the surface—it touches me inwardly—it reminds me of my origin—for
I am such a plant—so native to N.E. methinks as springs from the
sand cast up from below.

4 P M I find ice under the north side of woods nearly an inch
thick—where the acorns are frozen in. which have dropped from
the orehanging oaks and been saved from the squirrels perchance by
the water. W. E. C. says he found a ripe strawberry last week in
Berkshire. Saw a frog at the swamp bridge on back road

Nov 9th

The boat which we paddled that Elysian day—Oct 7th was made
of 3 distinct boxes shaped like bread-troughs—excepting the bough
piece which was rounded ⊏▢▢⊐ —fastened together by screws
& nuts—with stout round leather handles by which to carry the
separate parts— It was made of the thinnest & lightest material
without seats or thole pins—for portability. So that three passengers

could sit in three different boats which by turning the *hand*-nuts? they might separate & steer different ways.

The river has fallen more than a foot since I last observed it. I see minute yellow coccoons on the grass as I go across the field behind Dennis'—reminding me of some late flower as the cinquefoil What is the insect.? I hear a cricket singing the requiem of the year under the clam-shell bank— Soon all will be frozen up & I shall hear no cricket chirp in the land. The very rabbit forms & squirrel holes will be snowed up and walking in the winter days in the sunny forenoons after a light snow has fallen in the night covering up the old snow already deep & the gentle wind from time to time shakes down a golden dust from above—I shall see still the gray squirrel or the red still cheery & lifesome making tiny tracks over the snowcovered rails & riders When the sun shines aslant between the stems of the pines.

In our walks C. takes out his note-book some times & tries to write as I do—but all in vain. He soon puts it up again—or contents himself with scrawling some sketch of the landscape. Observing me still scribbling he will say that *he* confines himself to the ideal—purely ideal remarks—he leaves the facts to me. Sometimes too he will say a little petulantly—"*I* am universal I have nothing to do with the particular and definite." He is the moodiest person perhaps that I ever saw. As naturally whimsical as a cow is brindled—both in his tenderness & his roughness he belies himself.

He can be incredibly selfish & unexpectedly generous— He is conceited, and yet there is in him far more than usual to ground conceit upon—

I too would fain set down something beside facts. Facts should only be as the frame to my pictures— They should be material to the mythology which I am writing. Not facts to assist men to make money—farmers to farm profitably in any common sense. Facts to tell who I am—and where I have been—or what I have thought. As now the bell rings for evening meeting—& its volumes of sound like smoke which rises from where a cannon is fired—make the tent in which I dwell. My facts shall all be falsehoods to the common sense. I would so state facts that they shall be significant shall be myths or mythologic. Facts which the mind perceived—thoughts which the body thought with these I deal— I too cherish vague & misty forms —vaguest when the cloud at which I gaze is dissipated quite & nought but the skyey depths are seen.

James P Brown's retired pond now shallow & more than half

dried up— Seems far away and rarely visited—known to few—though not far off. It is encircled by an amphitheater of low hills on two opposite sides covered with high pine woods—the other sides with young white oaks & white pines respectively I am affected by beholding there reflected this grey day—so unpretendly the gray stems of the Pine wood on the hill side & the sky—that mirror as it were a permanent picture to be seen there—a permanent piece of idealism— What were these reflections to the cows alone! Were these things made for cows' eyes mainly? You shall go over behind the hills, where you would suppose that otherwise there was no eye to behold—& find this piece of magic a constant phenomenon there. It is not merely a few distinguished lakes or pools that reflect the trees & skies but the obscurest pond hole in the most unfrequented dell does the same.

These reflections suggest that the sky underlies the hills as well as overlies them, and in another sense than in appearance

I am a little surprised on beholding this reflection—which I did not perceive for some minutes after looking into the pond—as if I had not regarded this as a constant phenomenon.— What has become of nature's common sense & love of facts when in the very mud puddles she reflects the skies & trees. Does that procedure recommend itself entirely to the common sense of men.? Is that the way the New England farmer would have arranged it?

I think it is not true what De Quincey says of himself that he read Greek as easily & copiously as other men do French—for as murder will out so will a man's reading—and in this author's writings the amount of reference to Greek literature does not at all correspond to such a statement.

I knew that this pond was early to freeze— I had forgotten that it reflected the hills around it.— so retired! Which I must think even the sordid owner does not know that he owns.

It is full of little pollywogs now— Pray when were they born?

To day the mts seen from the pasture above are dark blue so dark that they look like new *mts* & make a new impression—and the intervening town of Acton is seen against them in a new relation—a new neighborhood.

The new monument in Acton rising by the side of its *mt* houses like a tall & slender chimney looking black against the sky—!! I cannot associate that tall & slender column or any column in fact with the death of Davis & Hosmer—& Concord fight & the Am. revolution. It should have been a large flat stone rather covered with

lichens—like an old farmers' door step which it took all the oxen in
the town to draw—— Such a column this as might fitly stand
perchance in Abysinia or Nubia but not here in middlsex Co—where
the genius of the people does not soar after that fashion. It is the
Acton flue. to dissipate the vapors of patriotism in the upper air—
which confined would be deleterious to animal and vegetable health.
The Davis & Hosmer Monument might have been a doorstep to the
Town House.

Pitch pine cones very beautiful—not only the fresh leather colored
ones but especially the dead grey ones—covered with lichens— The
scales so regular & close—like an impenetrable coat of mail. These
are very handsome to my eye— Also those which have long since
opened regularly & shed their seeds

An abundance of the rattlesnake Plantain in the woods by
Brown's Pond—now full of a fine chaffey seed?

Now the leaves are gone the birds nests are revealed—the brood
being fledged & flown. There is a perfect adaptation in the material
used in constructing a nest—there is one which I took from a maple
on the causeway at Hubbards bridge. It is fastened to the twigs by
white woolen strings. out of a shawl? which it has picked up in
the road though it is more than half a mile from a house— And the
sharp eyes of the bird have discovered plenty of horse hairs out of
the tail or mane—with which to give it form by their spring—with
fine meadow hay for body—and the reddish wooly material which
invests the ferns in the spring—apparently—for lining

Nov 10th

This morning the ground is once more whitened with snow—but
it will apparently be gone in an hour or two. I live where the pinus
rigida grows—with its firm cones almost as hard as iron—armed with
recurved spines

In relation to politics—to society—aye to the whole out-ward
world I am tempted to ask—Why do *they* lay such stress on a
particular experience which you have had?— That after 25 years you
should meet Cyrus Warren again on the sidewalk! Haven't I budged
an inch then?— This daily routine should go on then like those—it
must be conceded—vital functions of digestion—circulation of the
blood &c which in health we know nothing about. A wise man is as
unconscious of the movements in the body politic as he is of
digestion & the circulation of the blood in the natural body.

These processes are *infra*-human. I sometimes awake to a

consciousness of these things going on about me—as politics—society—
business & &c—as a man may become conscious of some of the
processes of digestion—in a morbid state—& so have the dyspepsia as
it is called.

It appears to me that those things which most engage the
attention of men—as politics, for instance, are vital functions of
human society, it is true, but should unconsciously performed like
the vital functions of the natural body.—   It is as if a thinker
submitted himself to be rasped by the great gizzard of creation.
Politics is, as it were, the gizzard of society—full of grit & gravel and
the two political parties are its two opposite halves—which grind on
each other. Not only individuals but states have thus a confirmed
dispepsia—which expresses itself—you can imagine by what sort of
eloquence.

Our life is not altogether a forgetting but also alas to a great
extent a remembering of that which perchance—we should never
have been conscious of.—   the consciousness of what should not be
permitted to disturb a man's waking hours.—   As for society why
should we not meet not always as dyspeptics—but some times as
eupeptics?

No true & absolute account of things——of the evening & the
morning & all the phenomena between them—but ever a petty
reference to man—to society—aye often to christianity. What these
things are when men are asleep. I come from the funeral of mankind
to attend to a natural phenomenon. The so much grander
significance of any fact—of sun & moon & starrs—when not referred
to man & his needs but viewed absolutely—   Sounds that are wafted
from over the confines of time

Nov. 11th

Nov. 11th

When pointing toward Cap Tourment I asked the name—of a
habitant when we met—he hazzarded the name of Belange—or fair
angel or perchance he referred to some other sort—   At any rate my
interrogations of this nature gave—vent to such a musical catalogue of
sweet names though I did not know which one to fix on—that I
continued to put them to every habitant I met if only for this
pleasure.

Living much out of doors in the air—in the sun & wind—will no
doubt produce a certain roughness of character—will cause a cuticle
to grow over the finer sensibilities of a man's nature as on his face &
hands—or those parts of his body which are exposed to the weather

As staying in the house on the other hand may produce a softness &
smoothness not to say thinness of skin—accompanied by an increased
sensibility to certain impressions.— And no doubt it is a nice matter
to proportion rightly the thick & thin skin. Perhaps we should be
more susceptible to some influences important to our intellectual
growth—if the sun had shone on us & the wind blown on us a little
less. As too much labor calluses the hand and deprives it of the
exquisitness of the touch.

But then methinks that is a scurf that will fall off fast enough—that
the natural remedy is to be found in the proportion which the night
bears to the day— The winter to the summer &c. Thought to
experience.

2 Pm

A bright but cold day—finger cold— One must next wear gloves
put his hands in winter quarters. There is a cold silvery light on the
white pines as I go through J. P. Brown's field near Jenny Dugan's.
I am glad of the shelter of the thick pine wood on the Marlboro'
road—on the plain. The roar of the wind over the pines sounds like
the surf on countless beaches—an endless shore—& at intervals it
sounds like a gong resounding through halls & entries. How the
wind roars among the shrouds of the wood i.e. there is a certain
resounding woodiness in the tone— The sky looks mild & fair
enough from this shelter.— every withered blade of grass & every
dry weed—as well as pine needle—reflects light— The lately dark
woods are open & light—the sun shines in upon the stems of trees
which it has not shone on since spring— Around the edges of ponds
the weeds are dead and there too the light penetrates— The
atmosphere is less moist & gross & light is universally dispersed. We
are greatly indebted to these transition seasons or states of the
atmosphere—which show us thus phenomena which belong not to
the summer or the winter of any climate. The brilliancy of the
autumn is wonderful—this flashing brilliancy—as if the atmosphere
were phosphoric.

When I have been confined to my chamber for the greater part
of several days by some employment or perchance by the ague—till I
felt weary & house-worn—I have been conscious of a certain softness
to which I am otherwise & commonly a stranger—in which the gates
were loosened to some emotions— And if I were to become a
confirmed invalid I see how some sympathy with mankind & society
might spring up

Yet what is my softness good for even to tears— It is not I but nature in me. I laughed at myself the other day to think that I cried while reading a pathetic story. I was no more affected in spirit than I frequently am methinks—the tears were merely a phenomenon of the bowels—& I felt that that expression of my sympathy so unusual with me was something mean—& such as I should be ashamed to have the subject of it understand. I had a cold in my head withal about those days. I found that I had some bowels—but then it was because my bowels were out of order.

The *fall* of the year is over—& now let us see if we shall have any Indian summer.

White Pond is prepared for winter. Now that most other trees have lost their leaves the evergreens are more conspicuous about its shores & on its capes. The view of the S horizon from the lane this side still attracts me—but not so much as before I had explored those wayland hills—which look so much fairer perhaps than they are. Today You may write a chapter on the advantages of travelling—& to-morrow you may write another chapter on the advantages of not travelling. The horizon has one kind of beauty and attraction to him who has never explored the hills & *mts* in it—and another I fear a less etherial & glorious one to him who has— That blue mountain in the horizon is certainly the most heavenly—the most elysian which we have not climbed—on which we have not camped for a night. But only our horizon is moved thus farther off—& if our whole life should prove thus a failure—the future which is to atone for all where still there must be some success will be more glorious still.

Say's I to my-self should be the motto of my Journal.

It is fatal to the writer to be too much possessed by his thought— Things must lie a little remote to be described.

Nov 12th

Write often write upon a thousand themes—rather than long at a time— Not trying to turn too many feeble summersets in the air—& so come down upon your head head at last— Antaeus like be not long absent from the ground— Those sentences are good and well discharged which are like so many little resiliencies from the spring floor of our life.— a distinct fruit & kernel itself—springing from terra-firma. Let there be as many distinct plants as the soil & the light can sustain. Take as many bounds in a day as possible. Sentences uttered with your back to the wall. Those are the admirable bounds when the performer has lately touched the spring board. A good bound into the air from the air is a good &

wholsome experience but what what shall we say to a man's leaping
off precipices in the attempt to fly–he comes down like lead. In the
mean while you have got your feet planted upon the rock with the
rock also at your back and as in the case of King James and
Roderick Dhu can say come one come all   This rock shall fly

                    From its firm base as soon as I.

Such uttered or not is the strength of your sentence. Sentences in
which their is no strain. A fluttering & inconstant & quasi inspiration
–and ever memorable Icarian fall in which your helpless wings are
expanded merely by your swift descent. into the pelagos. beneath.

   C. is one who will not stoop to rise (to change the subject) He
wants something for which he will not pay the going price. He will
only learn slowly by failure–not a noble but disgraceful failure–
This is not a noble method of learning. To be educated by evitable
suffering. Like De Quincy for instance. Better dive like a muskrat
into the mud & pile up a few weeds to sit on during the floods–a
foundation of your own laying–a house of your own building
however cold & cheerless

   Methinks the hawk that soars so loftily & circles so steadily &
apparently without effort–has earned this power by faithfully
crawling on the ground as a reptile in a former state of existence.
You must creep before you can run–you must run before you can
fly. Better one effective bound upward upward with elastic limbs
from the valley–than a jumping from the mountain tops in the
attempt to fly. The observatories are not built high but deep–the
foundation is equal to the superstructure. It is more important to a
distinct vision that it be steady than that it be from an elevated point
of view.

   Walking through Ebby Hubbards Wood this afternoon with
Minott who was actually taking a walk for amusement & exercise–
he said on seeing some white pines blown down–that you might
know that ground had been cultivated by the trees being torn up so
–for otherwise they would have rooted themselves more strongly–
Saw some very handsome canoe birches there, the largest I know–a
foot in diameter & 40 or 50 feet high. The large ones have a reddish
cast–perhaps from some small lichen. Their fringes & curls give
them an agreeable appearance. Observed a peculiarity in some white
oaks. Though they had a firm & close bark near the ground–the
bark was very coarse & scaly in loose flakes above. Much coarser
than the swamp white oak. Minott has a story for every woodland
path– He has hunted in them all. Where we walked last he had
once caught a partridge by the *wing*!

7 P m to Conantum

A still cold night— The light of the rising moon in the East—
Moonrise is a faint sun-rise. & what shall we name the faint aurora
that precedes the moonrise? The ground is frozen & echoes to my
tread. There are absolutely no crickets to be heard now. They are
heard then till the ground freezes. Today I heard for the first time
this season the crackling vibrating sound which resounds from thin
ice when a stone is cast upon it. So far have we got toward winter.
It is doubtful if they who have not pulled their turnips will have a
chance to get them.. It is not of much use to drive the cows to
pasture. I can fancy that I hear the booming of ice in the ponds. I
hear no sound of any bird—now at night—but sometimes some
creature stirring—a rabbit or skunk or fox—betrayed now by the dry
leaves which lie so thick & light. The openness of the leafless woods
is particularly apparent now by moonlight—they are nearly as light as
the open field. It is worth the while always to go to the water side
when there is but little light in the heavens & see the heavens & the
stars reflected— There is double the light that there is elsewhere—&
the reflection has the force of a great silent companion. There is no
fog now o'nights— I thought tonight that I saw glow worms in the
grass—on the side of the hill—was almost certain of it & tried to lay
my hand on them—but found it was the moonlight reflected from
apparently the frost crystals on the withered grass & they were so
fine that they went and came like glowworms.

It had precisely the effect of twinkling glow worms.

Nov 13   To Fair Haven Hill

A cold & dark afternoon the sun being behind clouds in the west
The landscape is barren of objects——the trees being leafless—& so
little light in the sky for variety. Such a day as will almost oblige a
man to eat his own heart. A day in which you must hold on to life
by your teeth— You can hardly ruck up any skin on nature's bones
— The sap is down—she wont peel. Now is the time to cut timber
for yokes & ox bows—leaving the tough bark on—yokes for your
own neck. Finding yourself yoked to matter & to Time.

Truly a hard day—hard Times these. not a mosquito left Not an
insect to hum. Crickets gone into winter quarters— Friends long
since gone there—& you left to walk on frozen ground—with your
hands in your pockets. Ah but is not this a glorious time for your
deep inward fires?— & will not your green hickory & white oak
burn clean—in this frosty air?

Now is not your manhood taxed by the great Assessor? Taxed for
having a soul—a rateable soul. A day when you cannot pluck a

flower—cannot dig a parsnip nor pull a turnip for the frozen ground—
what do the thoughts find to live on? What avails you now the fire
you stole from heaven? Does not each thought become a vulture to
gnaw your vitals? No Indian summer have we had this november—
I see but few traces of the perennial spring.

Now is there nothing—not even the cold beauty of ice crystals—&
snowy architecture. Nothing but the echo of your steps over the
frozen ground no voice of birds—nor frogs— You are dry as a
farrow? cow. The earth will not admit a spade All fields lie fallow—
Shall not your mind? True the freezing ground is being prepared for
immeasurable snows.— but there are brave thoughts within you that
shall remain to rustle the winter through like white oak leaves upon
your boughs—or like scrub oaks that remind the traveller of a fire
upon the hill sides—or evergreen thoughts cold even in mid summer
by their nature shall contrast the more fairly with the snow.

Some warm springs shall still tinkle and fume? and send their
column of vapor to the skies.

The walker now fares like cows in the pastures—where is no grass
but hay—he gets nothing but an appetite. If we must return to hay—
pray let us have that which has been stored in barns—which has not
lost its sweetness.

The poet needs to have more stomachs than the cow—for for him
no fodder is stored in barns— He relies upon his instinct which
teaches him to paw away the snow to come at the withered grass.

Methinks man came very near being made a dormant creature.
Just as some of these animals—the ground squirrel for instance which
lays up vast stores—is yet found to be half dormant, if you dig him
out. Now for the oily nuts of thought— Which you have stored up.

The *mts* are of an uncommonly dark-blue today— Perhaps this is
owing not only to the greater clearness of the atmosphere which
brings them nearer, but to the absence of the leaves. They are many
miles nearer for it— A little mistiness, occasioned by warmth would
set them further off—& make them fainter

I see snow on the Peterboro hills reflecting the sun. It is pleasant
thus to look from afar into winter We look at a condition which
we have not reached. Notwithstanding the poverty of the immediate
landscape—in the horizon it is simplicity. & granddeur— I look into
valleys white with snow & now lit up by the sun—while all this
country is in shade. This accounts for the cold northwest wind.

There is a great gap in the mountain range just south of the two
Peterboro hills—methinks I have been through & that a road runs

there—at any rate humble as these *mts* are compared with some yet at this distance I am convinced that they answer the purpose of Andes— And seen in the horizon I know of nothing more grand & stupendous than this great *Mt* gate or pass. A great cleft or sinus in the blue banks as in a dark evening cloud—fit portal to lead from one country from one quarter of the earth to another—where the children of the Israelites may file through Little does the N.H. farmer who drives over that road realize through what a sublime gap he is passing— You would almost as soon think of a road to wind through and over a dark evening cloud. This prospect of the *mts* from our low hills—is what I would rather have than pastures on the *mt* sides aye than townships at their base. Instead that I drive my cattle up in May I turn my eyes that way. My eyes pasture them & straight-way the yearling thoughts come back. The grass they feed on never withers—for though they are not ever green they're ever blue to me. For though not evergreen to you—to me they're ever blue.

> I do not fear my thoughts will die
> For never yet it was so dry
> as to scorch the azure of the sky.
> It knows no withering & no drought
> Though all eyes crop it ne'er gives out
> My eyes my flocks are
> Mountains my crops.
> I do not fear my flocks will stray
> For they were made to roam the day
> For they can wander with the latest light
> Yet be at home at night.

Just spent a couple of hours (8 to 10) with Miss Mary Emerson at Holbrook's. The wittiest & most vivacious woman that I know— Certainly that woman among my acquaintance whom it is most profitable to meet—the least frivolous who will most surely provoke to good conversation and the expression of what is in you. She is singular among women at least in being really & perseveringly interested to know what thinkers think. She relates herself surely to the intellectual where she goes.

It is perhaps her greatest praise & peculiarity that she more surely than any other woman gives her companion occasion to utter his best thought.

In spite of her own biases she can entertain a large thought with hospitality—and is not prevented by any intellectuality in it—as

women commonly are. In short she is a genius—as woman seldom is
—reminding you less often of her sex than any woman whom I
know— In that sense she is capable of a masculine appreciation of
poetry & philosophy. I never talked with any other woman who I
thought acompanied me so far in describing a poetic experience.
Miss Fuller is the only woman I think of in this connection—& of
her rather from her fame than from any knowledge of her. Miss
Emerson expressed tonight a singular want of respect for her own
sex—saying that they were frivolous almost without exception—that
woman was the weaker vessel &c That into whatever family she
might go she depended more upon the "clown" for society than
upon the lady of the house. Men are more likely to have opinions
of their own.

The cattle train came down last night from Vermont with snow
nearly a foot thick upon it. It is as if in the fall of the year a swift
traveller should come out of the north with snow upon his coat. So
it snows. Such some years may be our first snow.

Just in proportion to the outward poverty is the inward wealth.

In cold weather fire burns with a clearer flame.

Friday Nov 14

Surveying the Ministerial lot in the S W part of the town.
Unexpectedly find Heywoods pond frozen over thinly it being
shallow & coldly placed.

In the evening went to a party. It is a bad place to go to.— 30 or
40 persons mostly young women in a small room—warm & noisy.
Was introduced to two young women— The first one was as lively
& loquacious as a chic-a-dee—had been accustomed to the society of
watering places, and therefore could get no refreshment out of such
a dry fellow as I. The other was said to be pretty looking, but I
rarely look people in their faces, and moreover I could not hear
what she said there was such a clacking—could only see the motion
of her lips when I looked that way. I could imagine better places for
conversation—where there should be a certian degree of silence
surrounding you & less than 40 talking at once. Why this afternoon
even I did better. There was old Mr Joseph Hosmer & I ate our
luncheon of cracker & cheese together in the woods. I heard all he
said, though it was not much to be sure & he could hear me. &
then he talked out of such a glorious repose—taking a leisurely bite at
the cracker & cheese between his words—& so some of him was
communicated to me & some of me to him.

These parties I think are a part of the machinery of modern

society—that young people may be brought together to form
marriage connections.

What is the use of going to see people whom yet you never see—
& who never see you? I begin to suspect that it is not necessary that
we should see one another.

Some of my friends make singular blunders. They go out of their
way to talk with certain young women of whom they think or have
heard that they are pretty—and take pains to introduce me to them.
That may be a reason why they should look at them, but it is not a
reason why they should talk with them. I confess that I am lacking a
sense perchance in this respect—& I derive no pleasure from talking
with a young woman half an hour—simply because she had regular
features.

The society of young women is the most unprofitably I have ever
tried.

They are so light & flighty that you can never be sure whether
they are there or not there. I prefer to talk with the more staid &
settled—*settled for life*, in every sense.

I met a man yesterday afternoon in the road who behaved as if he
was deaf, and I talked with him in the cold in a loud tone for 15
minutes—but that uncertainty about his ears & the necessity I felt to
talk loudly—took off the fine edge of what I had to say—and
prevented my saying anything satisfactory. It is bad enough when
your neighbor does not understand you—but if there is any
uncertainty as to whether he hears you—so that you are obliged to
become your own auditor—you are so much the poorer speaker—and
so there is a double failure.

Nov. 15th

Here is a rainy day which keeps me in the house.

Asked Therien this afternoon if he had got a new idea this
summer— Good Lord says he a man that has to work as I do, if he
does'nt forget the ideas he has had—he will do well. May be the man
you work with is inclined to race then by Gorry your mind must be
there—you think of weeds.

I am pleased to read in Stoever's Life of Linnaeus (Trapp's
Translation) that his father being the first learned man of his family,
changed his family name & borrowed that of Linnaeus (Linden-tree-
man) from a lofty linden tree which stood near his native place. "a
custom," he says "not unfrequent in Sweden, to take fresh
appellations from natural objects." What more fit than that the

advent of a new man into a family should acquire for it & transmit
to his posterity a new patronymic. Such a custom suggests, if it does
not argue, an unabated vigor in the race.— relating it to those
primitive times—when men did indeed acquire a name—as memorable
and distinct as their characters. It is refreshing to get to a man whom
you will not be satisfied to call Johns' son or John'-son's son—but by
a new name applicable to himself alone he being the first of his
kind. We may say there have been but so many men as there are
sir-names & of all the John-smiths there has been but one true John
Smith—& he of course is dead. Get yourself therefore a name—&
better a nickname than none at all.

There was one enterprising boy came to school to me whose
name was "Buster"—& an honorable name it was— He was the only
boy in the school to my knowledge who was named.

What shall we say of the comparative intellectual vigor of the
ancients & moderns, when we read of Theophrastus, the father of
botany, that he composed more than 200 treatises in the 3d cent.
befor C. & the 17th before printing, about 20 of which remain and
that these fill six vols in folio printed at Venice— Among the last
are two works on natural history & the generation of plants. V Class
dict V Scrap Book

What a stimulus to a literary man to read his works! They *were*
opera. Not an essay or two which you can carry between your
thumb & finger.

Dioscorides (ac. to Stoever) who lived in the 1st century after
Christ was the first to inquire into the medicinal properties of plants
—"the literary father of the *materia medica*" his work remains.

And next comes Pliny the elder—& "By his own avowal, his
natural history is a compilation from about 2500 different authors."

Conrad Gesner of the 16th cent—the first botanist of note among
the moderns— Also a naturalist generally.

In this century botany first "became a regular Academical study".

I think it would be a good discipline—for Channing—who writes
poetry in a sublimo-slipshod style to write Latin—for then he would
be compelled to say something always—and frequently have recourse
to his grammar & dictionary. Methinks that what a man might write
in a dead language could be more surely translated into good sense
in his own language—than his own language could be translated into
good Latin—or the dead language.

Sunday Nov 16th

It is remarkable that the highest intellectual mood which the
world tolerates is the perception of the truth of the most ancient

revelations, now in some resets out of date—but any direct revelation
—any original thoughts it hates like virtue. The fathers and the
mothers of the town would rather hear the young man or young
woman at their tables express reverence for some old statement of
the truth——than utter a direct revelation themselves. So far as
thinking is concerned—surely original thinking is the divinest thing.
Rather we should reverently watch for the least motions the least
scintillations of thought in this sluggish world—and men should run
to and fro on the occasion more than at an earthquake. We check &
repress the divinity that stirs within us to fall down & worship the
divinity that is dead without us.

I go to see many a good man or good woman so called & utter
freely that thought which alone it was given to me to utter—but
there was a man who lived a long long time ago & his name was
Moses—& another whose name was Christ, and if your thought does
not or does not appear to coincide with what they said, the good
man or the good woman has no ears to hear you.

They think they love God! It is only his old clothes—of which
they make scarecrows for the children. Where will they come nearer
to God than in these very children?

A man lately preached here here against the abuse of the sabbath
& recommended to walk in the fields & dance on that— Good
advice enough which may take effect after awhile But with the
mass of men the reason is convinced long before the life is— They
may see the church & the sabbath to be false—but nothing else to be
true

One woman in the neighborhood says "Nobody can hear Mr
preach,—hear him through, without seeing that he is a good man"—
"Well is there any truth in what he says?"— "O yes, it's true
enough, but then it wont do; you know it wont do. Now there's
our George, he's got the whole of it; and when I say 'come George,
put on your things & go along to Meeting—he says No—Mother I'm
going out into the fields. It wont do.' " The fact is this woman has
not character and religion enough to exert a controlling influence
over her children by her example, and knows of no such police as
the church & the minister.

If it were not for death & funerals I think the institution of the
Church would not stand longer. The necessity that men be decently
buried—our fathers & mothers—brothers & sisters & children
(notwithstanding the danger that they be buried alive) will long if
not for ever—prevent our laying violent hands on it. If salaries were
stopped off—& men walked out of this world bodily at last—the

minister & his vocation would be gone. What is the church yard but a grave yard? Imagine a church at the other end of the town, without any carrion beneath or beside it, but all the dead regularly carried to the bone mill! The cry that comes up from the churches in all the great cities in the world is—How they stink!

What more fatal vengeance could Linnaeus have taken than to give the names of his enemies to pernicious & unsightly plants—thus simply putting upon record for as long as the Linnaean system shall prevail who were his friends & foes. It was enough to record the fact that they were opposed to him. To this they could not themselves have objected nor could he have taken a more fatal vengeance. V Scraps.

Noticed this afternoon that where a pitch pine 3 inches in diameter had been cut down last winter, it had sent out more than a hundred horizontal plumes about a foot long close together & on every side. Plenty of ripe checquer berries now—. Do they blossom again in the spring? The ferns which are almost the only green things left now—love the crevices & seams of moist cliffs & boulders —& adorn them very much. They become more conspicuous now than at any season

I had a thought this morning before I awoke. I endeavored to retain it in my mind's grasp after I became conscious—yet I doubted, while I lay on my back, whether my mind could apprehend it when I should stand erect. It is a far more difficult feat to get up without spilling your morning thought—than that which is often practised of taking a cup of water from behind your head as you lie on your back & drinking from it. It was the thought I endeavored to express on the first page of today.

Thinkers & writers are in foolish haste to come before the world—with crude works. Young men are persuaded by their friends or by their own restless ambition, to write a course of lectures in a summer against the ensuing winter— And what it took the lecturer a summer to write it will take his audience but an hour to forget. If time is short—then you have no time to waste.

That sounds like a fine mode of expressing gratitude—referred to by Linnaeus— Hermann was a botanist who gave up his place to Tournefort who was unprovided for— "Hermann", says Linnaeus, came afterwards to Paris, and Tournefort in honor of him ordered the fountains to play in the royal garden".

Nov 17

All things tend to flow to him who can make the best use of them, even away from their legal owner. A thief finding with the

property of the Italian Naturalist Donati, whom he had robbed
abroad, a collection of rare African seeds, forwarded them to
Linnaeus from Marseilles. Donati suffered shipwreck and never
returned.

Nov. 18th

Surveying these days the ministerial-lot. Now at Sundown I hear
the hooting of an owl—hõohoó hóo—hoorer—hóo. It sounds like
the hooting of an idiot or a maniac broke loose. This is faintly
answered in a different strain apparently from a greater distance—
almost as if it were the echo—i.e. so far as the *succession* is concerned.

This is my music each evening. I heard it last evening. The men
who help me call it the "hooting owl" and think it is the cat-owl. It
is a sound admirably suited the swamp & to the twilight woods—
suggesting a vast undeveloped nature which men have not
recognized nor satisfied. I rejoice that there are owls. They represent
the stark twilight unsatisfied thoughts I have. Let owls do the idiotic
& maniacal hooting for men. This sound faintly suggests the infinite
roominess of nature—that there is a world in which owls live— Yet
how few are seen even by the hunters! The sun has shone for a day
over this savage swamp where the single spruce stands covered with
esnea? moss—which a Concord merchant mortgaged once to the
trustees of the ministerial fund & lost—but now for a different race of
creatures a new day dawns over this wilderness—which one would
have thought was sufficiently dismal before. Here hawks also circle
by day & chicadees are heard—& rabbits & partridges abound.

The chopper who works in the woods all day for many weeks or
months at a time becomes intimately acquainted with them in his
way. He is more open in some respects to the impressions they are
fitted to make than the naturalist who goes to see them He is not
liable to exaggerate insignificant features. He really forgets himself—
forgets to observe—and at night he *dreams* of the swamp its
phenomena & events. Not so the naturalist; enough of his
unconscious life does not pass there.

A man can hardly be said to be *there* if he *knows* that he is there—
or to go there, if he knows Where he is going. The man who is
bent upon his work is frequently in the best attitude to observe what
is irrelevant to his work. (Mem. Wordsworth's obs. on relaxed
attention) You must be conversant with things for a long time to
know much about them—like the moss which has hung from the
spruce—and as the partridge & the rabbit are acquainted with the
thickets & at length have acquired the color of the places they
frequent. If the man of science can put all his knowledge into

propositions—the wood man has a great deal of incommunicable knowledge

Dea. Brown told me me today of a tall raw-boned fellow by the name of Hosmer who used to help draw the sein behind the Jones' House—who once when he had hauled it without getting a single shad—held up a little perch in sport above his face—to show what he had got— At that moment the perch wiggled and dropped right down his throat head foremost—and nearly suffocated him—& it was only after considerable time, during which the man suffered much that he was extracted or forced down.— He was in a worse predicament than a fish hawk would have been.

In the woods S of the swamp are many great holes made by digging for foxes

Nov 19th

Old Mr. Joseph Hosmer who helped me to-day—said that he used to know all about the lots—but since they've chopped off so much & the woods have grown up—he finds himself lost. 30 or 40 years ago when he went to meeting he knew every face in the meeting house —even the boys & girls looked so much like their parents—but after 10 or 12 years they would have outgrown his knowledge entirely (they would have altered so—but he knew the old folks still—because they held their own & did'nt alter. Just so he could tell the boundaries of the old wood which had'nt been cut down, but the young wood altered so much in a few years, that he could'nt tell anything about it.

When I asked him why the old road which went by this swamp was so round about, he said he would answer me as Mr— — — did him in a similar case once Why if they had made it straight they would'nt have left any room for improvement.

Standing by Harrington's pond-hole in the swamp—which had skimmed over—we saw that there were many holes through the thin black ice—of various sizes from a few inches to more than a foot in diameter all of which were *perfectly* circular. Mr H. asked me if I could account for it. As we stood considering we jarred the boggy ground and made a dimple in the water—& this accident we thought betrayed the cause of it—i.e. the circular wavelets so wore off the edges of the ice when once a hole was made. The ice was very thin. & the holes were perfect disks. But what jarred the ground & shook the water? Perhaps the wind which shook the spruce & pine trees which stood in the quaking ground—as well as the little life in the water itself. & the wind on the ice & water itself. There was a more permanent form created by the dimple but not yet a shell-fish.

Nov 20th

It is often said that melody can be heard farther than noise—& the finest melody farther than the coarsest. I think there is truth in this—& that accordingly those strains of the piano which reach me here in my attic stir me so much more than the sounds which I should hear if I were below in the parlor—because because they are so much purer & diviner melody. They who sit farthest off from the noisy & bustling world are not at pains to distinguish what is sweet & musical—for that alone can reach them That chiefly comes down to posterity.

Hard and steady & engrossing labor with the hands especially out of doors—is invaluable to the literary man—& serves him directly— Here I have been for 6 days surveying in the woods—and yet when I get home at evening somewhat weary at last, and beginning to feel that I have nerves—I find myself more susceptible than usual to the finest influences—as music & poetry— The very air can intoxicate me or the least sight or sound—as if my finer senses had acquired an appetite by their fast.

As I was riding to the ministerial Lot this morning about 8½ Am I observed that the white clouds in the west were disposed ray wise in the W and also in the east as if the sun's rays had split & so arranged them? A striking symetry in the heavens. What its law?

Mr J. Hosmer tells me that one spring he saw a red squirrel gnaw the bark of a maple & then suck the juice—and this he repeated many times

What is the bush where we dined—in Poplar hollow? Hosmer tells of finding a kind of apple—with an apple seed? to it on scabbish which had been injured or cut off.

Thinks ploughed ground more moist than grass-ground. That there are more leaves on the ground on the N Side of a hill than on the other sides—& that the trees thrive more there—perhaps because the winds cause the leaves to fall there—

Nov 21st

My mother says that visiting once at Capt. Pulcifer's at the North End, two sea-captains' wives told the girl, when the things were carried out to be replenished, not to turn out their slops as it would drown their husbands who were at sea.

Frank Brown shewed me today the velvet duck (White winged coot) & the surf duck— These two as well as the Scaup? duck he says are called coots.

Saw also a fine brant a shore lark—a pine gross-beak—kittiwake

gull & buonaparte's do—(the last very like the first but smaller) all
shot at Clarke's island. Also a little brown creeper with a
woodpecker tail & curved bill, killed here.

Old Mr. Joseph Hosmer, who lives where Hadley did—remembers
when there were two or three times as many inhabitants in that part
of the town as there are now— A blacksmith with his shop in front
where he now lives—a Goldsmith (Oliver Wheeler?) at the fork in
the road just beyond him, one *in front* of Tarbel's—one in the
orchard on the S side of the lane in front of Tarbels—one further
Nathan Wheeler on the right of the old road by the Balm of Gilead
—3 between Tarbels & J P Brown's, a tavern at Lorings—a store at
The Dodge cottage that was burnt also at Derbey's?—&c &c The
farms were smaller then— One man now often holds 2 or 3 old
farms. We walk in a deserted country.

The Major Heywood & Mill road together turn out of the Marl.
Road just beyond the Desert—the the former keeps the left to the
Powdermills—the Latter the right to the saw-mill.

The main Road beyond Lorings used to be called Law's path—
where is Laws brook (S branch of Nagog—i.e. Fort Pond?)

The old roads furrow the 2nd division woods like trenches.

Better men never lecture than they hire to come here. Why don't
they ask Edmund Hosmer or George Minot? I would rather hear
them decline than most of these hirelings lecture.

Nov 22nd The milkweed pods by the roadside are yet but half
emptied of their silky contents— For months the gales are dispersing
their seeds. Though we have had snow.

Saw E Hosmer this afternoon making a road for himself along a
hill side—(I being on my way to Saw Mill Brook) He turned over a
stone & I saw under it—Many crickets & ants still lively, which had
gone into winter quarters there apparently. There were many little
galleries leading under the stone indenting the hardened earth like
veins. Mem. Turn over a rock in mid winter & see if you can find
them. That is the reason then that I have not heard the crickets
lately. I have frequently seen them lurking under the eaves or
portico of a stone even in mid summer.

At the brook the partridge berries chequer the ground with their
leaves—now interspersed with red berries. The cress at the bottom of
the brook is doubly beautiful now because it is green while most
other plants are sere. It rises & falls & waves with the current. There
are many young hornbeams there which still retain their withered

leaves– As I returned through Hosmers field–the sun was setting
just beneath a black cloud by which it had been obscured–and as it
had been a raw & windy afternoon, its light which fell suddenly on
some white pines between me & it lighting them up like a
shimmering fire–and also on the oak leaves & chestnut stems was
quite a circumstance. It was from the contrast between the dark and
comfortless afternoon and this bright & cheerful light almost fire
The eastern hills & woods too were clothed in a still golden light.
The light of the setting sun just emerged from a cloud and suddenly
falling on & lighting up the needles of the white pine between you
& it after a raw and louring afternoon near the beginning of winter
is a memorable phenomenon. A sort of Indian summer in the day,–
which thus far has been denied to the year.

    After a cold grey day this cheering light almost warms us by its
resemblance to fire

Sunday Nov. 23d

    The trees (counting all 3 inches in diameter) in Conantum swamp
are

Bass	6	
Black Ash	8	
Elm	16	see if all are really elms
Red? oak	2	
White ash	2	
Walnut	3	
Apple	5	
Maple	9	
Hornbeam	2	and a great many smaller still with leave still on
Swamp Wht? oak	1	covered with ivy

    Dogwood also there is & cone bearing willow & what kind of
winter berry with a light colored bark?

    Another such a sunset to-night as the last while I was on
Conantum.

Nov. 24

    Setting stakes in the swamp (Ministerial) Saw seven black ducks
fly out of the peat hole. Saw there also a tortoise still stirring. The
painted tortoise I believe.

    Found on the S side of the swamp the Lygodium palmatum
which Bigelow calls the only climbing fern of in our latitude–an
evergreen called with others–snake tongue as I find in Loudon.

    The Irishman who helped me says when I ask why his country

men do not learn trades—do something but the plainest & hardest
work—they are too old to learn trades when they come here

Nov 25

This morning the ground is again covered with snow deeper than
before

In the afternoon walked to the east part of Lincoln— Saw a tree
on the turnpike full of hickory nuts which had an agreeable
appearance— Saw also quite a flock of the Pine Grosbeak a plump
& handsome bird as big as a robin— When returning between Bear
Hill & the RR. the sun had set & there was a very clear amber light
in the west—& turning about we were surprised at the darkness in
the east—the crescent of night—almost as if the air were thick a thick
snowstorm were gathering—which as we had faced the west we were
not prepared for—, yet the air was clear.

That kind of sunset which I witnessed on saturday & Sunday is
perhaps peculiar to the late Autumn. The sun is unseen behind a hill
— Only this bright white light like a fire falls on the trembling
needles of the pine.

When surveying in the swamp on the 20th last—at sundown I
heard the owls. Hosmer said "If you ever minded it, it is about the
surest sign of rain that there is. Don't you know that last Friday
night you heard them & spoke of them—& the next day it rained?".
This time there were other signs of rain in abundance "But night
before last," said I, "when you were not here they hooted louder
than ever & we have had no rain yet.". At any rate, it rained hard
the 21st and by that rain the river was raised much higher than it
has been this fall.

Sunday Nov. 30th

A rather cold and windy afternoon with some snow not yet
melted on the ground. Under the south side of the hill between
Brown's & Tarbel's, in a warm noook—disturbed 3 large grey-
squirrels & some partridges—who had all sought out this bare and
warm place. While the squirrels hid themselves in the tree tops I sat
on an oak stump by an old cellar hole and mused.

This squirrel is always an unexpectedly large animal to see frisking
about. My eye wanders across the valley to the pine woods which
fringe the opposite side, and in their aspect my eye finds something
which addresses itself to my nature. Methinks that in my mood I
was asking nature to give me a sign— I do not know exactly what it
was that attracted my eye— I experienced a transient gladness at any

rate at something which I saw. I am sure that my eye rested with
pleasure on the white pines now reflecting a silvery light—the infinite
stories of their boughs—tier above tier—a sort of basaltic structure—a
crumbling precipice of pine horizontally stratified. Each pine is like a
great green feather stuck in the ground. A myriad white pine boughs
extend themselves horizontally one above & behind another each
bearing its burden of silvery sun-light with darker seams between
them—as if it were a great crumbling piny precipice thus stratified—
On this my eyes pastured while the squirrels were up the trees.
behind me That at any rate it was that I got by my afternoon walk
—a certain recognition from the pine. some congratulation. Where
is my home? It is indistinct as an old cellar hole now a faint
indentation merely in a farmer's field—which he has ploughed into &
rounded off its edges—years ago and I sit by the old site on the
stump of an oak which once grew there. Such is the nature where
we have lived— Thick birch groves stand here & there dark brown?
now with white lines more or less distinct—

The Lygodium palmatum is quite abundant on that side of the
swamp—twining round the golden rods &c &c.

Dec 12th

In regard to my friends I feel that I know & have communion
with a finer & subtler part of themselves which does not put me off
when they put me off—which is not cold to me when they are cold
—not till I am cold. I hold by a deeper and stronger tie than absence
can sunder.

Ah dear nature—the mere remembrance, after a short forgetfulness,
of the pine woods! I come to it as a hungry man to a crust of bread.

I have been surveying for 20 or 30 days—living coarsely—even as
respects my diet—for I find that that will always alter to suit my
employment— Indeed leading a quite trivial life—& tonight for the
first time had made a fire in my chamber & endeavored to return to
myself. I wished to ally myself to the powers that rule the universe—
I wished to dive into some deep stream of thoughtful & devoted life
—which meandered through retired & fertile meadows far from
towns. I wished to do again—or for once, things quite congenial to
my highest inmost and most sacred nature— To lurk in crystalline
thought like the trout under verdurous banks—where stray mankind
should only see my bubble come to the surface.

I wished to live ah! as far away as a man can think. I wished for
leisure & quiet to let my life flow in its proper channels—with its
proper currents. When I might not waste the days—might establish

daily prayer & thanksgiving in my family. Might do my own work
& not the work of Concord & Carlisle—which would yield me
better than money. (How much forbearance—aye sacrifice & loss,
goes to every accomplishment! I am thinking by what long discipline
and at what cost a man learns to speak simply at last) I bethought
myself while my fire was kindling to open one of Emerson's books
which it happens that I rarely look at—to try what a chance sentence
out of that could do for me. Thinking at the same time of a
conversation I had with him the other night—I finding fault with
him for the stress he had laid on some of Margaret Fuller's whims &
superstitions— But he declaring gravely that she was one of those
persons whose experience warranted her attaching importance to
such things—as the sortes Virgilianae for instance of which her
numerous friends could tell remarkable instances—

At any rate I saw that he was disposed regard such things more
seriously than I. The first sentence which I opened upon in his book
was this.— "If, with a high trust, he can thus submit himself, he will
find that ample returns are poured into his bosom, out of what
seemed hours of obstruction and loss. Let him not grieve too much
on account of unfit associates in society of perfect sympathy, no
word, no act, no record, would be. He will learn, that it is not
much matter what he reads, what he does. Be a scholar, and he shall
have the scholar's part of everything. &c &c"

Most of this corresponded well enough to my mood—and this
would be as good an instance of the sortes virgilianae as most to
quote. But what makes this coincidence very little if at all
remarkable to me is the fact—of the obviousness of the moral—so that
I had perhaps *thought* the same thing myself 20 times during the day
—& yet had not been *contented* with that account of it—leaving me
thus to be amused by the coincidence rather than impressed as by an
intimation out of the deeps.

The Irishman (MacCarty) who helped me survey day before
yesterday would not sit on a rock with me to eat his dinner (there
being snow on the ground) from a notion that there was nothing so
deadly as sitting on a rock—sure to give you a cold in the back. He
would rather stand. So the doctors said—down in the Province of
New Brunswick— But I warranted him that he would not get a
cold in his back & so he minded me as a new doctor. A grey
headed boy good for nothing but to eat his dinner. These Irishmen
have no heads. Let me inquire strictly into a man's descent, and if
his remotest ancestors were Erse let me not have him to help me

survey. One or two I have seen—handy men—but I learned that their
fathers who came from Ireland were of the Scotch Irish. This fellow
was sure to do the wrong thing from the best motives—& the only
time he was spry was when he was running to correct his own
blunders out of his own head—then I saw the broad red soles of his
new cowhide boots—alternately rising & falling like the buckets of a
waterwheel.— When he had lost his plum & went to get it—then he
showed the red soles of his boots.

Nothing is so sure to make itself known as the truth—for what
else waits to be known?

Sat Dec 13th

While surveying today saw much Mt Laurel for this
neighborhood in Mason's pasture—just over the line in Carlisle. Its
bright yellowish green shoots are agreeable to my eye We had one
hour of almost Indian summer weather in the middle of the day. I
felt the influence of the sun— It melted my stoniness a little. The
pines looked like old friends again. Cutting a path through a swamp
where was much brittle dogwood &c &c I wanted to know the
name of every shrub. This varied employment to which my
necessities compel me serves instead of foreign travel & the lapse of
time— If it makes me forget somethings which I ought to
remember, it no doubt enables me to forget many things which it is
well to forget. By stepping aside from my chosen path so often I see
myself better and am enabled to criticise myself. Of this nature is the
only true lapse of time. It seems an age since I took walks & wrote
in my journal— And when shall I revisit the glimpses of the moon?
To be able to see ourselves—not merely as others see us—but as we
are—that service a *variety* of absorbing employments does us.

I would not be rude to the fine intimations of the Gods for fear
of incurring the reproach of superstition.

When I think of the Carlisle man whom I saw today—& the
filthiness of his house—I am reminded that there are all degrees of
barbarism even in this so called civilized community. Carlisle too
belongs to the 19th century.

Saw Perez Blood in his frock. A stuttering sure—unpretending
man. Who does not speak without thinking, does not guess— When
I reflected how different he was from his neighbors Conant—Mason—
Hodgman—-I saw that it was not so much outwardly—but that I saw
an inner form.— We do indeed see through & through each other—
through the veil of the body—& see the real form & character—in

spite of the garment—any coarseness or tenderness is seen and felt under whatever garb. How nakedly men appear to us—for the spiritual assists the natural eye.

Dec 14th

The boys have been skating for a week, but I have had no time to skate for surveying. I have hardly realized that there was ice—though I have walked over it about my business. As for the weather, all seasons are pretty much alike to one who is actively at work in the woods. I should say—that there were two or though remarkably warm days—& as many cold ones in the course of a year—but the rest are all alike—in respect to temperature— This is my answer to my acquaintances who ask me if I have not found it very cold being out all day.

Mc.Kean tells me of hardy horses left to multiply on the Isle of Sable— His father had one—(for the shipwrecked to eat) Can they be descendants of those beasts Champlain or L Escarbot refers to?

I hear the small wood-pecker whistle as he flies toward the leafless wood on Fair Haven—doomed to be cut this winter. The chicadees remind me of Hudson's Bay for some reason— I look on them as natives of a more northern latitude.

The now dry & empty but clean-washed cups of the blue curls spot the half snow covered grain fields. Where lately was a delicate blue flower now all the winter are held up these dry chalices. What mementoes to stand above the snow!

The fresh young spruces in the swamp are free from moss—but it adheres especially to the bare & dead masts of spruce trees often times half destitute of bark. They look like slanting maypoles with drooping or withered garlands & festoons hanging to them.

For an emblem of stillness—a spruce swamp with hanging moss now or at any season.

I notice that hornet's nests are hardly deserted by the insects—than they look as if a truant boy had fired a charge of shot through them —all ragged & full of holes— It is the work either of the insects themselves or else of other insects or birds.

It is the Andromeada (panicled?) that has the fine barked stem—& the green wood in the swamps.

Why not live out more yet—& have my friends & relations altogether in nature—only my acquaintances among the villagers? That way diverges from this I follow not at a sharp but a very wide angle   Ah nature is serene and immortal. Am I not one of   the Zincali?/?

There is a beautifully pure greenish blue sky under the clouds
now in the S.W. just before sunset.– I hear the ice along the edge
of the river cracking as the water settles. It has settled about 2 feet
leaving ice for the most part without water on the meadows–all
uneven & cracked over the hummocks–so that you cannot run
straight for sliding. The ice takes the least hint of a core to eke out a
perfect plant–the wrecks of bullrushes & meadow grass–are
expanded into palm leaves & other luxuriant foliage. I see delicate
looking green pads frozen into the ice. And here & there where
some tender & still green weeds from the warm bottom of the river
have lately been cast up. onto the ice.

There are certain places where the river will always be open–
where perchance warmer springs come in. There are such places in
every character genial & open in the coldest days.

I come from contact with certain acquaintance whom ever I am
disposed to look toward as possible friends It oftenest happens that I
come from them wounded. Only they can wound me seriously–and
that perhaps without their knowing it.

Dec 17th

The Pitch pine woods on the right of the Corner road. A
piercing cold afternoon–wading in the snow– R. Rice was going
to Sud. to put his bees into the cellar for fear they would freeze–
He had a small hive–not enough to keep each other warm. The
Pitch pines hold the snow well. It lies now in balls on their plumes–
and in streakes on their branches–their low branches rising at a small
angle and meeting each other–A certain dim religious light comes
through this roof of pine leaves & snow–it is a sombre twilight–yet
in some places the sun streams in–
producing the strongest contrasts of
light and shade.

The winter morning is the time to see the woods & shrubs in
their perfection wearing their snowy & frosty dress. Even he who
visits them half an hour after sunrise will have lost some of their
most delicate & fleeting beauties. The trees wear their snowy
burden but coarsely after mid day–& it no longer expresses the
character of the tree I observed that early in the morning every
pine needle was covered with a frosty sheath–but soon after sunrise
it was all gone. You walk in the Pitch pine wood as under a
penthouse The stems & branches of the trees look black by contrast
You wander zigzag through the aisles of the wood–where stillness &
twilight reign.

Improve every opportunity to express yourself in writing as if it were your last

I do not know but a pine wood is as substantial and as memorable a fact as a friend. I am more sure to come away from it cheered than from those who come nearest to being my friends. It is unfortunate for the chopper & the walker when the cold wind comes from the same side with the sun for then he cannot find a warm recess in which to sit. It is pleasant to walk now through open & stately white pine woods. Their plumes do not hold so much snow commonly—unless where their limbs rest or are weighed down onto a neighboring tree. It is cold but still in their midst—where the snow is untracked by man—and ever & anon you see the snow dust shone on by the sun falling from their tops & as it strikes the lower limbs producing innumerable new showers. For as after a rain there is a second rain in the woods so after a light snow there is a second snow in the woods when the wind rises. The branches of the white pine are more horizontal than those of the pitch—and the white streaks of snow on them look accordingly. I perceive that the young black oaks and the red oaks too methinks still keep their leaves as well as the white. This piercing wind is so nearly from the west this afternoon that to stand at once in a sheltered and a sunny place you must seek the SSE S S E side of the woods.

What slight but important distinctions between one creature & another—what little but essential advantages one enjoys over another— I noticed this after noon a squirrels nest high in the fork of a white pine. Thither he easily ascends—but many creatures strive in vain to get there.

The lower branches of the hemlock point down & even trail on the ground The whole tree making a perfect canopy.

When they who have aspired to be friends cease to sympathize it is the part of religion to keep asunder.

One of the best men I know often offends me by uttering made words—the very best words of course or dinner speeches—most smooth and gracious & fluent repartee a sort of talking to Buncomb ——a dash of polite conversation—a graceful bending—as if I were master Slingsby of promising parts from the University. O would you but be simple & downright. Would you but cease your palaver— It is the misfortune of being a gentleman & famous. The conversation of gentlemen after dinner. One of the best of men & wisest to whom this diabolical formality will adhere. Repeating himself— Shampooing himself. Passing the time of day as if he were just introduced. No words are so tedious. Never a natural or simple word or yawn. It produces an appearance of phlegm & stupidity in me the auditor. I am suddenly the closest & most phlegmatic of mortals. And the conversation comes to naught. Such speches as an ex member of Congress might make to an ex member of Parliament.

To explain to a friend is to suppose that you are not intelligent of one another. If you are not, to what purpose will you explain?

My acquaintances will sometimes wonder why I will impoverish myself by living aloof from this or that company—but greater would be the impoverishment if I should associate with them.

Dec 19th

In all woods is heard now far & near the sound of the woodchopper's axe—a twilight sound now in the night of the year— Men having come out for fuel to the forests— As if men had stolen forth in the arctic night to get fuel to keep their fires agoing. Men go to the woods now for fuel who never go there at any other time. Why should it be so pleasing to look into a thick pine wood where the sunlight streams in & gilds it? The sound of the axes far in the horizon sounds like the dropping of the eaves. Now the sun sets suddenly without a cloud—& with scarcely any redness following so pure is the atmosphere—only a faint rosy blush along the horizon

Sat. 20th

2 Pm to Fair Haven Hill & plain below— Saw a large hawk circling over a pine wood below me—and screaming apparently that he might discover his prey by their flight— Travelling ever by wider circles What a symbol of the thoughts now soaring now descending —taking larger and larger circles or smaller and smaller— It flies not directly whither it is bound but advances by circles like a courtier of the skies No such noble progress—how it comes round as with a wider sweep of thought— But the majesty is in the imagination of the beholder for the bird is intent on its prey. Circling & ever circling you cannot divine which way it will incline—till perchance it dives down straight as an arrow to its mark. It rises higher above where I stand and I see with beautiful distinctness its wings against the sky—primaries & secondaries and the rich tracery of the outline of the latter? its inner wings within the outer—like a great moth seen against the sky. A Will-o-'the wind. Following its path as it were through the vortices of the air. the poetry of motion—not as preferring one place to another but enjoying each as long as possible. Most gracefully so surveys new scenes & revisits the old. As if that

hawk were made to be the symbol of my thought how bravely he came round over those parts of the wood which he had not surveyed—taking in a new segment.— annexing new territories

Without heave yo! it trims its sail,— It goes about without the creaking of a block— That America Yacht of the air that never makes a tack—though it rounds the globe itself—takes in and shakes out its reefs without a flutter.— its sky scrapers all under its control— Holds up one wing as if to admire—and sweeps off this way then holds up the other & sweeps that. If there are two concentrically circling, it is such a regatta as South hampton waters never witnessed.

Flights of imagination—Coleridgean thoughts. So a man is said to soar in his thought— Ever to fresh woods & pastures new. Rises as in thought

Snow squawls pass obscuring the sun—as if blown off from a larger storm.

Since last monday the ground has covered half a foot or more with snow & the ice also before I have had a skate Hitherto we had had mostly bare frozen ground— Red—white—green—& in the distance dark brown are the colors of the winter landscape. I view it now from the Cliffs. The red shrub oaks on the white ground of the plain beneath make a pretty scene. Most walkers are pretty effectually shut up by the snow.

I observe that they who saw down trees in the woods with a cross-cut saw carry a mat to kneel on.

It is no doubt a good lesson for the woodchopper the long day alone in the woods & he gets more than his half dollar a cord.

Say the thing with which you labor—it is a waste of time for the writer to use his talents merely. Be faithful to your genius—write in the strain that interests you most— Consult not the popular taste.

The red oak leaves are even more fresh & glossy than the white.

A clump of white pines seen far westward over the shrub oak plain which is now lit up by the setting sun a soft feathery grove with their grey stems indistinctly seen—like human beings come to their cabin door standing expectant on the edge of the plain—impress me with a mild humanity. The trees indeed have hearts. With a certain affection the sun seems to send its farewell ray far and level over the copses to them. & they silently receive it with gratitude like a group of settlers with their children. The pines impress me as human. A slight vaporous cloud floats high over them—while in the west the sun goes down apace behind glowing pines & golden clouds like mountains skirt the horizon—

Nothing stands up more free from blame in this world than a pine tree.

The dull and blundering behavior of clowns will as surely polish the writer at last as the criticism of men of thought.

It is wonderful—wonderful—the unceasing demand that Christendom makes on you—that you speak *from a moral point of view*. Though you be a babe the cry is repent repent. The christian world will not admit that a man has a just perception of any truth—unless at the same time he cries Lord be merciful to me a sinner.

What made the hawk mount? Did you perceive the manoever? Did he fill himself with air? Before you were aware of it he had mounted by his spiral path into the heavens.

Our County is broad and rich—for here within 20 miles of Boston I can stand in a clearing in the woods and look a mile or more over the shrub oaks to the distant pine copses and horizon of uncut woods without a house or road or cultivated field in sight.

Sunset in winter from a clearing in the woods. about well meadow head They say that the Indians of the Great Basin live on the almonds of the pine. Have not I been fed by the pine for many a year?

Go out before sun-rise or stay out till sun-set.

Sunday 21st

My difficulties with my friends are such as no frankness will settle There is no precept in the New Testament that will assist me. My nature it may is secret— Others can confess & explain. I can not. It is not that I am too proud, but that is not what is wanted.

Friendship is the unspeakable joy & blessing that results to two or more individuals who from constitution sympathise— And natures are liable to no mistakes but will know each other through thick & thin— Between two by nature alike & fitted to sympathize there is no veil & there can be no obstacle. Who are the estranged? Two friends explaining.

I feel sometimes as if I could say to my friends My friends I am aware how I have outraged you how I have seemingly preferred hate to love—seemingly treated others kindly & you unkindly— sedulously concealed my love—& sooner or later expressed all and more than all my hate— I can imagine how I might utter something like this in some moment never to be realized— But let me say frankly that at the same time I feel it may be with too little regret— That I am under an aweful necessity to be what I am. If the truth were known, which I do not know, I have no concern with those friends whom I misunderstand or who misunderstand me.

The fates only are unkind that keep us asunder—but my friend is ever kind. I am of the nature of Stone. It takes the summer's sun to warm it.

My acquaintances sometimes imply that I am too cold—but each thing is warm enough for its kind— Is the stone too cold which absorbs the heat of the summer sun and does not part with it during the night? Crystals though they be of ice are not too cold to melt—but it was in melting that they were formed. Cold! I am most sensible of warmth in winter days. It is not the warmth of fire that you would have—but everything is warm & cold according to its nature. It is not that I am too cold—but that our warmth & coldness are not of the same nature—hence when I am absolutely warmest, I may be coldest to you. Crystal does not complain of crystal anymore than the dove of its mate. You who complain that I am cold—find Nature cold— To me she is warm. My heat is latent to you. Fire itself is cold to whatever is not of a nature to be warmed by it. A cool wind is warmer to a feverish man than the blast of a furnace. That I am cold means that I am of another nature.

The dogwood & its berries in the *swamp* by the R.R. just above the red house—pendant on long stems which hang short down as if broken—betwixt yellowish? & greenish? white ovoid pearly? or waxen? berries— What is the color of them? Ah give me to walk in the dogwood swamp—with its few coarse branches— Beautiful as satan.

The Prinos or Black Alder berries appear to have been consumed —only the skins left for the most part sticking to the twigs—so that I thought there were fewer than usual. Is it that our woods have had to entertain arctic visitors in unusual numbers? Who have exhausted their stores—

Sunlight on pine needles is an event of a winter day.

Whoever saw a partridge soar over the fields— To every creature its own nature. They are very wild—but are they scarce? or can you exterminate them for that?

As I stand by the edge of the swamp (Ministerial) a heavy winged hawk flies home to it at sundown just over my head in silence

I cross some mink or muskrat's devious path in the snow—with mincing feet and trailing body.

Tonight—as so many nights within the year—the clouds arrange themselves in the East at sunset in long converging bars—according to the simple tactics of the sky— It is the melon rind jig.— It would serve for a permanent description of the sunset— Such is the morning & such the evening.— Converging bars inclose the day at each end as within a melon rind & the morning & evening are one day.

Long after the sun has set & downy clouds have turned darked—& the shades of night have taken possession of the east—some rosy clouds will be seen in the upper sky over the portals of the darkening west.

How swiftly the earth appears to revolve at sunset—which at midday appears to rest on its axle.

Dec 22d

If I am thus seemingly cold compared with my companion's warm—who knows but mine is a less transient glow—a steadier & more equable heat like that of the earth in spring—in which the flowers spring & expand.

It is not words that I wish to hear or to utter—but relations that I seek to stand in—and it oftener happens methinks that I go away unmet unrecognized—ungreeted in my offered relation—than that you are disappointed of words.

If I can believe that we are related to one another as truly and gloriously as I have imagined, I ask nothing more and words are not required to convince me of this. I am disappointed of relations, you of words.

I have seen in the form in the expression of face of a child 3 years old the tried magnanimity—and grave nobility of ancient & departed worthies. Just saw a little Irish boy come from the distant shanty in the woods over the bleak rail-road to school this morning—take his last step—from his last snow drift onto the school house door-step—floundering still saw not his face or his profile only his mien & imagined—saw clearly in imagination his old worthy face behind the sober visor of his cap— Ah! this little Irish boy I know not why—revives to my mind the worthies of antiquity—he is not drawn he never was drawn in a willow wagon—he progresses by his own brave steps— Has not the world waited for such a generation. Here he condescends to his abc without one smile who has the lore of worlds uncounted in his brain— He speaks not of the adventures of the causeway— What was the bravery of Leonidas & his 300 boys at the pass of Thermopylae to this infants!— They but dared to die— he dares to live.— And take his "reward of merit" perchance without relaxing his face in to a smile—that overlooks his unseen & unregardable merits. Little Johnny Riaden. Who faces cold & routs it like a Persian army— Who yet innocent carries in his knees the strength of a thousand Indras.– That do not reward the thousandth part of his merit–

While the charitable waddle about cased in furs–he lively as a cricket passes them on his way to school.

An innocent child is a man who has repented once for all, and is born again. Has entered into the joy of his Lord.

Almost the whole world is orthodox–and look upon you as in a state of nature– In conversation with people of more than average wit, I find that the common assumption is that they have experienced a new birth but–you are in a state of nature.

Dec. 23d

It would give me such joy to know that a friend had come to see me and yet that pleasure I seldom if ever experience.

It is a record of the mellow & ripe moments that I would keep.

I would not preserve the husk of life–but the kernel.

When the cup of life is full and flowing over–preserve some drops as a specimen-sample. When the intellect enlightens the heart & the heart warms the intellect.

Thoughts will sometimes possess our heads when we are up and about our business which are the exact counterpart of the bad dreams which we sometimes have by night. And I think that the intellect is equally inert in both cases. Very frequently, no doubt–the thoughts men have are the consequence of something which they have eaten or done. Our waking *moods* and *humors* are our dreams but whenever we are truly awake & serene–and healthy in all our senses we have memorable visions. Who that takes up a book wishes for the report of the clogged bowels–or the impure blood?

Yesterday afternoon I walked to the Stone bridge over the Assabet and thence down the river on the ice to the leaning hemlocks–and then crossed the other branch to the house– Do I not see two kinds of black alder–one blotched the other lighter colored–the former with many small berries crowded–the latter larger & single? Scared up partridges into the tops of the hemlocks where they thought to conceal themselves–

Observed where a woodchopper had come to the river & cut a hole for water some days before. The river frozen unexpectedly even –but few open places–had gone down since it froze–& the ice was accordingly bulged up over the rocks in its channel with many fine cracks in all directions. It was a good opportunity to examine the fluviatile trees. I was struck by the amount of small interlaced roots–

making almost a solid mass—of some red? oaks—on the bank which
the water had undermined—opposite Sam. Barrets. Observed by a
wall beneath Nawshawtuct where many rabbits appeared to have
played and nearly half a pint of dung was dropped in one pile on
the snow.

This morning when I woke I found it snowing—the snow fine &
driving almost horizontally as if it had set in for a long storm—but a
little after noon it ceased snowing & began to clear up——& I set
forth for a walk. The snow which we have had for the last week or
10 days has been remarkably light & dry. It is pleasant walking in
the woods now when the sun is just coming out & shining on the
woods freshly covered with snow— At a distance the oak woods
look very venerable—a fine hale wintry aspect things wear—and the
pines all snowed up even suggest comfort. Where boughs cross each
other much snow is caught—which now in all woods is gradually
tumbling down— By half past 3 the sun is fairly out. I go to the
cliffs. There is a narrow ridge of snow a white line on the storm side
of the stem of every exposed tree. I see that there is to be a fine
clear sunset. & make myself a seat in the snow on the cliff to
witness it. Already a few clouds are glowing like a golden sierra just
above the horizon— From a low arch the clear sky has rapidly
spread eastward over the whole heavens—and the sun shines serenely
—and the air is still—and the spotless snow covers the fields. The
snow storm is over—the clouds have departed—the sun shines serenely
—the air is still—a pure & trackless white napkin covers the ground—
and a fair evening is coming to conclude all— Gradually the sun
sinks—the air grows more dusky & I perceive that if it were not for
the light reflected from the snow it would be quite dark— The
wood chopper has started for home. I can no longer distinguish the
color of the red oak leaves against the snow but they appear black.
The partridges have come forth to bud on the apple trees. Now the
sun has quite disappeared—but the after-glow as I may call it—
apparently the reflection from the cloud beyond which the sun went
down from the thick atmosphere of the horizon—is unusually bright
& lasting— Long broken clouds in the horizon in the dun
atmosphere (as if the fires of day were still smoking there) hang with
red & golden edging like the saddle cloths of the steeds of the sun.
Now all the clouds grow black—& I give up to night— But
unexpectedly half an hour later when I look out having got home I
find that the evening star is shining brightly & beneath all the west
horizon is glowing red—that dun atmosphere instead of clouds

reflecting the sun—and I detect just above the horizon the narrowest
imaginable white sickle of the new moon.

Dec 24th

It spits snow this afternoon. Saw a flock of snowbirds on the
Walden road— I see them so commonly when it is beginning to
snow that I am inclined to regard them as a sign of a snowstorm—
The snow bunting *Emberiza nivalis* methinks it is—so white & arctic.
Not the slate colored. Saw also some Pine gross-beaks—magnificent
winter birds—among the weeds & on the apple trees—like large Cat
birds at a distance—but nearer at hand some of them when they flit
by are seen to have gorgeous heads breasts & rumps? with red or
crimson reflections—more beautiful than a steady bright red would
be. The note I heard a rather faint & innocent whistle of two bars.
Now & long since the birds nests have been full of snow.
I had looked in vain into the west for nearly half an hour to see a
red cloud blushing in the sky— The few clouds were dark—and I
had given up all to night but when I had got home & chanced to
look out the window from the upper—I perceived that all the west
horizon was glowing with a rosy border, and that dun atmosphere
had been the cloud this time which made the days adieus. But half
an hour before that dun atmosphere hung over all the western
woods & hills—precisely as if the fires of the day had just been put
out in the west and the burnt territory was sending out volumes of
dun & lurid smoke to heaven As if Phaeton had again driven the
chariot of the sun so near as to set fire to earth.

Thursday Dec 25

Via Spruce swamp on Conantum to hill top returning across river
over shrub oak plain to Cliffs. A wind is now blowing the light
snow which fell a day or two ago into drifts—especially on the lee
now the south side of the walls—the outlines of the drifts
corresponding to the chinks in the walls and the eddies of the wind.
The snow glides unperceived for the most part over the open fields
without rising into the air (unless the ground is elevated) until it
reaches an opposite wall which it sifts through and is blown over—
blowing off from it like steam when seen in the sun. As it passes
through the chinks it does not drive straight onward but curves
gracefully upwards into fantastic shapes—somewhat like the waves
which curve as they break upon the shore— That is, as if, the snow
that passes through a chink were one connected body detained by
the friction of its lower side. It takes the form of saddles & shells &

pooringers— It builds up a fantastic alabaster wall behind the first—a
snowy sierra. It is wonderful what sharp turrets it builds up builds up
—i.e. by accummulation—not by attrition—though the curves upward
to a point like the prows of ancient vessels look like sharp carving—
or as if the material had had been held before the blow-pipe. So
what was blown up into the air gradually sifts down into the road or
field & forms the slope of the sierra— Astonishingly sharp & thin
overhanging eaves it builds even this dry snow—where it has the least
suggestion from a wall or bank—less than a mason ever springs his
brick from. This is the architecture of the snow. On high hills
exposed to wind & sun it curls off like the steam from a damp roof
in the morning. Such
sharply defined forms it
takes as if the core had
been the flames of gass lights.

I go forth to see the sun set. Who knows how it will set—even
half an hour before hand? Whether it will go down in clouds or a
clear sky? I feel that it is late when the mountains in the north and
north-west have ceased to reflect the sun. The shadow is not partial
but universal

In a winter day the sun is almost all in all.

I witness a beauty in the form or coloring of the clouds which
addresses itself to my imagination—for which you account
scientifically to my understanding—but do not so account to my
imagination. It is what it suggests & is the symbol of that I care for—
and if by any trick of science you rob it of its symbolicalness you do
me no service & explain nothing.

I standing twenty miles off see a crimson cloud in the horizon—
You tell me it is a mass of vapor which absorbs all other rays &
reflects the red—but that is nothing to the purpose—for this red vision
excites me, stirs my blood—makes my thoughts flow—& I have new
& indescribable fancies and you have not touched the secret of that
influence. If there is not something mystical in your explanation—
something unexplainable—some element of mystery, it is quite
insufficient. If there is nothing in it which speaks to my imagination
—what boots it. What sort of science is that which enriches the
understanding but robs the imagination. Not merely robs Peter to
pay Paul—but takes from Peter more than it ever gives to Paul.

That is simply the way in which it speaks to the understanding
and that is the account which the understanding gives of it—but that
is not the way it speaks to the Imagination & that is not the account

which the Imagination gives of it. Just as inadequate to a pure
mechanic would be a poets account of a steam engine.

If we knew all things thus mechanically merely—should we know
anything really?

It would be a truer discipline for the writer to take the least film
of thought that floats in the twilight sky of his mind for his theme—
about which he has scarcely one idea (that would be teaching his
ideas how to shoot) faintest intimations—shadowiest subjects—make a
lecture on this—by assiduity and attention get perchance two views
of the same—increase a little the stock of knowledge—clear a new
field instead of manuring the old— Instead of making a lecture out
of such obvious truths—hacknied to the minds of all thinkers— We
see too soon to ally the perceptions of the mind to the experience of
the hand—to prove our gossamer truths practical—to show their
connexion with our every day life (better show their distance from
our every day life) to relate them to the cider mill and the banking
institution. Ah give me pure mind—pure thought. Let me not be in
haste to detect the *universal law*, let me see more clearly a particular
instance. Much finer themes I aspire to—which will will yield no
satisfaction to the vulgar mind—not one sentence for them—
Perchance it may convince such that there are more things in
heaven & earth than are dreamed of in their philosophy. Dissolve
one nebula—& so destroy the nebular system & hypothesis. Do not
seek expressions—seek thoughts to be expressed. By perseverance you
get two views of the same rare truth.

That way of viewing things you know of—-least insisted on by
you however—least remembered—take that view—adhere to that—insist
on that—see all things from that point of view— Will you let these
intimations go unattended to and watch the door bell or knocker?
That is your text. Do not speak for other men— Speak for yourself.
They show you as in a vision the kingdoms of this world—and of all
the worlds—but you prefer to look in upon a puppet-show. Though
you should only speak to one kindred mind in all time—though you
should not speak to one—but only utter aloud that you may the
more completely realize & live in the idea which contains the reason
of your life—that you may build yourself up to the height of your
conceptions—that you may remember your creator—and justify his
ways to man—that the end of life may not be its amusement— Speak
though your thought presupposes the non existence of your hearers.
— thoughts that transcend life & death. though mortal ears are not

fitted to hear absolute truth.– Thoughts that blot out the earth are best conceived in the night when darkness has already blotted it out from sight.

We look upward for inspiration.

Dec 26th

I observed this afternoon that when Edmund Hosmer came home from sledding wood and unyoked his oxen–they made a business of stretching and scratching themselves with their horns & rubbing against the posts–and licking themselves in those parts which the yoke had prevented their reaching all day– The human way in which they behaved affected me even pathetically. They were too serious to be glad that their day's work was done–they had not spirits enough left for that. They behaved as a tired wood-chopper might. This was to me a new phase in the life of the laboring ox. It is painful to think how they may sometimes be overworked. I saw that even the ox could be weary with toil.

Sat Dec 27.

Sunset from Fair Haven Hill. This evening there are many clouds in the west into which the sun goes down so that we have our visible or apparent sunset and red evening sky as much as 15 minutes before the real sunset. You must be early on the hills to witness such a sunset by half past 4 at least. Then all the vales even to the horizon are full of a purple vapor–which half veils the distant *mts* and the windows of undiscoverable farm houses–shine like an early candle or a fire– After the sun has gone behind a cloud–there appears to be a gathering of clouds around his setting and for a few moments his light in the amber sky seems more intense brighter & purer than at noon day.

I think you never see such a brightness in the noonday heavens as in the western sky sometimes just before the sun goes down in clouds, like the extasy which we told sometimes lights up the face of a dying man–that is a *serene* or evening death–like the end of the day. Then at last through all the grossness which has accumulated in the atmosphere of day–is seen a patch of serene sky fairer by contrast with the surrounding dark than midday–and even the gross atmosphere of the day is gilded and made pure as amber by the setting sun as if the days sins were forgiven it. The man is blessed who every day is permitted to behold anything so pure & serene as the western sky at sunset–while revolutions vex the world.

There is no winter necessarily in the sky though the snow covers the earth. The sky is always ready to answer to our moods– We can see summer there or winter. Snow & drifts on the earth—it swiftly descends from the heavens & leaves them pure. The heavens present perhaps pretty much the same aspect summer & winter.

It is remarkable that the sun rarely goes down without a cloud.

Venus—I suppose it is—is now the evening star—and very bright she is immediately after sun set in the early twilight.

Dec 28th

All day a drizzling rain—ever & anon holding up with driving mists— A January thaw— The snow rapidly dissolving, in all hollows a pond forming—unfathomable water beneath the snow. Went into Tommy Wheelers house—where still stands the spinning wheel and even the loom home made. Great pitch pine timbers overhead 15 or 16 inches in diameter—telling of the primitive forest here. The white pines look greener than usual in this gentle rain— and every needle has a drop at the end of it— There is a mist in the air which partially conceals them and they seem of a piece with it. Some one has cut a hole in the ice at Jenny's Brook—and set a steel trap under water, and suspended a large piece of meat over it for a bait for a mink apparently.

Dec 29th

The sun just risen. The ground is almost entirely bare. The water is the puddles are not skimmed over—it is warm as an April morning. There is a sound as of blue birds in the air, and the cocks crow as in the spring. The steam curls up from the roofs & the ground. You walk with open cloak— It is exciting behold the smooth glassy surface of water where the melted snow has formed large puddles & ponds—and to see it running in the sluices.— In the clear atmosphere I saw far in the eastern horizon the steam from the steam engine like downy clouds above the woods I think even beyond Weston.

By school-time you see the boys in the streets playing with the sluices—and the whole population is inspired with new life.

In the afternoon to Saw Mill Brook with W. E. C. Snow all gone from Minott's hill side— The willow at the red house shines in the sun. The boys have come out under the hill to pitch coppers Watts sits on his door step. It is like the first of April. The wind is west. At the turnpike bridge water stands a foot or two deep over the ice— Water spiders have come out and are skating against the stream. How much they depend on January thaws! Now for the frozen thawed apples. This is the first chance they have had to thaw this winter. It feels as warm as in summer— You sit on any fence rail and vegetate in the sun & realize that the earth may produce peas again. Yet they say that this open & mild weather is unhealthy—that is always the way with them. How admirable it is that we can never foresee the weather—that that is always novel. Yesterday nobody dreamed of to-day—nobody dreams of to-morrow— Hence the weather is ever the news. What a fine & measureless joy the gods grant us thus—letting us know nothing about the day that is to dawn. This day yesterday was as incredible as any other miracle— Now all creatures feel—it even the cattle chewing stalks in the barn yards. & perchance it has penetrated even to the lurking places of the crickets under the rocks.

The artist is at work in the deep cut. The telegraph harp sounds.

Tuesday Dec 30th

Mem. Go to the Deep Cut. The flies now crawl forth from the crevices all covered with dust, dreaming of summer—without life or energy enough to clean their wings

This afternoon being on fair Haven Hill I heard the sound of a saw—and soon after from the cliff saw two men sawing down a noble pine beneath about 40 rods off. I resolved to watch it till it fell—the last of a dozen or more which were left when the forest was cut and for 15 years have waved in solitary majesty over the sproutland. I saw them like beavers or insects gnawing at the trunk of this noble tree, the diminutive mannikins with their crosscut saw which could scarcely span it. It towered up a hundred feet as I afterward found by measurement—one of the tallest probably now in the township & straight as an arrow, but slanting a little toward the hill side.— its top seen against the frozen river & the hills of Conantum. I watch closely to see when it begins to move. Now the sawers stop—and with an axe open it a little on the side toward which it leans that it may break the faster. And now their saw goes again— Now surely it is going—it is inclined one quarter of the quadrant, and breathless I expect its crashing fall— But no I was mistaken it has not moved an inch, it stands at the same angle as at first. It is 15 minutes yet to its fall. Still its branches wave in the wind as if it were destined to stand for a century, and the wind soughs through its needles as of yore; it is still a forest tree—the most majestic tree that waves over Musketaquid.— The silvery sheen of the sunlight is reflected from its needles—it still affords an inaccessible crotch for the squirrel's nest—not a lichen has forsaken its mastlike stem——its raking mast—the hill is the hull. Now' now's the moment —the mannikins at its base are fleeing from their crime—they have dropped the guilty saw & axe. How slowly & majestically it starts—as if it were only swayed by a summer breeze and would return without a sigh to its location in the air—& now it fans the hill side with its fall and it lies down to its bed in the valley from which it is never to rise, as softly as a feather, folding its green mantle about it like a warrior—as if tired of standing it embraced the earth with silent joy.— returning its elements to the dust again—but hark! there you only saw—but did not hear— There now comes up a deafening crash to these rocks—advertising you that even trees do not die without a groan. It rushes to embrace the earth, & mingle its elements with the dust. And now all is still once more & forever both to eye & ear.

I went down and measured it. It was about 4 feet in diameter where it was sawed—about 100 feet long. Before I had reached it— the axemen had already half divested it of its branches. Its gracefully spreading top was a perfect wreck on the hill side as if it had been made of glass—& the tender cones of one years growth upon its summit appealed in vain & too late to the mercy of the chopper. Already he has measured it with his axe—and marked out the mill logs it will make. And the space it occupied in upper air is vacant for the next 2 centuries. It is lumber He has laid waste the air. When the fish hawk in the spring revisits the banks of the Musketaquid, he will circle in vain to find his accustomed perch.— & the henhawk will mourn for the pines lofty enough to protect her brood. A plant which it has taken two centuries to perfect rising by slow stages into the heavens—has this afternoon ceased to exist. Its sapling top had expanded to this January thaw as the forerunner of summers to come. Why does not not the village bell sound a knell. I hear no knell tolled—I see no procession of mourners in the streets —or the woodland aisles— The squirrel has leapt to another tree—the hawk has circled further off—& has now settled upon a new eyre but the woodman is preparing lay his axe at the root of that also.

Dec 31st

The 3d warm day. now overcast and beginning to drizzle. Still it is inspiriting as the brightest weather—though the sun surely is not agoing to shine, There is a latent light in the mist—as if there were more electricity than usual in the air. These are warm foggy days in winter which excite us.

It reminds me this thick spring like weather, that I have not enough valued and attended to the pure clarity & brilliancy of the winter skies— Consider in what respects the winter sunsets differ

from the summer ones. Shall I ever in summer evenings see so
celestial a reach of blue sky contrasting with amber as I have seen a
few days since— The day sky in winter corresponds for clarity to
the night sky in which the stars shine & twinkle so brightly in this
latitude.

I am too late perhaps, to see the sand foliage in the deep cut—
should have been there day before yesterday it is now too wet &
soft.

Yet in some places it is perfect. I see some perfect leopard's paws

These things suggest—that there is motion in the earth as well as
on the surface; it lives & grows. It is warmed & influenced by the
sun—just as my blood by my thoughts. I seem to see some of the life
that is in the spring bud & blossom more intimately nearer its
fountain head—the fancy sketches & designs of the artist. It is more
simple & primitive growth. As if for ages sand and clay might have
thus flowed into the forms of foliage—before plants were produced to
clothe the earth. The earth I tread on is not a dead inert mass. It is a
body—has a spirit—is organic—and fluid to the influence of its spirit—
and to whatever particle of that spirit is in me. She is not dead but
sleepeth. It is more cheering than the fertility & luxuriance of
vineyards—this fundamental fertility near to the principle of growth.
To be sure it is somewhat foecal and stercoral—. So the poet's
creative moment is when the frost is coming out in the spring but
as in the case of some too easy poets—if the weather is too warm &
rainy or long continued it becomes mere diarrhea—mud & clay
relaxed. The poet must not have something pass his bowels merely—
that is women's poetry.— He must have something pass his brain &
heart and bowels too, it may be, altogether.— so he gets delivered—
There is no end to the fine bowels here exhibited heaps of liver—
lights & bowels. Have you no bowels? Nature has some bowels.
and there again she is mother of humanity. Concord is a worthier
place to live in—the globe is a worthier place for these creations
This slumbering life—that may wake.. Even the solid globe is
permeated by the living law. It is the most living of creatures. No
doubt all creatures that live on its surface are but parasites.

I observed this afternoon the old Irish woman at the shanty in the
woods—sitting out on the hill side bare headed in the rain & on the
icy though thawing ground—knitting. She comes out like the ground
squirrel at the least intimation of warmer weather. She will not have
to go far to be buried—so close she lives to the earth.— While I
walk still in a great coat & under an umbrella— Such Irish as these

are naturalizing themselves at a rapid rate—and threaten at last to displace the Yankees—as the latter have the Indians— The process of acclimation is rapid with them they draw long breaths in the sick room. What must be the philosophy of life to that woman—ready to flow down the slope with the running sand! Ah what would I not give for her point of view. She does not use any ths in her style—Yet I fear that even she may have learned to lie.

There is a low mist in the woods— It is a good day to study lichens. The view so confined—it compels your attention to near objects—& the white background reveals the disks of the lichens distinctly— They appear more loose-flowing—expanded—flattened out—the colors brighter—for the damp— The round greenish yellow lichens on the white pines loom through the mist (or are seen dimly) like shields—whose devices you would fain read. The trees appear all at once covered with this crop—of lichens & mosses of all kind—flat—& tearful are some—distended by moisture— This is their solstice—and your eyes run swiftly through the mist to these things only. On every fallen twig even that has lain under the snows—as well as on the trees, they appear erect & now first to have attained their full expansion. Nature has a day for each of her creatures—her creations. To day it is an exhibition of lichens at forest Hall— The living green of some—the fruit of others. They eclipse the trees they cover.— And the red-club pointed—(baobab tree like) on the stumps—the *erythrean* stumps.— ah beautiful is decay. True as Thales said—The world was made out of water—that is the principle of all things.

I do not lay myself open to my friends!? The owner of the casket locks it, and unlocks it.

Treat your friends for what you know them to be—regard no surfaces— Consider not what they did, but what they intended. Be sure as you know them, you are known of them again. Last night I treated my dearest friend ill. Though I could find some excuse for mysellf, it is not such excuse as under the circumstances could be pleaded in so many words— Instantly I blamed myself—& sought an opportunity to make atonement—; but the friend avoided me, and with kinder feelings even than before I was obliged to depart— And now this morning I feel that it is too late to speak of the trifle—and besides I doubt now in the cool morning, if I have a right to suppose such intimate & serious relations as afford a basis for the apology I had conceived—for even magnanimity must ask this poor earth for a field. The virtues even wait for invitation. Yet I am resolved to know that one centrally—through thick & thin—and though we should be cold to one another—though we should never speak to one another—I will know that inward & essential love may exist even under a superficial cold—& that the law of attraction speaks louder than words. My true relation this instant shall be my apology for my false relation the last instant.

I made haste to cast off my injustice as scurf— I own it least of anybody for I have absolutely done with it. Let the idle & wavering & apologizing friend appropriate it. Methinks our estrangement is only like the divergence of the branches which unite in the stem.

Last night I heard Mrs Oakes Smith lecture on Womanhood. The most important fact about the lecture was that a woman said it and in that respect it was suggestive.

Went to see her afterward. But the interview added nothing to the previous impression, rather subtracted. She was a woman in the too common sense after all. You had to fire small charges— I did not have a finger in once, for fear of blowing away all her works & so ending the game. You had to substitute courtesy for sense & argument It requires nothing less than a chivalric feeling to sustain a conversation with a lady. I carried her lecture for her in my pocket wrapped in her handkerchief—my pocket exhales cologne to this moment. The championness of womans rights still asks you to be a ladies' man— I can't fire a salute even for fear some of the guns may be shotted. I had to unshot all the guns in truth's battery and fire powder & wadding only. Certainly the heart is only for rare occasions—the intellect affords the most unfailing entertainment. It would only do to let her feel the wind of the ball. I fear that to the last woman's lectures will demand mainly courtesy from man.

How deceptive the size of a large pine— Still as you approach it—even within a rod or two it looks only like a reasonable stick—fit for a string piece perchance—the average size of trees one foot in diameter—big as a keg or a half barrel it may be. Fit for the sill or the beams of an old fashioned house.— This you think is a generous appreciation & allowance. Not till you stand close to its foot, upon one of its swelling insteps & compare its diameter with the diameter of your own eyeballs, do you begin to discover its width. Stand by its side & see how it shuts out a hemisphere from you. Why it is as wide as a front door. What a slender arrow—a light shaft now that you stand a rod or two off— What a ballista—a battering ram—a mighty vegetable monster—a cannon, near at hand! Now set a barrel aye a hogshead beside it. You apply your measures— The foot rule seems suddenly shrunk. Your umbrella is but half as long as it was—

The pine I saw fall yesterday measured today 105 feet—& was about 94 years old—

There was one still larger lying beside it. 115 feet long—96 yrs old—4 feet diam— the longest way. The tears were streaming from the sap wood—about 20 circles—of each. pure amber or pearly tears.

Through the drizzling fog now just before night-fall I see from the Cliffs the dark cones of pine trees that rise above the level of the tree tops—and can trace a few elm tree tops where a farm house hides beneath.

Denuded pines stand in the clearings with no old cloak to wrap about them. only the apexes of their cones entire—telling a pathetic story of the companions that clothed them. So stands a man. It is clearing around him. He has no companions on the hills— The lonely traveller looking up wonders why he was left when his companions were taken.

Notes

These brief notes are intended primarily to help readers follow Thoreau's activities and interests during 1851, and to facilitate the understanding of passages that might otherwise seem obscure. For full annotation, see the Princeton Edition. Its annotations give detailed accounts of the sources of Thoreau's many literary, classical, biblical, historical, botanical, and ornithological references. The Princeton annotations also describe many geographical sites mentioned in the Journal and render biographical sketches of Thoreau's Concord neighbors and other New England figures. Another excellent resource for those who wish to pursue Thoreau's literary and scientific references is Robert Sattelmeyer's *Thoreau's Reading*, cited in "Suggestions for Further Reading." For the location of some of the places in the Concord area referred to in this volume, see the map on page 338. Assisting in the development of the following notes were former Vassar College students Laura Chamorro, Jennifer B. Johnson, and Alphonso Lopez.

6.9–14   Here and in several subsequent passages, Thoreau is referring to a work by François André Michaux, *The North American Sylva* (1819). He occasionally refers to Michaux with the abbreviation "MX." See his references to another of Michaux' works, *Voyage á l'Ouest des Monts Alléghanys* (1808), at 62.8–63.18.

8.1–9.14   All the references in these passages quoting Ovid are from the *Metamorphoses*, II.

9.24–36   The panorama called "The Rhine and Its Banks" was exhibited in Boston from December 1848 to June 1849. Panoramas were landscape scenes drawn on long rolls of canvas, which were slowly opened to the audience.

10.13–11.10   Thoreau is referring here to a work by Arnold Henry Guyot, *The Earth and Man: Lectures on Comparative Physical Geography, in Its Relation to the History of Mankind* (American edition, 1851).

11.28–35   Thoreau's source here is J. O. Halliwell, *The Voiage and Travaile of Sir John Maundevile* (1839).

12.7–12   From Cicero's first oration against Cataline (I, ii) in *Orationes*, this passage, in the Loeb translation, reads: "For we have a senate's decree of this kind. But it is merely inserted in the records like a sword buried in its sheath. According to this decree of the senate, Cataline, you should have been instantly executed. You are living—and you are living not to repent, but to augment, your effrontery. I wish, Conscript Fathers, to be merciful.

I wish not to seem lax when the perils of the state are so great, but now I condemn myself for inaction and remissness. There is in Italy a camp of enemies of the Roman people, situated in the passes of Etruria, their number is increasing daily; but you behold the commander of that camp and the leader of the enemy inside the walls and even in the senate plotting daily from within the city the destruction of the state."

12.27   Thoreau is quoting the last line of John Donne's poem "The Triple Fool."

12.28–33   Thoreau is quoting from the 1820 London edition of Ralph Cudworth, *The True Intellectual System of the Universe.*

12.34–35   The quotation is from the 1794 edition of John Caspar Lavater's *Aphorisms on Man.*

13.38–39   The *New England Farmer* was a midnineteenth-century agricultural magazine published in Boston.

14.18–21   The first two lines are the well-known opening of *The New England Primer*, to which Thoreau adds the closing lines.

21.31–22.3   Thoreau is here quoting from Robert Hunt, *The Poetry of Science* (1850). Hunt is quoted from again at 24.9–14 and 24.19–20.

23.6–7   This visual observation, like those in many other entries, was made as Thoreau surveyed a property, in this case a woodlot owned by Cyrus Stow.

26.12–14   This quotation is from Hugh Miller, *The Foot-prints of the Creator* (1850).

26.20–32.14   These passages record Thoreau's responses to an incident related to the recently passed Fugitive Slave Law. On April 12, 1851, a runaway slave from Georgia named Thomas Sims was taken by militia to the ship in Boston Harbor that would return him to slavery. This incident, along with the Anthony Burns affair three years later, prompted Thoreau's lecture and essay titled "Slavery in Massachusetts." The reference at the beginning of the passage is to Thomas De Quincey's *The Caesars* (1851), in which De Quincey cites Thomas Blackwell's *Memoirs of the Court of Augustus.*

30.15   The *Liberator*, expressing the views of William Lloyd Garrison (the leading radical abolitionist), and the *Commonwealth* were antislavery newspapers.

30.31–31.5   Thoreau is quoting from Washington Irving's *Mahomet and His Successors* (1850).

31.26   Major John Buttrick, Captain Isaac Davis, and Abner Hosmer were killed in the battles of Concord and Lexington at the outset of the Revolutionary War in 1775.

33.35–36   The quoted lines are from an elegy to Sir Philip Sidney that Thoreau read in an 1815 collection of Elizabethan poetry.

34.40   The quoted phrase is from an 1826 American edition of Thomas Campbell's works.

44.23–45.12   Intermittently through this passage Thoreau refers to Asa

Gray's *A Manual of the Botany of the Northern United States* (1848), one of numerous works of natural history he read during 1851. Gray's *Manual* is also cited at 203.34–35 and at later points in this volume.

47.27   Whenever Thoreau refers to "Emerson" in this botanical context, he means George B. Emerson, author of *A Report on the Trees and Shrubs Growing Naturally in the Forests of Massachusetts* (1846).

55.10–60.17   Intermittently through this section, Thoreau refers to Jacob Bigelow's *American Medical Botany* (1817–1820).

58.6   The lecture Thoreau refers to here is "The Wild," a part of which later became a separate lecture titled "Walking." The two talks, reassembled, constitute the essay "Walking," which was published in 1862 shortly after Thoreau's death.

67.24   This work by Charles Darwin, now known as *The Voyage of the Beagle* (American edition, 1846), is referred to by Thoreau intermittently from this point through page 82.

76.8   Conantum, mentioned often in the Journal, is a tract of land along the Concord River named (after its owner, Ebenezer Conant) by Thoreau himself. See map, J4.

94.29   " 'Sam' the jailor" is Samuel Staples, who had arrested Thoreau in July 1846 for not paying his poll tax.

99.34   "Porter's Cambridge" is the stop on the Fitchburg Railroad where Thoreau would disembark on his visits to the Harvard library.

99.42   William Cranch Bond (1798–1859) was director of the Harvard College Observatory.

100.14–15   See, for example, Wordsworth's observations on the poet's "pleasure" in Preface to *Lyrical Ballads* (1798).

101.34   "W.E.C." is William Ellery Channing the Younger (1817–1901), who accompanied Thoreau on many of the walks described in this volume. Channing is also referred to as "C."

107.14   The phrase "Our Life is a forgetting" echoes Wordsworth's "Ode: Intimations of Immortality from Recollections of Early Childhood."

119.28–29   The "eccentric & melancholy minister whom I have heard of" alludes to Nathaniel Hawthorne's story "The Minister's Black Veil," collected in Hawthorne's *Twice-Told Tales* (1837).

120.22–23   The phrase "Juan Fernandez did Crusoe" alludes to Daniel Defoe's *Robinson Crusoe* and the figure Alexander Selkirk, whose experiences Crusoe's adventures were based on.

125.9–14   Here, as at 125.26 and 125.34–36, Thoreau refers to a recent trip to Quebec in the autumn of 1850. The trip provided the material for his *A Yankee in Canada*, first presented as lectures and serial essays; it later appeared in *Excursions* (1906).

125.34–36   Both James Wolfe (1727–1759) and the Marquis de Montcalm (1712–1759), commanders of the British and French troops respectively, were killed on the Plains of Abraham in the battle of Quebec in 1759. See also the references to Wolf at 130.7 and 163.6–7. Richard Montgomery

(1738–1775), a general in the American forces during the Revolution, was killed during a battle at Quebec in 1775; in the same battle, Benedict Arnold was wounded.

128.21–22   Thoreau refers here to a trip he took, by rail and boat, to Plymouth, during which he stayed on Clark's Island for four days.

129.4–15   Here Thoreau retells a legend about Nix's Mate, a shoal in Boston Harbor that was once an island.

132.13–15   Thoreau refers here to his first trip to Cape Cod in the fall of 1849.

134.4–12   "Webster" is U.S. Senator Daniel Webster, whose support of the Fugitive Slave Law had angered Thoreau. His farm is described in the preceding paragraph. Charles Emerson was Ralph Waldo Emerson's brother, a lawyer.

136.6   The "Gurnet" is a peninsula in Plymouth Harbor.

136.21   "Uncle Ned" is Edward Winslow Watson, proprietor of Clark's Island, referred to on the previous page at line 26.

139.24   "The Pines" refers to the salt meadow on Clark's Island.

141.37   Caroline Sturgis Tappan (1818–1888) wrote for the Transcendentalist journal *The Dial*.

142.5   George Partridge Bradford (1807–1890), a schoolteacher, was another of the Concord Transcendentalists.

142.8–33   Here Thoreau describes various Plymouth relics, including Plymouth Rock. "Phillip" is the Indian chief Metacomet, whom the English named King Philip.

143.5   Édouard Desor (1811–1882) and James Elliot Cabot (1821–1903) were natural scientists whom Thoreau may have visited in Boston on his return trip from Plymouth.

143.13   The Zoological Institute of June, Titus and Angevine, and Van Amburgh's Menagerie were major traveling menageries of the midnineteenth century.

146.24–25   The *Annual of Scientific Discovery* was published in Boston in 1851.

148.38–40 and 149.23–25   These passages reflect Thoreau's reading of William Bartram's *Travels* (1791).

152.24   The word "fulgor" means a brilliant light.

159.28–29   Thoreau refers here to Napoleon Bonaparte ordering the construction of a carriage road over the Simplon Pass in the Alps (1800–1807); the road joined Italy and Switzerland.

161.40   Champ de Mars is a military parade ground that Thoreau had seen during his 1850 trip to Montreal.

162.11–12   Thoreau is here consulting George Warburton's *Hochelaga; or England in the New World* (1846).

164.9–15   This passage derives from *The Animal Kingdom* (1827–1832), by Baron Georges Cuvier, one of several natural scientists Thoreau read during 1851.

165.31   This Latin phrase means "Let not the shoemaker go beyond his last."

167.27   See the entry for November 15th, in which Thoreau identifies Buster (Henry Kendall) as a former student.

170.25–171.5   This passage was drafted for inclusion in Thoreau's "An Excursion to Canada," which was based on his visit to Quebec in the autumn of 1850.

173.22–41   This entry begins with a draft version of the beginning of the lecture on Canada that Thoreau gave five months later at the Concord Lyceum.

174.33   This passage refers to the family of Patrick Riordan, an Irish immigrant who lived in a shanty near Walden Pond.

179.38–180.8   The Vermont and Boston Telegraph Company line, whose construction Thoreau describes here, ran through Concord.

180.31–32   Thoreau here refers to Fort Independence, on Castle Island in Boston Harbor, and Castle William, a fort on Governor's Island in New York Bay.

180.34   Jean Froissart was the author of a fourteenth-century history of Europe.

180.36   Sir Walter Scott (1771–1832) was the author of *Ivanhoe* and other novels with medieval settings.

183.5–7   The quoted lines are from Milton's "Lycidas," ll.3–5.

186.30   Kalmia is an American plant named after the botanist Peter Kalm by his teacher, Linneaus.

187.16   The North Branch is an alternate name for the Assabet River. See map, E3.

188.28   The phrase "Morses or Houses or Bain's" refers to competing telegraph companies of the early 1850s.

189.32   The work referred to here is the Latin agricultural writer Marcus Porcius Cato's *De Re Rustica* (On Agriculture).

189.40   Thoreau refers here to Jesse Buel's *The Farmer's Companion*, published in Boston in 1839, and Solon Robinson's contributions to New England agricultural magazines.

193.1   Thoreau may be contrasting the fate of the two Greek heroes, Nestor living into old age and Achilles dying in his prime.

194.5–10   In his *The Human Body and Its Connexion With Man* (1851), James John Garth Wilkinson offered an elaborate theory of analogy, comparing moral truths to functions of the human body. See other references to this work in subsequent entries.

196.1   The phrase "vale of Tempe and of Arcadey" alludes to John Keats's "Ode on a Grecian Urn."

201.8   Peter Kalm's *Travels into North America* (1770–71) is one of several works of natural history that Thoreau read in 1851.

202.11–27   The figure Thoreau encounters walking on the railroad is Samuel Hoar (1778–1856), Concord's leading citizen; he was a U.S. Congressman from 1835 to 1837.

204.13   The English philosopher Thomas Carlyle had been the subject of Thoreau's 1847 essay "Thomas Carlyle and His Works."

204.15   The book Thoreau refers to here is probably *Letters on the Laws of Man's Nature* (1851), by the liberal-minded British author and traveler Harriett Martineau.

206.20   Barred from the promised land, Moses was instructed by God to view it from Pisgah (Mount Nebo).

209.17   Thoreau is referring here to a lake he saw on his first trip to Maine in 1846.

212.23–24   These lines echo the closing lines of William Cullen Bryant's poem "Thanatopsis."

215.23   The cities of Sodom and Gomorrah, according to legend, lie at the bottom of the Dead Sea.

216.28–30   Here Thoreau refers to the famous incident, in 1844, in which he and a friend accidentally set fire to the woods outside Concord.

219.40–220.23   This passage, which Thoreau used in *Walden*, derives from Benvenuto Cellini's *Memoirs*, of which a translated version was published in Boston in 1845.

220.26–29   In classical legend, the shepherd Endymion asked the god Jupiter for eternal youth and unlimited sleep.

222.14–33   Concord's selectmen had asked Thoreau, as a professional surveyor, to perambulate and verify with them the town's boundaries. See also the passages at 225.41–226.2 and 238.30.

224.30   Cheronaea, a Boeotian town, was the setting for several famous battles of antiquity.

227.4   James Baker owned the farm that titles the *Walden* chapter "Baker Farm."

227.33   To punish Apollo for slaying the Cyclopes, Zeus sent him to serve Admetus, king of Pherae. Apollo's service was to tend Admetus's flocks for nine years.

229.24   Robert Smith (1689–1768) was a professor of astronomy at Cambridge University.

235.27–29   The prophets referred to here are the biblical Daniel and William Miller (1782–1849), founder of the Millerite sect, who said Christ would return in 1843.

238.13   Louis Anselm Lauriat (1785–1858), a balloonist, made several ascents in the Boston area during the 1830s and 1840s.

240.27–30   The U.S. Exploring Expedition, under congressional auspices, set out from Virginia for the Pacific in the summer of 1838, returning in the spring of 1842. Thoreau is alluding to the fact that the publication of its findings was much delayed. In 1851 a popular account of the expedition, *Voyage Round the World*, was published by its leader, Charles Wilkes.

243.2–3   In 1845 Robert Chambers had published *Vestiges of the Natural History of Creation*, a highly controversial book that argued for a theory of organic evolution.

245.17   Edmund Hosmer (1798–1881) is a familiar presence in the Journal and a lifelong friend of Thoreau's. He assisted Thoreau in the building of the Walden hut and was with him the night before he died.

246.31–33   This passage refers to violins made in Cremona, Italy.

247.2–19   In the period following the passage of the Fugitive Slave Law, Thoreau was active in helping escaped slaves, such as "Henry Williams," flee to Canada. As this passage makes clear, one of the routes of escape was through Concord by rail. Frederick Minkins, known as Shadrach, mentioned here, was a fugitive slave who worked at a Boston coffee house until he was captured early in 1851. A group of African-Americans freed him on the day of his capture, and he eventually found his way to freedom in Canada. "Augerhole Burns" may refer to Frederic D. Byrnes, a U.S. deputy marshal who was among those who arrested Shadrach at the coffee house. "Lovejoy" is probably the Reverend Joseph Cammett Lovejoy (1805–1871), minister of an abolitionist church in Cambridgeport. William Lloyd Garrison (1805–1879) was the foremost figure in radical abolitionist politics of the day.

249.4–250.14   George Minott (1783–1861), like Edmund Hosmer, is a familiar figure in Thoreau's Journal. Also a Concord farmer, he is often invoked by Thoreau as a source for local legends and natural history.

256.27   Thoreau here refers to a classical legend about the Cynic philosopher Diogenes, who walked about Athens in a state of misery, with a tub on his head.

259.3   "This Dodonean fruit" is the acorn, which in classical mythology has sacred associations.

261.34–262.15   The "friend" is almost certainly Ralph Waldo Emerson, intellectual leader of the Transcendentalist movement and Thoreau's mentor until their relationship began to fray in the late 1840s.

267.41–268.21   During this period Thoreau was reading *Principles of Zoology* (1848), by Louis Agassiz and A. A. Gould, one of several works of natural history he studied in 1851.

268.35   John Goodwin (1803–1860), a hunter and fisherman, was a local figure with whom Thoreau often talked. He appears frequently in the Journal as a source for descriptions of natural phenomena.

273.33   Amos Bronson Alcott (1799–1888), a key member of the Concord Transcendentalists, was noted for his theories and experiments in educational reform.

273.39–40   The first quotation is from Thomas Storer's poem "The Life and Death of Thomas Wolsey, Cardinall" (1599), and the second is from Robert Southey's poem "Remembrance."

274.25–28   Some have speculated that the woman referred to here is Emerson's wife, Lidian.

274.34   "My friend" is probably Ralph Waldo Emerson.

275.33 and 275.35   "RWE," here and elsewhere, is Ralph Waldo Emerson.

280.13   In Old Norse, "Thing" is a term for a public gathering.

282.15   In classical legend, "Pactolus" refers to a river of golden sands in ancient Lydia.

283.2–3   Isaac Van Amburg (1801–1865) was the manager of one of nineteeth-century America's most successful menageries.

283.3   The phrase "World's fare" refers to the great 1851 international exhibition in London's Crystal Palace.

283.4   Thoreau here alludes to Aeneas carrying his father, Anchises, out of Troy's ruins (*Aeneid*, Book II).

283.16   This Greek passage, from Aeschylus (*Prometheus Bound*), was translated by Thoreau himself for the January 1843 issue of *The Dial*: "countless smilings / Of the ocean waves."

284.16–17   This passage is revealing because it shows that Thoreau took notes during his walks. These notes were the raw material from which he crafted his Journal entries, often on the following morning.

287.15   The phrase "Our life is not altogether a forgetting" is a paraphrase of a line from Wordsworth's "Ode: Intimations of Immortality."

289.33–34   In classical mythology, the giant Antaeus was strengthened by his contact with the earth when opponents wrestled him to the ground.

290.2–6   This passage alludes to Sir Walter Scott's *Lady of the Lake*, in which the Saxon chieftain Fitz-James and the Gaelic hero Roderick Dhu battle one another.

292.2–4   Prometheus's punishment for stealing fire from the gods was being chained to a rock, where an eagle came every day to devour his liver because he was immortal, the punishment lasted forever.

293.7   This sentence alludes to the Israelites' passage through the Sea of Reeds, as described in Exodus.

293.29   Mary Moody Emerson (1774–1863), who visited Concord in the autumn of 1851, was Ralph Waldo Emerson's paternal aunt.

294.6   Margaret Fuller Ossoli (1810–1850) was one of the major figures in the American Transcendentalist movement. She edited the Transcendentalist journal *The Dial* and wrote for the New York *Tribune*. When she perished in a shipwreck off Fire Island during July of 1850, Thoreau was sent by the community of Concord to search for her remains.

295.30   Alek Therien is the unnamed French-Canadian woodchopper to whom Thoreau devotes a large portion of the chapter "Visitors" in *Walden*.

295.35–298.39   Intermittently in this section passages reflect Thoreau's reading of D. H. Stoever's biography, *The Life of Sir Charles Linnaeus* (translated London edition, 1794).

296.20–21   "V Class dict" refers to Lempriere's *Classical Dictionary*; "V Scrap Book" refers to Thoreau's own "Fact Book," a gathering of his natural history observations. See also the reference at 298.12.

299.37–38   See Wordsworth, *The Excursion* (I, 618–619): "And attention now relaxed, / A heart-felt chillness crept along my veins."

306.13   The phrase "sortes Virgilianae" (Virgilian lots) refers to a practice from antiquity in which lines of poetry were written on individual leaves and then drawn by lot, in the belief that such chance selections carried prophetic meanings. As Thoreau's remarks suggest, the practice continued into the nineteenth century. Also note the reference at 306.25.

306.17—23   The passage is from Emerson's lecture "Literary Ethics."

307.26   This sentence alludes to *Hamlet* (I, iv, 53): "Revisit'st thus the glimpses of the moon."

308.16   Samuel de Champlain (1567?—1635) and Marc L'Escarbot (d. 1630?) were French explorers of North America, both of whom had written about Sable Island in Nova Scotia.

308.41   The "Zincali" were a Spanish gypsy people.

309.21   Reuben Rice (1790—1888), a farmer and beekeeper with whom Thoreau often talked, is a familiar presence in the Journal.

310.34   This phrase, from which the slang term "bunk" may derive, refers to a congressman from Buncombe County, North Carolina, whose windy speeches made his home district a nineteenth-century euphemism for insubstantial expression.

310.36   Jack Slingsby, a tinker, is a character in George Borrow's 1851 novel *Lavengro*.

312.5—11   Thoreau here refers to a regatta in August 1851, in which an American yacht of revolutionary design, the *America*, beat the British ship *Titania*.

312.12   The phrase "Coleridgean thoughts" refers to inspiration derived from Samuel Taylor Coleridge, a British romantic poet and philosopher whose writings deeply influenced Thoreau.

316.1   In the Hindu scriptures, the Vedas, Indra is the god of battle.

320.21—22   This passage alludes to *Hamlet*, I, v, 166—167.

320.36—38   This passage may allude to Ecclesiastes 12:1 and Milton's *Paradise Lost*, I, 26.

323.12—16 and 325.6—35   Few readers are aware that these passages describing the earth flowing from the Deep Cut, which became central to Thoreau's climactic chapter "Spring" in *Walden*, were written from observations made in late December.

323.37   Thoreau refers here to the Concord River by its Indian name, "Musketaquid," which means "grass-ground river."

326.24   By "*erythrean*," Thoreau apparently means to evoke the Greek word for "red," *erythros*.

326.24—25   Thales (640—546 B.C.) was an Ionian philosopher who posited that water, as Thoreau writes, "is the principle of all things."

327.10—12   Elizabeth Oakes Smith (1806—1893) was a feminist reformer and one of America's first female lecturers. Thoreau heard her lecture at the Concord Lyceum.

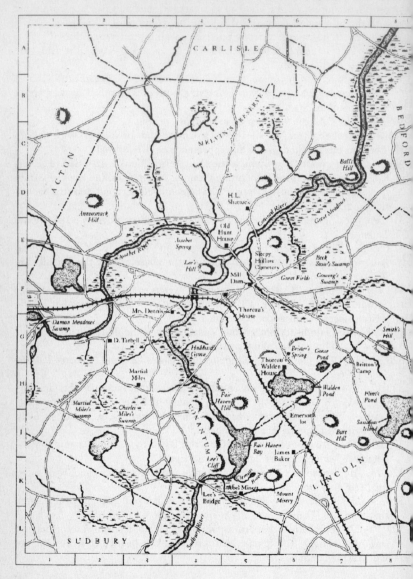

Concord, Massachusetts